THE PLURAL OF US

The Plural of Us

POETRY AND COMMUNITY IN AUDEN AND OTHERS

BONNIE COSTELLO

PRINCETON UNIVERSITY PRESS

PRINCETON & OXFORD

Published by Princeton University Press,
41 William Street, Princeton, New Jersey 08540
In the United Kingdom: Princeton University Press,
6 Oxford Street, Woodstock, Oxfordshire OX20 1TR

press.princeton.edu

ISBN 978-0-691-17281-1

Library of Congress Control Number: 2016960848

British Library Cataloging-in-Publication Data is available

This book has been composed in Classic Arno Pro

Printed on acid-free paper. ∞

Printed in the United States of America

10 9 8 7 6 5 4 3 2 1

How do you make a plural of us, my sweet Master of Arts?
—LOUISE BOGAN TO THEODORE ROETHKE, OCTOBER 3, 1935

CONTENTS

ACKNOWLEDGMENTS

I AM GRATEFUL to the American Council of Learned Societies and the Cullman Center at the New York Public Library for a fellowship in 2011–12 that gave me the time and space to develop this project. Thanks to NYPL Berg Collection director Isaac Gewirtz and librarian Anne Garner for their assistance in helping me explore the remarkable Auden papers at the Berg.

Auden's literary executor, Edward Mendelson, has been generous throughout the project in answering my questions and granting permission to quote unpublished material by Auden. I completed a draft of the book in 2014–15 with funding from the National Endowment for the Humanities, in combination with sabbatical support from Boston University. Thanks also to the Boston University Center for the Humanities for help in covering permissions fees.

Credits

1

Speaking of Us

POETRY IS THE EXPRESSION of individuals, prompted by experience and imagination to record their feelings, their ideas, their fears and desires. It also springs from culture and community. The poet presumes, or at least hopes, that his expression speaks for others, that what he feels and thinks is not merely personal but shared, representative, even universal. And the thoughts and aspirations the poet presents from his individual perspective are not only those of the private and inward self. They may concern his interpersonal and social relations, or his participation in the common, which is established in his address to the reader. How the poet makes use of the first-person plural may tell us a lot about how he imagines his intimate, social, and artistic relations. "We" can be partisan, tribal, authoritarian, and even demagogic. Yet many of our greatest poets have often meant by "we" "not the collective singular We of tradition" but rather an open-ended "You-and-I united by a common truth" or at least together "seeking truth to which we shall both be compelled to assent"; they have said "we" to create community rather than to divide groups or impose majority.[1]

As Walt Whitman draws to a close his long poem "Crossing Brooklyn Ferry," he poses a set of rhetorical questions. "We understand then, do we not? / What I promis'd without mentioning it, have you not accepted?"[2] How many are included in this "we"—one or a multitude? Does Whitman speak as an intimate or as an orator? Is the reader included in this group, or is she overhearing an address to someone else? Is the assent here merely intellectual and emotional, or is it also implicitly political? With Whitman the reader has richly and dialectically imagined the meaning of "we." It remains interrogative, collaborative, improvisatory, invitational, and above all in the optative mood. As a reader, I meet Whitman's vision on my own terms, not by the assent of the group or the necessity of logic. Whitman's closing questions emerge from the acknowledgment of deep paradoxes concerning the one and the many—paradoxes of democracy and of poetry. At the very end of "Crossing Brooklyn

Ferry," Whitman's "we" is no longer a potential between a speaker and those he addresses but a congregation, turned to the physical world's "dumb beautiful ministers": "We fathom you not—we love you."[3] The collective subject in these lines is not so much presumed as brought about by the poem, and in a way this "we" is the very thing "promised without mentioning it." This "we," a relation emerging in the constant shuttle of "I" and "you," is indeterminate and open, public and yet private, many and few, of the mind and of the body. Whitman's promise of democratic community is linked to the plurality of readers and is a thing always in the making, not something fixed and imposed. Whitman's "we" is agglomerated but also individuated; it is reciprocal and engaged, with indefinite edges and continuously varying interlocutors, infinite but not a totality. In speaking of "us," Whitman foregrounds the nuanced social meanings and varied tonalities of the first-person plural. He also highlights its performative nature. It makes something happen. Whitman opened up a pronominal poetics that has become a hallmark of recent American poetry. However, as Whitman well knew, the relation of this imaginary community and literary-symbolic effect to a realizable social presence is ambiguous and indeterminate.

W. R. Johnson celebrated Whitman as a rare "choral" voice in modern lyric. Even Whitman's "I," he argues, is really a "we" since it speaks of a culture's aspirations. Whitman's choral lyric, Johnson avers, is not a reflection of the realities of America but a vision of American potential: "What choral poets do is not so much to state the fact of good community as to imagine the possibility of good community."[4] Separating the man from the art, and selective in his choice of texts, Johnson finds this drive toward *communitas* even in Pound, whose *Cantos*, he argues, "exists only *in potential*," as a collaboration with each reader. In the *Pisan Cantos* especially, in his anguish and humility, "muttering only to himself, suddenly and amazingly he begins at last to talk to all of us, *for* all of us," "about the survival of *communitas*, in its utter ruin."[5] For Johnson, modern choral lyric speaks for a *potentiality* that it also helps realize, at least in the virtual world of reading.

Poetry has its own special language, but it is built up from, and often imitates, ordinary language and draws out implications of our usage, thus helping us reflect on speech in our public and private lives. While this is a study focused entirely on poetry (and the "we" as narrative voice in fiction produces quite different effects), some preliminary reflection on the perils and controversies surrounding common usage of the first-person plural helps frame the discussion. We allow a great deal of license to the literary imagination, but in public speeches, journalism, or politics, for instance, this same invocation of an indeterminate "we" can sound hollow, coercive, or presumptuous. Does the orator or writer presume to speak for *me*? Does "we" have any real antecedent for an unbounded, diverse populace? This is a foundational question in

American history, one that resonates throughout in the struggles of balance or alignment between I and We, Us and Them. Patrick Henry protested in response to the Philadelphia Convention: "What right had they to say 'we, the People?' . . . who authorized them to speak the language of We, the People?'"[6] One might argue that here too was *potential*, a community posited rather than represented, something envisioned more than authorized; but our founding documents have real-world consequences fundamentally different from literary contracts with unknown readers. Patrick Henry's question resounds through American political and social debate, right through to red-hot (and very blue) patriot Molly Ivins, who famously quipped in response to the promiscuous use of "we" in economic journalism: "We is not me or a lot of us." Ivins is provoked by a reporter's inclusion of all of us as beneficiaries of financial gain: "Who you callin' 'we,' white man?"[7] She would be surprised to find any company with Ayn Rand, but radical individualism has its own objections to the first-person plural: "The word 'We' is as lime poured over men, which sets and hardens to stone, and crushes all beneath it."[8] The point is that even at contrasting poles of political orientation, this pronoun raises hackles. But if the presumed inclusiveness of "we" is inconsiderate, hegemonic, or dystopic in some contexts, it is a democratic imperative in others. President Obama quoted himself and others in Selma when he said, "The single most powerful word in our democracy is the word 'We.' We the People. We Shall Overcome. Yes We Can. It is owned by no one. It belongs to everyone."[9] A fragmented society, a society of "us" and "them," turns away, or looks on in disdain, at the suffering of minorities. But if "we" includes all "the people" of America, then the degraded condition of some reflects on everyone. For James Baldwin in 1960, Harlem becomes, not a place apart, but a measure of who we are. He finds rhetorical power in the grammatical ambiguity of the first-person plural through a small modifying clause that closes his essay "Fifth Avenue, Uptown." Baldwin implicitly calls Americans to honor the promise of inclusiveness: "Walk through the streets of Harlem," Baldwin invites his reader, "and see what we, this nation, have become." For better or worse, "we" is a powerful communicative tool, perhaps the quintessential pronoun of oratory, if also of intimacy. Poetry reflects and sometimes seeks to alter the language we use, publicly and privately, and the meanings we form. The study of literature, especially poetry, can raise our awareness of the force and risk of pronouns. Literature does not always want to serve an ameliorative function, nor should it. But some poetry seeks to harness the rhetorical power of the first-person plural to posit and promote community, often where there is social fragmentation. It can also alert us, intentionally or not, to the pronoun's dangers and exclusions, probing the implications of our usage and making us attentive to what we really mean when we say "we."

Poetry, more than any other genre, when it wrestles with political and ethical concerns, does so within the arena of *language*. Though linguists seldom venture into the special realm of literature, their questions and insights about the function of pronouns help foreground the opportunities that poets exploit. Whatever the historical setting, "we" is an ambiguous pronoun in English. Just as each of us is connected to many overlapping and conflicting units and communities, so we mean lots of things by "we," depending on context. "We" is an indexical pronoun, a deictic floater like "here" and "now." There is of course a referential meaning of sorts—more like a kind of aura around the word. It means the speaker (or a character the speaker is pretending to be) and at least one other. But that formula doesn't get us very far. Some languages distinguish "we" that includes the listener and "we" that does not, but English is not among them.[10] "We" in English can be bounded or unbounded. First-person plural might better be called first-person plus, where the second term of the equation $I + X = We$ needs to be solved. And the equation would also perhaps involve two forms, $I + X\text{-}hearer = We$, or $I + X + hearer = We$. "We" is sometimes weighted plural (an assemblage of individuated I's) and sometimes singular (a collective or corporate unit with a uniform identity or solidity). And perhaps most important for the lyric and its textual subjectivities, the "I" behind the "We" may be strongly present, almost inaudible, or without iteration. But as linguists interested in relevance theory have pointed out, speech is rarely explicit—it depends on the inferences listeners make, based on their expectations. For all the maxims of cooperative efficiency in conversation (quality, quantity, relation, manner) outlined by Paul Grice in "Logic and Conversation," implication in the use of the first-person plural can be imprecise: we often don't really know exactly what others are saying when they say "we." Exclusions and inclusions are often unconscious, as Ivins and Baldwin are pointing out. The boundaries are at times unclear even to the speaker, which is why the ambiguity of deictic words works in a joke or a poem—two places where ambiguity has value. "We" is often hard to disambiguate, and readers and listeners tolerate a large area of confusion or uncertainty about the identity of "we" in a given sentence. Poetry can exploit that ambiguity to show us something about what it means to be or to say "we," and to stretch and revise that meaning.

"We" can register many different forms of togetherness. It can be royal or communal, universal or parochial, intimate or public, personal or impersonal, inclusive or exclusive, majestic, universal, or corporate, intellectual or social. But ambiguity is a virtue in poetry, if also sometimes a problem. Gertrude Stein in "Poetry and Grammar" preferred pronouns to nouns precisely because they indicate but do not fix identity, eliding past conceptions that attach to names, allowing for more open and immediate thought: "Pronouns represent some one but they are not its or his name. In not being his or ~ her name they already have a greater possibility of being something than if they were as a noun is the name of anything."[11]

The freedom that Stein identifies is a central motivation of many poets as they play with pronouns. Poetry is not just an imitation of the world, but in creating its own world of interactions, it sometimes models values and possibilities occluded in social reality. This need not be a didactic project. As Auden himself said, "poetry makes nothing happen." But he went on in the same poem to say that poetry is "a way of happening, a mouth."[12] I follow him there in the sense that poetry performs and voices our deepest human relations. Poetry also exploits the oratorical power of "we"—as exhortation, as seduction, as tribal affiliation. My interest is not in presenting poetry as ethically exemplary—the faults of poets are the faults of us all. Rather, I am interested in how the poetry of Auden and others, in their use of the first-person plural, raises rhetorical and ethical problems and possibilities—implicitly and explicitly, inadvertently and deliberately.

Poets may not be the unacknowledged legislators of the world (Auden frequently expressed his disdain for Shelley's famous declaration), but many are certainly interested in the governance of the tongue. One of the functions of poetry is to play us back to ourselves, and it can test those little function words that shape our thought. Poetry, though we mostly associate it with "I," speaks often of or as "we," and not only the "we" ("us," "our") of private relations, since poetry's roots are partly in oratory. Yet criticism about the lyric has mostly overlooked poets' uses of the first-person plural, attending instead to "I" and "You." Lyric has been defined primarily as the genre of the individual, and hence of the first-person singular, though contemporary critics have turned to its social dimension in their attention to lyric address.[13] An I/You address often brings a "we" into being, both grammatically and in a more dramatic sense, and many poets keep the "I" and "You" audible even in speaking for the group. But it would be a mistake, I think, to treat the first-person plural simply as a byproduct of lyric address. For one thing, "we" in poetry often arises without a clear situation of address. And since a collective pronoun exists for that meeting of I and You, it would seem to point to something distinct, something at least potentially more than or different from the sum of its parts.

Wallace Stevens invokes this emergent unit in his "Final Soliloquy of the Interior Paramour," which is not final but recurrent in its sense of ultimate arrival, in which "we collect ourselves, / Out of all the indifferences, into one thing" where "we forget each other and ourselves." Stevens's pronoun is moving in its ambiguity, linking the private experience of poetic thought (the lovers' space of a "room" and the narrower individual's space of "the mind" and imagination) with the social experience of love and potential community.[14] Is this the usurpation of everything by a single mind, a form of the royal we? Such a reading would link Stevens back to Matthew Arnold's ideal where man's soul is "centered in majestic unity."[15] Or is Stevens suggesting a loss of self in the collective "one thing" that, for the poem, exists externally and potentially in "the evening air" and as an optative "world imagined"? "We say," "out of," and other phrases hover between these meanings and others. This intimate encounter within the space of literature, this textual "we" with its unlocalized "here," would seem to have little to do with actual social relations—might even appear antagonistic toward the social. But it can posit connections that history has restricted, and it can imagine a reality—a future—less fragmented than the one we live in. As Holocaust survivor Paul Celan observed, echoing the persecuted Russian poet Osip Mandelstam's "To the Addressee," a poem "can be a message in a bottle, sent out in the—not always greatly hopeful— belief that somewhere and sometime it could wash up on land, on heartland perhaps. Poems in this sense . . . are under way: they are making toward something."[16] The "you" of poetry, then, is propulsive, making its way toward "we," acknowledging a distance from the other but wishing for a union. Poems can make "we" happen in fictive or readerly time, even if it is blocked in history.[17] In Celan's beautiful poem "In Memoriam Paul Eluard," for instance, he recalls the French poet's St. Peter-like ethical failure when he denied his friendship with poet Zavas Kalandra before a Stalinist tribunal. The poem redeems him by looking beyond death to a "stranger" and deeper "blue" of the soul, and by uttering and making us utter what Eluard failed to say: "the one who said Thou to him / will dream with him: We."[18] Poems can be "making toward" a potential alliance, a group, even a community—because poetry deals in possible worlds rather than simply representing history.

The connections that form "we" above are private and intimate, but they are not ultimately separate from the civil impulse of poetry. The paradox of poetry, that it is often a private communication but also often an unrestricted and open-invitational one, not only overheard but also indirectly addressed to many if not all, makes the "we" of poetry peculiarly layered. But as criticism has stressed the "I" and "you" of lyric, it has overlooked the shared, collaborative, or generalized subjectivity that may be confrontational and oppositional but may also create a space for "we" to happen. This flexibility and ambiguity in the referential boundaries of the first-person plural allows "we" in poetry to be at once a singular meditation ("in the mind") and a space of shared, even common experience, and a granulated meeting of I's and You's. Whether directly addressing another person or group or representing that plural subject to outsiders, the poet's "we" conjures a complex and powerful unit of being for the reader.

Poetry thrives on the gaps and imprecisions of natural language and inten-
sifies them even as it seeks clarity. The indexical indeterminacy of pronouns,
their dependence on inference, creates a space for new meanings. The "we"
of modern lyric evokes, often with deliberate elasticity and ambiguity, and
sometimes with tension and contradiction, a range from intimate to public
life, often within the same text, and sometimes even simultaneously. Elizabeth Bishop underscores this ambiguity with her quasi-epiphany near the
end of "The Moose" when she writes: "why do we feel / (we all feel) this
sweet / sensation of joy?"[19] Who is included in this "we"? Is it the passengers
on the bus from Nova Scotia to Boston, awakened from the drowsy rhythms
of travel to behold this "grand, otherworldly" animal? Nameless, they are
still individual voices. Is the reader included as well as the speaker? What
about the moose that "looks the bus over"? Bishop's parenthesis, though it
gathers and frames her words, paradoxically highlights the openness of the
pronoun's inclusion and gives it extension beyond any direct reference in
the poem. Poetry depicts small communities, those parentheses of our lives.
But in using "we," poetry can also metonymically suggest broader gatherings
so that the sense of the general does not withdraw from the particular into
impersonal abstraction, or the local hide itself in a false universal. Poetry's
"we" can be highly nuanced and variable, then, marking overlapping and con-
centric circles.

In celebrating Whitman and Pound, W. R. Johnson called for the renewal
of "choral poetry": "What matters, for literary choral, is that the agent and
the object of choral mimesis be present: the universal representative of the
community singing for and to the community about the hopes and passion
for order, survival, and continuity that they all share."[20] He laments that since
classical times the dominant mode has been the solo lyric, emerging from
and speaking of alienation and fragmentation: not "wir und weld" but "ich
und weld."[21] But for many modern poets that "wir" was the mantle for failed
social orders and dangerous totalitarian impulses, carrying the presumption
of a dominant group. Whitman may claim to speak for the unvoiced, but for
much of literary tradition the male covered up the female voice. An inclusive
"we" could not be so easily projected. In "Diving into the Wreck," Adrienne
Rich refuses the "assiduous team" and dives alone, though once descended she
discovers a faceted "we" within, a Jungian Unconscious, but also a potential
social form that bends the first-person plural out of its patriarchal exclusions.
"We are, I am, you are // . . . the one who find our way."[22] When Langston
Hughes declares, "Let America be America Again," he begins with a singular voice, "ME," one that speaks for America's oppressed minorities. Yet like
Baldwin he also exhorts a potential community, "We the people," and calls it
into action to fulfill the nation's promise of inclusive diversity. The poet must,

to invoke Whitman, be vigilant in creating a voice "differentiated yet a part of the whole." Modern poetry's "we" has sometimes been a hiding place for the embarrassed I. Yet if the drive to *communitas* comes and goes in the history of lyric, the desire not only to identify universals, but also to speak of them in the first-person plural, remains strong.

While function words such as pronouns don't have content in the usual sense, they do convey and perform social arrangements, and their use reflects changes in social awareness. In our age, sensitive to diversity and wary of coercive power structures, speaking for others is difficult. Yet the first-person plural is a troublesome pronoun in any era. In a historical view of lyric subjectivity, the shifts in the first half of the twentieth century are especially marked. The problem of "we" as a functioning pronoun—referring to the group, or the common, or the artist's relation to the public—was central not only to the political but to the cultural conversation, especially in the years between the Depression and the end of World War II, when artists were drawn to solidarity and yet often horrified by emerging forms of authoritarian statism and collectivism. What did it mean in those years to speak for others, or for many to speak as one? Modernist poetry had formed in small avant-garde circles, but the culture of the arts had shifted in the 1930s, looking beyond itself for its origin and justification. A subsequent age that emphasized collective ideologies, historical process, and public responsibility over aesthetics and individual consciousness put new pressures on the art world and fostered new reflections on voice, audience, and address. As collectivism led to division and debate in the thirties and forties, "we" became contested ground. Diverse thinkers emerged from the thirties— Ortega, Burke, Wilson, Weil, Arendt, Niebuhr, and many others—to express concerns about the voice and spectacle of the masses and the weakening of individual voice and conscience.

The strong demand for poetry to offer "public speech" and invoke "the social muse" put the collective "we" in the foreground.[23] Carl Sandburg confirmed Whitman's optimism with *The People, Yes*. The critic Cary Nelson has led a major recovery of protest poetry and proletarian poetry, highlighting writers of the thirties such as Kenneth Fearing, Edwin Rolfe, Genevieve Taggard, and Horace Gregory, who eschewed the poetry of aesthetics and interiority in favor of a public voice.[24] The anthologies and critical studies of the period identified work in collective terms: Kreymborg's *A History of American Poetry: Our Singing Strength* (1934); the collective *We Gather Strength* (1933); H. H. Lewis's *We March Toward the Sun* (1936), Langston Hughes's *Let America Be America Again* (1938). There was certainly substantial resistance to this idea of poetry's role as public speech. Archibald MacLeish might declare a new set of imperatives for poetry, but Louise Bogan, writing to Rolfe Humphries on July 8, 1938, objects in capital letters: "I STILL THINK THAT POETRY HAS

SOMETHING TO DO WITH IMAGINATION. . . . I STILL THINK THA[.]
IS PRIVATE FEELING, NOT PUBLIC SPEECH."[25] Malcolm Cowley, editor of
The New Republic from 1929 to 1944, puts the question "who is we?" directly
at the beginning of a memoir of the thirties: "Great changes would surely take
place and . . .—most of us felt at one time or another—that it was our duty as
writers to take part in them, at least by coming forward to bear witness. I say
'we' and 'us' while conscious of their being treacherous pronouns."[26] But this
is written in 1980, looking back at the 1930s.

The first-person plural was not only taken up by a left-leaning subgroup of
social-realist writers. Agrarians, objectivists, and classical formalists complicate the account of poetic voice in the thirties. The major American modernists reimagined their art in this environment, altering their style and subject
matter. Wallace Stevens, for instance, in "The Man with the Blue Guitar"
(1936), enters into dialogue with an audience that clamors for that reflexive
yet transformative "tune beyond us yet ourselves."[27] The end of World War II
and the advent of the Cold War changed the nature of the poetic "we," in part,
at least in reaction against the uses that had been made of public speech by
fascist and other collectivist movements. Many poets shifted away, at least for a
time, from political and social activism and group identity, and moved toward
the self as representative figure, the "we," not of "all of us," but of "each one of
us" in our individual lives of human faults and aspirations. Such evocations
of everyman have sometimes seemed normative and presumptive, falling in
with Cold War ideology, but they were often more self-conscious and anxious than has been generally acknowledged. Robert Lowell often distances
himself not only from the public and patriotic "we" but from the comfortable
village conformity of "our Independence Day."[28] But if choral lyric disappeared
with the Cold War cultivation of privacy, civil poetry has been perennial, and
the first-person plural has maintained its hold on poetic voice. Indeed, it has
had a considerable comeback in contemporary poetry, as I will suggest in my
conclusion. As we continue the critical project of theorizing and historicizing
lyric subjectivity, we might well turn to the fluent and problematic modes of
connection registered in modern poetry's use of this plural pronoun. In what
circumstances, and in what terms, might the poet—whose generic default
position is I—speak of "we"?

Poetry's first-person plural often prompts us to pose questions central to
modern social thought: For whom does the poet write, and what authority
does she have to speak for others? Is there a prior selfhood standing behind
the collective, or is the "I" suspended in the voicing of "we"? Is "we" one or
many? Can the poet construct a "we" that retains multiplicity within its choral
force? When does the poem give assent to this claim of collective identity, and
when does it distance itself? Modern poetry often creates a face of "we" that

is volatile in character as well as number and avoids masking a restricted as a universal interest. Modern poetry's "we," exploiting the inherent instability of the pronoun, is especially reflexive, highly sensitive to political and historical circumstance, and often speculative. The pronoun's ambiguity, especially in the abstract realm of poetry, also provides freedom to dislodge labels and imagine potential communities.

While this is the first generic study of "we" in modern poetry, the topic has been richly addressed in modern philosophy, especially in the Continental tradition with its ethical turn and attention to community. Philosophical theories of social phenomenology and ontology do not directly inform my discussion of poetry, but they do indicate how an emphasis on language can foster fresh thinking about social reality. Martin Buber stands at the forefront of a long tradition that looks at ontology, ethics, and society in relation to language, not only with his seminal book *I and Thou* (1920) but also in lectures he gave in Germany (under great controversy) after the war, especially "What Is Common to All" (1951). The question of what it means to say "we" has special pressure in this post-Holocaust context; though Buber's lecture avoids mention of contemporary history, he is clearly arguing against the collectivist and totalitarian models of "we" that had destroyed the public sphere and enabled the genocide and destruction of war. He argues too against an Eastern tradition that finds unity in a mystical "All" which obliterates individual will and consciousness. His praise is for the Western liberal idea of "the common" first articulated by Heraclitus, in which the single voice retains integrity in entering into discourse and harmony with others, either within the polity or more freely in the exchange of ideas and beliefs. "The genuine We," Buber writes, "is to be recognized in its objective existence, through the fact that in whatever of its parts it is regarded, an essential relation between person and person, between I and Thou, is always evident as actually or potentially existing. For the word always arises only between an I and a Thou, and the element from which the We receives its life is speech, the communal speaking that begins in the midst of speaking to one another."[29] For Buber this We that takes its life from speech is dynamic and full of risk, akin to fire and water. "All this flowing ever again into a great stream of reciprocal sharing of knowledge—thus came to be and thus is the living We, the genuine We, which, where it fulfills itself, embraces the dead who once took part in colloquy and now take part in it through what they have handed down to posterity." This "we" is not only of the past but also of the future: "As potentiality it lies at the base of all history of spirit and deed; it actualizes itself and is no longer there. It can actualize itself within a group which then consists of just a fiery core and a drossy crust, and it can flare up and burn outside of all collectives. . . . Leaping fire is indeed the right image for the dynamic between persons in We."[30] And "the between" is,

for Buber, the difficult and turbulent space of "the common," the space
course and dialogue, where the true meaning of "we" arises. Thus the "gen...
we" requires not only gathering but also distinction to maintain that space.

Later Continental thinkers echo and develop these concepts, resisting the
premise of classical liberalism that an integral "I" remains existentially prior
to the common. Both Emmanuel Levinas's *Entre Nous* and Jean-Luc Nancy's
Being Singular/Plural, for instance, explore the ethical implications of the
collective pronoun. Recent philosophical attempts to imagine community
beyond existing models (Blanchot, Agamben, Nancy) refuse the priority of
the individual but prefer, like Buber, *potentiality* to mastery in communal relations. Their ideas of open, flexible discursive communities often manifest in
imaginative works and literary community. For Levinas, "we" remains centered in the problem of "*between*," but he questions Buber's idea of reciprocity
and focuses ethics on the responsibility to the other. In *Being Singular/Plural*,
Jean-Luc Nancy, echoing and revising Heidegger, changes the preposition to
"*with*"—we must think of being as "being with."[31] Like Levinas, Nancy asserts
that "there is no meaning if meaning is not shared,"[32] and like Levinas his goal
is to get beyond horizons, views, or perspectives that objectify the other to
"Being" as something at once arising in plural relation and circulating back
to individual consciousness, the singular as the site of necessary and limited
understanding. Nancy emphasizes the term "*poesis*" in connection with art and
community, something that is posed, made, produced, inevitably exposed and
disposed. Nancy, like others writing out of Europe's late twentieth-century
stresses, finds that "liberalism is exhausted"; at the same time he is seeking
a "we," a concept of community, that is "no longer a matter of organizing . . .
according to the decrees of a sovereign Other, or according to the *telos* of
a history." He avoids "*the we*" (collectivism) and seeks a "we [that] always
expresses plurality" and "avoids generality."[33] Coming out of the postwar and
Cold War era (Levinas) and facing globalization (Nancy), their philosophies
express as much as they *analyze* their particular historical context. Roberto
Esposito in his recent book *Communitas* offers a different starting point for
considering the meaning of community. By emphasizing the etymology of
the term he foregrounds the importance of gift and debt bonds (*mundus*),
rather than property (*propria*) and belonging, in the forming and experience
of community bonds. "We" is not only situational, as Émile Benveniste has
said of I-and-you; it is also historical.[34]

I have been struck, in my readings of the texts mentioned above, by the
struggle with words, the strained usages (even allowing for translation), and
the pressure not only on etymologies (Nancy finds that *poesis* both ex-poses
and dis-poses) but also on pronouns and prepositions to set the analytical
terms of relation. There is a sense that the pronoun "we" needs renovation

(etiolated by journalism and constrained in identity politics) and that the available language of commonality and community is inadequate to the ideals these writers seek. But there is also a sense that the habits of language are difficult to bend. Here is where poetry—which often foregrounds, troubles, and renovates language, and which presents possible or virtual worlds more than actual ones—has a special role to play, though it is not its only or necessary role. Buber's lecture "What Is Common to All," focused as it is on "the genuine We," closes with a work of imagination, a quotation from J. C. F. Hölderlin's poem "Celebration of Peace":

> Man has learned much since morning,
> For we are a conversation, and we can listen
> To one another. Soon we'll be song.

Jean-Luc Nancy acknowledges that the obstacles of definition lead him toward the imagination: "At what point must ontology become . . . what? Become conversation? Become lyricism? . . . The strict conceptual rigor of *being-with* exacerbates the discourse of its concept."[35] He turns to Goethe, to Baudelaire, to exemplify poetry's singular plurality. Nancy's question, "Who is it that says we?" has long been asked in a lyric voice.[36]

The philosophical idea of *potentiality* so central to recent discussions of community among these Continental philosophers intersects with the sociolinguistic idea of *performativity* in the Anglo-American tradition, first introduced by J. L. Austin and revised and extended by other speech act theorists and philosophers of language such as Paul Grice, John Searle, and Stanley Cavell. This idea has engaged literary critics in a variety of ways, but its specific implication for poetic pronouns has not been discussed. Speech act theorists are interested in what language *does* in a communicative framework, more than in any prior reality that it retroactively describes or to which it refers. As J. L. Austin long ago argued, language sometimes proposes or establishes rather than represents reality, and it has affective as well as descriptive functions. Poets are intensely aware that language is not just a system of rules but a community of users who shape it in their direct and indirect speech acts. At the same time, poetry's use of pronouns is complicated by the absence of explicit context.[37] Poetry sometimes (1) wants to refer to or speak for a preexisting group or (2) wants to expose or critique "we" as social performance rather than something natural or given. But (3) it also often tries to bring into being a particular "we" that has been obstructed in history; hence the appeal of poetry in emerging cultures. (4) Finally, though, poetry is not action, its ultimate performance may be abstract; it calls up human feeling without confining it to historical particulars or divisions, perhaps even interrupting these.

This "we" is projective, parabolic, and provisional. It is also historical, an have located my discussion of poetry's "we" not only generically but also in the particular, historically inflected example of W. H. Auden. We are now in a rather different historical environment, but it has much in common with Auden's formative thirties, which may explain the recent resurgence of the first-person plural in poetry.

My subject, then, is the communal possibilities of lyric in general. But the topic is vast and its interest arises in specific examples. In order to follow out the nuanced implications of poetry's many uses of the first-person plural, I have chosen W. H. Auden as my case study, as a poet singularly concerned with what he called "the human pluralities"—societies, communities, and crowds. I proceed on two fronts, then: what sort of genre does the use of "we" produce under the burden of modern history, and how is Auden's case a particularly interesting one in this respect? I examine markers of plural voice in relation to lyric theory and practice, ethics and sociolinguistics, though my focus is always on the poetry. I consider "we" from its most constricted and intimate to its fully unbounded forms, while at the same time showing the movement, overlap, and ambiguity within its range. Throughout, I am concerned with how "we" becomes a term absorbing reflections on voice in democracy.

Two broad themes emerge in this wide-ranging analysis. The first is that the first-person plural in poetry is often modulated and palimpsestic, moving between restrictive and inclusive forms within and beyond particular communicative frameworks. The poet tests and stretches the boundaries of his community. "We" remains open and dynamic as it returns to and moves out from various subjectivities and interactions. The second theme is that poetry as an art not only refers and reflects but also imagines and formulates *potential community*.[38]

In *Must We Mean What We Say?* Stanley Cavell asks: "Who is to say whether a man speaks for all men?"[39] "By what right does the philosopher say 'we'? We speaks of a consent that is not common, that by rights is yours."[40] The philosopher is speaking for himself, and yet he knows that the test of his seriousness is the worth of his thought for all men, which is why he writes in the first-person plural. He must dwell in this contradiction and ambivalence. Few would be willing to do away with this plural pronoun in the public sphere. The desire to say "we" and thus to refute the essential atomization of the social reality remains, even if he cannot "'postulate' that 'we,' you and I and he, say and want and imagine and feel and suffer together."[41] For Cavell, at least implicitly, the "we" of reason's presumptive assent touches on ethical and political concerns. Cavell's aim is not to prohibit the invocation of "we," only to call our attention to its indeterminacy and our need to return constantly to conversation, to the fact that we do not know the minds of others and must both acknowledge this fact and the fact that "we," and meaning itself, is constituted in the continual discourse of you and I. He continues: "Why are we so bullied by such a question [of the right to say we]? Do we imagine that if it has a sound answer the answer must be obvious or immediate? But it is no easier to say who speaks for all men than it is to speak for all men. And why should that be easier than knowing whether a man speaks for me? It is no easier than knowing oneself, and no less subject to distortion and spiritlessness."[42] The solution is not silence or a return to privacy or parochialism, or the formation of some special philosophical language that can transcend our limits; the answer is mindfulness about the imprecisions of language and about how ordinary language shapes thought, and how we nevertheless communicate and understand within it. Literature is especially formed to such mindfulness, which is perhaps why Cavell so often turns to it in making his arguments. Cavell aligns philosophy and art in this sense: both invoke a "we" that recognizes the limits of authority and acknowledges an unknowable other, even an unknowable self. Cavell's remarks make it clear that this question about philosophy is not different from questions about how we speak, practically and without certainty, in ordinary situations—in communities, in marriages. Nor is it fundamentally different from questions about how the poet speaks. One of my aims in this book is to consider how the literary imagination develops this mindfulness about our claim to speak as "we." Poetry, while it often acknowledges the Other and the limits of our knowing, nevertheless aspires (at times with urgency and great seriousness) to speak for others, for each of us, for a group, even at times for all of us together.

"We" does not always suggest a universal, of course, though poetry's abstraction can create a boundless implication, a universalized voice if not a platform of universals. Poetry's universal "we" is built up out of many smaller, overlapping, or contending forms of togetherness. I take a taxonomic approach to my subject, looking broadly at different classes of "we" usage, especially in modern poetry, even as I note slippage and envelopment among these uses. How does the first-person plural function in self-dialogue, in intimate address, in partisan groups? What is the social relation between poet and audience? What "imagined communities," to borrow from Benedict Anderson, does poetry create? How is a crowd different from a congregation? What is the relationship between the impersonal, the general, and the universal? It might seem that these classes of usage raise separate issues distinct from the problem of universals, of speaking for "us all," but poetry often reveals how connected and overlapping they are, how the personal can be mistaken for the universal and, on the other hand, how models of intimate conversation might inform public language. This principled We is reimagined as a network of shifting I/Thou relations without completely abandoning the ideal of the impersonal or of clustered communities. Poetry has been called the most intimate art and also the most universal, and it achieves this double function in part by constantly modulating among various "we's" and checking one against the other.

W. H. Auden seems to try them all. He is perhaps the preeminent modern poet for thinking about groups and group organization, intuitively and in the abstract, but he is rarely fixed to a particular theory or ideology for long.[43] He is the poet of "private faces in public places," and of "private stuff" and "public spirit," interested in the tensions and continuities between our intimate lives and our historical relations. He loves theories and doctrines, sometimes to the detriment of his verse, and passes through them like pages of a calendar, but the questions remain the same and give coherence to the process. He is a writer not only interesting to think *about* but interesting to think *with*, in part because he is always thinking, always changing position and genre. Auden was always reading, reviewing, and versifying the social, theological, and ethical philosophers of his time (Niebuhr, Buber, Arendt, Weil, Tillich, Rosenstock-Huessy, and many others) who were preoccupied with pronouns as a lens through which to understand human relations in history. Auden moves from coterie writing to public rhetoric but eventually warns against the "chimaera" of the crowd and the false ontology of "the public." As a poet beginning with English cultural and socialist sentiments, witnessing the rise of fascism, immigrating to the U.S., and, like a latter-day Tocqueville, beginning to explore American democracy, he had a wide experience of the ideologies and embodiments of the notion of "we, the people." He was deeply engaged in questions pertaining to the poet's relationship to audience and to the public more broadly, and he thought a lot about marriage and brotherly love. But Auden's interest in groups was not only conceptual; it was emotional and practical. His attraction to dramatic and dialogic form as a figure of community survives even to his late poems in which he takes counsel with himself, and he explores multiple genres for the possibilities they offer to encompass and express group relations. As a ventriloquizing poet, always playing us back to ourselves so that we may hear what we mean, he is highly sensitive to the many postures and tonalities that can arise in the use of the first-person plural. In the chapters to follow I will be exploring Auden's use of "we" through its various contexts, from his quarrels with himself and reflections on narcissism, to his didactic and liturgical modes. Auden is the central figure because he is preoccupied throughout his life with the relation between public and private, the artist's responsibility to the public and to history, the need for community, the dangers of oratory, the connections between aesthetics, politics, and ethics.

Auden's career-long reflection on the differences between crowds, societies, and communities is at the core of this study.[44]

Every writer brings particularity to the problem of saying "we," and the permutations of poetry's first-person plural are innumerable. But just as "we" is constituted in the shifting relations of "I" and "You," so the conversation across poetries of different styles and periods forms a dynamic space for considering what is common to all.

2

The Demagogue and the *Sotto Voce*

PRONOUNS ARE CRUCIAL tools for any poet. They create dramatic relation and perspective, but because they are insubstantial they allow for abstraction and inclusion. They engage us with persons, places, and things while avoiding the fixity of names. No poet was quite so preoccupied with pronouns as W. H. Auden, who reflects on them often in his poetry and essays. Their social, ethical, and religious ramifications, not to mention their artistic potential, were a career-long fascination for him. His understanding of "the human pluralities" often comes down to the structure and meaning of pronouns.

The pronoun "we" arises variously (and with varying poetic success) throughout Auden's poetry and prose to suggest distinct structures of togetherness: a coterie, a romantic couple, a congregation, or a whole culture, sometimes within the same poem. To highlight the importance of this pronoun in its objective case, Auden frames his essay collection *Forewords and Afterwords* with titles containing "us." He starts forward with a broad generational divide—"The Greeks and Us" (we are the moderns)—and closes with a narrow and backward-glancing trio—"As It Seemed to Us" ("us" being in this case just three "diffy" thinkers all old enough to be writing autobiography: Waugh and Woolf, with Auden as moderator; *F&A* 493). This scaling of plural subjectivities is typical of Auden's writing.

But "us" is a perilous pronoun for any artist and was especially so in the 1930s, as Auden responded to the aspirations and consequences associated with various ideologies of "Collective Man" and to the force of crowds and publics in contemporary history (*SP* 96). How might the poet speak for others without totalizing claims? Auden's use of pronouns rewards study and suggests the subtle and strategic engagement with groups that forms the subject of so many of his essays.[1]

It is in his stance as a public poet writing in the "low dishonest decade" of the thirties that the pronoun gives him the most trouble. "We" is a powerful and intimidating tool of political rhetoric.[2] Precisely because he had a penchant for this rhetoric, Auden would sometimes attack it. If he could rally a public, he also feared this power, for as Kierkegaard writes (and Auden later included the comment in his selections from Kierkegaard): "the public is everything and nothing, the most dangerous of all powers and the most insignificant."[3]

In order to introduce my Auden focus, I want to consider here his relatively neglected poem "Law Like Love," which incorporates many of the pronominal registers I explore throughout this book. In this poem Auden reveals his skepticism about public orators and their absolutes, and turns against the rhetoric of his own most famous public poems, "Spain" and "September 1, 1939." In "Law Like Love," which may count as his first "American" poem though not the first he wrote in America, Auden finds alternatives for realizing the civic function of poetry. From the "we" of oratory he removes to the "You" and "I" of conversation, but this *sotto voce* is not a retreat into privacy. As Edward Mendelson writes, "In 'Law Like Love' the acts and velleities of individual persons, not large historical movements, are the analogues of events that occur on a universal scale."[4] I will offer a close reading of the poem in the last section of this chapter, but first I want to explore how pronouns function in some earlier, explicitly public works, and how the conversation he has with himself about public voices leads to this dialogic turn.

Auden's uneasy sense of the state of English and European society, and of his role in its redemption, pervades his last "English" volume, *Look, Stranger!* (called *On This Island* in the American edition). As he will do again after the Second World War, the poet claims a plural voice in a moment of national crisis and uncertainty, but he seeks a more positive principle of unity. Eschewing an earlier, more alienated stance, the poet writes inclusively as a concerned observer of Europe between the wars, speaking in a public voice and rousing the populace to the plight of the *polis*. This is especially true in the final poem of this volume, "Epilogue" ("Certainly our city") of 1936.[5] Auden dropped the poem from his *Collected Poems*, but not before putting it through several changes, notably in the title, where he seems to be looking for the right stance in relation to his public subject: the rise of malice and tyranny in Europe and the distortion of ideals. "Europe, 1936" became "Epilogue" when it closed *Look, Stranger!* Later, in the less focused context of his first *Collected Poems*, he called the piece "As We Like It" (1945) and "Our City" (1950). The pronouns "we" and "our" held different, less local resonances for Auden as he moved off the island of England to become an American and increasingly take a "cosmopolitan path."[6]

The incomplete sentence that begins this poem and forms the entire first stanza ("Certainly our city . . . the glass") seems to answer a question or confirm a speculation made before the poem began. What city is this? Whose city is this? But without an antecedent, the "certainly" potentially becomes an adverb intensifying "our." The poem's first-person plural calls us out of numb neutrality into an active connection. This is "our city," not someone else's, though it has changed in troubling ways. "Our" connotes not so much property as responsibility. The second stanza of "Certainly our city" draws attention to its pronouns, using enjambment to give them emphasis, and introducing proper nouns only later. After scanning a generic urban industrial scene (its "byres of poverty" and its "cathedral") in the detached, descriptive voice of stanza one, Auden shifts to a more urgent tone in viewing "our city," "built by the conscience-stricken, the weapon-making, / By us." The constantly enjambed first-person plural creates emotional connection to the scene:

> By us. The rumours woo and terrify the crowd,
> > Woo us. The betrayers thunder at, blackmail
> > Us. But where now are They
>
> Who without reproaches shewed us what our vanity has chosen.

By emphasizing the first-person plural, the poem compels readers, as fellows of a *polis*, to look on and acknowledge their involvement and their lack of honest leaders. It's the same banal and troubled place, but the healers and heroes are gone, leaving terrified crowds amidst those who "have the power" and "wish to wound." As with other poems in the 1936 volume, Auden here urges the group (a nonpartisan populace of a generic European city) to confront its condition and rouse itself from apathy and complacency. He emphasizes, therefore, the possessive and objective forms of the pronoun: "our" and "Us"; not identity but responsibility is at stake. He looks "on this island" from a deliberate distance in order to face the facts. But knowledge is not action. The passive voice ("by us") works thematically here to underscore the lag in agency, or the helpless alienation of the modern inhabitants compared to the energetic founders of their civilization. Auden provokes "us" to re-engage, to face "our" part in the crisis (and to take ownership of "our city" in order to heal it) before turning to blame others—the inchoate "crowd" or vague "betrayers." We wait in vain for heroic rescue—"they," the redeemers of the past, are gone. This strategic use of pronouns to prod a public to self-reflection and action is characteristic of Auden's work in the thirties. He speaks not only *to* a troubled public but also *as* a member of that community, urging it to confront its condition and its loss of heroic initiative and idealism. There is no singular personal voice in this poem, no I or You, only Us (the populace) and Them (past leaders and healers). A dejected public mourns past heroes and pronounces the death of the modern city. But the poetic voice does not retreat into private anguish or alienation. The poem draws to its end in rhetorical questions that seem designed to admonish the *polis*: "Can / Hate so securely bind? Are They dead here? Yes. / And the wish to wound has the power. And to-morrow / Comes." This is oratory, which is perhaps why Auden omitted the poem from *Collected Poems* despite its powerfully abbreviated images and panoramic scope. "Certainly our city" ends in a resigned rather than an admonitory voice. "It's a world, it's a way" is not Auden's way but a disdainful echo of the public complacency he faults. Public recognition of the city's plight is the beginning of transformation, and the insistent pronouns push the audience toward change. Auden imagined a social love that would transcend self-interest and narcissism and "think no thought but ours," and he sought a hero who thought in terms of "we," not "I."

Auden employs his oratorical voice a year later in "Spain," which speaks with an implied purpose: to raise concern for the Republican cause and the International Brigade. The poem arouses an urgent feeling through its incantatory lines, suggesting that existence gathers meaning through choice in history. While Auden would eschew the rallying rhetoric of the thirties, the theme stays with him. (In the 1972 poem "Aubade," he writes that "Time, the domain of Deeds" calls for "the Imperative" and unites us under a capitalized first-person plural. "We are free to choose our paths / but choose We must.")[7] "Spain" (1937) picks up where he left off in "Certainly our city" and uses similar anaphora and metonymic compression as well as many of the same words and symbolic strategies. The poem incites the moribund public to seize "To-day" and create a "really better / World" (*EA* 165). "We are left alone with our day, and the time is short" (*SP* 57), Auden warns at the end of "Spain," echoing and advancing the epilogue to *Look, Stranger!* Auden's later antipathy toward this public exhortation is well known. As he famously wrote to Mrs. E. R. Dodds, "I suddenly found I could really do it, that I could make a fighting demagogic speech and have the audience roaring. . . . My dear, it is so exciting . . . but so absolutely degrading; I felt just covered with dirt afterwards."[8] We can see Auden wrestling with this rhetoric throughout the late thirties, especially in his nuanced deployment of pronouns.

Auden said he came to America, in part, to stop writing these kinds of public poems, which he marginalized as "occasional" when he collected them in *Another Time*. "September 1, 1939" was written in his first year in the U.S., but while it puts the "I" before the "We," it has a great deal in common with "Spain." The line he disavowed even before he abandoned the poem, "We must love one another or die" (*SP* 97), may be his most famous, and it certainly carries over the rhetoric of the public orator with his imperative "we." In "New Year Letter," which Auden started writing at about the same time, he speaks of "The preacher's loose immodest tone" (*CP* 202), and his embarrassment about that tone may be one reason he turned against "September 1, 1939" despite its humility *topos*. But in many poems, especially those he would compose in

America, Auden shifts and varies the identity associated with the first-person plural, returning it to local and particular sites from its oratorical perch, as if to restrain an imperial tone or humanize a public voice. In such poems the *sotto voce* of the private individual, "the untidy and unintimidated personal voice," checks the impulse of the demagogue.[9] As Edward Mendelson has remarked, "whenever Auden wrote a poem he recognized as grand, emphatic, and false, he immediately followed it with one that was quiet, tentative, and truthful."[10]

"Law Like Love," for instance, if we accept Mendelson's dating (September 1939), may be read as Auden's repudiation of his own forms of public address, especially "Spain" and "September 1, 1939," well before he abandoned those poems in gathering the *Collected Poems*. All three poems appear in *Another Time*, although "Law Like Love," which has received the least critical attention, is the only one of the three Auden would keep. There has been much commentary on Auden's excisions and revisions but less detailed attention to the way his poems respond to previous poems in a long conversation with himself, especially about the meaning of community and the ability of the poet to speak for others. In "Law Like Love," Auden expresses his skepticism toward those who make absolute claims and commands from interested and limited perspectives. The poem satirizes those perspectives and postures but goes on to build up a different, more qualified "we" from horizontal relations rather than from vertical, abstract principles. This "we" derives from conversation and deliberation, not oratory or decree, from acts of saying, not from what has been said. It is an ethical rather than a political, institutional, or societal "we." By returning to the interpersonal in this way, Auden may also be recalling, and modifying, some of the principles that guided him in his Berlin period of 1929, before he developed his public voice, even as he absorbs new influences in America, where he moved a decade later.

I have suggested that "Law Like Love" (1939) may be read in dialogue with Auden's public poetry of the thirties, "Spain" and "September 1, 1939" in particular. To establish this point, I need to look first at his disposition toward collective groups in those works, and at specific verbal and formal gestures that he may be echoing in "Law Like Love." For instance, is Auden cueing us to his 1937 "Spain" in the last line of the first stanza of "Law Like Love": "To-morrow, yesterday, to-day" (*SP* 98)? The line certainly reiterates, in a jauntier mood, the repeated time frames that organize the earlier poem. A review of pronoun use in "Spain" suggests the difficulty Auden was having at the time in defining a community for which he could speak (and this may reflect his ambiguous role in the war itself). Pronouns suggest inclusions and exclusions, as well as agency and possession, and reflect troubled conditions in the thirties, when causes and courses of action were so much in dispute. In "Spain" (I cite the March 1937 version in *SP* 54–57), we can observe Auden's deliberate pronoun avoidance as he substitutes anaphoric noun phrases and passive constructions for complete structures of intervention and ownership. Not "our yesterday is all past" but "Yesterday all the past"; history is spectacle rather than owned experience. Auden opens "Spain" with a kind of impersonal, newsreel-pageant of images. Unlike the impersonal survey of the industrial landscape in the opening of "Certainly our city," this account presents incontrovertible realities, past and present. History has its own momentum, like a force of nature or, later, a metaphysical power. Verbs convert to gerunds, nouns, or participles, confusing cause and effect: "the shadow-reckoning," "the carving of angels," "the taming of horses"; "the assessment of insurance by cards"; "the bustling world of the navigators," and so on. Some of this cataloging is conventional for public speeches, but given Auden's later emphasis on faces and responsibility, the absence of agents here is significant. As the poet shifts from "Yesterday" to "To-day," "the struggle" in "Spain" remains without an actor: "the fall of the curtain," "the adoration of madmen." Auden is building up to a call for collective intervention, but, as Mendelson has argued, the poem remains at the threshold of commitment between necessity and choice.[11] Anticipating Auden's later ideas, we might say that he views choice as a necessity.

In the second section of "Spain," the pronoun "I" briefly emerges, beginning with "the poet" who "whispers" (presumably in contrast to the politicians who shout). This is a dramatic, not a lyric "I" since the "the poet" is distinguished from the voice of the poem. Indeed, much of the first part of the poem is in quotation, including words of "the poet." Auden goes on to cite other segments of society—the scientist, the poor. Each "I" speaks for or as a group constituency loosely consolidated, not as individual voice. The verb mode is the imperative plea "send me" or intransitive reflection "I inquire. I inquire." "The poor" are not given a direct subjectivity ("we") but only a possessive "our" that ironically describes their lack of possession: "Our day is our loss." The ventriloquized voices build until "the nations combine each cry," not only becoming international but melting social and class distinction in order to form an imagined community around Spain's plight. Auden does not so much absorb this diversity of voices as merge them into one transcendent voice— something that would become more typical of the fascist enemy's rhetoric. With an ear always listening for the dangerous seductions of rhetoric, he may have heard a resemblance to the voice of the enemy.

Abstraction is answered with abstraction in "Spain" when this "cry" produces in response a disembodied voice of "the life" and a chain of predicates: "I am your choice, your decision. Yes I am Spain." We do not suffer History but make it, the poem suggests by these nouns. But the abstraction of choice in this "I" complicates the transition. "I" is an indexical pronoun—but the "I" here is imaginary, abstract and impersonal, invented by and internal to the text. This "I," floating above the helpless spectators and sufferers in the poem as a projection of their moral conscience, is the catalyst of the emergent "we" in a forming I-We relationship. The public gathers into one perceiving body—"the heart / And the eyes and the lungs"—and thus becomes the "I" of a collective entity: "the life" that is entirely transpersonal, despite the poet's reference to the "individual belly." (Mussolini's campaign slogan "One heart, one will, one decision" comes uncomfortably to mind with these lines.) "The life" thus becomes the higher voice, a host incarnate (as sacrificial blood seeds the arid land), haunted by the transcendental fictions it wants to reject. "Our thoughts have bodies" suggests turning intention to action. But since there is really only one "thought," individual bodies are really one corporation in the service of "it." Here the first person is not the embedded voice of "the poor" but a collective and unspecified "we." I/Thou relations have been converted into a unified force: "Our hours of friendship into a people's army." No individual conscience or consciousness takes responsibility in this impersonal and passive construction: "The conscious acceptance of guilt in the necessary murder." And later even the vision of the future forms as crowd imagery and a collective voice rather than a return to private life. The future promises "the beautiful roar of the chorus under the dome." Auden would soon delete the line, though the promised future of the "pageant-master," oddly akin to some rather sinister figures in *The Orators*, survives all versions of "Spain."

Thus when Auden finally claims the pronoun "we" at the end of "Spain," its function and potential agency is ambiguous. "We are left alone with our day" does not seem to suggest isolated individuals but rather an aroused mass that has been swept together in the momentum of a speech. "Alone" here may suggest the absence of superhuman forces to intervene in human "History," but "History the operator," a vaguely Marxist idea, still animates an abstraction. Auden is not just capitalizing the beginning of the line; he is giving History metaphysical power. The personification of Spain has kept in place the authoritative "I-We" relationship (with "I" again the voice of an abstraction), as if "We" might act as a historical agent subsuming a fearful and hesitant you and I. Who is this compelling "We" that would join forces with History? Auden would later suggest that only free and equal individuals—faces, not numbers—constitute a community and make ethical choices that determine the course of history. The individual may be a threat to community when, like Coriolanus, he "cannot say 'we' and demands a special place."[12] But in dialogue with other persons, the singular forms the core of community in Auden's later liberal vision. In "Spain," however, the collective seems to take on a power and will of its own, indeed to become a force of nature, part of what he would later call the Dynamo, that takes the individual up into its impersonal vortex. "Spain" has the magnificence of a great mural (not *Guernica*, however, with its individual foci), and it is rightly considered one of the essential public poems of modern literature.

When Auden later revised and then rejected "Spain," it was not only because of the scolding from George Orwell over the unfeeling phrase "necessary murder" or because he sensed there was something "degrading" in his ability as an orator to "have the audience roaring." The roar itself bothered him, not just his own demagogic tendencies, but also the capacity of individuals to yield to a crowd, or even to become subsumed into social or political groups. Articulate discourse, he would later suggest, dissolves in a crowd, and words become noise. People are all too ready to become aroused as a mass, to merge into a herd and roar from a daemonic "we" voice that subsumes individual responsibility.

No wonder that in writing "September 1, 1939" Auden began with an emphatic first-person *singular* pronoun, a voice far from the crowd, albeit in a public house, or rather an American "dive." In this poem Auden tries to reassert lyric's individual voice in place of the impersonal oratorical voice of "Spain." This is not a rally platform or a broadcasting studio (where we might imagine Auden delivering "Spain"). But the poem passes quickly from the individual to the oratorical voice. As with Yeats's "I" in "Easter, 1916," Auden's initial anecdotal passivity and alienation are quickly replaced with oratory, addressing matters of History, destiny, and human choice. Drunks in bars do like to make speeches sometimes. Auden's initial "I," drinking alone, is speaking to himself or nobody; but the local, colloquial voice is a temporary persona and does not represent the rhetoric the poem will pursue.

Auden increasingly hated the faceless demographic view of humanity, finding it antithetical to the ethical life. But his imagination was drawn to multitudes. "September 1, 1939" (*SP* 95–98) still seems concerned with numbers, "the dense commuters," "the helpless governors," the "ironic points of light," "faces along the bar," rather than with individual faces, despite the quick sketches of iconic figures like Hitler and Diaghilev. Auden may be mimicking public rhetoric to expose hollow media concepts such as "Collective Man" and "Important Persons," but he does not exhibit clear alternatives to public rhetoric. Indeed, one theme of the poem is the necessary intrusion of the public into the private and the need to transcend excessive self-love. The condition of the times forces itself on *us*, indeed, creates "us" by (in a strained transitive grammar) "obsessing our private lives," and we are helpless to resist. Quickly, Auden shifts to an I-We alliance: "I and the public know"; he is back in the realm of oratory, though not in the register of the demagogue. Here "the public" has authority and backs the poet's assertions, though later, in "Horae Canonicae," he writes of "our public. / The faceless many who always / Collect when any world is to be wrecked." Auden laments that "the unmentionable odour of death" has entered the private life. Yet his response to this invasion

is not to reanimate the private world but to create an "odorless" public that
after the war he would find toxic precisely because one can't sense it. But in
"September 1, 1939" Auden's characterization of "the public" is affirming. From
"I and the public" Auden moves to I-and-the-Just; at least he implicitly numbers himself with "the Just" when he announces he is "Beleaguered by the
same / Negation and despair." Who "the Just" are or what specifically constitutes justice, he never makes clear. While Auden may distance himself from
"the police," there is more than a bit of the Judge looking down his nose in
his notorious sentence: "We must love one another or die."[13] Auden doesn't
strictly follow poetry's conventional expansion from I to We here, since after
the famously troublesome line he backs off and returns to the first-person
singular—"All I have is a voice." But this "voice" has become strangely faceless
and radio-like in speaking for others. The humility of the "I" in "September 1,
1939" is a *topos*. Auden seems more interested in the I/We relation here than
the I/Thou that the commandment "we must love one another" implies or
that he emphasized in later work. "September 1, 1939" is a great work of anti-
oratorical oratory, critical of the "windiest militant trash," aligned with "Thu-
cydides" yet clearly a didactic poem. Even while composing "September 1,
1939," Auden had doubts about its claim to speak for "everyone." For instance,
he excised a stanza that once came after stanza 7, ending:

> No promises can stay
> The ruling of the court
> In session on an act
> Nor magic wish away
> Its summary effect:
> What can I do but recall
> What everyone knows in his heart,
> One law applies to us all;
> In spite of terror and death
> The continuum of truth
> May not be torn apart.[14]

The scene is of a judicial court, and the stanza makes a grandiose pronounce-
ment on "law" such as Auden would soon satirize. Is the "act" historical and
dangerous while the "law" is a higher moral principle that calls to us "in spite
of" the "terror and death" that the act may bring about? What "court" and "act"
might Auden have in mind in the first of these canceled stanzas? Is this court
generic or historical? Is Auden alluding, say, to the "Enabling Act" of 1933 that
led to Hitler's dictatorship? Is the "law" in the second part of this stanza, the
one that applies to "everyone" and "us all," the same one that sponsors the
courtroom scene? Is it a universal law of historical forces or a moral law of

human justice? As with the other excised stanza and several retained stanzas of this poem, Auden's assertive tone does not always support a coherent or substantive idea of "truth." The "law" remains hidden even though the poem does not consider it mysterious.[15] Like "Spain," this is a masterpiece of public poetry, but Auden would seek other stances for forming community, where the authority of the poetic voice works more by example than by precept, more by humor and implied conversation than oratory.

Scholars have stressed Auden's self-conscious Americanness in "September 1, 1939," and indeed in revising, the poet (or perhaps the *New Republic* copyeditor) changed all the spelling to American norms.[16] But as he later wrote to Naomi Mitchison, this poem was a "hang-over from the U.K." and not at all the kind of poem he came to the U.S. to write.[17] In writing "Law Like Love" Auden may be retracting the very claim in the excised stanza of "September 1, 1939," to "know" "one law [that] applies to all." Is "Law Like Love," with its plurality of voices, its shift from public to private discourse, and its humor, a more "American" poem?[18]

———

"Law Like Love" (*SP* 98–99), also written (according to Mendelson's dating) in September 1939, offers a reflection on the claim to universal "laws" that such public poems as "Spain" and "September 1, 1939" proclaim. "Law Like Love," while it does not respond to contemporary events, is much more qualified and localized in its ethical commands and claims to know what is right and true. Even if we account for generic differences, categorizing "Law Like Love" as a love poem rather than a public poem, we can see how directly Auden has set the poem as a response to those earlier oratorical voices. The poem reverses the default logic of modern poetry that so often moves inevitably from the local "I" to the universal "We." It moves instead through competing absolutes, to more qualified claims, and ends with a "we" voice that seems more choral than oratorical and built as much on acknowledgment of difference and limit as on consensus or mandate. "Law Like Love" turns from public faces to private ones, addressing a "dear" in a quiet encounter. The poem makes a considerable swerve from Auden's more political understanding of human fundamentals. Now, Mendelson writes: "The affirmation of a unique 'I' can claim the fullest understanding of the law because the law, like love, is concerned (so Auden believed) with personal uniqueness, not with political generalization."[19] But it is just as clear that the "I" requires a "You" in loving conversation in order to discover the law. The poem shifts from speeches and decrees to an I/Thou relationship in which propositions are provisional and qualified, and involve commitments that are subject to response from other minds. This "we" forms around a conversation as in a friendship or marriage, rather than around the consensus of a tribe, bureaucracy, or aroused mass. It does not rely on the idea of "the public," yet in its reserved way it might be considered a civic poem.

"The problem for the modern poet, as for everyone else to-day, is how to find or form a genuine community," Auden remarked in 1938, in his introduction to *The Oxford Book of Light Verse* (*Prose* I 436).[20] We can read "Law Like Love" in relation to this problem of finding or forming community, and the role of humor in its solution, in establishing a "we." "Poetry which is at the same time light and adult can only be written in a society which is both integrated and free." The introduction to *Light Verse* is retrospective and laments the absence of those conditions in the contemporary world. Auden had turned away from light verse since "Letter to Lord Byron" (1936) in order to face a fractured and subjugated modern world. But he seems to have retrieved some of the features of light verse in "Law Like Love," perhaps hoping for the corollary that "poetry which is at the same time light and adult" might do something to advance a society that is "integrated and free." In a fragmented society, poetry becomes a place of *potential* community. In fact Auden's concept of community is bound up with this idea of *potentiality*. A community, because it is inclusive, is never fully formed. As he wrote in "The Virgin & the Dynamo," a community exists "neither by chance, like a crowd, nor actually, like a society, but potentially, so that it is possible to conceive of a community in which, at present, n=1" (*DH* 64). That potentiality describes, among other things, a condition of writing, since the relation to a reader is projected, not actual.

Does the modern community require a belief in universals? "Law Like Love" asks this question. Or does the conversation between even two individuals connected by mutual interests and acknowledgments rather than abstract laws create the potential for integrated community? In "The Virgin & the Dynamo," Auden distinguishes societies, crowds, and communities. Societies are necessary. Crowds are numbers without faces and disturbing to the poet. But communities, which are always *becoming* rather than fully embodied (at which point they are societal), are clearly where he places his faith. "Spain" moves through the first two, from various social roles (poet, scientific investigator, the poor, nations) to the aroused collective, transpersonal "life." In "Law Like Love," Auden moves through the full sequence.

The groups Auden catalogs through the first half of the poem are social, indeed institutional types (gardeners, priests, judges, scholars, etc.), each operating according to a law-driven "system" and its respective propositions. The satiric tone quickly builds in the poem. "Law is the wisdom of the old" seems a palatable truism until it is situated, in the next line, in the scolding voice of "the impotent grandfathers" and set against the "treble" of their troublesome grandchildren, to create a kind of societal chamber music. From the family, Auden builds to broader institutions.

> Law, says the priest with a priestly look,
> Expounding to an unpriestly people,
> Law is the words in my priestly book,
> Law is my pulpit and my steeple.

Priest and judge (the latter comes next in the nine-stanza procession), as figures with authoritarian power in society, are singular orators. Auden was always interested in faces—and so is the satirist. The face the poem puts on as it presents the various voices reciting their laws is certainly satiric, though remarkably modulated and tuned to types within that mode. The first stanza, "Law, say the gardeners, is the sun," has the neutral tone of a primer whereas the poem builds to mimicry and irony.

The satiric effects in "Law Like Love" are created not only by sound but also by imagery. One source might be Honoré Daumier, the visual artist Auden most admired, and who was fascinated by orators and crowd spectators. Consider "the judge as he looks down his nose" or the "priest with his priestly look." "The Just" of "September 1, 1939" are not so much sober as faceless; one cannot argue with them; but judges and priests here make faces and we can read them and look behind them. They are men, not angels, and the laws they propound are man-made. Ultimately, though, Auden's satire inheres in sound and rhetoric more than in imagery. The simple declarative language of the opening initially suggests matters of fact. But the echo of nursery rhyme in Auden's "people" / "steeple" rhyme (recalling "here is a church, here is a steeple / open the doors and see all the people") undermines the priestly pontifications. The form varies from couplets to alternating rhymes to unrhymed lines as the poem fits itself to various social formations—each may presume to speak for all, but Auden gives each its own sound, relativizing the plurality of voices. The judge is said to speak "clearly and most severely," but Auden moves toward his conclusion with the tautology of an orator who assumes rather than argues his case: "Law is The Law." (Auden combines the priest and judge stanzas in *Collected Poems*, perhaps suggesting they are two of a kind.) As speakers they are satirized, but their "laws" are not dismissed or displaced with the poet's alternative absolutes. Auden's stanza-long catalog of what "others say" itself creates a dialogical quality missing from each of these absolutist voices. It forms a chain of opinions. But the poem doesn't rest in contingency just because it acknowledges others. Humor is linked to skepticism, but this skepticism involves an awareness of limits to knowledge rather than negation or relativism.

As he wrote in 1952, modifying his earlier remarks on light verse, "A sense of humor develops in a society to the degree that its members are simultaneously conscious of being each a unique person and of being all in common subjection to unalterable laws" (*DH* 372). These "unalterable laws" are not social or institutional but are laws of necessity—especially of the body and its limits, to which even those with institutional power must submit. This is a singular "we" but also a basis for uniting a plurality. In this way humor fosters community, and American humor appealed to him. Auden wrote to Mrs. Dodd early in his emigration to America that he had discovered "one of the best poets in America . . . Ogden Nash." Ogden Nash? He quotes Nash's poem "Spring Comes to Murray Hill," which begins "As I sit in my office / on 23rd St. and Madison Avenue."[21] At least from Auden's point of view, then, light verse was thriving in the United States, and perhaps this was a sign of societal health. Anyone coming across this letter immediately connects it to the opening of "September 1, 1939." But there is really nothing at all Nash-like about *that* poem. "Law Like Love," on the other hand, shows the influence sharply. Becoming American might have meant learning from Walt Whitman, Henry James, and Marianne Moore, but it also meant channeling the lighter spirits of Ogden Nash and even the American songbook. John Fuller identifies the verse rhymes of "Law Like Love" with the much softer, and English, A. A. Milne, but the acerbic, more consequential, and *American* Nash seems the likelier source.

With the breakdown of social order in the middle stanzas, however ("others say / . . . / Law has gone away"), the lighter satire of the poem falls away. "Satire flourishes in a homogeneous society where satirist and audience share the same view as to how normal people can be expected to behave" (*DH* 385). Modern society has little of this consensus, but it does have hearsay and crowd mentality. Rumor (figured in refrain and repetition) and that chimera, public opinion, follow the presumption of authority. This idea seems to resonate in the etcetera of the poem's catalog: "others say, others say." The poem tracks a collapse of discourse into noise, and noise into roar. Instead of the polyphonies of the old and young, we hear a voice becoming sinister, chant-like, and univocal until the "loud angry crowd" whose "Law is We" drowns out the *sotto voce*. The "soft idiot softly Me," fades out in the crowd and with it goes any plurality such as was heard in the family treble and bass at the poem's opening. Auden would later describe irony as a *sotto voce*, difficult to hear in a public crisis and perhaps not adequate, but important as a dimension of the human voice if it is not to lose its plurality.[22] If satire can't survive the angry times, humor at least remains a necessity. The congenial spirit of humor continues in the poem, but not the voice of satire, which requires shared beliefs and cultural values. Instead of mocking others where there is no one to listen, the *sotto voce* turns toward the intimate other. Auden replaces the vocative "O" of the orator in "Spain" with the interpersonal "dear" of the lover and friend in "Law Like Love."

If we follow the categories of "The Virgin & the Dynamo"—societies, crowds, communities—the last third of the poem is devoted to the potential of "community," as a corrective to this frightening momentum toward the authoritarian or mob "We" in earlier parts of the poem. Community is formed not from injunctions or out of consensus but out of I/Thou relations that are reciprocal, engaged, and shifting. Auden swerves in his use of "we." Instead of an I/We of the loud crowd versus the mumbling *sotto voce* of the alienated "me," he turns to an I/Thou of conversational deliberation. A community can be as few as two or even one deliberating with himself and inclined toward another. Auden's "dear" at this time is of course Chester Kallman, whom he had met in April, and many of Auden's I/Thou exchanges in the poetry of his American period are grounded in this difficult quasimarital relationship. But he may also be looking back to the intense conversations of his Berlin days, when he was reading and taking notes voraciously, and when his sexual experiences were matched in intensity only by emotionally charged conversations with his intimates about the nature of human drives and attachments. Auden writes in his Berlin journal: "John [Layard] in the evening talked a lot about Law as love. I was ashamed in fact of Christopher, though on other occasions I agree with a great deal of what he says. That what we think we believe varies with our company."[23] Auden's affair with Layard was deeply troubled at the time he wrote these words, and Layard's attempted suicide was surely something Auden could not have forgotten even more than a decade later, so perhaps, even if the idea of "law as love" is not especially original philosophically, Auden would have associated it with Layard.

Halfway through "Law Like Love," Auden finally takes his turn away from the sequence of commentators on the nature of "the law" to speak in his own voice. He begins not with the assertion of an absolute to match theirs, not with a decree, but with a qualification and an implicit double negative: "If we, dear, know we know no more." The "If" marks a return to quiet reasoning (after the loud crowd's rage) through the marker of a syllogism, but this is not a new relentless "law" of logical necessity. Reason in fact encounters "the absurd," a subject very much on Auden's mind as he has recently been reading Kierkegaard. Auden keeps a balance of simple vocabulary and an increasingly complex syntax that, with the couplets and other repetitive sounds, heightens the feeling of light verse.

> If we, dear, know we know no more
> Than they about the law,
> If I no more than you
> Know what we should and should not do
> Except that all agree

Gladly or miserably
That the law is
And that all know this,
If therefore thinking it absurd
To identify Law with some other word,
Unlike so many men
I cannot say Law is again,
No more than they can we suppress
The universal wish to guess
Or slip out of our own position
Into an unconcerned condition.

His thought pursues a circuitous and nuanced path full of condition and conversation with indefinite borders—if, given, therefore . . . "Although." Ironically, the only universal the poem seems to arrive at is that we all yearn for impersonal truths, yearn to "slip out of our own position / Into an unconcerned condition." Conversational deliberation (even within this one-sided form) leads, however, to fellow feeling, and to community formed in acknowledgment of limit.

Auden has shifted ground so that by the end of the poem "Law," even the law of logic with its identity principle is a ghostly subject, its predicate displaced by simile—Law simply "is." Auden is as good as his word: "I cannot say Law is again," and like Wittgenstein, he passes over it in silence. His interest shifts away from law. The real law is hidden and outside discourse, but we can say what it resembles, "A timid similarity / We shall boast anyway: / Like love I say." Though the syntax implies the lingering subject "law" for the prepositional "like love," by dropping the subject of the sentence he shifts to the relative condition of simile to suit the relative condition of human communication and commitments. But *are* similes "timid"? He does not forswear his will to pronounce general truths. Layard "talked about love *as* Law." Auden says "like" and so stays short of saying what "Law is," but how short?

When the syntax of the deliberating mind gets into knots of nots, the "timid" qualifying voice finds a new "boast" (though the content seems modest it is daring and interpersonal), and the rhetoric changes again. The deontic modal verb "we shall" before the "I say" puts the emphasis on entering into commitment rather than on the thought as revealed truth—a vow even as vows are not kept. Indeed, the line "Like love I say" calls up the form of the vow. Vows and boasts are not true or false statements, not claims but acts; they are what J. L. Austin called *performatives*.

If stanza 8 has shaped a lyric "we" of I/Thou exchange, Auden allows himself a more choral voice at the end, dropping the "I" for a "we" that is communal, not hegemonic. All members are free and equal. The last stanza is in the voice of a congregation (a "collect" in the lexicon of English prayer) though not a collective, and without a priest (or judge or poet-orator) singing a kind of hymn to something outside his own "vanity," a hymn to community based on mutual limit rather than the authority of named universals. It might seem in "Law Like Love" that Auden has retreated from the public sphere, but the open-ended quality of this final voice suggests that the boundaries between public and private are not so sharp.

> Like love we don't know where or why,
> Like love we can't compel or fly,
> Like love we often weep,
> Like love we seldom keep.

These last lines seem to speak not for others but with others. He hasn't quite echoed Layard in seeing Law as Love, but by dropping "law" in the last stanza he does more than compare—he displaces, as in a trope, and what is lost in absolutes is gained in repetition and unison. In fact, "like" might be said to lose its function as a term of comparison and become a term of endearment. To my ear there's more here than just one more interested perspective continuing the poem's parataxis (*law say the lovers is love*). Though love is not quite a disinterested, transcendent principle, the poem shows how love poetry might have a civic function. Impersonal truth claims have little appeal for Auden as they either mask an interest (of gardeners, judges, priests, for instance) or remove themselves from human historical struggle. Love is not offered as an abstract principle so much as a proximate and present condition of mutual interest and attachment.

In "Law Like Love," we have an example of Auden's attempt to perform community, which as he says later "can only exist in potential" and is in this sense especially a formation of imagination rather than society. I hear a chorus in these last lines in part because Auden uses the chorus so much in his drama and his sense of dramatic ritual is alive in his poetry; the origins of lyric poetry are after all choral, and Auden tries to revive them in such moments. The reader can join in since a community does not change, Auden says, by the addition of members.

Edward Mendelson described Auden's later "I" as "an I who tried to escape the limits of the solitary self not by pretending to *be* something different but by learning to *become* something different."[24] In this poem we can see a similar poetics of becoming in the expression of a "we." By the end of this poem, at least, Auden's preference for the World of the Virgin over the World of the Dynamo is clear: "In this World [the Historical World of the Virgin] Necessity is the consciousness of Freedom and Justice the love of my neighbor as a unique and irreplaceable being. (*One law for the ox and the ass is oppression*)" (*DH* 61–62). Years after "Law Like Love," Auden would invoke Simone Weil: "belief in the existence of other human beings as such is love."[25]

Community is formed out of love, not laws, and out of acknowledging the existence of the other. Though he used the pronoun regularly, Auden never defined a "We-feeling" perhaps because, as this poem shows, it has so many moods and treacherous as well as loving relations. But in describing the "I-feeling" and the "You-feeling" he implies a We-feeling: "Common to both the I- and the You-feeling: a feeling of being-in-the-middle-of-a-story" (*CP* 655). The second person precedes the first; we respond and obey before we can summon and command.

3

Song of My Selves

I was of three minds,
Like a tree
In which there are three blackbirds.

—WALLACE STEVENS, "THIRTEEN
WAYS OF LOOKING AT A BLACKBIRD"

"A TRUE FIRST person plural is an impossibility," wrote Franz Boas, "because there can never be more than one self."[1] But he could as easily have asked, "How can there be only one self?" Whitman's "I am large, I contain multitudes"[2] has been taken up as a common theme of recent cognitive and behavioral psychology.[3] We think of the inward-looking poet as antagonistic to the social order, but the pluralized self may be the beginning of the lyric's ability to imagine community. The poet's communing with himself may create a foundation for imagining other minds. Forms of the pluralized self that might seem to be distinct—such as self-dialogue, narcissism, aristocratic elevation, empathy—overlap and pull against each other in the poet's interaction with the world. Instances of what linguists call "nosism"—the use of "we" when "I" is implied—have a surprising persistence in poetry.

Rather than suggesting inner plurality and psychological or cognitive enlargement, the majestic we is most often associated with imperiousness, distance, and public presentation of the self's authority—hardly the prelude to democratic sociality.[4] King Lear preempts the speech of others with a "we" that doubles back on itself in self-circulating love: "which of you shall we say doth love us most?"[5] Is his "shall" marking a possibility, a prediction, or a command? That deontic "shall" slips from invitation to decree. Shakespeare's royal we is rarely mere convention; it is an opportunity for dramatic character development. In poetry the majestic we has sometimes been reconstructed as a metaphor for the aristocracy of the imagination. Emily Dickinson makes prolific use of the royal we. "And now We roam in Sovereign Woods"; "We—would rather / From Our Garret go / White—Unto the White Creator—/ Than invest—Our Snow—."[6] This "royal air" is not only imperial, however. It also registers the plurality of the self as fundamental. We hear Dickinson's royal we, her sense of the difficult aristocracy of the poetic imagination, in many contemporary poets, from John Berryman ("we cry oursel's awake") to Kay Ryan ("The Test We Set Ourself"). We are accustomed to thinking about duality and conflict rather than plurality and expansion within the self. Modernism often emphasized the divided self—tensions between public and private, ego and id, self and soul, mind and body. Matthew Arnold anticipated this theme in his preface of 1853: "The calm, the cheerfulness, the disinterested objectivity have disappeared: the dialogue of the mind with itself has commenced." That dialogue has a tragic aspect for him: "We hear already the doubts, we witness the discouragement, of Hamlet and of Faust."[7] But must the self be unified, suppressing competing thoughts and impulses? Many writers have treated the self as a manifold rather than a monarchy, with equilibrium and liminal being rather than opposition or final synthesis as the desired states. "Do I contradict myself?" asks Whitman. He's not troubled by it. "Very well, then, I contradict myself."[8] The imperial aspect of the American self has ever been connected to the idea of self-improvement. The majestic we can serve this motive as we imagine an alternative version of our being. This is what Stanley Cavell calls "nextness."[9] He means "next" in the sense of *beside* ourselves, different from ourselves, a plural self, and "next" also as in the temporality of a self that would move forward in vision and being, without a particular goal, to perfection. Contemporary psychology is also catching up to Whitman. Paul Bloom has observed that "the capacity to spawn multiple selves is central to pleasure" and that literature contributes to that capacity, allowing us to entertain imaginatively potentialities that we can't live out but that enrich our well-being.[10] The modernist use of personae is an obvious example of this spawning, though its affect may be agitation more than pleasure. Contemporary poetry has extended this technique with a proliferation of portraits of the self "as" another, often removing the anguish and pathology of self-division and seeing plurality as health.[11]

But the plurality of the self is not only a matter of private well-being. The capacity to expand or transform the self through imagination is also directly linked, according to philosopher Ted Cohen in *Thinking of Others*, to our ethical development and the capacity for empathy. (The doctor's "we," often associated with condescension, has more to do with compassion, this capacity to understand another's pain.) To imaginatively become another is for Cohen a metaphoric act. Literature, which enhances our inherently double, metaphoric thinking and our ability to entertain other selves, thus plays an important role in moral development. And like metaphor, these acts of imagining oneself as another through literature do not simply reflect antecedent similarities but spawn and establish connections, again linking literature to *potential* community. While Paul Bloom's work is focused on expanding the self and Ted Cohen's on imagining the other, their arguments overlap in how we might understand the capacity of an "I" to thrive in plurality. The openness to being what Auden called a "double man" can involve a greater facility for interpersonal awareness. To see "oneself *as* oneself" is already a primary metaphoric act (italics mine).[12] Works of art can also "teach me something about myself, or allow me to discover something about myself."[13] The sense of potential in imagining oneself as another, or allowing difference within the self, has temporal as well as social implications. "To gain a sense of oneself at a future time" is for Cohen another metaphoric act that depends on the capacity of the imagination, enhanced in literature, to pluralize identity. Self-reflection and acknowledgment of the other are, then, related and mutually supporting metaphoric acts.

The plurality of the self is now often viewed as health rather than pathology. But it was not always so. Whitman aside, in a great deal of modern literature the mind's dialogue with itself represented inner crisis in need of structured opposition or final synthesis. We think of people who talk to themselves in the plural as lonely, solipsistic, or insane. (E. A. Robinson's Old Eben Flood in "Mr. Flood's Party" would serve as an example.) But Eliot's interiorized, forestalled love song might point to a more meaningful communication than Prufrock finds in the available scenes of social life. True recognition and fostering of plurality within the self, rather than turning us away from others, can be a way to strengthen social and ethical relations. Thought and speech fundamentally orient themselves in dialogue between a self and another who is not "I." Plato clearly understood that cognition depends on the mind's dialogue with itself, and later philosophers have shown that such dialogue both reflects and opens the mind to others. Heidegger's "existential solipsism," for instance, interacts with the "being-with" of *Dasein* in a way that allows one to truly care for others rather than appeasing others in an inauthentic way through "talkative fraternizing."[14] Stanley Cavell recognized that "Understanding how we form a community with the other is . . . akin to understanding how we form it with ourselves."[15] Poetry often operates in a liminal space in which these poles are made flexible and productive. Something of this may be heard in Yeats's "Dialogue of Self and Soul," in which the self has the last word but chooses the first-person plural, "we must laugh and we must sing."[16] Yeats's poem evokes an imperial scene, suggesting a royal we. But it is ambiguous whether this is a chorus of self and soul, emerging from the dialogue, or an inclusive human imperative, uttered by the self in alliance with the soul. Poetry has given form to the way we encounter our secret lives, the selves that lie "incognito." It is in the nature of human consciousness to form a sense of separateness within the world, and a plurality in the inner life can be a kind of empowerment as well as expansion. At the same time, the plurality within our sense of ourselves opens us to instability, and this too poets explore.

The mature Auden would increasingly see the plurality of the self as an inevitable condition of being and consciousness, and a check to narrow subjectivity and repressive will, rather than a flaw to be overcome. *The Double Man* (1941) does not decide questions but poses them. Its major poem, "New Year Letter," offers a dialogue between poetry and prose and between his own words and those he has read (presented in "Notes"). The epigraph cites Montaigne (by way of Charles Williams): "We are, I know not how, double in ourselves, so that what we believe we disbelieve, and cannot rid ourselves of what we condemn."[17] Auden would go on to write a sonnet on Montaigne and include many quotations from him in his *Aphorisms*. Indeed, Auden is in many ways a modern-day Montaigne, looking at his society by engaging in a dialogue with and about himself—not in the form of idealizing self-love, but rather humble and skeptical self-regard, "Our faith well balanced by our doubt" (*CP* 222). "Human personality in its full depth, its inner dialectic, is self-disclosure and self-concealment," he would write in 1954 in "Balaam and His Ass" (*DH* 110). Yet the self-dialogue and multivocality within the community of one is not always a withdrawal from social life, as Auden reveals. It may be a prelude to or precondition of social being. "Man is a creature who is capable of entering into Thou-Thou relationships with God and with his neighbors because he has a Thou-Thou relationship with himself" (*DH* 109). Narcissism in this context wears a new, perhaps a nicer face.[18]

The Orators: Auden as Narcissus

"Ariel's other name is Narcissus," Auden wrote in an essay on Robert Frost (*DH* 340). *The Orators* opens on an image of a narcissist, aware of his attractiveness to others, perhaps, but fully absorbed in solitary echoic contemplation, "Bending a beautiful head, worshipping not lying, / 'Dear' the dear beak in the dear concha crying" (*EA* 61). If the bent head indicates worship, it certainly also, since this is a "swan," marks narcissistic self-reflection and romantic self-communing. Yeats's "Song of the Happy Shepherd" comes to mind: "Go gather by the humming sea / Some twisted, echo-harbouring shell, / And to its lips thy story tell / And they thy comforters will be."[19]

Auden's lifelong argument with romanticism surely derives in part from his recognition of its tendencies in his own early thought and art. Though he disdained the elevation of the self to godlike stature and disavowed any magical powers of the poetic imagination, he was certainly fascinated by the hero as a type and by the romantic figure of the alienated artist. The element of "self-regard" is a particular habit of mind that Auden seems at once to advance and despise. He saw the glorification and consequent solipsism of the romantic hero as a major cause of contemporary inertia, a mutually defeating co-dependency with a passive public. The romantic hero becomes, in turn, dictatorial and alienated. *The Orators* is built around a tension between the solitary hero's self-regard and the proper formation of the group. Yet Auden also saw introspection and self-dialogue as crucial to art and even to the ability to imagine change. In *The Orators*, this ambivalence plays out in the poet-protagonist's quarrel with himself, a quarrel that manifests not only thematically but also formally and rhetorically. In his 1968 book on Auden, *Quest for the Necessary*, Herbert Greenberg argued that "Divided consciousness . . . is the principal subject matter of his poetry, and it provides the conceptual foundation for his way of looking at things."[20] Mendelson's reading of *The Orators* also emphasizes division, less as foundation than as discovery: "Its bafflingly elusive tone emerged from the divisions Auden recognized in himself only while he was writing it." *The Orators* is not only social analysis; it is also "expressionist autobiography" and "self-analysis."[21] Auden often saw self-division as a troubling conflict, related to the breakdown of the relation of the individual to the group. Yet in many ways *The Orators* works against this diagnosis. While the tensions between self-regard and cultural imperatives may appear as a sickness, inner and outer divisions also become parallel and interrelated problems in *The Orators* and may be linked in a process. Seen this way *The Orators* offers more than a portrait of futility. By allowing conflict full expression and ordering it for the imagination, Auden points to a direction of civic health that he may not have recognized, especially later when he distanced himself from his early poetry.

The Orators describes the failure of both the hero's independence and the group's cohesion and momentum. It portrays the perversion of the group through the work of quasifascist orators. But in the last section, the odes, the work develops an internalized rhythm of assertion and doubt that directs the audience against authoritarian voices and the crises that come from violent opposition. Mendelson argues that the odes "are not sure whether they celebrate or parody the positions they take. . . . Auden's abandoned 1932 preface called them personal reflections on the question of leadership in our time. The question remains open."[22] But is this a problem, or is openness precisely their poetic and civic virtue? Auden's "self-analysis" as he works through his ambivalence about the relations between groups and individuals points away from hierarchical and adversarial social forms toward a dialectical civic order. This alternative structure is glimpsed in the work more at the level of linguistic and formal innovation than representation or statement. The form points where the characters cannot yet go. In *The Orators'* difficult, polyphonic, experimental styles, Auden gives voice to contending selves and searches for a poetic-language alternative to violent public rhetoric and oratory. He creates a language that allows for divisions within the mind and tensions between belief and doubt, civil and hermetic impulses. Self-dialogue and self-regard are not simply insular; they acknowledge ambivalence and make a step toward absorbing difference into a richer and more complex relation to the other. By making the quarrel within a principle of composition, Auden also provides an antidote to the repressive and monolithic oratory that is built on exclusions and entertains no doubts or differences. Auden's text is constantly answering back to its orators through irony, shifts of style and perspective, questions, paradoxes, opacities, and other counterpoints to "argument[s]." Auden moves from an inward-turning, crisis-driven meditation in "Letter to a Wound" to a choral voice that absorbs modernist tensions and paradoxes while overcoming alienation; he moves, that is, from paralyzing division to productive pluralism.

The Orators is "an English study," mimicking a variety of English oratorical and poetic styles (some classical in origin), and exploring a range of group formations, from close friendships and kinships to national identity. The quarrel is within English culture. But it is also Auden's "song of myself," just as Whitman's "Song of Myself," with its many, often contradictory styles and selves, offers an American study. Private and public, self and community influence each other and merge in Auden's poetic imagination, for the tensions in Auden's environment are also within him. The anxious, self-regarding mirror of Narcissus, with its effects of doubling and division and its prompts to self-dialogue, provides a crucial stage, even a threshold, in the poet's search for a fresh, creative relation to the world.

From his early days as a writer Auden associated his craft with the archetype of Narcissus and with the self-division central to that figure's story. Auden's "Well of Narcissus" is an inkwell. The "we" in his youthful poem "Narcissus" is explicitly the pluralized self of self-regard: "The words we stuck together on the nursery floor / Broke in our jammy fingers. We rose as the clock struck, / Our tongues ashamed, deceived by a shake of the hand."[23] The image here is of childhood masturbation, and an alliance of the body and the will. The self-doubling "we" becomes, as the poem continues, an ontological as much as a physical phenomenon, and very much a linguistic matter, connecting writing to narcissistic urges. Language both structures and pluralizes being: "We meet at last, this film between us, / Between the perception and the noun / The desire, and the assurance, I and AM." The emergent poet exists in this liminal film. Language marks the division of the self as the threshold and also the promise of union in the plural first person. But it remains a comical and unconsummated union, marked by betrayal and shame as well as self-deception. Auden later emphasizes the frustrations of Narcissus rather than his secret meeting. In "Balaam and His Ass," Auden focuses on the paradoxes and inversions of master/slave relations, even those that occur within the double man: "Narcissus falls in love with his reflection; he wishes to become its servant, but instead his reflection insists upon being his slave" (*DH* 115). Narcissus is increasingly a double figure in Auden, rather than merely a self-absorbed one. Auden's own double nature involves not just his life on two continents, or the tensions of his private and public self, but also the scope of his will in relation to his bodily being. "What we call the 'I,' in fact, is the area over which our will is immediately operative. Thus, if we have a toothache, we seem to be two people, the suffering 'I' and the hostile outer world of the tooth. His penis never fully belongs to a man" (*EA* 394). Many of Auden's late poems (e.g., "Loneliness," "Talking to Myself," "You," "Profile") are "*tête à têtes*" with himself in which the "we" is a conversation between his sense of a higher consciousness and his attachment to the body, not always a comfortable conversation. "Our marriage is a drama." The quarrel with the self has eased with age. "Bound to ourselves for life, / we must learn how to / put up with each other" (*CP* 887). These internal conversations have become tolerant and amused, but they are also a point of return and a check on oratory.[24]

Our double nature and self-regard are often a problem for Auden, but at the same time they can be a source of dynamic creativity. The issue arises in Auden's earliest work. The Oxford poems are rife with pronoun trouble. They shift from You to He to a "two-faced," dreaming "I" or avoid grammatical subjects altogether. Part of what makes the early poetry so difficult is the deferral of agency that comes with the expression of inner conflict. Pronoun subjects don't emerge until late in sentences and seldom have noun antecedents. This is particularly true of the "Megalopsych" sonnet sequence in *Poems* (1928). There is little evidence of the strong, expansive spirit Aristotle imagined as the "megalopsych," though it is not entirely clear that Auden's proposed title is ironic. Out of the disintegrated experience of self, some kind of wisdom is emerging. The ability to destroy the creations of the self may not be ultimately self-destructive; such ability may instead be part of new wisdom and strength.

In a lyric sequence originally titled "1929" (*EA* 37–40), Auden proceeds in this autobiographical narrative of death and rebirth on the "track which is himself." The poem opens with a straightforward narration and an "I" that has been absent from Auden's previous poetry: "It was Easter as I walked in the public gardens." But if the poem offers a sense of renewed life with others ("altering speech for altering things"), this "I" is also a retrospective and reminiscing figure, lingering around weaker selves, and especially around the site of Narcissus ("the pond"). The figure of a "solitary man" is ugly as "embryo chicken"—not mature and not human, but Narcissus is not wholly banished. In section 2 the self is constituted of imperfect verbs, suggesting a being and consciousness that is emergent and *potential* rather than complete or coherent: "Coming out of me living is always thinking / Thinking changing and changing living, / Am feeling as it was seeing." The lines describe not static or stunted self-regard but a lively self-consciousness associated with growth. Auden in "1929" may be imitating Anglo-Saxon grammar and syntax as he drops noun and pronoun subjects and articles, but this also recalls the language of Gertrude Stein, and it explores Stein's notions of the self, loosened from fixed identity. Auden avoids the subject here, replacing personhood with gerunds like "living" and "feeling," "me" as their mere site of origin. The sequence offers a growing social awareness and sense not only of "mother" but also of "the other." Near the end of section 2 Auden incorporates a dialogue that may be internal and is certainly critical. He shifts from self-presentation of a first-person "I" to an impersonal third-person "he" who says "We" but is "unforgiving" and incapable of meaningful love of another. In section 3 ("Order to stewards and the study of time"), the third person is an abstraction, "the frightened soul," likely a version of the self that is contemplated from a reflective distance. As he meditates on the conditions necessary for "independent delight" of the maturing soul, Auden uses a social image of plurality and procreation and calls for a new language of being: "as foreign settlers to a strange country come, / By mispronunciation of native words / And by intermarriage create a new race / And a new language, so may the soul / Be weaned at last to independent delight"—"independent," that is, of old forms and social expectations, and of the limits of the embryonic state of solitude. The new "I" has the aspect of a megalopsych in Aristotle's sense of expansive being, capable of ethical action. This new self arises, if we follow the metaphor, out of intermarriage with its strangeness, its otherness. Having released the soul from its dependencies, the speaker turns in section 4 to another, a "You whom I gladly walk with" in the present tense, the pronouns foregrounded, the thought united: "We know it, we know that love . . . / Needs death," death of the old self and its complacent, retentive self-confidence. Yet the last lines suggest how difficult this liberation is. The poem ends with a scene of Narcissus gazing at his image, "deep in the clear lake / The lolling bridegroom, beautiful, there." Does Auden mean that the reflection of Narcissus has receded into the unconscious, leaving the conscious mind "clear" of his image? Or is this unconsummated love still lingering in the newly formed self? He is not done with Narcissus, it would seem, even if his mirror-love is one that detains him from love's work in the world.

There is an element of resignation in this sense of inner dualities, and certainly in *The Orators* the problem of competing selves and consequent inertia remains unresolved. Yet the condition of the double man is not decisively a lamentable condition; nor does doubleness inevitably produce either sterile repetition or paralyzing dualism. It is the precondition of writing, as Auden would indicate years later in "Nones": poetry leads back "to a room, / Lit by one weak bulb, where our Double sits / Writing and does not look up" (*CP* 634). True, narcissism is not dialogical; on the contrary, it involves repetition and self-circulation. As Jacques Derrida put it, "Narcissism has no contrary, no other side, no beyond, and love for the other, respect for the other, the self-denial in favor of the other do not interrupt any narcissistic movement."[25] Neither does self-regard foreclose acknowledgment of another, nor dialogue with the self preclude dialogue with another. Indeed, these acknowledgments are mutually supportive. Self-circulating as it is, narcissism, as a form of self-address, does include an absurd kind of dialogue. In the spirit of a stand-up comic, Auden creates portraits of Narcissus that remind us of the dialogical element of self-regard: "Narcissus (drunk): 'I shouldn't look at me like that, if I were you. I suppose you think you know who I am. Well, let me tell *you*, my dear, that one of these days you are going to get a very big surprise *indeed!*'" (*DH* 94). In a more sober mood Auden links the origin of language to self-regard: "only man has a language by means of which he can disclose himself to his neighbor, which he could not do and could not want to do if he did not first possess the capacity and the need to disclose himself to himself. . . . But subjective communication demands dialogue and dialogue demands a real language" (*DH* 109).

For later Auden, then, Everyman is Narcissus, to whose well he returns often and to whom he devotes an entire section in *The Dyer's Hand*. "Every man carries with him through life a mirror, as unique and impossible to get rid of as his shadow" (*DH* 93). "We shall be judged, not by the kind of mirror found on us, but by the use we have made of it, by our *riposte* to our reflection" (*DH* 94). Poetry itself is a kind of mirror, and one that has special advantages over social interaction: "Like an image in a mirror, a poem is a pseudo-person, i.e. it has uniqueness and addresses the reader face to face or person to person, but, like all natural beings and unlike historical beings, it cannot lie" (*Prose* IV 64). The double man of belief and skepticism is deeply related to this archetypal mirror man, for it is through introspection, as Montaigne revealed while looking "outside his library window," that skepticism first arises (*CP* 299).

Auden introduces the mirror often in his poetry, and it is sometimes a prelude to the window. One must confront the self and make a riposte to its image before one can properly look out at the world of others and offer correction. In "As I Walked Out One Evening," the speaker has judged the world without self-knowledge. The clocks tell him to turn toward the image of the self, confronting its conflicts and limits, as a prelude to brotherly love. "O look, look in the mirror," they say, but they demand a two-way gaze: "look in your distress" but also "stand, stand at the window," and "love your crooked neighbor / With your crooked heart" (*SP* 67).

The turn from mirror to window is already implicit in *The Orators*. One of the best uses of the mirror, one of the best *ripostes*, is self-questioning and humility, the lover's quarrel with himself. Narcissus, even as he turns away from community, is in this sense an ally to the civil poet, potentially a defense against both the hollow man and the tyrant. Self-consciousness inoculates against the hubris of the orator who consolidates his image by subjugating others to his point of view. The double man creates productive skepticism within his point of view.

————

The Orators: An English Study, a modernist, genre-bending work, marks a threshold in Auden's career as a poet concerned with diagnosing his society, its institutions and its leadership, and with the individual as he relates to social groups. But this "English Study" is also a self-study, or a study of selfhood, in which the poet takes stock of his own troubled motivations and actions, and those of his friends, as they live and reflect within a culture that is "ill." External battles form an allegorical map of a self in conflict and crisis. Stephen Spender recognized this double function early on, and other critics have echoed his view: "The struggle in fact while existing externally is also taking place within the poet himself."[26] The heterogeneous language of the work reflects this double function, at once oratorical and meditative, satiric and earnest. At times the language imitates, in order to expose, familiar rhetorical situations and voices of public authority; at other times it ruptures or strains language to undermine this discourse, expose its dangerous logic, and explore new meanings. But the aim is as much to encounter and explore the plurality of the self as to defeat and expel "the enemy within."

"We make of the quarrel with others, rhetoric, but of the quarrel with ourselves, poetry."[27] Yeats's remark is often quoted, but what does he mean by "ourselves"? The pronoun is intrasubjective, but does "ourselves" evoke a personal or collective first person? Does poetry come from a local culture's internal debates or from individual struggle and self-scrutiny? Once we recognize the ambiguity of the first-person plural here, the distinction between rhetoric and poetry similarly becomes difficult to maintain. How easily may we distinguish between the private place of the self and the public space of others? It is likely that Auden was familiar with Yeats's remark, given the affinities between Yeats's "An Irish Airman Foresees His Death" and Auden's "Journal of an Airman" at the center of *The Orators*. Auden's poem makes ample use of the first-person plural, sometimes arising from a group, at other times arising from the counsel with himself. In any case, it is possible to see the mixed language of *The*

Orators not only as a convergence or coexistence of these two "quarrels" but as an extension of the long battle between rhetoric and poetry.[28] For all the oppositional "us vs. them" polemics of *The Orators*, its poetry emerges from recognizing multiple points of view in disequilibrium and from looking for open and flexible community beyond the norms of the broken system or the solipsistic view of the alienated self. Auden's sense of himself at this point in his career was certainly conflicted and his position liminal. He was still not far from his student days and identified in many ways with his students. At the same time, as a teacher he participated in an institution devoted, among other things, to the continuity of a culture about which he was critical but not detached. *The Orators* does not resolve this conflict. The student/teacher overlap is but one of many such tensions, sometimes painful, but also, as they are acknowledged, brought into creative equilibrium through poetic language and form.

In celebrating the early Auden of radical technique and "special language" over rhetoric, Randall Jarrell admired the poet's nondidactic quarrel with himself. Charles Altieri, by contrast, admires Auden's "return to rhetoric," which shows him conscious of the limits of discourse and the artifice of shared forms, but also of the possibilities of forging values and engaging community through language. For Altieri, as for many others, *The Orators* represents Auden's impasse, for while he takes his private anxieties for a measure of public crisis, he retreats from creative agency, collapsing back into the alienated modernist poetic stances he would surpass, rather than imagining a new order for the times. For Altieri, the Auden of *The Orators* offers no options for civil discourse, only "Eliot's alternatives—a cry and a prayer."[29] But as Eliot himself anticipates in "Rhetoric and Poetic Drama," the distinction between rhetoric and poetry remains an unstable and relative one. Perhaps this is what Stan Smith means when he argues that Auden offers "a rhetorical attempt to wring the neck of rhetoric."[30]

The verse passages of *The Orators* have received relatively little attention, at least in terms of their genre distinction. Yet in these passages, which increase as the work progresses, we see the push-pull of internal and external quarrels taking place and the external battle increasingly absorbed into a pattern of creative disruption rather than violence and crisis. The epigraph to *The Orators*, "Private faces in public places / Are wiser and nicer / Than public faces in private places," establishes a chiasm rather than a gap of alienation or a strict dichotomy of realms (*EA* 59). When the "private face" of poetry (the quarrel with ourselves) enters the "public place" of oratory and social address (the quarrel with others), it brings its inner dialogue, and imagination of the other, with it.

Justin Replogle's early study, *Auden's Poetry,* caught one aspect of the doubleness in Auden's voice as he navigates between rhetoric and poetry, between high and low tones, and between lyricality and quotidian speech. His argument provides particular insight into *The Orators*. In his chapter "Pattern of

Personae," Replogle identified interplay between "Poet" and "Antipoet," and we might extend this dichotomy to "orator" and "antiorator." "The danger of the Poet lies mainly in his pomposity, that of the Antipoet in his crudeness."[31] It is wrong, Replogle argues, to imagine that the antipoet is the real poet; in successful poems they are joined. "Apart they just contradict each other." Replogle wants this to become a stable, integrated relation yielding a unitary authorial voice, what Stan Smith claims *The Orators* strategically refuses: "a meaning and a meaningful person with whom to associate."[32] But even if we disagree with his evaluation, Replogle's remark is useful: "Poems that explode and collapse under pressure from the incompatible parts of Auden's temperament are the most striking features of his early work and the seed ground for later growth."[33] We can read *The Orators* as a dramatic record of a divided mind and plural selfhood, always permeable and subject to social forms, working through mixed impulses as it seeks agency in the public realm. As the two quarrels, external and internal, coexist within the work, they keep up a dialectic between rhetoric and poetry, turning the us vs. them logic of the first into an internal dynamic and pushing the hermetic impulses of the latter back into social relevance.

This would not be the only time Auden would relate internal with social pluralities, or see the "verbal system" of a poem in relation to the social order, which the feeling individual internally contends with in order to write. "The final poetic order of a poem is the outcome of a dialectical struggle between the feeling and the verbal system . . . every feeling competes with every other, demanding inclusion and a dominant position. . . . To the degree that a poem is successful, society and community form one common order, and the system may justly love itself because the feelings which it embodies form a true community loving each other" (*DH* 68). While at first the struggle seems to be between some authentic sense of personal feeling and imposed social order represented by writing, by the end of the passage it is clear that feelings themselves are multiple and that writing has more to do with establishing equilibrium within that plurality. Auden's description of the poem here fits well with the kinds of problems that arise in reading *The Orators*, and that likely arose in writing it. Notably, this is a productive tension and struggle and an inevitable part of poetry for Auden, not something to be fixed or repressed. I will focus on the poetry in section 3 of *The Orators* in the latter part of this chapter, but first I want to situate it in the book as a whole.

———

Among the many illnesses explored in *The Orators,* "self-regard" comes up most often, and most ambivalently. Auden introduces the theme of narcissism in a sympathetic third-person voice in "Prologue" and again through the unsympathetic voice of an orator in "Address for a Prize-Day" (*EA* 61–64) who warns against "excessive lovers of self." His portrait implicitly condemns poets among others, those "habituees [*sic*] of the mirror" who pursue orphic ambitions in "diaries full of incomprehensible jottings," an allusion, perhaps, to "Journal of an Airman" in section 2. As readers have noted, the creator of this disdainful portrait is himself morally dubious and sadistic.[34] The haranguing address here makes the reader wish to defend these purgatorial beings. The speaker's use of first-person plural is coercive and tolerates no dialogue or internal doubt or reflection, no free will or individuality on the part of the audience. He voices the culture's imperatives, indoctrinating the listeners not in terms of I and We but Us vs. Them. The questions that begin the speech are rhetorical and do not await answers: "Commemoration. . . . What does it mean to us, here and now?" Indoctrination, not dialogue, is the goal: "Let's try putting it in another way." The speaker invokes "you" ("imagine to yourselves") only as a directive toward "our type of thinking." Having established this coercive, imperative "we" lets the speaker go on to create exclusions by enumerating Dantesque circles of perversion. "They" threaten the values shared by "us." He is the admiral, and the audience must all be onboard, or overboard: "We can't afford skrimshankers [shirkers] or passengers." The momentum of the speech is toward single-minded consolidation of troops set for unreflective action based on tradition. What becomes clear in "Address for a Prize-Day" is that any form of inward reflection, any questioning of the system and its axioms, is viewed as illness, and those who pause and think for themselves are "excessive lovers of self."

Auden obviously does not share the Prize-Day orator's desire to isolate and exclude the impulse of introspection. By changing the point of view (and revising "self-love" to "self-regard"), Auden garners sympathy for self-regarders even if he portrays them as ultimately stymied by their self-circulation. The scorn of "Address for a Prize-Day" contrasts with the more sympathetic, first-person image of self-regard (and self-pity) presented in "Letter to a Wound," where the self-regarder entertains doubt, struggles with conflicted feelings, and speaks for himself of feelings he fears to make public. But by the time we reach "Journal of an Airman," the middle section of *The Orators*, self-regard has become hermetic and solipsistic.

"Letter to a Wound" (*EA* 71–73) makes use of the first-person plural in self-address but offers a riposte to the coercive "we" of the Prize-Day orator. "Letter to a Wound" appears after a gradual transformation of the voice of book 1 in which parodies of oratory and responsive readings become more and more obscure and delirious. The poem moves from familiar public rhetoric to Gertrude Stein–like opacity in "Statement," in which the dominant pronoun is "one," marking fragmentation as well as impersonality. The letter genre itself makes the argument, replacing intimidating propaganda with intimate conversation. Although this is a relatively short passage, it is given prominence as the closing words of book 1. "Letter to a Wound" anticipates the airman's journal, and "the wound" returns frequently as an unspecified figure throughout the volume (*EA* 68, 90, 95, 100). In "Letter to a Wound," the quality of self-regard is suffering, not erotic pleasure, though of course these are intertwined. Instead of the juvenile Narcissus who hovers at the threshold of being and identity, the speaker of "Letter to a Wound" reflects a later stage, the internalized conflict between private and public versions of the self. The "Letter to a Wound" is *not* oratory, not public speech—quite the opposite: "Better burn this." Yet the letter's overstatement may not be entirely ironic in its claim that self-regard leads to knowledge beyond the self: "Thanks to you, I have come to see profound significance in relations I never dreamt of considering before."

In many ways "Letter to a Wound" is a fictional rendition of Auden's Berlin journal of 1929, a unique and expansive document in Auden's archive, in which he recorded his erotic experiences as well as his philosophical reflections. Auden's early understanding of the importance of plurality in the self can be seen in this journal, though he understands the plurality not in terms of multiple selves but in modified Cartesian dualities: "Body and Soul (not-Me and Me) can have no independent existence, yet they are distinct, and any attempt to make one into the other destroys" (*EA* 297). Berlin was the "strange country" where Auden put aside the forms and obligations of his family and culture— "took down all those photographs from my mantelpiece"—and turned to pursue his private desires. "Mr. Gangle" the surgeon (Mendelson sees him as a figure for Auden's own brain, hence another figure of self-division) is "afraid," but the speaker's dialogue with the wound has overcome his sense of failure and formed a new communion with his suffering. The double man was a hollow man in consort with himself, but he becomes a loving pair in the first-person plural: "I saw nothing, walked, not daring to think," he writes, as if describing one of Eliot's living dead. "And now, here we are together, intimate, mature." Of course this is not maturity but a stage, short-circuiting sociality in self-absorption: "Once I carved on a seat in the park 'We have sat here. You'd better not.'" But in the course of his "year" of intimacy with the wound, he has outgrown alienation and developed a conscience. Indeed, the wound has in some ways improved his manners, is "making [itself] felt whenever I had been particularly rude or insincere." The speaker of "Letter to a Wound" wears a private face, but he will need to bring it into public places.

"Letter to a Wound" is central, pivotal, and paradigmatic as we experience the contradictions and ambiguities of *The Orators*. Most readers of *The Orators* find either that the work falls short because its meaning and politics are confused in the recourse to varied and contradictory models, or that the point of the work is purely negative, to expose the treachery of public speech and the inability of language itself to convey a truth. Auden himself found the work confusing. His many explanations to correspondents (Mitchison, Parkes) are inconsistent. And he famously stated in his preface to the 1966 edition: "my name on the title page seems a pseudonym for someone else."[35] He is appalled by the protofascist tendencies he finds in the work. But less often cited are the remarks Auden makes next in the preface, remarks that reveal a division not just between the younger, more mature, and politically correct self but within the creation itself. "My guess to-day is that my unconscious motive in writing it was therapeutic, to exorcise certain tendencies in myself by allowing them to run riot in phantasy. . . . I realise that it is precisely the schoolboy atmosphere and diction which act as a moral criticism of the rather ugly emotions and ideas they are employed to express."[36] Here is the strategy of the double man who wishes to vent certain feelings and at the same time condemn them and distance himself through antirhetorical "antics." He does not stand outside these discourses, emotions, and ideas of the orators, commenting on them from a purer position; he is participant and critic at once. But the poem in its linguistic innovations may be wiser than its later poet, or those seeking a coherent statement. The poem refuses to reduce its meanings to a unified ideology or discursive claim; it gives vent to Auden's quarrel with himself even if that should be an impediment to the didactic function. Irony in *The Orators* is not produced from a single satiric position in which an "us" of reader and writer might form an alliance against a "them" of satirized stances.[37]

After the grotesque procession of fragmented, hateful multitudes of "our-selves" in "Statement," it is no wonder that an "I" figure turns to make company with himself in "Letter to a Wound." Here at least there is a kind of community as Auden absorbs the condition of the double man. His plurality becomes a poetic strategy. The poet himself is the focus of struggle, not just its diagnostician. The speaker addresses his wound: "Do you realize we have been together now for almost a year?" The first-person plural continues to the end: "we know what to expect, don't we? . . . Nothing will ever part us." Auden satirizes this self-love that hugs its wounds, but he does not condemn it. If "Letter to a Wound" is a contraction and withdrawal into self-regard, it is not without awareness of the social world. The preoccupation with doors, first passed through in adventure, then closed in fear and suspicion, modifies to thresholds here and to a liminal state of mind. The writer's self-absorption is interrupted and the letter restarts. "*Later.*" He brings his social interactions back into the private reflections. John Boly sees only contradiction between the letter writer as either an "unhealthy," "solipsist" or "honest," "unillusioned" speaker; Auden's irony is momentarily out of control. "Probably this is because Auden began his literary career as a late twenties aesthete, and only gradually came to accept a qualified notion of the poet's social responsibility. In 'Letter to a Wound' it is possible to see Auden struggling to reconcile two contradictory impulses within his own literary identity."[38] But must the writer reconcile contradictory impulses? And is that Auden's goal? Poet-critic David Lehman offers a somewhat more positive analysis of the divisions in tone and attitude in "Letter to a Wound."

> "Letter to a Wound" . . . is a poignantly ironic description of the salutary effects of disease. "You" throughout refers to the wound, with which the writer lives in a state of intimacy, like a spouse. . . . The letter writer is guilty of the excessive love of self that culminates in perversity if not perversion, yet the wry note Auden strikes makes us regard the letter as a parabolic description of the modern artist, at odds with himself, yet deriving inspiration from this division and from the incessant dialogue, like ongoing peace negotiations, between stalemated factions.[39]

In "Journal of an Airman," the middle book of *The Orators*, self-dialogue collapses into hermeticism and solipsism, and "the enemy" is again external. The airman's obscurity is appropriate to the private nature of the journal as a form, even compared with the more liminal "Letter to a Wound." The airman is "the agent" of a transcendent "central awareness," an awareness that would foster "love" and "sympathy" (he may be modeled on John Layard) rather than "partial priority" (the enemy's struggle for domination) (*EA* 75). But there is a paradox in the very way he presents his "central awareness." A narrative secrecy concerning retribution and espionage forms the drama of the journal, rather than any dialogue or "interdependence." He is above dialogue. As an airman, often enclosed in a cockpit thousands of miles above the earth, he is a figure of the isolated individual, though in an obscurely indicated plotline he has recruited a small band of forces to defeat "the Enemy" who has falsely accused his uncle, presumably a rival to the patriarchal line that dominates society. There is little point in trying to sort out these cryptographs, especially since the coding of alphabetical tags—A, B, E—suggests they are abstract counters in a war game more than real people, and indeed the boundary of the real is continually "crossed" into fantasy. The sense of plots, of things happening, of preparations and execution of plans, of allies and enemies overrides any particular historical context. This very elusiveness of external reference also gives the airman's battle between "Us" and "Them" a psychological turn. "The Enemy" for the airman is repression and domination, just as it is deviance for the speaker of "Address for a Prize-Day." They form a pair. Randall Jarrell read early Auden entirely within this schema of Us against Them.[40] Jarrell prefers earlier works such as *Poems* and *Paid on Both Sides* in which a more searching and experimental stance is apparent, but he fails to recognize how that stance informs *The Orators* despite the hard lines of its speakers. While Auden's sympathies may lie with the exile, the airman and the Prize-Day speaker resemble each other precisely in the Us vs. Them logic they employ. The Us and Them groups are each so heterogeneous that they collapse into one another. The airman resists the dominant system, but he has a system of his own and considers himself "the agent of this central awareness."

The airman of book 2, though he writes mostly in prose and charts, is the first versifier among the orators, if we exclude the prologue. In allowing him verse, Auden marks him as a figure of imagination and a thinker more inclined to see recursive pattern than dialectic or linear narrative. The airman's poetry is notable for his virtuosity and mastery of elaborate, fixed forms that predict the poem's course. He is in this sense the descendant of Yeats's Irish airman. His formalism is consistent with his worldview: "the system organizes itself," as if he could stand outside the system and observe it as a poet might his form; "the enemy" is any force that would intervene to determine the course of "the system" through social coercion. There is no internal quarrel going on in the airman's forms—his rhyme royal and sestinas, alphabetical and other systems, removed from sense and feeling, are consistent with his diagrams, formulas, and genetic algorithms.

The airman's first poem, "After the death of their proud master" (*EA* 75), is blank verse, fairly strict in meter and without enjambment after the first line. The voice is that of the antipoet who uses slang and crude imagery: "Beethameer, Beethameer, bully of Britain" with blunt rhymes of "bum "and "dumb." The narrative of "After the death" follows a thermodynamic "law" of the degeneration of the hero, of disparagement and betrayal of the dead, followed by the subsequent death of the disaffected. The airman's next poem, a sestina, is the narrative of a single figure positioned either as savior or scapegoat (the one become the other) against the group. The airman does not include himself in the poem though he may be telling his own story. The first "we" is also a "they" in his narrative. "We have brought you, they said, a map of the country." If the speaker is the airman, whom "they" address as "you," he quickly becomes an impersonal figure, a "he" of sacrifice and crucifixion. The sestina's permutations of repeated nouns enhance this detached perspective. But the shifts of orientation in the poem anticipate the more fluent structures of the odes. As often with the sestina form, the poem tells a story of leakage and disintegration of the distinct categories it sets up, one displacing another: the hero is handed a map of the country, but the experience that follows deviates completely from the dictates of those who send the hero out. The opposition of authorized "bay" and forbidden "wood" collapses, through pun and repetition, in the closing three-line envoi: "Sees water in the wood and trees by the bay." But the airman is not writing from inside this story of reversals—he tells it fatalistically, dispassionately, from a point of view after events.

In the next verse passage the airman organizes experience into other impersonal systems—an alphabet (ace to zero), a division by three, and a calendar countdown. The airman often writes in mnemonic couplets ("Last day but ten / It's moving again. / Last day but nine / I've forgotten the sign . . ."). Lines that are not in strict form sound like impersonal prose or aphoristic jotting. Though he is writing a "journal," the airman hovers above experience, locked in his thoughts, trying to master a spatial reality with formulas and abstractions. In his physical stance, then, he embodies the vertical structure of the heroic ideal that *The Orators* calls into question. The airman's abstract notation is not an answer to the stresses of plurality and choice that history presents.

———

The mix of genres and modes in the airman's journal typifies modernist heterogeneity. But what the airman does not write is odes. Auden labels all of book 3 "odes," and the generic distinction deserves attention. Odes are certainly associated with oratory, public ceremony, and the celebration of the heroic individual. Auden's precursor here is Pindar, who readily used the first-person plural, and perhaps also Laurence Binyon, who in 1914 used the Pindaric ode to exalt the sacrifice of soldiers going to World War I. But the odes of book 3, many written in first-person plural, do not come from a commanding or firm epideictic oratorical voice. They contain romantic turmoil and create a rhythm of merging voices and shifting points of view that suggests a more horizontal and vibrant potential order. Auden in book 3 turns from the airman's solipsistic height to a dramatic quarrel without and within. While the poems upset the confidence of the Pindaric originals, these are not anti-odes, exactly. Rather, they employ the language of private faces in public places—oratory in which the inner struggles and conflicts of the speaker are made part of the turn to the civic sphere.

To write civil poetry is at some level to be an orator, and for Auden this means entering the purgatory of language, the struggle between rhetoric and poetry. *The Orators* has, until book 3, presented two kinds of linguistic purgatory—the one of cynical lies and repression, and the other of modernist opacity. If private faces must ultimately enter public places and speak a language that communicates in more than secret codes, how are they to avoid the distorting lies and incitements to paranoia and crucifixion that have characterized the romance narratives of Western culture and supported so much recent folly? In *The Orators*, Auden worries over this question rather than answering it.

Why does Auden devote book 3 of *The Orators* entirely to "Six Odes," highlighting the genre in the section title and setting it beside "Address," "Argument," "Statement," "Letter," and "Journal" as alternative rhetorical forms? Surprisingly, no critic has investigated the meaning of genre as such in *The Orators*. The odes section counterbalances the exclusively prose dimension of book 1 and the genre mixing of book 2. But what values or stances are associated for Auden in the prose/poetry distinction? In book 3, Auden gathers up a series of group portraits under a formal rubric. Is he simply undermining the classical public ode with the doubts and anxieties of romantic division and uncertainty? Or is he finding a language for the double man in his purgatorial state, turning rhetoric to poetry? We can read *The Orators* not only as diagnosis of postwar culture but also as a search for the artist's function in that culture as someone who reflects and redirects its language and thought. The odes suggest that Auden is trying to unite the self-reflective and the civil impulses of the writer.

The structure of *The Orators* reveals a changing relationship of the group to the individual. A sinister orator inculcates youth with a system of exclusions; a disconsolate and fragmented populace longs for deliverance from a catalog of woes; a search for new initiatives and leadership begins, accompanied by anxieties and suspicions; a single figure withdraws into self-address. In book 3, "Six Odes," the individual is returned to the group, however problematically. Conqueror and conquered exchange places often as each of the odes struggles with the question of leadership and the search for new order. They express the suffering of a collapsed society and its call for a "savior."[41] The concentration and compression of poetry brings the cyclical condition of the violence into relief for the reader, while the point of view remains invested in the scenes of action. The alternating rhythm of rallies and routs creates a new kind of consciousness in which skepticism is gradually seeping into oratory so that poetry can "illumine, and not kill" (*EA* 110). The odes internalize oppositional struggle as each position implies and mirrors the other; "us" and "them" are predicated on one another until the distinctions are hard to maintain. The book remains purgatorial, however, presenting triumph and loss as one cyclical movement, still without a direction out of this pattern.

While each ode of book 3 is formally and tonally distinct, together they create a different kind of poetry from the airman's: less inane, less abstract, more emotional, and more dramatic and unpredictable, with greater metrical variety. The voices in the odes (whether of individuals or groups) are often divided from within, creating a rhythm of assurance and doubt that is marked earlier only by opposition. Here, then, we have "continuity and discontinuity" that the airman, from his height, could see but not feel. The speakers of book

3 frequently employ the first-person plural, indicating a relation to others, but the poems are not fully choral until the end. They are often interrupted by moments of deliberation that produce a dialogical tension. The shifts from confidence to desolation convert hubris and self-pity into a compassionate mirror. The groups do not consolidate interests but have in common a purgatorial history of struggle and conflict, hoping and doubting, searching for a form of expression other than lies or madness. In comparison to the Prize-Day speaker's harangue or the airman's poetic stunts, this is a poetry where impassioned rhythms and assertions are constantly qualified and undercut. Ultimately, in the sixth ode, the alternating moods and stances become a choral prayer that, rather than silencing negations, incorporates them in a searching, ambiguous music.

While the imagery of opposing teams and the longing for heroic rescue continue, these odes are characterized by digression and leakage more than antagonism and antithesis. Oratory has led to deceptions, expulsions, crucifixions, and bloody conflict. What kind of dialectical energies might be engaged in poetic form to provide an alternative that comes closer to generating peace without subjugation? The compression of poetry, which increases with each poem in book 3, converts crises into a rhythm of assertion and doubt, confidence and discouragement, elegiac but also anticipatory. The patterning of the poems exposes a cycle that, once internalized, might condition the mind for openness to knowledge and growth rather than violence and suppression. This is not the only way to read these poems, but it is in line with the language of warning and hope that would characterize Auden's work just a few years later in poems like "Hearing of Harvests" and "Out on the Lawn." Only through close reading and attention to the form can we appreciate the work that poetry does in channeling the quarrel with ourselves into a new relation to others.

In ode 1 (*EA* 94–96), we see most clearly how Auden imagines a first-person plural that is ambiguously internal and communal. The first ode follows directly from "Journal of an Airman," as if the speaker had just descended from his height. The speaker's liminal state, between waking and dreaming, blurs the distinction of self and others, past and present, local and global awareness. The poem begins awake. The point of view is different from the airman's distant and singular perspective; here the "I" speaker is pluralized, "watching in three planes from a room overlooking the courtyard." Wordplay disorients us. "Three planes" seems to multiply the perspective of the airman's *plane* and bring it closer to the ground, though still elevated, transforming, perhaps, into a three-*paned* bay window. The "three planes" also connect Auden to a trio, later identified as "Wystan, Stephen, Christopher, all of you," who hold distinct but conjoined points of view. This initially pronoun-less, wakeful "watching" of the past "year decaying" turns to recall the previous night and its dream, which is a kind of assessment of the year. An "I" emerges to tell the dream, but the consciousness is again permeable, not contained in the isolated cockpit of the airman. A disembodied, prophetic "voice" speaks to the three friends, calling them to "read your losses," and as the poem goes on other voices intercept the ode. Setting and time are indeterminate and disjunctive, a jumble of personal memories cast in archetypal, biblical contours, perhaps in imitation of *The Waste Land*. These young poet-philosophers have put forth various ineffectual utopian plans, but they confront a society still caught in "fatal error." The speaker presents himself as "a spectator," but he is also one of the sufferers hoping for rescue. "'Save me!' the voice commanded" in the penultimate stanza, but it may be his own voice, for while he is "spectator" to the sick society, he is tapped by one of the "captains" and asked, "'How did you fall, sir?'" The speaker's Icarus-like "fall" from the airman's height is complete by the end of the ode, when we are removed from the dream space to a beggar's grounded plea for rescue. The vertical ideal of the hero has collapsed. Auden reinforces the sense of a Dantesque purgatorial space by employing the medieval dream allegory: "Lo, a dream met me in middle night, I saw a vision." The form perhaps exposes the archaic nature of the fallen order, but the Anglo-Saxon idiom of dropped subjects or verb/subject inversions ("shaped me a Lent scene"; "came summer like a flood") also enhances the strange sense of spectatorship of one's life.

As the poem goes on, from Lent to New Year, other voices become embedded within this dream voice—a troop of healers offers competing diagnoses and cures for a sick society. But the speaker of ode 1 witnesses rather than acts: "I saw," "I paused, hesitant," "I stood spectator." He sees the "general sorrow," perpetuated in a self-defeating adversarial culture: "the brain-track perfected, laid for conveying / The fatal error." The unspecified "voice" of the dream is not an oratorical voice exhorting or lamenting, nor a frightened voice of hound or hare. The voice comes from within, calling the group to confront not only its "losses" but also its fatal errors. The "losses" of course refer to the events of the past year, but there is also the sense of self-reckoning and awareness that the utopian "cures" proposed by the friends are the wrong track. There is little Pindaric celebration or steady resolve in this inward-turning, self-reckoning ode, but neither does it express solipsism or paralysis.

Throughout the odes, the language of sleep and awakening recurs. The recruiters promise "the right sleep" of untroubled, confident victors sure of their righteousness (*EA* 98), but the poems testify to uneasy dreams and wakefulness of inner doubt. Ode 1 reinforces this uneasiness in its mix of anapests and trochees, its long and pulled-in lines, giving the feeling of sweeping movement of events and the halting, anxious consciousness that observes them. While line length is predictable within the eight-line stanza, rhyme is not; it is sometimes exact, sometimes barely audible. Verbs and gerunds loosed or severed from subjects complicate the syntax to convey an unsettled awareness.

Ode 2 (*EA* 96–98) does not answer the beggar's questions on the state of Eastern Europe that arise in ode 1, and it is probably wrong to view the odes as a narrative sequence. Instead, the second ode shifts to another scene altogether. It returns us to the boarding school environment with which *The Orators* began and reminds us that the "brain-track" that leads to "fatal error" is "initiated" in this place of youthful study. The scene of ode 2 is a rally suggesting the Olympian games in Pindar, and the rousing rhetoric lurches us out of the dreamy divagation of ode 1. The "we" here is raising team morale.

After ode 1, *The Orators* is set in Helensburgh, Scotland, where Auden was a teacher at the Larchfield school, though he continually reminds us of events in the wider world that are relevant for contemporary Europe. This off-center northern school setting allows Auden to look awry on the "English" culture he is examining and to imagine community in a way that the larger scope of the nation obscured. It also allows Auden to move out from the solipsism of the airman. Saying "we" within small communities remains a strong value throughout Auden's work, though such communities must be mindful of the suffering and instability that surround them. Helensburgh suggests a place where community can go on even as the larger culture repeats its destructive patterns—but this pastoral setting must ultimately remind us of that darker and larger world. Like a poem, a small marginal community becomes both a space in which to diagnose the larger mainstream culture and a space in which a community of alternative values and ordering principles can be conceived. We are reminded continually that the boarding school is the place of initiation into the codes and values of the dominant culture, and the scene of the playing field often morphs into a theater of war, exposing the dangerous logic of indoctrination. As instructor, Auden is necessarily a participant in and an agent of that process, even as he might, as a recent graduate and writer, both identify with the students and wish to "study" that cultural initiation. This double role, and the conflicts that arise from it, are central to the tone and style of *The Orators*, especially in book 3.

While ode 1 expresses uncertainty, ode 2 returns to overreaching confidence and hubris: "Walk on air do we? And how!" As with all the odes, this boast incorporates its opposite. Here, the dismissal of fears merely points to them: "Not, as the desperate need to, do we clutch at arm, / . . . we to the right sleep

come." This denial looks back to the uneasy dreams of the first ode and anticipates the death-shadowed state of ode 3. In ode 2, Auden works with a pattern
of off rhymes and line length variation typical of the rhapsodic form and with
Hopkins-like alliteration and sprung rhythms, enhanced by hyphenations,
rhetorical questions, and exclamations. These effects bolster the excitement of
the game, but there is something of the mock-heroic in their application to a
high school sporting event. Auden apparently decided early that this ode was
unsuccessful since he left it out of the second printing of *The Orators*. However,
the omission of this ode breaks the symmetry of the sequence, which alter-
nates stances of acknowledged loss and anticipated success.

Ode 3 (*EA* 98–101) retains the school setting by its dedication ("to Edward
Upward, Schoolmaster"), but the "we" group now is more generic; Auden
would later retitle the poem "The Exiles." The effect of ode 2 was expansive,
and the alternate rhymes propel us forward, as if the single pulled-in line was
the speaker catching his breath. In the third ode the form has the opposite
effect; the two unrhymed tetrameter lines break in half with caesurae and with
pauses, as in old English. The constrictions of off-rhyme dimeter couplets
recall some of Wilfred Owen's uneasy lines in "Futility." The weary weight
and sorrow, the enervated trudge of the routed, are established in alliterative
mass, evoking medieval laments. The landscape is frozen again and language
ineffectual: "vows have no virtue," "voice is in vain." Instead of "the right sleep"
we feel "the touch" of the "old wound." These purgatorial "ghouls" form a bond
in discouragement, but it's a soulless and passive community with no direction
or purpose, no deliberative capacity. This would seem to be the choral lyric in
its negative form, not the voice of community in all its diversity, with an "I"
speaking to "you," but a uniform voice of weakness and hopelessness, speaking
to itself or nobody. Yet this is not another subjugated elegy such as "Argument"
in book 1. If this group is incapable of imagining a different future, it is also
removed from fear and violence, "in groups forgetting the gun in the drawer."
The implication is mixed: both suicide and murder have been contemplated
but also suspended through group association.

Ode 4 (*EA* 101–6) jolts us out of despair with a "birthday" ode. A piece of
light verse heraldry announces a nativity after the near death knell of ode 3.
The variance in line lengths, overriding the heroic couplets (eventually breaking into alternate rhymes), underscores the impromptu, occasional air. The
pattern is repeating itself in a scrambling of Latin declension, "a birth / On
English earth / Restores, restore will, has restored," and concludes in an echo
of Wilfred Owen: "To English story / The directed calm, the actual glory." The
first-person plural includes the celebrants as family members and friends in
hyperbolic praise of their newborn as the savior. The satire here is convivial,
though the betrayal of the adolescent in the prologue to *The Orators* haunts

this celebration of "youth." The ode stands somewhere between repetition and a pastoral parody of the old heroic narrative.

The envoi to ode 4 (*EA* 106) reminds us that we are still in the borderlands of Helensburgh, not in the more troubling heart of culture. The atmosphere suggests the classical refrain: *Et in arcadia ego*. As a pastoral incorporates loss and death into natural cycles, so here too the mood modulates, though without a sense of crisis. The poem checks the hyperbolic hopes and weighs both the value of local community and the uncontrollable forces of nature in the calculation of redemption. The last section of 4 is a send-off, invoking seasonal cycles rather than cycles of human history. Its advance knowledge of darkness, the speaker reminds us, is not a premonition of doom—"I'm going to sleep, not going to be dead." The birthday poem ends in the dark but reminds us that history and nature are not the same. The next ode may not be intended as a continuation of this story, but in shifting from the family birthday party to the boarding school setting, Auden again maps out the stages of education and the doubts and betrayals that inevitably follow hyperbolic hopes.

Ode 5 (*EA* 106–9) is one of the few parts of *The Orators* that Auden retained for his *Collected Poems*, yet it has seemed to many critics among the most confused sections of the work. Justin Replogle says it may be "a consistent poem whose consistency fails to be clear."[42] But is this very ambiguity one of the reasons Auden valued it? In dedicating the fifth ode "To My Pupils," Auden provides a strong contrast to the peroration, "Address for a Prize-Day." In later titling the ode "Which side am I supposed to be on?" Auden questions the idea of taking sides and makes betweenness the substance of the poem. As instructor, he is an agent of the system that initiates young men into English hierarchy and nationalism, but he also imagines this system from the point of view of the questioning youth, for whom the heroic legacy is only lore. The "we" of this poem makes the speaker one of the troops rather than its commander, someone "alert to obey orders" rather than a top gun, someone who has been initiated into the code but is conscious of its cracks. The poem recognizes the role of hubris and fear rather than courage in the enforcement of the old repressive code. "We must stop the leakage," declares the speaker in a moment of bad faith, ventriloquizing official authority. But his poetry—full of qualification, countering voices, and border crossings—has registered that leakage. The speaker of 5 is the double man rather than the double agent; he is "watching with binoculars."

In this ode Auden uses form and syntax to enhance this feeling of ambivalence and inner division, assertion and doubt; he is an insider into whose awareness outliers have entered. Qualifying clauses crowd out the main clause on either side.

Though aware of our rank and alert to obey orders,
Watching with binoculars the movement of the grass for an ambush,
The pistol cocked, the code-word committed to memory;
      The youngest drummer
Knows all the peace-time stories like the oldest soldier,
      Though frontier-conscious,

About the tall white gods who landed from their open boat,
Skilled in the working of copper, appointing our feast-days,
Before the islands were submerged, when the weather was calm,
      The maned lion common,
An open wishing-well in every garden;
      When love came easy. (*EA* 106–7)

This first long sentence encapsulates all the paradoxes of the paranoiac code that violently defends a nostalgic ideal, "When love was easy." This indoctrination into cultural myth binds young and old. The first qualifying clause undermines "rank" even as it invokes it, the youngest drummer supplanting the oldest soldier. "Frontier-conscious" in anticipation of ambush, they yet pledge to a primitive myth of founders as "tall as white gods." They seem unable to inhabit the present or imagine the future as other than repetition. The lack of rhyme and the variability of line length over long sentences add to this uneasy, unsettled feeling.

    Stanza 3 proceeds in a similar way, impacting assertions with qualifiers and syntactic ambiguity, pulling away from a propositional thrust that the speaker mouths without faith: "Perfectly certain, all of us, but not . . ." introduces doubt in the same breath as confidence, and all the evidence is on the side of doubt as various "agents." Messengers appear to bring news of defeat, pulling away from the consensus of "all of us." Stanza 4's "yes" thus quickly shifts to a "yes, but," and stories of defeat seep further into the collective conscience, which has now divided as the lines become more dialogical, enfolding dissonant voices, the "recruit" wanting more information from the messenger, the "veteran" attempting to silence all skepticism, as if "the right sleep" were still possible. The voice of the poem describes the code into which the youths are indoctrinated and the obligations that are part of that code, but it's the voice of a double man, undermining the code behind the "very full programme" it oversees and exposing the anxiety beneath the bravura version of history that supports it. Irony replaces qualification here as "you" replaces "we." Auden adopts the voice of authority sardonically, imitating a superior addressing young recruits and informing them of their duties. The "us vs. them" mentality dominates as the speaker returns to the first-person plural in stanzas 8 and 9. But these stanzas form a kind of chiasm; "we" and "they" exchange places.

The patriotic pageantry of a "we" in stanza 8 gives way to the rising challenge of "them" in stanza 9, who in turn describe the flourishing band of stanza 8 as "they." Stanza 10 suggests this emboldened group of stanza 9 is a projection of the fears of those in stanza 8: "What have we all been doing to have made from Fear / That laconic war bitten captain addressing them now." This paranoiac description of the enemy incites mutiny. The irony of stanza 10 is that the image of a mighty enemy as a projection from our fear produces an echo of the hubris of those readying for ambush. Auden reinforces this mirror/echo effect by using the first-person plural in quotations as he imagines an enemy leader exhorting his own troops.

The enemy is us, or provoked by us; that we "have caused their shout" is nothing to celebrate. This becomes clear with the roll call of the deadly sins— Wrath, Envy, Greed, Lust, etc.—the sins that perpetuate the code of murder and martyrdom. The idea of sin is of course part of the code of repression. But for the poet these behaviors and attitudes that perpetuate the cycle of prov- ocation and violence are the real source of evil. The ode imagines facing the invisible enemy (who is felt to be lying in ambush), loving them even while strangling them, "put our arms round their necks and looked in their eyes." Increasingly with the turn in "we were unlucky," the poem opens the "we" to imagine the "frontier" outside official report. "They are brave, yes, though our newspapers mention their bravery / in inverted commas." But by stanza 16 the imagination is pulled "back to our lines" and censorship and caution return, hatred once again overtaking the dream of human fellowship. Evoking the Christmas truce of the First World War, Auden imagines what the official voice cannot: human connection that could collapse the system of winners and losers. The ventriloquizing voice of authority is challenged between the lines: "you're holding us up."

The last two stanzas of ode 5 amplify the divided voice that has been build- ing throughout the poem. The ode has moved from a defensive to an offensive position as the "enemy" looms larger. Ode 5 goes from protection of the home- land to maneuvers of attack at the frontier. What is the speaker's position in this process? Auden seems unsure of how to situate his voice; he sometimes quotes or mimics the official authority, addressing youth; but at other times he seems on the receiving end of oratory, part of a "we" that hears the bravura skeptically, noting its contradictions.

Whose is the voice of the final stanza of ode 5? Not the orator who puts up "the bunting" but someone alienated from a system that dooms us to attack. The bunting celebrates the retreat into the shelter of nationalism and old values, "Indoors before it is too late." The language of necessity in this stanza is instructive: "we must say goodbye," "we're doomed to attack." But it is already too late; the final words are uttered by another voice, one without quotations, that will find no shelter in a cultural code that dooms it: "We shall lie out there," says the outlier, and the pun cancels all the lies of authority. The power of this ode comes less from an alienated voice in mockery of the official culture than from one who is inside, willing to doubt, and to imagine another point of view than the official one.

The sequence's closing sixth ode (*EA* 109–10) is what is called in Anglican tradition a "collect." It turns oratory to its root meaning of prayer and its association with a religious society of secular priests. It is voiced in first-person plural, suggesting a church chorus. As Auden would later write, a community comes into being by expressive gathering (*DH* 64). While this prayer looks superficially like a conventional appeal to God to take sides, its peculiar language creates ambiguities to suggest a different, more internal struggle, for spiritual transformation and an end to violent oppositional ways. A close reading of this poem reveals some writing between the lines and grammar-undermining rhetoric. This final choral poem is not a pathetic lament from the passive crowd but an expression of supplication and hope such as Auden will use to close many of the long poems and plays he writes after 1936.

Given the emphasis on groups throughout *The Orators*, it is easy to imagine this as a scene in a local chapel, especially as the Scottish metered psalm, the model for ode 6, emphasizes the regional locale of Helensburgh. Ode 6 has abandoned hero worship for communal expression of yearning and hope. It brings the reader back to the beginning of *The Orators*, in a spirit of second thoughts rather than plot fulfillment. In the second stanza of the prologue, antecedent to the betrayal of the hero, there were echoes of Psalm 23: "among green pastures straying he walks by still waters."[43] The image of the swanlike hero in the prologue, head bent, "worshipping, not lying," has been contradicted by the many lies and self-aggrandizements that follow in the book. The waters of *The Orators* have not been still, nor have the pastures been green. But in returning to the psalms in the sixth ode, Auden offers an image of community reconciled in defeat, now truly "worshipping, not lying." This final ode also recalls the second section of "Argument" in book 1, with its responsive readings in first-person plural ("O Four Just Men, spare us," "O Dixon Hawke, deliver us," etc.). But that earlier prayer is utterly sardonic and secular, whereas ode 6, the closing prayer of book 3, suggests a struggle between grammar and rhetoric that might break through to salutary speech.

Many readers have understood this final ode negatively, as another in the sequence of failures, mocking the conventions of an archaic institution and pointing to the hollowness of traditions. But Auden found in the linguistic errors of the Scottish renditions of the Psalms a space for modernist indeterminacy of meaning, "like Mallarmé."[44] How can one worship and not lie in the tainted medium of language? Only by a language of errancy. Within this community of prayer, some articulation of truth may occur, some performance of language that can "illumine and not kill." Here is the Lord's Prayer from the Scottish book of the Psalms, Auden's source for ode 6:

> The Lord's my shepherd, I'll not want.
>   He makes me down to lie
> In pastures green: he leadeth me
>   the quiet waters by.
>
> My soul he doth restore again;
>   and me to walk doth make
> Within the paths of righteousness,
>   ev'n for his own name's sake.

Given this quaint antecedent, it would be easy to dismiss ode 6 as a piece of light verse, more "school boy antics." But the placement and matter of this ode give it gravitas and respectful humility. Gone are the uncertain, expanding and contracting lines of the ode. Here is a hymn stanza and a scene of prayer, the "narrow strictness" that will characterize the next volume of poetry he writes. Indeed, the form seems associated with the divine "organised blockade" of stanza 5. Auden has transferred the military imagery from a struggle with an "enemy" to a "necessary defeat" that becomes a precondition to illumination rather than violence. But this is not the partisan God quoted in stanza 8 of ode 5. Indeed, the poem maintains skepticism even in its gesture of prayer, for surely Auden knew, in his peculiar word order, that an address to "Not, Father" was a modernist wager of the double man, embedding skepticism in belief; later in the poem he appeals to this not-Father to "be not another than our hope." That Auden intended some reverence in this awkward syntax is evident from another source, Baudelaire's *Intimate Journals*, which opens: "Even though God did not exist, Religion would be none the less holy and divine."[45]

Auden uses the awkward Scottish translation to create ambiguity in the location of divinity:

> Against your direct light, displayed,
>   Regardant, absolute,
> In person stubborn and oblique
>   Our maddened set we foot.
>
> These nissen-huts if hiding could
>   Your eye inseeing from
> Firm fenders were, but look! To us
>   Your loosened angers come. (*EA* 109–10)

The language of the gaze pervades these stanzas, and again the distorted syntax collapses boundaries of inner and outer exposure. The warped sentences break open language to admit "direct light" against the "nissen huts" of prefabricated rhetoric. Here is Hopkins's "inseeing" and an invitation to "Look!" at defeat rather than hide or counterattack. The adjectives of stanza 2 hang between object and subject. "Displayed" ambiguously modifies both the "direct light" and the "stubborn and oblique" persons it reveals; "regardant" suggests the backward, nostalgic consciousness of the supplicants, who can only think of the present and future in terms of the past. But the words also, through their punning, suggest the divine "regard" that turns them from that retreat and false shelter of retrograde thinking. The ambiguous language creates a reciprocal relation between supplicant and "father." The poem seeks direction and authority but posits it from within and without. Self-regard and divine regard come together.

The last line of stanza 2 of ode 6 has given critics the most trouble. "Our maddened set we foot," makes "set" and "foot" both nouns and verbs, and thus makes "maddened" a modifier for both "foot" and "set." Presumably the anger and derangement of the deluded culture causes them, they confess, to stand obliquely and stubbornly (and perversely and futilely) against the clear light of truth. Stanza 4 describes the failure of that obliquity. It exposes the false protections of wit and magic such as we find in the airman's illusory world of "magical countersigns" and "airy sacrifice." But there is perhaps a positive connotation here too: the maddened foot of the metrical line deranges syntax and forces familiar rhetoric into unfamiliar shapes. But in doing so it may open the thought to what language usually covers up. If poets "set foot" against the light, if they (and their maddened set) hold their failures against the light, turning them to poetry, they expose them rather than disguise them. Thus turning "against" might become a turning "toward," as something held against the light reveals what might not be visible in the shadows.

This modernist punning and ambiguity offer a different way toward the life of the double man than the oppositional cycles of assertion and defeat, violence and suffering, that have characterized other sections of *The Orators*. Ode 6 surrenders without fear and without a division of "us" and "them." Only here does the poem expect "peace" and evoke illumination rather than violence. A community expressing itself in the first-person plural, "We routed," stands in an attitude of anticipation and prayer. But the ambiguity of the syntax allows the speakers to be the agents of their own redemption. The line "Be not another than our hope" implores the "Not, Father" to present himself in the image of their hopes, not the image of their fears; yet it also suggests that this power is itself an inward one. The final verbs of the poem, "disarm . . . illumine . . . and not kill" are applied to the "Father," presumably, but might also be actions of the "routed" themselves, empowered by their hope; they might not only passively "expect" some future state but work to achieve this potentiality by laying down arms and taking up the language of illumination. There is no enemy outsider here, no autonomous hero. It is not a call to arms but a call to disarm and to end the bloody cycle. This ambiguity of language, in the manner of Mallarmé, is one way not to "lie." It is not the way Auden will choose to pursue his truth in the thirties.

The epilogue to *The Orators* (*EA* 110) exits from the cycle of victory and defeat. Is this the end of the story begun in the prologue, with the hero now abandoning his suffering culture, betraying it as he was betrayed? Perhaps it is, but the auditory link of "reader and rider," "hearer and horror," "fearer and farer" suggests they are doubles, not antagonists but siblings, an internal pair. The romantic hero abandons his dependents, but perhaps a more collaborative, horizontal relation can now take place without him.

Auden's poetry would not in fact retreat. A year later he is still writing from the Helensburgh school, calling on the "Lords of Limit" to "look leniently upon us all to-night" (*CP* 63). His use of the first-person plural in this poem ("we know you there / Whose sleepless presences endear / Our peace to us with a perpetual threat" [*CP* 64]) speaks from within the community, not as an airman, antagonist, or outlier.

4

Private Stuff and Public Spirit

We in us find the eagle and the dove.
—JOHN DONNE, "THE CANONIZATION"

We see us as we truly behave.
—JOHN ASHBERY, "SOME TREES"

WHEN DOES LOVE poetry say "we"? Not as often as you would think. In what sense is love poetry mindful of the social world, even civic-minded? More often than you would think. This chapter looks at some of the ways the "we" of love poetry expands to perform a civil or didactic function, and it connects this function to the puzzle of love's number, tense, and grammar, which constitutes the subject matter of many love poems. Plato argued that *eros* could be a rung on the ladder to other forms of love. Love's number may involve not only addition but also an exponential process, in sublimation "mounting upwards from one to two, and from two to all fair forms."[1] But a great deal of thinking since has set romantic love at odds, not only with truth and reason, but with social and ethical thinking. Later philosophers saw romantic love as exclusive and private, indifferent or even hostile to the world beyond itself and inscrutable to that world.

Poetry has also explored these tensions and antagonisms between lovers and the rest of us and asked how the experience of lovers might be reconciled to broader moral and civic values. On the one hand, lovers are subject to human laws and patterns of behavior and desire, to the general "we" that is all of us, and these laws and patterns are often evoked in love's appeals and seductions. On the other hand, lovers often see themselves as exceptional, transcending or defying the common lot through love's powerful union and offering alternative modes of being together that provide correction to a

64

world of strife. This hyperbolic theme resonates throughout John Donne's love poetry. One hears it, for instance, in the insistent, mobile pronoun "we" of "The Anniversary," as subject, as object, as possessive adjective; declarative, interrogative, and imperative, part of humanity and yet exceptional.

> But we no more than all the rest.
> Here upon earth we're Kings, and none but we
> Can be such Kings, nor of such subjects be;
> Who is so safe as we? where none can do
> Treason to us, except one of us two.
> True and false fears let us refrain,
> Let us love nobly, and live, and add again
> Years and years unto years, till we attain
> To write threescore: this is the second of our reign.

Inward-turning as it may be, love poetry in all periods has often provided a mirror for the social world, whether as an idealized model of intersubjectivity or as a troubled symptom or reflection of social domination, fragmentation, or polarity. In lyric poetry the "we" of lovers, exclusive to the extreme, sometimes turns to widen its circle, forming relations with a specific community, with invisible listeners, or with an unrealized, indeterminate future community. The epithalamium is the most obvious and deliberate form of this social turn in love poetry, reflecting the way the institution of marriage reconciles the tension between the erotic and the civic. But the pattern can be seen even in lyrics of unsanctioned or unhappy love.

Lyric poetry, which takes romantic and erotic love as one of its quintessential subjects, has endured some of the same criticisms hurled at lovers. "The lunatic, the lover and the poet / are of imagination all compact."[2] As the genre most associated with the private life, lyric poetry is often seen as insular, hermetic, irrational, bound to pleasure and illusion, irrelevant and even subversive to moral and social consciousness, certainly a world unto itself. The "you" of love poetry feels exclusive even when the particular beloved is unidentified, and the "we" that arises in the love relation, if it does (Petrarchan love poets sigh alone), seems to have little room for public spirit, justice, or even brotherly love, locked as it is in erotic mystery, secrecy, obsessive intimacy, ecstasy, or dejection. The reader must either enter into the madness of love, identifying with the speaker, or wonder at its absurdity. Nowhere so much as in love poetry is the ideal of a first-person plural so fully imagined, its paradoxes so intensely contemplated. Love makes its own community, but it is troubling for civil community, seeming both exclusive and unrealistic. Auden's "we" in the early love poetry is fraught within and without. And yet the speaker in love poetry sometimes steps back from his enthrallment to take on the voice of a wise spectator, who seeks not to court or swoon but to understand love and to guide its impulses to social good.[3] These two units, the "we" of lovers and the "we" of sober reflection and civil community, may mirror or follow each other, compete, overlap, or merge in the course of the poem. Love poetry's shifts between an intimate "we" and a philosophical "we" involve the audience in a nuanced relationship with the utterance, as Eliot makes clear in "The Three Voices of Poetry." He includes love lyric in the second voice, of poems addressed to other people, not only because it is addressed to a beloved but because it contains a hint of oratory.

Poetic address can be considered as practice or paradigm, then, for social and ethical engagement. But the social connections are not only symbolic ones. Referentially ambiguous deictic words—"here" and "now" and a range of pronouns—can function on different planes of the poem; they can be internal to the story (diegetic) or to the poet's commentary reaching outside the bounds of the story and its interlocutors (nondiegetic). These levels of reference are never very tightly distinguishable in poetry as compared with prose. Poetry moves freely among discursive orientations and shifts its objects of address and implied reference from one framework to another.[4] The tonalities and dispositions of lovers toward their beloveds introduce relations of domination or recognition of the other that are relevant to human relations more generally, and the drama of the poem engages us in these dynamics. The shifting registers of a poem create layers of private and public address as it moves (sometimes seamlessly or ambiguously, sometimes abruptly) out of story or character into the scene of writing, or as it turns to philosophical reflection, which may serve the dramatic context but also lift out of it to involve the reader more directly. The "we" of lovers thus posits a more inclusive community, to which they belong and return, even when they seem to turn away. The pronoun can call the reader into an imaginary unit with the poet, a moment of mutuality and consent, even when the poem may be creating a divide between "us" (the loving pair) and "the world"; or it can release speaker and reader from the exclusive zone of lovers into human connection on a wider scale.[5] Though the lover's praise or desire may remain in the I/You interaction, his experience can be set in relation to general truths. But the pronouns can work in the opposite way as well, as the lover invokes general truth in his appeal to a beloved. In the use of general propositions, the line between seduction and civil purpose is not always clear. Shakespeare's first sonnet begins "From fairest creatures we desire increase."[6] The sonnet seems at once an act of persuasion and a reflection on human nature. This "we" is not intimate but inclusive. When the poet draws on a general "we" to argue a specific case to an intimate, the reader is pulled in, considering how this general truth applies in the instance of loving address.

If there be nothing new, but that which is
Hath been before, how are our brains beguil'd,
Which labouring for invention bear amiss
The second burthen of a former child.
Oh that record could with a backward look,
Even of five hundred courses of the sun,
Show me your image in some antique book,
Since mind at first in character was done,
That I might see what the old world could say
To this composed wonder of your frame;
Whether we are mended, or where better they,
Or whether revolution be the same.[7]

As Helen Vendler explains it, "speaking as *we*, he is a mind, speaking as *I* he is a lover."[8] While the lovers feel exclusive and unique to each other, they are subject to general laws and belong to wider communities. This "we" is also generational, comparing its view to the backward gaze of a "they" the poet cannot conjure. Such shifts remind us that love exists in a world of many over-lapping human groups and that love poetry draws out a variety of tones and dispositions as it invokes and presents the conditions of love. Shakespeare's sonnets were on Auden's mind throughout his career, and this ambiguity in the voice, between lover and wise spectator, likely provided a model of how to integrate, or at least entangle, private and public speech. Shakespeare also offered Auden a model for moving between an ideal of union and a reality of separateness. Shakespeare uses the first-person plural more often than his Petrarchan predecessors do, but when speaking of lovers, "we" usually bears the burden of division, presence called up through absence. "Let me confess that we two must be twain, / Although our undivided loves are one" begins sonnet 36.[9] And the "*we, our*" that dominates the octave, as Vendler points out, is supplanted by "*I, thou*" in the sestet.[10] In sonnet 39, the speaker is resigned to this separation, which he understands in terms of number: "Even for this, let us divided live, / And our dear love lose name of single one."[11] These sonnets are rife with compensatory paradoxes of inverted temporality and active embrace of what is already accomplished. Here, "let us divided live" proposes a state already established as a human condition.

The Dialogue of One

One of the arguments of this book is that "we" is a problematic pronoun as it designates the puzzle of a plural unit; love poetry presents this psychologi-cal and spiritual paradox with particular intensity. As Marianne Moore writes in "Marriage," "everything to do with love is mystery"; lovers are "opposed each to the other, not to unity." Lovers are one and yet two, unique and yet joined, part of the common but apart from it. Love's number varies in lyric tradition—it may be singular, as in Sidney, double, as in Shakespeare, or even triple, as in Barrett Browning, where God is witness. It may be a decimal, as in Frost's "Meeting and Passing": "less than two / But more than one as yet." But Frost has also imagined love as a trio: "We must be something. / We've said we two. Let's change that to we three."[12] Poetry parses this indeterminacy in the pronoun in order to imagine a variety of active and elastic human relations. Love poetry is the subgenre in which ideas of unity in human connection, both domination and intersubjectivity, have been most often explored. When lovers talk, they talk about love, and an obsessive counting often arises in the meditation of love's unit. Poetry is full of monads, dyads, even triads, as it calculates love's sum. John Donne's love poetry ("The Canonization," "Lecture on a Shadow," or "The Anniversary," for instance) provides some of the most interesting uses of the first-person plural, both in its shifts between lover and wise counselor and in its pondering of love's number and grammar. Is love's "we" one or two? Is it more than the sum of its parts? Does ecstatic feeling between lovers introduce infinity into love's counting? Does consciousness of time or the social environment fracture and obstruct love's ideal, or do these conditions give romantic love its distinction? The answers to these questions might map onto a history of love poetry, though various forms and formulas are recurrent. Love poetry ponders these enigmas and explores their permutations in every age, reflecting and even following shifting philosophical, religious, and cultural traditions.[13] Denis de Rougemont's *Love in the Western World*, C. S. Lewis's *The Allegory of Love*, Anders Nygren's *Eros and Agape*, among others, have given us histories of the Western idea of romantic love and traced its philosophical and literary traditions, revivals, and modifications. Auden was drawn to this history, read and reviewed these books, which helped him shape his conception of love in the modern world.

In connection with the amorous counting in love poetry there is a grammatical testing and modeling of the structure of intimate relation. Western love poetry, from Song of Solomon to the present, often employs chiasmus and other binding and reciprocal syntax as it structures romantic connection, and the first-person plural takes up various grammatical positions in this process. The most intense states of erotic and spiritual union provoke silence rather than talk. Lips that meet do not speak. Souls that unite need no language but silence. But love's unit is also predicated on difference, and love poetry constantly reasserts the space it seeks to overcome. Absence, temporal and spatial, rather than presence; other minds, rather than one mind; time, rather than the eternal present tense, provoke poetic address, which is why love poetry so often hypothesizes separation or imagines the beloved asleep. Yet the temporality of love propels itself toward an imaginary "we" and toward a layered "here" and "now" in which relations are proposed, remembered, or invented. This dynamic is mapped onto the grammar and syntax of love's declarations.

The poet may speak of shared feelings or actions, using "we" as a grammatical subject or "our" as a possessive. He may imagine a joint voicing, preserving difference in duet (Frost's "Today will be the day of what we both said").[14] Or he may place their unit in an objective position as "us," as a target of the lovers' own or an outsider's contemplation or agency. The speaker may seek reciprocity ("each other") or reflexivity ("ourselves"). Or the speaker may hail the pair with invitation or imperative ("let us"). As love poetry probes the paradoxes, pains, and pleasures of love's unit, it moves around in this grammatical field in order to define the space of betweenness and to view it inside and out. The grammar of love reflects how love's "we" is seen: as a genderless "neutral thing," a doubling, a fusion, a polarity, a magnetic intersubjectivity of I and Thou, an infinite intimacy beyond time and space, a newly established entity where nothing was before, an "us" that "we" might contemplate in wonder, or a shadow figure—a trace of what once was or an illusion dispelled.

In exploring these variables in number and grammar, Western love poetry has often been the exemplary or allegorical figure for other kinds of desire and relation with another—human, divine, social, and even textual. The grammar of love poetry may also turn outward explicitly, in exclusion or inclusion. The speaker may take an antagonistic stand presenting "us" (private, ideal, sacred) against a hostile "them" (public, imperfect, profane) that threatens love's unity and harmony with its strife and division. Or, in the case of epithalamium and other poems of forming bonds, the speaker may welcome the world and expand love's unit, making the lovers an anchor of communal joy or continuity, the intimate "we" resounding in a choral "we" of active community. Patterns of exclusion and inclusion may involve an exchange of one focus of love, *eros*, for another, *communitas*, as the speaker turns from the scene of his private affection to take up civic and didactic work. There are myriad ways in which the reader is pulled into the love lyric and its relational unit—through identification with the speaker or addressee, as an overhearing witness or bystander (vicarious, judging, even voyeuristic), or simply as someone subject to the same human conditions (desire, time, history, power, art, society) that arise in the discourse of love, where "we" is no longer the exclusive unit of lovers but a term that includes interlocking groups or "us all." "We" involves a complex layering that connects to the reader in ways that are not just metaphoric; "we" relations in love lyric are elastic, and this flexibility reinforces the capacity of the genre not only to model but to activate or awaken other social relations.

Terrifying Mottoes and the Language of Love

"Some say it makes the world go round / And some say that's absurd," Auden wrote in "O Tell Me the Truth about Love" (*SP* 69). He was interested in love poetry throughout his career, as both reader and author. He certainly learned from the social- and time-burdened love lyrics of his immediate predecessors. Modern poetry is full of such shadow-haunted, time-burdened meditations on love, presenting a fractured, socially burdened "we," more memory than desire, and often dominated by the past tense. George Meredith's *Modern Love* developed this new kind of love poetry, warping Renaissance conventions, and we find it also in Hardy, Eliot, Millay, Frost, Larkin, and many others. "We" is not an ideal, worked toward or elusive, but an illusion coming apart, a morbid afterglow based on mutual disillusion and knowledge of failure. The pattern love makes here does not transfigure but reflects the world of social division, falsehood, and ephemeral connection. And the failure of love's "we" becomes a symptom and mirror of a broader social failure. But in his reflections on intimacy, Auden took up the long story of love in the Western world, from Petrarchan and Shakespearean sonnet conventions to the tragic romance of Tristan and Isolde and the predations of Don Juan. The civil and ethical thrust of this tradition, its contribution to *communitas*, is not straightforward. But in reviewing *Love in the Western World* in 1941, in the midst of war, Auden argues that *eros* is not the opposite of *agape*; the relation is not dualistic but "dialectical." "For Eros, surely, is '*amor sementa in voi d'ogni vertute, e d'ogni operazion che merta pene*' . . . a conversion, not an addition, the Law fulfilled, not the Law destroyed" (*Prose* II 139–40). Auden writes the review in a time when he is both deeply in love and deeply worried about the fate of the world, given the rise of fascism's "collective Eros." Much of Auden's love poetry was written in the shadow of social crisis and war, and it bears the burden of guilt as well as secrecy. Love can seem a stealthy indulgence before the spectacle of public suffering. His early love poetry sometimes sets itself against external forces or sees the failure of love in terms of a repressive and polluted environment. The push-pull of private desire and public obligation shapes the poems in various ways, as the language of love degenerates into lies or competes with the slogans, benign or hostile, of public life. Auden's epithalamia are especially aware of the divisive world that surrounds the embracing lovers. They send out loving vows in defiance of the "terrifying mottoes" that threaten human community (*SP* 35). When Auden committed himself to Chester Kallman, he also turned love into an ethical endeavor and potential social good, wanting to align erotic energy with rather than against the social surround, by making a pattern of their love. The "we" formed in "the arbitrary circle of a vow" (*SP* 122) becomes a template for community, a space where "private stuff" might be reconciled to "public spirit," allowing love, and by extension love poetry, a moral or civil function.

In October 1939 Auden wrote a rare poem of ecstatic union between lovers. It's a beautiful poem but seldom cited, perhaps because it does not appear in *Selected Poems*, or perhaps because it is uncharacteristically joyous and untroubled. As with much of Auden's love poetry, it avoids identifying the gender of the lovers.[15] Auden called the poem "Song" and placed it near the middle of what many consider his most accomplished volume, *Another Time*. That volume's dedicatory poem to Chester Kallman reminds us "every eye must weep alone." But there are no tears in "Song," no loneliness, and no borders.

> Warm are the still and lucky miles,
> White shores of longing stretch away,
> A light of recognition fills
>   The whole great day, and bright
> The tiny world of lovers' arms. (*CP* 265)

Auden's poem establishes a special present tense for erotic love and a space at once intimate and expansive, stretching out to gather up a world. "Whole" modifies a temporal unit, "day," but time is given a spatial breadth with "great." The lovers' "tiny world" becomes a wide totality. Though this is not an epithalamium, its "happy miles" suggest Spenser's confidence that "the woods shall to me answer and my Eccho ring."[16] The ease between lovers radiates out into the world and brings it back so that "the tiny world of lovers' arms" is continuous with the universe; body and landscape are one being, animated with desire. Marvell's "The Garden" echoes through the poem. The next stanza reverses direction, "the learned shade" bringing the wisdom and calm of time, perhaps, without its ravages. With "silence" it "invade[s]" the "breathing wood" of the lovers' world, but these are benign features, falling "greenly" and stirring "their secret to a smile." The lyric "now" at the center of the middle stanza suggests the bliss of consummated love. The poet of "borders" discovers a boundless feeling in this lovers' embrace. Limbs, brows, a smile forget their separate bodies. Perhaps for this reason (rather than merely for gender secrecy) the poem is without pronouns at first, the voice speaking from both inside the experience and outside it, praising the fulfillment. "A light of recognition" turns a verb of their mutual acknowledgment into a noun of condition, requiring no agency of You or I. The praise itself takes on an erotic charge, a bursting forth of language after the "dry dumb past" and even the blissful silence. The third stanza shifts from indolent ease to an exclamation of joy. Erotic "seas of shipwreck" paradoxically bear them "home," from a green shade to a "fire of praising." The exclamation "Restored! Returned!" continues the trope of reciprocity and of departure and return, the anonymous "lost" castaways redeemed and "home at last." Only in the penultimate line does the first-person plural appear, but its late introduction suggests a unity achieved and recognized in the embrace, the enjambment creating emphasis, the inversion converting love's reciprocity to a time-trumping effect: "and we / Our life-day long shall part no more." The inversion of the familiar idiom "live long day" may qualify the temporality of love (this is an eternal moment, not an eternity of moments), but most importantly the happiness seems to break over the borders of time. Aspiration and achievement are one; no "I" and "You" remain, only love's "we." The song, its fifteen lines overrunning the sonnet's "narrow strictness," establishes the feeling of holism and boundless union by melding words through assonance and alliteration, and finding rhymes inside of lines, or in half-rhymes, rather than creating a pattern of sharp closing oppositions and antitheses.

Auden seems in "Warm are the still and lucky miles" to have stepped away from the social and political concerns of his recent poetry, indulging in a moment of private bliss. But his thinking about romantic love has a communal reach. Here, the generalizing images at the end, of "the lost" ones (presumably including the lovers in their earlier lives) and the "the dry dumb past," seem to extend out from the private moment, inviting all, not just each other but the world, to "See!" the pattern of their love. Rather than simply creating "private spheres out of public chaos," the poem suggests how private union might extend its redemptive and harmonizing influence by sheer force of feeling. "Warm are the still and lucky miles" is a rare moment of ecstatic ease in modern poetry, and especially in Auden's love poetry. None of Auden's didactic abstraction "invades" this inviolable "song." As he would write in "Heavy Date" during the same month: "When two lovers meet, then / There's an end to writing / Thought and Analytics" (CP 260). Auden would soon turn philosophical and indeed analytical about his relationship to Kallman as the "life-day long" of their blissful union proved fleeting in duration if boundless in consequence.

As we've seen, love shapes the grammar and syntax as well as number of its pronouns, whether it is a reciprocal chiasm or, as in Donne, a "new soul" emerging as a predicate.[17] The lovers' "we" in Auden's poetry returned to a fraught relation of you and I, even as their relationship continued to be a moral compass for Auden, informing his wider ethical vision with a "we" that generalizes from his urges and failures. The poem "Every eye must weep alone" (EA 456) begins in a struggle to overthrow the ego and its desires ("I Will"). The declaration "I Am become I Love" (in which love becomes a predicate object) projects itself as a line that "all I's" might utter, but in the context of the dedication it is Auden speaking for himself, not for the two as a unit. Indeed, he acknowledges: "I Have Not I Am Loved." Narcissus remains ungratified, his love unreciprocated. There is no meeting the world in each other's eyes in this repetition of I's. The "we" that might arise when "all I's can meet and grow" is ostensive. Auden represents the experience of love as a self-discovery through self-forgetting. As he writes in "Heavy Date": "I have / Found myself in You" (*CP* 260). But if Auden's work chooses the I/You relation, with all its tensions, over narcissistic gratification, this very recognition of the other becomes a basis for reconciling romantic love with ethical and social awareness.

———

Most of Auden's early poetry "about love" is nothing like "Warm are the still and lucky miles." Love is uneasy; there is no ecstatic "we." The tense is generally past and passive. Love's adversaries are everywhere; "I" and "you" find each other mostly at odds, and the repressive forces of the external world create division within the self and between lovers. Auden embodies love's tensions and evasions in stoical and sardonic tonalities and figures of incongruity. These are indeed voices of "the lost," recalling Meredith's and Hardy's elegiac love lyrics. The "birds up above" may converse "so sweetly on reciprocal love," awakening human desire, but the division between lovers is often "ten thousand miles deep" (*CP* 142–43). "Love," it seems, is an individual feeling of desire and its fulfillment or frustration, not something ecstatic or even shared. Even when love is imagined in a positive light, it tends to focus on personal gratification rather than mutuality. "Lover, sulk no more," Auden sings in "Underneath the abject willow," "come, / . . . Into your satisfaction" (*SP* 45). The imperative mood gives the poem didactic force. Where Auden uses the first-person plural in his early love poetry it tends to signify a past or evoke a memory rather than declare a fulfilling "now." The "we" may know itself only in loss. "The Letter" of 1927 ("From the very first coming down," *SP* 4) provides a striking contrast to "Warm are the still and lucky miles." Here, love does not reshape the world; instead, the world distorts love. The antipastoral poem marks out division not only in space and time references but also in the poem's form. "You" and "I" in this address are set on separate lines, with a landscape already marked by the ups and downs of erotic hope and disappointment. The "country god" Pan, frozen into a stone statue, inspires only passive voice and double negatives, certainly no "fire of praising." "We" arises only once in twenty-eight lines, and in reference to an impotent spectatorship that could as well apply to the reader who is following the account as to the couple whose experience the poem relays. All other pronouns drop out in the declensions, as if the course of love comes to pass by necessity rather than choice and is easily anticipated: "shall see, shall pass, as we have seen." "Pass" becomes "passed" two lines later, a word that hangs ambiguously between the former lovers (who "pass" each other emotionally) and the world around them. It's an enervated version of Petrarchan conflict. "As we have seen" speaks not as a lover in the recollection but impersonally, as a mind in a cool formal analysis, for which the lovers are exhibits and witnesses rather than grieving participants. Yet the mood is less of wisdom than regret.

In another early poem, "Taller to-day" (*SP* 5–6), "we" arises in the first line: "we remember similar evenings." The companions are jolted to childhood but separate childhoods, before any "we" had formed. The moment of union is already displaced, immediately shadowed by the past and by anxieties about the future. A qualified "We" is reasserted after "But" in the third stanza: "But happy now, though no nearer each other, / We see farms . . ." "Nearer" than when? When they were children and separate? The middle clause enacts what it says, keeping the distance between lovers; they share a view but not a view of each other. The final stanza inserts another "but" that would hold "this peace" as exceptional, transient, and far from ecstatic. This stanza also removes all pronouns and frames assertions in double negatives: "not this peace / No bird can contradict." Tenses undermine union. It is hard to invest much confidence in the "something fulfilled" of "this hour" (hinting at, without securing, this *our*). Whatever that "something" might be and whether that "something" is "loved or endured," it is far from rapturous. Feeling "endured" (not "enduring") is externalized, just as "something fulfilled" here suggests prophecy realized rather than a consummation achieved. "The Adversary," Auden's name for all the forces of division, social and psychological, set against love, is still at large "on lonely roads."

The sense that love arises within a public, social order marked by exclusions and antagonisms that obstruct personal bonds pervades all these poems, none so clearly as "The chimneys are smoking" (*EA* 116–18). The 1932 poem presents two related tensions that will continue to inform Auden's love poetry for several decades: first, the longing for lasting union and the inevitability of loss and separation; second, the conflict between private satisfactions and public imperatives. He feels the demands of the public sphere from which he is at once alienated as well as hostile to its repression, and toward which he is compelled by an authentic sense of obligation. In "The chimneys are smoking," Auden tries to address the first problem by solving the second. That is, he tries to overcome the loss that shadows his intimacy by exchanging that local and tentative "we" for political camaraderie, acknowledging the social imperative instead of feeling its constraints. Altruism and communal solidarity have a compensatory quality here. As Edward Mendelson has argued, the awkwardness and obscurity of the poem in places is a sign of Auden's doubts about the argument he is making, as if willed rhetoric could override cognitive dissonance and doubt.[18] The shifts in the use of the first-person plural are particularly symptomatic of this problem.

"The chimneys are smoking" begins with the absence of a lover and a self-distancing tone: "my magnet, my pomp, my beauty . . . / To-day is parted from me / And I stand on our world alone." The exceptional quality of the beloved and their brief "embrace" and consequent impact of the loss is the first impression—sea, Europe, hometown, the imperatives of nature and of politics are weaker than the compass of feeling ordered around this magnet of love. But it is the disorder of the outer world that seems to have brought about the romantic rupture. The purpose of the poem is not now, after "our hour of unity," forever to "stand alone," but instead to stand together with others, to reconnect with larger groups, distant and proximate—from the human to the local community. Love is referred to a broader social struggle. The public duty will take more than the words of the "communist" (later changed to "political") orator to fulfill. The orator arrives "like a sea god" at the poem's opening, but the speaker must work out a new perspective for himself. "I stand on our world alone" hovers between two meanings of "our," one private, one public. The "we" of the third stanza is punningly mathematical in its idea of redistribution, referring to the fragmented and unstable society in a "contest . . . for the carried thing / Divided in secret among us, a portion to each." But the poem then narrows back to a limited first-person plural, first as object, "that power that gave us our lives," then as subject, "we found when we met," remembering the lovers' embrace that puts the jigsaw together: "Out of the complex to be reassembled / Pieces that fit." This past moment of unity is returned to a natural law of gaps and separations, figured in the landscape. But a principle of universality keeps them united in a shared human condition; the "we" has shifted again, absorbing the unique, intimate pair into the general human condition:

> We ride a turning globe, we stand on a star;
> It has thrust us together; it is stronger than we.
> In it our separate sorrows are a single hope . . . (*EA* 118)

In "dreams" they sustain "linked arms" (not an "embrace" that creates an exclusive private world of "we," as lovers, but a show of brotherly solidarity). The "we" here is becoming inclusive, turning vaguely toward an image of social unity: "These millions in whom already the wish to be one / . . . is stealthily moving." A local political alliance has become a cause. Auden keeps pressing out the private, broken "we" into a new "dance" of social roles and relations among "the boatmen, virgins, camera-men and us." This utopian image of a private love enveloped in a universal love remains a remote ideal at best. The "we" of love's fulfilling moments does not endure by dissolving into the "sundering streams" between nature and mass humanity. Nor does the poem's embrace of fellow man in mutual subjection to nature's changes resolve the tension between private desire and public good.

Auden's conflicted allegiances to these two forms of "we" continue. He does not persist in his fantasy of "The chimneys are smoking" that brotherly love or class alliances can provide an alternative to inevitably fracturing interpersonal connection. Humanity, "the millions . . . [that has] the wish to be one," an agglomerating mass that has been "thrust . . . up together," cannot compensate for the failure of the erotic life any more than the erotic life can successfully turn its back on "the millions."

The style of "The chimneys are smoking" carries over from *Poems*. By contrast, Auden's love poetry in the mid-1930s clarifies syntax and relies less on the ambiguity of the early poetry's peculiar language to create its erotic unease and anxious movement between personal and public concerns. However, the situation of the "we" is no less fraught. In many of these poems a tension arises between the poet as impassioned lover and the poet as wise spectator. His stance as both erotic partner and worldly advisor has many literary antecedents and may also reflect Auden's desire for much younger men. Auden's poems sometimes suggest the Platonic model of pederasty in which the relationship between the *erastes* (the older male lover) and the *eromenes* (younger male lover) is both erotic and educational. But the effect of the didactic turn is often to expand or make ambiguous the audience for the poem. Here, wisdom reaches beyond the intimate scene toward the reader as audience. The most extreme case of this complexity of audience is "Lullaby," notably lacking in the first-person plural, where the addressee is sleeping and thus clearly not the primary audience for the poem, which quickly turns general and philosophical. The love sonnets of 1933 present the allegorical struggles of the Petrarchan tradition in which "Love" becomes a force outside individual will, a magnetism but not a mutuality, an allegorical third party, "He," rather than "us," arising between two people. In these sonnets "Love" seems to be the chief troublemaker: "He means to do no mischief but he would" (*EA* 146). The desiring poet is at odds with the wise spectator who has a sober understanding of this force and speaks not simply of the beloved but of a broadly humanistic "we" that includes all men. Instead of presenting the struggle between reason and passion as his own, he presents it as a pedagogical exhibit, his erotic purpose transformed into a didactic one. Reciprocity is explicitly forestalled in the address to a sleeping beloved though the push-pull of desire, and prohibition heightens erotic feeling: "Turn not towards me lest I turn to you" (*EA* 146). With the chiasm (a favored figure in love poetry of all eras) in these opening lines from the beseeching lover, Auden enters the closed loop of denial and yearning. Yet as the poem continues, the scene of the address figures their inequality, and the wise spectator takes over: "Love knows he argues with himself in vain." In the initial fantasy that "the stars watch us," "us" may be dramatically specific to the lovers, but the pronoun becomes impersonal and aphoristic in the sestet ("how easily may we do good / To those we have no wish to see again"). The speaker has taken the impersonal position of the stars even as he acknowledges their disinterest. He knows "Love"['s] ways, making his assertions more proleptic than dramatic or in the moment. These pronoun shifts map Auden's divided role as desiring lover (on the side of *eros*) and sober teacher (reflecting on moral action). In other poems, tension and resistance arise to dramatize the meditation. This older and wiser lover knows the ideal- izing tendencies of lovers and the truth of the world that belies their vows. In "Turn not towards me lest I turn to you," the basis of their mutuality and erotic union seems to be a dangerous inclination to experience love as autonomous and forgetful of the needs of the world ("love's preposterous guarantee . . . that there are no poor"). He brings the suffering social world into the bed- room, undermining the prerogatives of personal desire. The prolepsis opens and closes the sonnet, and the octave piles on negations and cancellations, keeping the social world before them rather than at bay. It is surprising to find a *volta* in "Yes," but it's the "yes" of unsettling suspension and denial rather than consummation. The *volta* seems to stand in for dialogue: "Yes, sleep." The speaker cannot, torn as he is between passion and wisdom.

Many other love poems from the thirties are narratives of disappointment in which the fragmentation of the public world infects the lovers' union. In "Fleeing the short-haired mad executives" (*EA* 149), Auden finally uses a "we" that refers to erotic relation and describes a mutual flight from the external public life. But the relationship is again unconsummated, at least in an emo- tional sense: "the rich interior still / Unknown." In "Dear, though the night is gone" (*EA* 161), the metaphor of love as a room continues, but it is now an exposed public space. The strong opening line suggests an aubade in sustained union, but the rest of the poem brings back a different night than the fulfilling one we expect him to describe. Paradoxically, it was night that separated them, not day, a night of troubled dreams in which all lovers' beds collect in the unro- mantic space of a "room / Cavernous, lofty as / A railway terminus," that is, a hollow public space of departures. Auden again shows his skill in imagining human relationships in spatial terms ("squares and oblongs"), finding geom- etry to match the grammar of love. Later Auden will look for circles, but here love is all angles. The pronoun "we" arises within a "far corner" of this "gloom" but offers no hiding place. In an aubade one expects an intimate space inter- rupted by a noisy world, but here the priorities are inverted. The emphasized erotic "we" of the second stanza ("our whisper," "we kissed") arises not within a bower but within a wider crowd of damaged lovers, a world that is "hostile." "Arms round each other's neck" suggests embrace but also hints at a violence infecting their union. Inevitably, then, the "we" of the middle stanza comes apart, leaving I and You again on separate lines. It's hard to tell where the dream ends. The poem does not close off the dream but lets it haunt the waking so that "dream" and "wish" are at odds. The final stanza creates a displacement; where reciprocal love (confession and submission) is wanted we get a skewed relation: "you . . . confessed another love," and "I, submissive, felt / Unwanted." Spatial boundaries of dream and waking, private and public, are confused. The slant rhymes and ending question—that nearly forgets its beginning—reinforce the unease. The story of the erotic "we" in these love poems of the early thirties is that of a common fate, an "ordinary swoon" subject to "human love," which tends toward hollow romantic idealism, lies, and infidelities.

Auden's suspicions about erotic "ease" become particularly clear in "Easily, my dear," soon after called "A Bride in the 30's" (CP 128–30). The sexual term "lucky," which Auden would use unironically five years later in "Warm are the still and lucky miles," here sets lovers' luck darkly against the "unlucky" landscape both rural and urban, crushed under the rising threat of fascism. "A Bride in the 30's" lays a corrective groundwork for the epithalamia of the war years, in which erotic life forms a foundation for social amelioration, or at least social hope. Auden addresses a beloved, giving drama and immediacy to the utterance, but the poem is pedagogical rather than amorous as it moves out from the intimate "we" to a broader alarm over fascism's "terrifying mottoes" that are seizing the world's attention.

"Easily" is repeated three times in the first lines of the poem, a sure sign that the ease won't be sustained. Auden already questions the "ease" of erotic and poetic connection by using the adverbial form of the word. There is something facile and complacent about lovers' contentment. Newly joined lovers think they are healthy and sealed off from the world, though the poem will go on, through the motif of a photograph album, to expose their proximity to mounting public evils. The camera eye widens love's narrow perspective; the "grouped invalids," and the "single assassins" who manipulate them, though overlooked in the honeymoon, peer out from the retrospective album pictures. The first-person plural enters the poem most explicitly under the burden of this awakening, where the incongruous "our first meeting" ends a catalog of troubling public images—"sterile farms," "the policed unlucky cities." Public orators on both sides—Hitler, Mussolini, Churchill, Roosevelt, and Van der Lubbe—distort the language of love with their propaganda and characterize the broader environment of hatred and violent order in which personal love arises. Rather than simply consolidate love's private haven, the speaker becomes didactic: love must be marshaled to a new purpose by a new moral imperative. "A Bride in the 30's" is a carpe diem poem urging "love, except at our proposal, / will do no trick at his disposal." "Trick" suggests sexual

availability, but here directed, as with the trickster, toward social transformation. Love must give up "ease" since there is work to do: love, "through our
private stuff must work / His public spirit." Auden turns away from the honeymoon memories and retrospective witness, addressed to the beloved, and
offers future-oriented imperatives. "The heart," generalized and separated now
from the erotic hopes of the lovers, "repeats" an imperative, turning a "we" to
imperative "you" that includes both the speaker and the beloved, and indeed
seems to hail to the wider community. By yoking the interpersonal (the colloquial phrase "private stuff" diminishing and concealing love's drives) to the
more formal "public spirit" that all can approve, Auden seeks a way to turn the
erotic toward the communal, without a naïve conflation of the two.

The added title for "Easily, my dear," "A Bride in the 30's," identifies the
photograph album as a honeymoon souvenir. Through marriage, the couple
is already entering the civil sphere. This is something new in Auden's poetry
and marks the relation of erotic love to social love as a continuum rather than a
conflict or alternative. In "Easily, my dear," this continuum is discovered rather
than assumed from the beginning. Love is no longer in or of the shadows, nor
does it dwell apart, in a space outside history and strife. It takes strength from
community and gives back its peace as a resource for hope and survival in
historical crisis. Marriage is one place where private stuff meets public spirit
and submits the interpersonal relationship to the public domain.

The Vow as Speech Act and Poetic Figure

The love poetry I have discussed so far is concerned with the past and the
present. Where it imagines the future, it tends to be directed away from personal attachment to social hope. But vows are inherently future-directed; they
establish potentiality as obligation, and Auden associates them with poetry.
"Words are for those with promises to keep" (SP 203). As performatives, vows
(J. L. Austin's chief example) are not true or false. Promises create bonds rather
than acknowledge them. One may stand alone in love, but a promise made out
of love, when the speaker is sincere and the hearer is receptive, makes a bond
between people even if the vow is not reciprocated. Auden's long-term interest
in vows is clear from his quotation of Hannah Arendt in his essay "Brothers & Others": "The remedy for unpredictability, for the chaotic uncertainty
of the future, is contained in the faculty to make and keep promises. Both
faculties depend upon plurality, on the presence and acting of others, for no
man can forgive himself and no one can be bound by a promise made only
to himself" (DH 218).[19] Promises introduce a principle of coherence into an
otherwise uncertain future. Promises also require witnesses, listeners, even if
the only listeners are the speakers themselves. In this sense vows are gestures

toward community. For Auden, a healthy human plurality involves a network of bonds, and marriage is the figure of their formation.

Auden's wartime marriage poems, "Epithalamion" (1939) for Borgese and Mann, and "In Sickness and in Health" (1940), emphasize the social and political significance of personal vows. The first is an occasional and perhaps commissioned poem, written for friends; the second, though unspecified as to gender, was motivated by the poet's commitment to Kallman, which he saw as a marriage. In both poems Auden draws from his own sense that the "we" formed in interpersonal commitment can be a foundation for social hope, thus swerving from earlier models of interpersonal strain or sacrifice of the private life to the public life. Auden's charge to love, that it not only acknowledge but also redeem the public world, produces some of his most inflated rhetoric, if also some of his most interesting layering of the plural first person.

Auden had written an epithalamium for his friend Cecil Day-Lewis in 1928,[20] but its tone and tenor serve as a contrast to his wartime marriage poems in that he still views love as a suspension of social concerns, even a turning away. From his early days in poetry Auden had written occasional verse, recruited by friends to offer epideictic toasts. Presumably this poem was read at Day-Lewis's wedding so that the community it gathers is a literal presence, not just an imagined one, its "we" an assembled group. He did not include this "Epithalamium" in any of his books, though he retained the phrase "taller to-day" as the first words of another early poem. "Epithalamium"—its title identifying with a long English tradition—first appeared in print in a memoir by Day-Lewis's son Sean Day-Lewis, *Cecil Day-Lewis: An English Literary Life* (1980). This early marriage poem is a kind of proletarian pastoral, with stanzas of eight lines, some rhymed and some uncoupled, hinting throughout at Spenserian conventions. While it may not be worth preserving as part of an Auden canon, it provides an interesting prelude to his later work in the genre, especially in its group orientation. The poet stands as a presiding witness and participant in the communal ceremony. The poem acknowledges the forms "unfamiliar" to those gathered, a group of "all of us who know" and sympathize with "workers" and "victims" of social oppression. Auden rhetorically gathers the community and serves as the agent of love's public spirit, the catalyst of its communal work. He speaks for the group in first-person plural, representing a politically minded community conscious of the labor to be done beyond the nuptial scene. He addresses the couple, "we speak to you," first pausing to remind the lovers of the troubled world beyond, asking them "now" to "stand . . . still" and survey it "like the sparrowhawk." The poet dispels the threat of fragmentation in love, then releases the pair from that trouble into the sensuous, pastoral *now* of their union. In this poem, marriage, though it gathers community, is not a foundation of social justice but a suspension of its responsibilities, except to "be quick" and engender a future. Auden's other early excursion into wedding verse is "Prothalamion," with six-line stanzas in couplets and toasting refrain, which he also removed from his canon. This is one of several marriage masques in Auden's poetry. Originally a bawdy parody following the vicar's sermon in *The Dog Beneath the Skin*, the poem appears in his *Collected Shorter Poems* very differently, without the demagogue's voice, as a celebration of premarital carnival spirit, a tribute to tolerance under the sign of permissiveness. But neither of these exercises, written between the wars, anticipates the somewhat grim wartime wedding poems he would write, when he was offering vows of his own.

Auden's relationship with Chester Kallman changed his attitude toward love and consequently the kind of poetry he wrote about love. That difficult relationship became the touchstone of his ethical vision. The marriage poem for Day-Lewis saw that union as a pause from leftist political action, which was the real center of belonging and purpose. But having abandoned by 1940 any sense that the poet has an activist role to play, Auden turns to interpersonal commitment and formal vows as a foundation and example for human community. Marriage offered a challenge to the nihilism and destruction prevailing in the public world. Love is now less a selfish or merely personal indulgence, a distraction from the work of social change, than a civil intervention. Auden's reflections on his emotional ties to Kallman provide an occasion to develop an idea of community already forming in "Out on the Lawn." In this light, promises made to a lover, whether kept or broken, are never a strictly personal matter; their force is not limited or bound to individual constancy. Like art, marriage displays a benign order and posits a future for it.

Auden writes these marriage poems at a time when he is also acknowledging the unknown, both in the world of events and in the mind of the beloved. "Narcissus disbelieves in the unknown" (*CP* 310), he writes in "Alone" (1940), not only because he thinks he knows everything, but also because he is only interested in himself. To turn to the other is by definition to turn to the unknown. Auden testifies to this again and again, in "If I Could Tell You," "Leap Before You Look," and other love poems of that year. He creates counterpoint as he sets his strict, predictable lyric forms against the acknowledgment of existential uncertainty and of the ultimate mystery of the other. The paradoxes of recognized difference and desire for union close "Alone": "every lover has a wish to make / Some other kind of otherness his own" (*CP* 311). Love is the interplay of desire for possession and acceptance of the other as a distinct subject. As he had learned from Marianne Moore, marriage is a paradox and an "enterprise," not a completed single event.

Central in the application of *eros* to the work of ethical community is the vow; it is the foundation of Auden's new vision of love and a swerve from earlier cynicism about human promises. Vows made freely in the knowledge of human frailty and in the face of historical ruin bespeak an existential leap of faith. Vows posit a future and affirm there is another way than destruction. In his early relationship to Kallman, Auden understood the vow as an exchange, but Kallman's infidelity would make him see the vow more in terms later described by Emanuel Levinas: responsibility to the Other as a one-directional movement from an I to a You.[21] The "we" created by a vow is not so much a reciprocal voicing of commitment as a surrendering of selfish will to an ethical bond, a bond of obligation rather than requital. A vow requires the recognition of another's subjective being and the receptive hearing of that other.

Auden's interest in vows long predates these marriage poems, and his ideas about vows developed gradually. Vows expand the self but can also be inflationary: "I am your vow," proclaims the disembodied conscience of "Spain" (*SP* 56). Private vows between lovers are mostly broken. Indeed, Auden's early poetry seems skeptical about all vows, focusing more on their breaking than on their making. In "A Bride in the 30's," Auden associates vows with propaganda in explicit parallel to romantic courtship ("Hitler and Mussolini in their wooing poses," *CP* 129). Other references to the vow bring up thoughtless youth's glib idealism ("Climbing with you was easy as a vow," *EA* 149), cynical seduction ("I'll love you till the ocean / Is folded and hung up to dry," *SP* 66), naïve commitment to authority ("the bars of love are so strong, their conspiracies / Weak like the vows of drunkards," *EA* 216), fallible resolution ("I *will* be true to my wife," *SP* 97), or weakness of resolve in the face of external threat ("Were the vows you swore me deceiving, deceiving? / No, I promised to love you, dear / But I must be leaving," *SP* 28). In the world of the early poems, humans seldom realize their vows. But for later Auden this fact of human lapse does not cancel the ethical and social importance of the vow. In the wedding poem Auden redeems the vow as a speech act. The "now" of the vow (importantly different from the "now" of erotic high noon in its relation to others) participates in ritual time, and its value transcends the inevitable betrayals of historical time. The marriage vow is a present-tense civil and spiritual act with meaning beyond the moment of swearing and the local and individual commitment it pronounces, and even beyond its test of fidelity. In the wedding poems the vow often modulates into performative modes such as prayer and benediction, further propelling the imagination toward the future. In the turn from breaking to making vows, Auden recenters his ethical vision. Even when honored in the breach, vows made freely make something happen. They have an illocutionary and even a perlocutionary force that reverberates into the life of the community. The word "lie" (punning or not) comes up often in Auden's writing, and poems might make us more aware of lies. But updating Sidney, Auden said a poem, unlike a historical person, "cannot lie," and so it is with the performance of vows, in poems, and in wedding ceremonies where "meaning and being are identical" (*DH* 68). An insincere vow is not a vow; a broken vow does not negate the meaning of the vow.

Wedding vows, like marriage itself, traditionally direct erotic energy that might be socially antagonistic into socially productive union. But writing at the beginning of World War II, Auden is especially aware of the breakdown of community and the antagonisms going on within and between nations. Marriage has a symbolic function for a world in crisis; it ritualizes a counterspace of love and peace. It models an amenable society even as an ominous reality lies all about. It gathers and orders humanity against the evidence of conflict and fragmentation. Auden at one time said that homosexuality was a narcissistic shortcut to sociality. But the marriage poems perhaps helped him place his relation to Kallman in a broader community of committed lovers. As such, he plays an ambiguous role in these poems, as someone both administering and, implicitly or explicitly, taking a vow.

Auden's "Epithalamion: For Giuseppe Antonio Borgese and Elisabeth Mann (Nov. 23, 1939)," written just two months after Britain declared war on Germany, attempts to see marriage as a foundational symbol of international peace.[22] This is not at all surprising. Likely, most wedding ceremonies in these months made the civil union a counterpoint to international strife, especially when the unions involved Europeans. In this case the Borgese/Mann union defies the antagonism of the "hostile kingdoms" (hostile to the Allies, that is) Italy and Germany. While Mussolini and Hitler spread hatred and violence, this marital union is a "seed" of "human unity," both figuratively and prospectively in the procreative authority of marriage. In performing their promises to each other the couple are "vowing to redeem the state." The line is awkward, but not unsubtle, suggesting how private commitments can create public good rather than deferring it.

There is no interpersonal address in the Borgese/Mann "Epithalamion." Auden is the presiding counselor, the wise spectator, not the lover. He has exchanged the intimacy of love poetry for a ceremonial platform. The poem turns first to dead artists and then, as the wise spectator, to "every girl and boy." Though the catalog of visual, literary, and musical artists in the second part of the poem might be considered relevant to a literary union like this one (Borgese was a writer and journalist, Mann the daughter of Thomas Mann), these figures shift our attention away from, rather than simply extending, the occasion of the marital union. In this wider community of artists and youth, Auden can be a full participant, not just a wedding guest or agent for a future state. "Kindly [according to nature, with goodwill] to each other turn," he instructs, administering the vows and conscious of the turns of inclusion and exclusion between the couple and the community characteristic of the genre of the epithalamium. But the poem does not go with them into an intimate space of love; the "we" remains public and general. Auden likely recognized its weaknesses since he chose not to include it in any collections after *Another Time*. As a poem to be read on the occasion of the marriage but written with a broader didactic purpose in mind, it has an awkwardly layered sense of audience and performance. One wonders what the newlyweds felt about having their celebration turned into a map of "modern policy." In shifting in the second half to the world of art from the world of the state, Auden makes a place for himself in the work of social correction, but "the heaven of the Great," the Parnassus of immortal artists, seems a limited basis for prayers and praises that might "redeem the state," or so Auden would have it. The congregation now gathered seems less a wedding group than an audience for an opera, as German and Italian artists become the real family of Mann and Borgese, and as Hölderlin, Wagner, Dante, Leonardo arrive, invited as the unacknowledged legislators of the world to displace Hitler and Mussolini. Here is where Auden focuses his first-person plural: "Looking down upon us all" from their immortal station, these greats convene a "we" less of local community or romantic love than of audience and abstract humanity to which their monumental works are addressed. The performative aspect of vows degrades into speechmaking and didacticism, into what Auden would soon condemn: "glittering generalities" (*SP* 120). His next epithalamium, "In Sickness and in Health" (*SP* 120–23), continues to present the vow as a pattern of love in a world subdued by hate. But perhaps since the proposed vow is his as speaker, the lovers retain their erotic being for each other rather than fulfilling a duty on behalf of the state. By affirming the commitment to "one dear" in the context of a performance of vows, Auden presents community not as a collective entity, a faceless, narcissistic "we" or a vague generational humanity, but as a vital network of affiliations and individual bonds.

"In Sickness and in Health" is, of course, not a real vow. It is a poem, what John R. Searle would call a "parasitic form of communication."[23] Thus in this poem, more than in previous epithalamia, the nuptial vow is connected to the *work* of art. In imitating a speech act, in creating a fictional ceremony, the poem not only explores the meaning of a vow but also engages the reader as a distant participant or witness, extending the force of the vow and the outline of its "arbitrary circle" beyond the unique circle of love and its witnesses, beyond the particular speaker and local hearer. The poem might be said to represent the possibility of vows and the potential community shaped by sincere promises. And the poem offers this possibility against the "noise" of the "terrifying mottoes" that teach the public a life-denying fear and caution. Unlike a vow, which imagines a future, a motto is static, an axiom that can descend to the level of a slogan; more threat than commitment. When a motto takes the imperative form it is addressed to everyone and no one; it is not a fundamentally ethical gesture. "In Sickness and in Health" is especially conscious of its speech acts and draws attention to them not only in the rhetorical modes it explores but also in its imagery and themes. The opening stanzas show Auden in his full poetic powers, with tightly woven metaphors and allusions, alliterative and assonantal musicality, elegant stanzas—all in counterpoint to the entropic and destructive world the poem describes. Art, like the marriage vow, is an "arbitrary circle" cut out of chaos and noise, and a raid on the "inarticulate." Though the poem does not describe a public ceremony, it becomes its own occasion, making the reader as well as Love witness to the vow.

The opening word establishes the poem as an address to a specific beloved, "Dear," and initiates a dramatic bond. Auden had begun an earlier love poem with "Dear" ("Dear though the night is gone") in an urgent and anxious telling of a dream of betrayal and abandonment. This "Dear" dispels that earlier darkness and turns instead toward commitment and faith, toward the utterance of a vow. But this drive must make its way through dramatically imagined obstacles external and internal. In particular, the poem performs the struggle to protect the vow from a world not only of "glittering generalities" but of "noise," "shuffle," "roar," "howling," and "loud foreign language." Auden often associated articulate language with man's moral distinction, especially his ability to make commitments to others. "Words are for those with promises to keep" (SP 203).

The traditional epithalamium delays the nuptial union in a rhythm of exclusions and inclusions, which gives culminating force to the vow. Threatened or endangered love sets up a drama of idealism. Auden's poem follows this convention; here the vow is repeatedly put off with warnings and conditions. In stanza 2 he writes (whether addressing himself or the beloved is unclear): "O, promise nothing, nothing, till you know" (later Auden changed "O" to "No," perhaps to emphasize the resistance or to nullify the romantic tonality; and such changes make clear how King Lear haunts this poem of vows and promises, as does Othello). He is still warding off dangers in stanza 4: "Let none say / I Love until aware." But this second exclusion is also an inclusion since the warning is directed impersonally, to anyone. At the end of the poem the speaker confirms that a vow is taking place, a "round O of faithfulness we swear." But the steps for performing a vow organize the poem throughout.

Though modeled to some extent on Spenser's "Epithalamium," this is not Spenser's pastoral world of echoing song, at least until the echoic effects of "rejoice" are sounded in its second half. And even then the rejoicing seems rather dour. Here the echoes suggest other, more troubling literary allusions, all admitting impediments to love. Dangers from abroad reverberate against love's hushed "benevolence of fingering lips." What the lovers can "distinctly hear" is the violence of contemporary history, a darker version of Marvell's "wingèd chariot" of Time. Auden evokes Petrarchan tradition with the image of the world mirrored in the "love lorn eyes," but the mirror is "warped" and the eloquence undercut with the terse account of what those eyes reflect, a Marvellian displacement: "A land of condors, sick cattle, and dead flies." Shakespeare echoes throughout the poem as well. The "Black Dog" may refer to fascist thugs, but it also reminds us of Iago's abusive language at the beginning of *Othello*, language aimed at obstructing a marriage. Stanza 2 calls up *King Lear* (a story of lies, false promises, and silence) with its double "nothing, nothing," especially in the context of the "round O's" and redundant "empty nought" arising further on to evoke and threaten the ties of love. Stanza 4's "O let none say I Love until aware" alludes to Shakespeare's sonnet 116, which will not "admit impediments" but certainly acknowledges them. The vow emerges stronger rhetorically for all it must resist. It performs hyperbolically, naming impediments in order to surmount them, and later even calling for temptation to test its strength.

Auden adopts a modern version of hyperbole from Kierkegaard: "the Absurd" is the illogical voice of faith essential to the vow. Human "love" is prompted and backed by a spiritual imperative that presides in this union. But does the speaker in "In Sickness and in Health" perform the vow, receive the vow, or administer the vow? Likely all of these roles are relevant since the "we" in this poem is multilayered and elastic. The vow is a line of defense, not a pastoral interlude as in the poem for Day-Lewis. It requires both realism and absurd faith. The lovers must "distinctly hear" the horrible noise of the world; at the same time they must remain deaf to its "language of revolt," which threatens love's drive toward union. But who are "we" in "we are the deaf"? The lovers take their place with others who would say "I Love" against the negations of the brutal and faithless world.

If noise is one dominant metaphor challenging the vow, "sickness" is another, and not only in the title's evocation of Christian vows. Lovers join most often when they are in robust health, but disease and entropy surround them in the first part of "In Sickness and in Health" in the "sick cattle," the "thermal wastes," the "contagious" negativity, and its "code of famine." Not only do these forces undo love's order, they "degrade" it, replacing it with tyranny's destructive codes. Against this dis-ease a great effort is required to "nurse" humanity, to protect "one ruining [that is, mortal, as well as adored] speck" in the beloved's form. Thus Auden makes "Love" not only a private gratification but also a healing counterforce to social sickness even as the vow speaks over the "terrifying mottoes" and hostile noise of the world. And this makes the lovers' commitment a civil amelioration, a way of healing the world without displacing their erotic intimacy with public service. Love does its social work in "nocturnal and mysterious" ways. In creating "the arbitrary circle of a vow" (however oblong in practice), the lovers do not exclude the world but instead make a pattern of their love.

The vow as speech act allows Auden to reconcile a passionate assertion of individual feeling to the needs of a larger community. In this it contrasts with fascism, which leaps upon the "individual back" and devours the private life. But Auden moves away in stanza 2 from the urgent address to a particular "Dear." In order to shift from the historical world that threatens "Love's imagination" to the sacred perspective that sanctifies the vow, he begins to depersonalize the poem. "Dear" is replaced with "dear heart," which may come from Thomas Wyatt ("Dear heart, how like you this?"), hinting at love's "continual change" ("They Flee from Me"). "Dear heart" may also suggest the possibility that Auden, like many a Petrarchan lover, is addressing himself, his own heart, or at least moving inward in meditation and then outward to a wider audience. The poem becomes increasingly didactic in its tonalities, as philosophical statement and mythic paradigm overtake the emotionally engaged, dramatic utterance of the first four stanzas. The performance of the vow recedes into explanation and illustration in stanza 5, focusing on failures of the past rather than newly formed or potential union. This didactic mode has its own mimetic eloquence, where Auden registers the state of Tristan and Isolde, the "two waterfalls" of romantic (but not dialogical) lovers, in the exalted, echoic effects of the line. Don Juan, "haunting the urinals," represents the opposite extreme of the same narcissistic pattern, a desolate figure of unhealthy love; the suddenly debased rhetoric and imagery, after the exalted formality the poem has established, reflects the degraded condition of his erotic drive. The collective narcissism that seems to have overtaken the world also perverts ardor as "the lovers of themselves collect" in the faceless fascist order. Auden defends against these fates as he anticipates the lovers' vows.

When Auden returns to a direct address to his "Beloved" in stanza 8, he brings the reader back out of impersonal reflection to the active performance of a vow that the poem imitates. But in addressing his "dear," Auden identifies the lovers as typically human, not exceptional. "We are always in the wrong." How might such imperfect voices offer a pattern of health to a sick society? The world's malice that was surveyed in stanzas 1–7 is now "our malice," at least potentially. (Auden in the 1940s seldom foregoes an opportunity to remind the reader of original sin.) This acknowledgment concludes the "passionate negation" that has mounted to make this a very gloomy wedding ceremony. And it's hard to see how such "private stuff," so burdened with guilt, can have much "public spirit."

At this impasse the poem shifts ground, calling on its listeners to "rejoice" after all the warnings and delays. But the rejoicing must find some other basis for hope than the erotic lovers, who are not exceptional but flawed humans.

It is time to focus on the *possible*, backed by spiritual actuality, rather than the *actual* lives of lovers and poets who are "always in the wrong." Grace is required, and a dialogical relation outside the scope of human interaction. The focus of address shifts away from the voice of the individual lover to his love, and a disembodied "love" speaks out, the difference marked in italics in stanza 9. The poet will later "pray" to this presence, but first the voice "preempts" the poet and replaces his negative and "makeshift" thoughts with rhetorical questions that assert a greater creative power underwriting the circle of the vow along with art's own arbitrary circle. The italicized stanza 9 inverts the opening stanzas of the poem, the "nothing, nothing" of imminent ruin belied by a *fiat lux*, a world made out of nothing. This stanza redirects the energy of the poem toward rejoicing and allows the poet to refocus his attentions from fear to love, and from man's inherent malice to a particular devotion to "one dear face."

The disembodied voice behind the italicized words of stanza 9 is that of "Love." Auden is explicit in this deferral and shift in reference, as the lover returns to address his dear: "Rejoice, dear love, in Love's peremptory word." Auden's repetition here equivocates as to the source and authority of human feeling, suggesting, as Shakespeare does in sonnet 116, that a metaphysical principle, not an external agent, guides errant human desire. Auden clearly wants to blend *eros* and *agape* here.[24] It is not simply that unsteady human love needs the higher blessing as a support and guide. Love's "peremptory word" suggests that the capacity to love has an incarnative quality, though its divine source is unknowable and even tautological; the very will to promise is provoked by grace within us, preempting our doubting, isolating narcissism. Auden's "now" in this poem connects historical time with ritual time, but the movement is not only vertical. Since the poem begins with a wide perspective on the crisis in Europe, the "circle" of the vow can be understood horizontally, not only to exclude the disease of modern history but also to extend to a peaceful future community. By layering local time and space with broader references (a common feature of epithalamia), Auden conditions the meaning of "we" in the poem. To whom is the command given to "Describe round our chaotic malice now, / The arbitrary circle of a vow"? Where is the perimeter of this circle? Is Auden addressing "dear love" or "Love" here? And is "Love" the fusion of You and I, an intervening grace, a third thing made by the loving connection, or all of these? Auden pulls many entities together in "All chance, all love, all logic, you and I, / Exist by grace of the Absurd." He is scrutinizing the meaning of "you and I" throughout. "And" is a sign of both distinction and union. It can be read as a conjunction that follows from the three "all's", so that the phrase "you and I" is equivalent to "all peoples" or as a conjunction that binds "you" and "I" into a singular you-and-I, which, as a loving unit, is separated from everyone and everything else, including "you" and "I" as distinct individuals.

As we have seen, "In Sickness and in Health" has both a narrative and a propositional aspect and modulates between an exclusive (personal) and inclusive (impersonal) use of the first-person plural as it works through intimate and didactic forms of address, which come together toward the end of the poem. As with Spenser's epithalamium, this marriage poem has worked its way through a ceremony (his own nuptials), using the devices of prospect and prolepsis to give layered space and time to the moment. As in a Renaissance epithalamium, the poem has repeatedly warded off what might threaten the union. It gathers and excludes in order to forge a harmonious community in which the marriage can succeed. Auden hints at consummation toward the end of the poem as he directs his lover to "lay your solitude beside my own." Auden structures the prayer, which covers the last four stanzas, in a sequence of "lest's" that ward off evil. Though the body is the focus, the rhetoric of prayer is marked in the elevated "Thy," addressed not to the beloved but to a spiritual, perhaps divine presence. Hence in the line "this round O of faithfulness we swear" the poem insists on the first-person plural, which is both specific to the newly united lovers and general to all who believe with them in the future that promises affirm. The pronoun arises insistently now, "we . . . lovers" committing themselves before "all."

Kallman's infidelity would soon confirm that "solitude" even in love, though Auden considered himself married for the rest of his life. The rededication of "In Sickness and Health" to Maurice and Gwen Mandelbaum in 1942 makes this in a way a poem of remarriage. Remarriage, as Stanley Cavell imagines it, puts aside romantic idealism and works from acknowledgment of the limits, not only of one's personal capacities but also of one's ability to know the mind of the beloved. For Auden this remarriage would involve a shift from desire for possession to recognition of the other. As Kallman left "to find his own life,"[25] Auden came to understand the place of "I" in love's work: "The singular is not Love's enemy; / Love's possibilities of realisation / Require an Otherness that can say I" (CP 384). Ultimately one does not marry "Love" (the site where "we" arises) but an individual beloved. The beloved is a very different kind of unknown from an abstract cipher like "Love," or even from the "nocturnal and mysterious" mood of sex. Perhaps this is also why Auden changed the ending to "In Sickness and in Health." In keeping with other late changes, his personal life is removed and he presents himself as Everyman, his "voluntary way" becoming an "ordinary way."

"In Sickness and in Health" is certainly dramatic, in the way of a good epithalamium. It works through gestures of warding off threats and bringing in community to define and protect the circle of love. And the many vocatives underscore the sense of action in the poem, which is gathering and excluding, slowing down narrative and pointing to the future, giving a sense of the now but locating it in multiple localities and temporalities. The poem's Shakespearean noughts fend off what they invoke, affirm with skepticism, like the best kind of faith. We accept the vocatives and hyperboles because, as in Shakespeare, the high ritual of the union calls for them, and the ideals describe Love without idealizing individual lovers. And yet the didactic elements of the poem overwhelm this dramatic ceremony. Especially as the poem turns to prayer and the lovers become instruments of the abstract work of Love, it is hard to believe in the presence of the beloved or the vitality of the vow. The future the poem imagines seems impersonal. The poems Auden would write immediately after "In Sickness and in Health" turn again from the general crisis to address the beloved with the knowledge of their share in its hazards. The unknown as a condition of love is better captured in a later poem of 1940, "Leap Before you Look," in which ambiguities and qualifications abound within the vow. The poet acknowledges "A solitude ten thousand fathoms deep / Sustains the bed on which we lie, my dear: / Although I love you, you will have to leap; / Our dream of safety has to disappear."[26]

Auden would revisit the subject of marriage vows just two years later in the lyrics he assigned to Ferdinand and Miranda in *The Sea and the Mirror*.[27] He returns to the themes and many of the structural elements of "In Sickness and in Health." Again, love's promise is "immured" within a world of strife, and the lovers are deaf to the foreign language of revolt. But the dramatic form of the sequence and the innocent personae of the lovers allow Auden to bracket out, for the lovers' lyrics, all the negating and skeptical voices of their elders. The poem can enter more fully into the lyric "now" of young lovers making their vows, because the perspective is theirs, and the qualifications to their idealism are part of the wider dramatic framework rather than registered from within. Auden was reading C. S. Lewis's *The Allegory of Love* in 1941–42, and he included it on his syllabus at the University of Michigan. Ferdinand and Miranda may be read as allegorical figures in this light.

Ferdinand's lyric address begins with the concept of the Other within marriage.[28] Auden plays with the love lyric's grammar and number to enhance the paradoxes common in the tradition. "You" are not only "unique" but also "secret," a "Dear Other[ness]" "retained" and complementary to the speaking "I." The language shifts in the second quatrain toward "me" and "I," but only to conclude the octave with a union: "two wonders as one vow / Pre-empting all, here, there, for ever, long ago." Here, the preemption comes not from a supernatural force but from the unit established in the vow itself. When Auden takes on the voice of Ferdinand, "You" and "I" are "unique" but not solitary. No external preemptive word is required. The vow itself is the voice of Love that "pre-empts" history and locates the lovers in their timeless ideal. Here, Auden imagines the reciprocity in the first-person plural. The sonnet closes in a doubling language of binding relation, mixing subject and object positions, in which the "we" of love is both the larger community and the beloveds: "Pleading with ours for us, another tenderness / That neither without either could or would possess." "Ours" might simply be a reference to relatives who hold sway over the union. Syntactically, "ours" refers back to the analogy "as world is offered world," suggesting that "ours" indicates "our world," though the shuttling lines are, perhaps intentionally, difficult to parse as they work to fuse two subjects and move between levels of belonging. Arthur Kirsch notes that in a letter to Isherwood, Auden says this sonnet "describes fucking in completely abstract words" (SM xxiii), but this reductive account seems designed to amuse Isherwood rather than to describe the poem's disposition. Auden gives a better account of the poem's power in the manuscript draft where he explains, "mutuality of love begets love." In this sense the poem recalls "Warm are the still and lucky miles" of just a few years before.

Auden follows Shakespeare's The Tempest in recognizing that the intrusions of another plot, one of violence and division, always threatens the matrimonial scene. The italicized voice of the singular, figured as Antonio, casts a shadow on each human connection in the sequence of poems. Auden would later write of The Tempest: "Ferdinand and Miranda, who seem as virginal and innocent as any fairy story lovers, are first treated to a moral lecture on the danger of anticipating their marriage vows, and the theme of the masque itself is a plot by Venus to get them to do so. The masque is not allowed to finish, but is broken off suddenly by Prospero, who mutters of another plot.... As an entertainment for a wedding couple, the masque can scarcely be said to have been a success" (DH 526). There is no masque in The Sea and the Mirror, so the individual songs retain the subjective integrity of their perspectives. Miranda does not address Ferdinand, though as Arthur Kirsch has noted, her speech immediately follows Ferdinand's in the Buffalo draft. Auden's decision to space them so widely apart perhaps suggests the reality of their difference from each other and the less than utopian world they must live in.

But a positive reading of Auden's restructuring is also possible. If Antonio's dissonance and selfish atomism opens and closes chapter 2 of The Sea and the Mirror, Ferdinand and Miranda are its bookends, framing the narrative with their love and harmony. Miranda's eleven-syllable villanelle (SM 25–26) contributes another highly ordered and recursive language of "integrated love," as Auden referred to it in the Buffalo draft. Antonio's possessive, self-regarding (but ultimately self-loathing) "alone" ends each song in dissonance and disjunction. But Miranda's praise of a "Dear One" answers back that in love, "mirrors are lonely" and that "mine" is surrender, not possession. Love shatters narcissism even as it expands the self into the other. For Miranda, in her admirable innocence and purity, love's number is not one or zero, or us against them, but both one and many, the lovers "in a circle dancing," the lively circle of a vow, that can extend itself to the community. Antonio's "figure," his negative O in the Dance of Death, does not cancel her promising circle of infinity.

The Living Room

Auden would continue to reflect on the bonds of love throughout his career, but the intimate "we" feeling that arose in "Warm are the still and lucky miles," which is voiced by Ferdinand and Miranda, is rarely expressed again. In the Dantesque "Canzone" (*CP* 328–30), with its end words that alternate "love," "will," "world," "day," and "know" as the competing forces of human experience, the "we" refers almost entirely to universals ("We are created from and with the world," etc.), not to personal bonds. The "beloved" turns out to be "Dear fellow-creature," hardly a unique being. In later Auden an intimate "we" gives way to a more ethically than erotically inflected interpersonal "I" feeling and "You" feeling. Having read Martin Buber, and in light of the crisis arising from Kallman's infidelity, Auden meditated at length on these pronouns in "Dichtung und Wahrheit" (1959). But it's a prose meditation in lieu of a poem, the voice of the wise spectator and his philosophic we, more than the lover with his raptures or entreaties, and far from the lyric idealism of his Shakespearean lovers for whom words do seem to "verify themselves" (*CP* 660).

Years later Auden's focus is the "living-room," a place of commonality, pointedly *not* the bedroom, not the place of "gratified desire." Here, Auden does propose a space where I and You might become "we." In "The Common Life" (*CP* 713–15), Auden wanders "about the house" (as he would call the volume of poems that contains it) that he sometimes shared with Kallman, the poem's dedicatee. "We, the inconstant ones" (a self-canceling "we") of "In Praise of Limestone"—both humanity in general and those two who share this domestic space despite infidelities—sustain something in this common room. The bond is more communal than erotic, the "You" become a "Thou, rather." It is not a space of vows but one where "I may enter / without knocking, leave without a bow." Though it is a "catholic" area in the secular sense, open to all, it remains a place of "protestant being" where "I" exists and can rebel. "There's no *We* at an instant, / only *Thou* and *I*." The first-person plural arises not out of their reciprocity or even faith in a common tradition but as they seem rational to others ("Sherlock Holmes," for instance). "A quick glance / at book-titles would tell him / that we belong to the clerisy and spend much / on our food." Soon enough Auden has moved to third person, as if inquiring of his life from Holmes's objective point of view, the wise spectator. But this is not the only point of view that counts for Auden. He inquires, neutrally, as to "what draws singular lives together in the first place." The poem examines a long marriage, though not the endurance of vows. And the first-person plural arises without reservation here in "our common room." A common room is not just a space for two—it is an emblem of community in discourse. Late in life, this is really what marriage means for Auden, as another "Epithalamium" makes clear. Playing witty master of ceremonies at the wedding of his niece, Rita Auden, he speaks for the community, not for the lovers ("we wish you"; "we're here to say so"). But while the poem gives Hymen his due and warns against the green-eyed monster, it is the wish to "common your lives" and turn "we" into a verb, that marks the significance of the ceremony for him.

5

Tribes and Ambiguities

We Blue They Yellow or orange
We Yellow They Blue or orange
We Yellow $_2$ They are Red or green   } "Peace"
We red They are Yellow or Blue
[But then:]
We are green they are orange   State War
We are Purple They are Yellow   Civil War

—FROM AUDEN'S MANUSCRIPT NOTES FOR
THE SEA AND THE MIRROR

POETRY HAS OFTEN supported group identity, resisting prejudice but making calls of solidarity, developing "the language of the tribe" and emphasizing difference to maintain cultural distinctness.[1] But it has also sometimes worked against oppositional models of identity, not only by invoking universals but also by creating ambiguity across boundaries. "We" can be formed not only in shifting relations of "you" and "I," but also in discovered commonalities across groups. Flexible or unassigned pronouns provide one source of that ambiguity; they allow us to enter into different subjectivities, recognize their relativity, and locate a permeable "we" beyond or between the divides.

Rudyard Kipling stands for many as the great apologist for empire, reinforcing boundaries even in narratives of their crossing, such as "The Ballad of East and West." The "we" of empire in "Recessional" checks hubris by calling on the "God of our fathers" for continued protection and guidance, but the point is to remain worthy of this God by avoiding the fate of "lesser breeds without the Law."[2] Auden was preoccupied with "Kipling and his views" in the war years. "What . . . makes Kipling so extraordinary" in Auden's view is not only his "civilization-barbarism antithesis" but, more so, its impact on internal relations.

The threatening "We" from outside, the "anxiety of encirclement," consolidates the "we" from inside. "It is precisely when We are threatened by Them that we can naturally think of . . . the ethical relation between Us and Them as one of self-interest. It is precisely when civilization is in mortal danger that the immediate necessity to defend it has a right to override the question of just what it is we are defending." Auden's Kipling is always "defensive" and incapable of ambiguity. He was "limit[ed] to one feeling at a time" (*Prose* II 198–202).

Yet Kipling recognized the arbitrary and historically determined nature of the negative out-group / positive in-group structure of racial and cultural identity. At times he can sound more like the skeptic Montaigne than the author of "The White Man's Burden." Kipling's satiric poem "We and They"[3] is a lesson not only in the ethics and politics of tribes but also in the ambiguity inherent in pronouns. It could be an Auden poem. Every "we" is a "they" in the eyes of others.

> Father and Mother, and Me,
> Sister and Auntie say
> All the people like us are We,
> And every one else is They.
> And They live over the sea,
> While We live over the way,
> But—would you believe it?—They look upon We
> As only a sort of They!

Kipling's five-stanza poem continues to show how difference congeals into hierarchical dichotomy. After a sequence of stanzas in which an imperial Western "We" depicts the colonial other in negative terms, the poem concludes:

> All good people agree,
> And all good people say,
> All nice people, like Us, are We
> And every one else is They:
> But if you cross over the sea,
> Instead of over the way,
> You may end by (think of it!) looking on We
> As only a sort of They!

Kipling's "We" and "They" don't interact in the poem and don't "cross over" except to "look upon" each other's customs with disgust. But Kipling's insistent chiasmic crossovers here work to underscore the speaker's eroding confidence in the stable and foundational nature of his group identity. "We" and its exclusions of "everyone else," the poem implies, might be based on little more than social proximity and the rituals and practices that form in social relation. Kipling's symmetrical play of us against them is only one model of how the ambiguity of pronouns works to put identity at risk and unsettle the line between Our Kind and Others.

Kipling's shuttle of perspectives and subject positions builds on the linguistic fact that pronouns are major "shifters," words that can change meaning depending on who is saying them and what the context is. They indicate relative position rather than referring to specific identity. They can be suddenly or gradually reassigned, migrating from one meaning to another, and, in the case of "we," can shift from an exclusive to an inclusive implication. Poetry's relative removal of boundaries and contextualizing markers means that this play of opposition may be abstracted; the specific tribe or community can become symbolic, moving toward wider identity. This is one of the ways that a regional or ethnic voice can be meaningful for someone not of that group. But the us/them symmetry implies exclusion, and the impulse to attach pronouns to referents continues to function when the context is ambiguous. Pronouns don't just float in the mind as abstract counterwords. This underspecified nature of poetic pronouns, their "weak implicatures," to use another term from linguistics, encourages the reader's translocation. "We" can start out local and become more inclusive, start out monarchical and end up nationalist or democratic, start out partisan and shift to the other side. It can move through, layer, or contrast affiliations.

In his seminal work *The Great War and Modern Memory*, literary critic Paul Fussell includes a chapter, "Adversary Proceedings," that identifies World War I as the beginning of a modern habit of "gross dichotomizing": "'we' are all here on this side; 'the enemy' is over there." The "versus habit" was figured, he argues, in the war's "physical confrontation between 'us' and 'them,' and it extended beyond armies at the front to include oppositions of past and present, civilian and combatant, and produced an ideological and cultural rigidity that still reverberates."[4] One of the great casualties of this "remorseless binary" thinking, he observes, is "ambiguity." Fussell likely exaggerates the war as an origin of dichotomous thinking, and in fact there is a great deal of border-crossing ambiguity in the war poets. Cooperation and affiliation among proximate, homogeneous groups who form identifying markers of their association is part of human evolution. And group identity seems to require a corollary of exclusion. In order to identify with *this* group, I must stand against *that* one. Cognitive scientists have demonstrated that we are hardwired for tribal association and thus tribal conflict.[5] Identity is relational and collective, established in connection with a series of differences that have become socially recognized. And difference easily develops into opposition. As political theorist William Connolly puts it, "Identity requires difference in order to be, and it converts difference into otherness in order to secure its own self-certainty."[6]

Polemics become part of the construction of identity as they translate difference into abnormality or moral failing. Plenty of literature has dramatized, and
even reinforced, this oppositional dynamic. But plenty of literature has also
worked against it. The complexities of group identity and a conflicted sense
of belonging are probably most widely and profoundly explored in the long
history of African American poetry, from the ambiguously marked "we" of
Paul Laurence Dunbar's "We Wear the Mask" to the implicitly layered "we" of
Robert Hayden's "Paul Laurence Dunbar" at the grave of the precursor. Melvin
Tolson's later work, full of formal and aesthetic as well as social risk, presents agonistic conjunctions of socially opposed identities. Tolson's "Afram-
erica" regrets the trap created for the Negro artist: "the white and not-white
dichotomy . . . the dialectic of / to be or not to be / a Negro."[7] Tolson's work
reflects a principle present in W.E.B. Dubois: moral universalism with special
devotion to a group. Gwendolyn Brooks's epistrophic "We Real Cool" may
be the most famous poem voiced in the first-person plural, and it shows what
a treacherous pronoun "we" can be when the dichotomizing mentality leads
the group to become an undifferentiated block, a swaggering collective ego
formed in defensive antagonism. Brooks calls out the shots in the enjambed
end-of-the-line "We," until the prophecy of the pool hall's name, "The Golden
Shovel," is fulfilled: "We / Die soon."[8] The irony turns on the logic of group
identity, which leads to the loss of identity in death. By using the first-person
plural rather than standing apart in judgment, Brooks draws the reader into the
pathos of others' experience and joins us to them. At the same time, Brooks
was profoundly aware of the pressures that led to this group consolidation,
especially the pressure of mainstream society and its law enforcement agents,
who view young black men in their nonconformity as a willfully hostile collective. From the outside, this "we" is only a sort of "They" to be generalized,
excluded, or eliminated: "There they are . . . / Black, raw, ready. / Sores in the
city." Brooks's "As Seen by the Disciplines" and other poems of oppositional
group identity resonate today in asking us to consider what it is like to be seen
as or by "them."[9]

Poetry's traditional emphasis on language, place, and identity makes it an
important site for the expression of group affiliation, confederacy, and alliances. But the elasticity of context and reference, and the abstraction of poetry
in particular, also make it available as a medium for crossing and redefining
boundaries, and opening out to new points of association. Pronouns are crucial
instruments in this work. If "ambiguity," to return to Fussell, is lost in the drive
to secure identity, especially when groups are in direct conflict and competition, ambiguity may on the other hand be precisely what is needed to overcome
those conflicts and allow democratic and peaceful relations among groups. References to universal values might rhetorically override human fragmentation,

but these are increasingly mistrusted as biased, interested, and totalizing projections, parts that represent themselves as wholes and that reinforce hegemony. What is the alternative to particularism and fragmentation? We do not escape our perspective; we view the world from a specific set of social and institutional affiliations, some more salient to our identity than others. We are this because we are not that. But we may recognize our identity as something we perform, in play with other appearances, rather than as an immutable property. In recognizing the multiplicity of our affiliations, the intersecting circles they produce, and the chance factors that set them in motion, in recognizing, that is, the contingency of identity, we get beyond "adversary procedures." Political scientist William Connolly's work is focused precisely on the importance of "ambiguity" (his insistent word) to democracy, especially the ambiguity that arises when the terms of identity and difference are understood as necessary but constructed, contingent, and relational forms of being. His ideas have relevance for poetry, which sometimes reinforces the idea of an essential and threatened identity but, as William Empson established for criticism in 1930, can also exploit ambiguity to challenge and expand our understanding.

The formation and support of group identity is surely one of the important functions of poetry when it is not bent on gross dichotomizing. Culture requires group identity, and despite modernist moves toward an international style, poetry survives by embedding itself in particular traditions, ideas, language practices, and evocations of place that associate it with a cultural group. But this work of cultural distinction may also make the work of ambiguity more compelling as it predicates connection on the acknowledgment of difference and opens life to new forms of being and knowing.

"Yes, we are going to suffer now": Auden's "In Time of War"

Auden's travels in the 1930s—to Iceland, Spain, Belgium, China—led him away from his "English study" and a focus on national identity in the direction of a more European, and eventually global, orientation toward the world. But the term "cosmopolitan," though it offers a fair descriptor of the poet's late work, seems wrong for this stage in Auden's personal and artistic development. A cosmopolitan is at home everywhere, whereas Auden's focus in the late thirties seems to be on the disruptions of traditional identity and the vulnerability of many rooted ways of life. Islands, Auden tells us in "Journey to Iceland," are "unreal," and even the "indigenous figure on horseback" (EA 203) holds strife and resentment, not community, in his heart. Likewise, "beauty's / Set cosmopolitan smile" (EA 204) is a lie. The troubled present touches him everywhere, and the "snowstorm" of crisis and conflict blinds him on his journey.

Randall Jarrell, in his second lecture on Auden, mocks the poet's "We-They system," "plainest in *The Orators*" and other work of the early thirties critiquing English society.[10] Critics of Auden's postwar work, most notably Philip Larkin, complained of the opposite—that a cosmopolitan Auden had removed himself from local and partisan writing and inhabited a featureless, inert space of abstract universals. Readers have objected not only to Auden's sermonic style but also to the pose of the bourgeois everyman in some of Auden's late work. But in the late thirties, especially as war was again breaking out in Europe and Asia, Auden overcame "the versus habit,"[11] even while he infused his poems with the urgencies of local experience. Auden's sonnet sequence "In Time of War" builds active connection across disparate groups through deictic shifts and ambiguities among "we" and "they," "here" and "now," implicitly linking them while acknowledging distinct perspectives. While these sonnets override difference, they are not impersonal; indeed, they resist the post-tribal, mechanized reality of modern warfare in which men are nonentities, not even "we" or "they," but instruments in a remote, impersonal system. The answer to this modern condition, Auden seems to suggest, is not to revert to regional tribes or remove to a cosmopolitan individualism. Instead, Auden imagines community in a new way that recognizes others as subjects to whom we are inextricably, and humanly, tied.[12] But "to accept all human beings on earth as brothers" and not as enemies or "algebraic cipher[s]" is a general proposition, not a practice (*DH* 235). To imagine the other as a subject, with unique feeling, location, and affiliation, requires dramatic engagement, not bland neutrality or detached generalization. The problem for poetry is how to achieve this effect without the constrictions of names and labels. Auden creates a flexible, pronominal abstraction that connects propositions to experience while avoiding the limits of names.

In "In Time of War," Auden turns poetry away from adversarial thinking and helps us to actively see others as brothers. In this way Auden performs a didactic function without preaching. He does so not by depersonalizing (reverting to abstract universals) or by particularizing (dwelling on the singular individual) but by migrating pronouns around dichotomous groups, undoing fixed identities and drawing close to those exiled to the margins of importance. In order to show this, in the first half of this section I place "In Time of War" in the larger context of the 1938 volume, *Journey to a War*, and distinguish it from the later, more remote "Sonnets from China" of *Collected Poems*. I outline the ways Auden has used the sonnet tradition, and the particular formal and syntactic properties of the sonnet, to dramatize the maze of human history across distinct and often polarized forms of identity. Finally, I show how reading for pronouns helps us understand Auden's distinctive mode of abstraction, one that allows him to generalize without abandoning perspective or falling into an impersonal, purely didactic stance.

"No, not their names," writes Auden in sonnet 24 of "In Time of War," the sequence of poems he published in *Journey to a War*.[13] Like so many poems since World War I, these sonnets argue against monuments and heroic chronicles. They eschew names, drawing us into "the little workshop of love" that is "Always far from the centre of our names" (*EA* 261). They memorialize the unseen, anonymous soldier, "Abandoned by his general," whose "name is lost forever like his looks" (*EA* 258). This is not the tomb of the Unknown Soldier, an abstract figure, but, paradoxically, an intimate look at Anonymous. The generals' names are left out too. Indeed, no one is identified in the sequence, in contrast to the prose diary that originally preceded the poems where important personages crowd the pages. Only three place-names arise in the original sequence of twenty-seven sonnets entitled "In Time of War." "China" is named in sonnet 23, and the iconic cities "Nanking; Dachau" are run together in sonnet 16 (*EA* 257). A comma would make them part of a series; a semicolon makes us pause longer and maintains distinction but also creates grammatical overlap. After so many nameless meditations, these place-names drop on the page like bombs from the air, and their conjunction establishes the war in China as part of a global struggle with many fronts. In the absence of names we may still be left with categories, classifications, stereotypes, distinctions. But the entire multigenre work *Journey to a War* evokes this mode of abstract sorting only to question it. In particular, "Us" vs. "Them" becomes a shifting, and ultimately meaningless, opposition. The travel-diary anticipates this ambiguity by creating a narrative in which positions, fronts, and allegiances are hard to pin down. The sonnet sequence abstracts and universalizes this ambiguity, in which identities of "them," "he," and "us" alter and merge.[14]

The absence of names in the sonnet sequence "In Time of War," the dominance of pronouns over proper nouns, is made especially noticeable by its contrast to the profusion of names in the first parts of the multigenre and multimedia *Journey to a War*. A sonnet dedicated to a novelist, "To E. M. Forster," opens the book and lists the names of some of his fictional characters. The initial sequence of six poems labeled "London to Hongkong" includes many place-names. The "Travel-Diary," which presents itself as an alternative to conventional travel narratives and in some ways a parody of conventional war reporting, further proliferates names, not only place-names but also the names of prominent people, European and Chinese, involved in the scene. "We had been invited to lunch, next day, with General Wu Teh-chen, the ex-mayor of Shanghai" (*Prose* I 505), and so on. About Hankow the diary declares, "This is the real capital of war-time China. All kinds of people live in this town—Chiang Kai-shek, Agnes Smedley, Chou En-lai" (*Prose* I 513)—eliding distinctions of political allegiance, social role, or nationality. The text is a parade of minor actors. "Auden" himself is named, since the text, while often based on his diaries, is penned by Christopher Isherwood. "We" in the travel-diary has a clear antecedent: Wystan and Christopher. There are anonymous figures, for sure, "generals, ambassadors, journalists, foreign naval officers, soldiers of fortune, airmen, missionaries, spies" (ibid.). There are "civilian victims" (*Prose* I 587). But pronouns in the diary are always clearly attached to antecedents and, if not particularized, at least identified as to types or social roles. The text immerses us in references, but the war itself remains something remote, the Japanese "enemy" obscure and never directly encountered, the meaning and motivations of the Chinese war effort shifting and elusive, as many critics have noted.

The identifying force of names shifts somewhat in "Picture Commentary," which follows the travel-diary and directly precedes "In Time of War." Here, group identification prevails. What is a picture commentary?[15] Does Auden mean "pictures with commentary," since there are strategic headings, labels, and captions throughout? Or is he inviting the reader to recognize intention and interpretation rather than transparency in the documentary mode—to see pictures as silent commentary? A complex dialogue goes on not just between the travel-diary and the pictures but also between the pictures and their labels and, indeed, in the arrangement of the pictures, mostly, but not always, presented in pairs to heighten comparison. The photographs, sequestered from the text, speak powerfully in their laconic language of angle, cropping, selection, and juxtaposition. In this picture gallery, duality is the prevailing principle of organization, though the kinds of duality vary considerably and are not always oppositional. Marsha Bryant notices "Auden's use of division and classification: north/south; communist/capitalist; Catholic/Protestant; officers/men; prisoner/sentry; intellectual/coolies." She concludes that Auden "invokes this hyperorganization only to undermine" dualistic thinking.[16] Here again we find names, or at least labels, but their hold on the images is unconvincing. Two images of obliterated bodies, "The Innocent" and "The Guilty," together ask us how such judgments might be made and from what angle. Auden's later use of pronoun shifters in the sonnet sequence follows from this disintegration of meaningful labels. The first subheading in the picture commentary is "UNITED FRONT" (*Prose* I 635), which would seem to suggest something broad and inclusive. But who is "united" and where the "front" might be remain in question throughout the diary. "Us" and "Them" have labile alignments as group affiliations overlap and interlock. When Auden and Isherwood arrived in China, they found evidence of Japanese occupation but also of Western imperialism. They also found internal conflict between Communists and the government of Chiang, only very tentatively "united" against the Japanese. The first images under "united front" are of the Chiangs, "united" as a married couple and heads of state. But instead of a male/female pairing, the couple on the left is matched with a single portrait of a decidedly Western-styled "Madame" alone in the right frame, creating asymmetry. (In the diary she is a force in herself but speaks very much for the generalissimo, speaks as "we.")[17] Two more pairs of portraits follow under this heading, to further complicate the notion of a "united front." "Feng You-hsiang (from the north)" beside "Li Tsung-jen (from the south)" and then, even more challenging, "Chou En-lai (communist)" and "Du Yueh-seng (capitalist)." Other oppositions and asymmetries follow, sometimes defining class or hierarchy, "Divisional Commander (Chang Tschen)" and "Staff Officer," who has no name label. Similarly, "Officer (Major Yang)" and "Men," again unnamed. As we move down in ranks, names increasingly disappear. The juxtapositions continue with their oppositional labeling by name or classification, but social division itself becomes the theme rather than national conflict.

The series of images labeled "WAR ZONE" (*Prose I* 653–66) asks us to reflect differently. The oppositional structure comes and goes, and it is harder to categorize the images according to dualisms. The first portraits in *Journey to a War* are close range and thus lack background and context, but context looms larger as the camera pans out and Auden replaces personal names with types and categories, while giving human faces to these loaded demographic labels: "Train Parasites." "Refugees." "Passengers." An image labeled "*La Condition Humaine,*" the title of a novel by André Malraux, and stills from the Chinese film *Fight to the Last,* the only place Japanese soldiers are represented, remind us that the truth of war is a mosaic of stories. But the final page in the gallery functions most powerfully. It is the only single full-page image, a portrait of "The Unknown Soldier." The sequence that began with eminent figures ends with an anonymous individual; his face obscured by hat and shadow, his thoughts unreadable, yet no longer "unknown" to us in the usual sense of the phrase. He is palpably there and decidedly Chinese, no mere abstract symbol or a generic Oriental. This concluding profile of the "Unknown Soldier" leads us in its ethical and formal implication into the sonnet sequence that follows the gallery. What does it mean to be "known" or "unknown"? How can we "know" another?

Many of the criticisms of the sonnet sequence "In Time of War" may be answered if we see it as part of this larger whole, each section offering its own generic meaning, not as a miscellany but in dialogue with the other genres, as a conversation about representing war and other groups. The sonnet sequence, in alliance with the other parts of *Journey to a War,* establishes a place where poetry both engages with events of the day and distances itself from the "folded lie" of newspaper rhetoric and documentary reporting with its presumption of transparent truth. Powerful as many of these sonnets are on their own, our experience of them is different when we see them in relation to each other as a sequence and as part of a broader project rather than in the revised and truncated version (the "Sonnets from China" in *Collected Poems*). In that later version, "China" seems remote and the war entirely emblematic, its participants archetypes. In their original context, however, the choice of namelessness and related kinds of generalization depend on the reader's awareness of other, more concrete, visual and verbal modes of reference and contextualization in the volume as a whole. The subjects of the sonnets are lifted from context rather than fundamentally abstract. The images and anecdotes that precede the sonnet sequence in other parts of the book do not provide identifying antecedents, but a texture of reality to which the sonnets are related without being confined.

Each part of *Journey to a War* has a distinct rhetorical approach to the through-line themes: class polarity, the dehumanizing force of the modern state and technological warfare, the chaos of war, and disconnect at every level between authority and local experience. Critics have oversimplified this heterogeneous work into a dichotomy of prose and poetry, but the sonnet sequence functions quite differently from other poetic sections of the book, including other sonnets.[18] The frequent critical conflation of the sonnet sequence and the long didactic "Commentary" is especially problematic.[19] The commentary's mountaintop synopsis, with its schematic abstract nouns derived from Confucian philosophy, contrasts with the embedded, wandering, and ambiguous world of the sonnets. Stuart Christie argues that Auden and Isherwood fail to represent the "Chinese reality" and write a work that is largely a reaction to that failure. (Self-conscious "failure" is also how Bryant characterizes Auden's antidocumentary stance.) He argues that Auden "rejects the material context" and turns China into "an occult imagining" against which the poet negotiates his liminal relationship to British nationalism. This may be true of "Commentary" or even the later version "Sonnets from China." But is "failure"—self-conscious or not—a fair assessment of this compelling sonnet sequence at it first appeared?[20] The 1966 "Sonnets from China," temporally removed from the war, gives precedence to geography over event and omits the poems most immediately involving the war; this disrupts the dialectic between the local and the universal that functions so powerfully in "In Time of War." "Sonnets from China" has a retrospective feel; "now" is a memory, even a fantasy. But the sonnet sequence in "In Time of War" is more fluent and less ideologically constrained. Even those sections Douglas Kerr calls a "*grand récit*" are dramatic and urgent, strategically designed to disorient us, not synoptic and philosophical. They engage feeling and sensation beyond their didactic function. What does it feel like to be "in" war, temporally or spatially, the poems ask.[21]

These qualities of experience are represented not only in the themes and scenes of the sonnets but in the way they are presented to the reader—narrative rather than didactic. We experience the sonnets as changing, embedded, and probing, their sequence more errant than teleological. The reader is not simply asked to reflect philosophically on the history of Western imperialism and its modern consequences, or to generalize from the China war to other sites of conflict. She is pulled into an unpredictable drama of locations, connections, and distances that makes the persistent "we" and "they" of the sequence an open, supple potentiality rather than a set of stable oppositions. The plastic forms of the sonnet are crucial to this effect, particularly their heavy use of deixis, of pronouns and adverbial pointers ("here" and "now") that lead us through the "intricate maze," which is the structuring trope of the sequence (*EA* 262).

Samuel Hynes argued that "Auden . . . was thinking and feeling not about one particular war, but about human history." In order to make that *feeling* powerful and inclusive, the sonnets present not just propositions but experiences, yet detached from their fixed referents, where they become vivid for the reader as dramatic exemplae of "the war that never ends."[22] If "In Time of War" is a sequence about "human history," it is not in itself a history, like those books into which the war will be "tidied" in sonnet 18 (*EA* 258). To feel "life instead of death," as Geoffrey Grigson put it, requires engagement more than abstraction, occult imagining, or panoptic reflection.[23]

The Work of Pronouns

As we have seen, one freedom that poetry has over prose, part of its distinctive form of abstraction, is that it can often use pronouns without fixing them to antecedents. We need to examine this device more closely, but first I want to make some general observations about the work of pronouns in "In Time of War." It is not unusual for sonnets to omit names as they aim at once for intimacy (in which case names are superfluous) and inclusiveness. In Auden the omission becomes thematically explicit, pointing to the anonymity of *war* (soldiers and victims treated as nonentities) and turning *poetic* anonymity to opportunity. While no one's name appears in Auden's sequence, there are of course plenty of personal pronouns, and with their antecedents removed, the pronouns work to gather and shuffle identities while acknowledging relational structures of difference. Any of us, high or low, central or marginal in world affairs, might be a "he" or "they" or "we." Our orientation to these positions alters from poem to poem, shifting the relative position of its victims and perpetrators. In an age marked by the vestiges of imperialism, adversarial nationalism, fascist collectivity, statist bureaucracy, and mechanized war, Auden's pronouns offer a flexible strategy for humanistic understanding. The shifting, unpredictable sense of experience in the sonnet sequence "In Time of War" produces a fluent and, at times, boundless feeling of "we," built up out of labile identifications among the pronouns rather than from generalizations, an impersonal group identity, or ideology. Pronouns in everyday use are function words; we hardly notice them. They suspend particularity rather than erase it. While antecedents are suspended, the sonnets are cognizant of the book's earlier, documentary relation to experience. Without obvious indexing, the pronouns and other function words ("here," "now") nevertheless remain pointers as we search for the links in the anaphoric chain. Thus "we" never indicates "General Will" or a statist collective such as "the nation" or "the Empire." "We" is an ever-changing, faceted, and fluent perspective that gets worked out through constant inversions and resettings of pronouns and other markers that create the urgency of things taking place, but without confining location. Even when Auden uses third person he remains close to the subject and embedded within the point of view even to the extent of free-indirect discourse ("They wondered why the fruit had been forbidden; / It taught them nothing new," EA 251). When the poem shifts from third- to first-person plural, the subjective view is not oppositional but part of a matrix of perspectives.

Many of the sonnets, then, through deictic strategies, indirect discourse, and other methods, achieve intimacy and immediacy, uniting experience and abstraction. The shifts of point of view from poem to poem affect the entire poetic sequence, which brings together related but disjunctive moments, locations, and subjectivities. The sequence as a form, where parts are independent yet linked, thus lends itself to this plastic sense of "we," fluid ethical relation in contrast to the static "positioned victories" of Us vs. Them. "In Time of War" loosens this dichotomy between eras and between cultures. The "Picture Commentary" explores the *geometry* of social space, its divisions and hierarchies, and the proximity to suffering. The sonnet sequence "In Time of War" explores the *grammar* of social relations. Without their antecedents, function words in the sonnets also take on meaning as social grammar, and relations rather than identities become important. A pronoun is referential in itself only in the typological sense that "They" refers to a group of people excluding the speaker and "We" refers to a group of people including the speaker. Patterns of social relation are thus revealed even as particular stories shift. In Auden's sequence, pronouns are reassigned from poem to poem. Other nonpronominal pointer words, especially adverbs of place and time, link to these anonymous figures in the sonnets and similarly activate the reader's search for context and connection. "Us" and "Them" are at different moments in the sequence past and present, Asia and Europe, Adam and Eve or the modern masses, enemy or ally. "He" may be an artist, a demagogue, or an unknown soldier but always "someone," not just an idea. Since it is difficult to discover distinct referents in the poems, we tend to link pronoun to pronoun—artist, demagogue, and soldier are no longer isolated singularities; they overlap and interlock for the reader. "We" is sometimes humanity, sometimes the suffering Chinese, sometimes the befuddled English observers, sometimes the West more broadly. "They" and "We" are the same and never the same, brothers and enemies. "We live here. We lie in the Present's unopened / Sorrow; its limits are what we are" (*EA* 259). This may apply to anyone, but it always applies to someone, to felt experience rather than to a concept. The line break activates the "Present" and opens the unopened sorrow for the reader.

"We" in these sonnets most often arises in the sestet, marking a shift from narrative situation to expansion or conclusion, a common rhetorical move in poetry. (The sequence itself makes a similar move.) The first appearance of "we" is in the sestet of sonnet 9, and "we," "our" or "us" appears in the sestet alone in 13, 16, 18, and 20. (Again, numbering is for "In Time of War," not "Sonnets from China.") But the pronoun "we" also becomes more and more prominent as the sequence continues, until it is the only personal pronoun in the concluding sonnet 27 where it shifts position in the lines as if "wandering lost." This inclusive "we," that is, passes through a labyrinth of variant positions before it emerges as a universal term. And these relational pronouns contribute to one of the central strategies and motives of "In Time of War": decentering our view of history and our particular place in it.

Sonnet Structure, Sequence, and Dynamics

Like most sonnet sequences, "In Time of War" is full of gaps and inversions, dramatic shifts of focus, without a seamless didactic authority. Readers who comment on the sequence at all focus on the first twelve poems that suggest a mythic and historical narrative, linking Genesis to contemporary history. Auden introduces the sequence with a genealogy, but he does not rely on it for understanding the present. Less than halfway through "In Time of War," Auden abandons the narrative logic that has seemed to govern the sequence, and we enter a maze.

While a few of the sonnets in "In Time of War" are well known, the sequence as a whole, the links between poems, and the choice of form have received little close attention. Line and syntax, rhyme, poetic conceit, diction and idiom, grammatical structures and tropes, grammatical structures *as* tropes, stanza divisions and the *volta*, all contribute to the *drama* of this section of *Journey to a War*. To read the poems in a *sequence* is to ask what relationship they have to each other. A sonnet sequence is not a strict narrative with its interpretive impositions. It is a series of episodes, distinct but associated, a paratactic principle that also organizes the individual poems. What experience do these poems convey or what conversation do they present as a group, and how do the formal and grammatical elements of the poems link them? The best approach to these poems, then, is one that considers individual sonnets as compressed structural and expressive units that loosely relate to one another and to sonnet history. They form, in a sense, a *community*. They are correlated through repeated formal and thematic tendencies, and through their creation of a story or conversation in discrete episodes or points of view that decenter the We.

If juxtaposition invites us to associate pronouns from one sonnet to another, the parallels often create irony. "He" emerges in the sequence in sonnet 4 (*EA* 252) as the exiled Adam, but gradually the culture endows him with godlike qualities that he begins to believe in until in sonnet 11 "He" has become Zeus pursuing Ganymede. Together the poems form a parable (not a myth) about the dangers of a man taking on godlike postures, which have been bestowed on him by a culture needing gods. In another story this demigod is just a man in the dust. What is the relationship of this demigod to the suffering and forgotten "he" of the famous dead soldier in sonnet 18, reduced to a subhuman state, "Abandoned by his general and his lice" (*EA* 258)? Even the notorious—gods, heroes, villains—are indicated by pronouns, and this puts them in the same class with the anonymous victims of war. The reader must make the transitions and find the links between figures and between events, links that may produce effects of irony or empathy. As the travel-diary is notable for its expansion and its mass of details, so the sonnet sequence is notable for its compression. Pronouns do some of that work of compression, enhancing juxtapositions and similes that often yield effects of irony. This is not the campy irony of the travel-diary but a more acerbic, graver portrait of human history. Shifts and variations in tone are a natural part of any sonnet sequence, which reflects varying moods and tonalities of a speaker. Here, tone changes as Auden gets to the contemporary world, and as "he" and "they" become "us."

One of the most distinctive features of these sonnets is their insistent use of "and" as a connective, both internally in each sonnet and externally in the movement from one sonnet to another. "And" conjoins subjects and is thus essential to "we"; it conjoins objects, providing a device of causation and correlation; "and" also conjoins events.[24] Randall Jarrell noted Auden's heavy use of "and," viewing it as a bad habit. We might instead consider the conceptual and emotional work the conjunction performs in juxtaposing images and events without the interpretive intrusion. These are poems about history, but by connecting events with "and" Auden makes the reader do the work of identifying causal relations, or acknowledging that history itself may not have a discernable pattern or *telos*, but is "an intricate maze" made of human choices. The poems pulse forward in the immediacy of "and," immersing the reader in situations rather than anticipating turns and consequences. The reader may draw the conclusions, but there is no end to the flow of history.

Beginning the sequence with "So" (*EA* 251), Auden marks the occasion as storytelling, but story told *in medias res,* without origin or destination. Without a causal antecedent, "so" becomes a variant of the paratactic "and." "And" is the term of errant wandering, which as the final sonnet makes clear, is from the first a guiding trope for human history in this sequence ("And looked for truth and was continually mistaken"). In a world held together by "and," everything is uncertain. "And" is epistemologically modest. "And" does not "tidy" events into books, does not subordinate minor to major figures and events. Auden sometimes seems to be revealing a grand plan (echoing biblical parataxis), at other times diverting us from that narrative logic into a present confusion. If history is a chain of events that marches on, we are always in a sense in the middle. Yet there is a feeling of amplification and weight as the series aggregates, though without summation. "And" is temporal, an ally of the "now" that is central to Auden's sonnets. But "and" is also spatial, creating perspective by incongruity, a "here" that unsettles our sense of geographic distance.

Perhaps most importantly for my argument, "and" also equalizes and equates. It coordinates rather than subordinates and undermines "versus." It is a form of "syntactic democracy," according to Richard Lanham.[25] But like democracy, it keeps things plural even as it brings things together. It finds unity in difference. Of course, "and" is also a term of understatement, allowing the reader to find the correlations and causations in juxtaposition, to judge and interpret. Finally, "and" links terms of extreme opposition, creating effects of irony, incongruity ("his general and his lice"), and other powerful tonal qualities—"and" upsets hierarchical orders; it also indicts.

Against the minimal ordering of parataxis, which produces effects of open-ended randomness, Auden sets the highly ordered and compressed formal structure of the sonnet. Sonnet structure often involves the recursive forms of repetition, comparison, and reversal rather than narrative progress. Auden uses the Petrarchan two-part form throughout the sequence, often subdividing into four- and three-line stanzas. But closing couplets, which were a feature of Auden's love sonnets from two years earlier, are rare here. Instead of closure, "In Time of War" uses the sonnet's formal divisions to create a drama of reversals in power and authority. For instance, while sonnet 10 reports: "The very poor saved up their pennies for him, / And martyrs brought him presents of their lives," the poem closes with the hero becoming the tormentor: "The poor saw there the tyrant's citadel, / And martyrs the lost face of the tormentor" (*EA* 255). Many of these poems have a strong *volta* at the turn from octave to sestet, marked by the conjunction "but" in place of "and," to mark ironies or inversions. Auden also often exploits the *volta* to mark a change in pronoun, especially from They to He or Them to Us. The relation of syntax to line produces more dramatic dimensions against the flattening march of "ands."

While Auden's lines are generally end-stopped, there are strategic moments of enjambment and caesura that create ambiguity and unsettle the reader's perspective. These moments tend to increase as the sequence goes on and the poems are dealing more fully with the unresolved present rather than the historical past. Most dramatically, Auden breaks a line in sonnet 25 (*EA* 261) into two lines, in a way that mirrors the subject matter (and perhaps recalls a similar break in Yeats's "Leda and the Swan").

> They speak of years before the big were lonely,
> And will be lost.
>   And only
> The brass bands throbbing in the parks foretell

Pulled-in lines at the ends of poems create similarly kinetic effects. Sonnets are highly dramatized speech acts, lending themselves less to didactic argument than to emotional turmoil and development.

Auden also exploits rhyme as a counterpoint to the weak connective of "and." The sonnet allows for a suspended rhyme, to associate ideas ("lying" and "dying") and create antithesis. Elizabeth Bishop may have borrowed her famous "master/disaster" rhyme from Auden,[26] who used it often, most dramatically in sonnet 20: "They cling and huddle in the new disaster . . . // Time speaks a language they will never master" (*EA* 259). In these and other ways, then, Auden uses the sonnet form to create a feeling of nonlinear (and supraverbal) order and pattern, an "intricate maze," even as the enumerative parataxis collapses difference and distance and emphasizes chance, equality, and flux. In writing sonnets for "In Time of War," Auden drew on the form's capacity to order volatile feeling, conflicting energies, irony, paradox, and ambivalence. Sonnets are more recursive than linear, more dramatic than expository or narrative, more dialectical than didactic. And most important for this argument, the sonnet form plays an important role in relativizing positions, in linking pronouns and other deictic terms so that identities become less oppositional and more relational, creating open networks of feeling and association.

Along with the conjunction "and," the adverbs "here" and "now" are key words for "In Time of War" that bind the reader to the diverse figures and bind those figures to each other since everyone lives in a here and now. This is a common deictic strategy in lyric, often awakening a sense of urgency and immediacy, but without a fixed referent or single register. Their meaning is relative, not only to context, but to their binaries, "there" and "then." And since poetry creates ambiguous boundaries between its story world and its utterance world, "here" and "now" can function at several levels. We can see Auden layering temporality in the first sonnets, those that create the archetypal backstory for the present crisis. In sonnet 2 (*EA* 251), for instance, the poem imagines the point of view and the deliberations of Adam and Eve, entering their "now." Consider the second stanza:

> They left: immediately the memory faded
> Of all they'd learnt; they could not understand
> The dogs now who, before, had always aided;
> The stream was dumb with whom they'd always planned.

While the pronoun "they" is meant to evoke Adam and Eve separated from nature and stranded in human history, the scene is less mythic than anecdotal; the names removed gives a sense of familiarity more than archetypal abstraction. Jarrell had argued that Auden's "We-They system" made the speaker superior to the past: "We are the Future, They are the Past. (Naturally the reader will side with Us and that perpetual winner, the Future.)"[27] But here the past is We as well as They. We enter into "their" uncertainty. Theirs is an unintelligible "now," haunted by what is absent or changed, "before." The ordering of words unsettles time: "They could not understand / The dogs now who, before, had always aided." Even as "the memory faded," "before" intrudes into the unfamiliar experience of separation from nature. The relative pronoun "who," though modifying "the dogs," feels lost in time, an interrogative identity wedged between before and now. These strategies add vitality to the story of the past and connect us with that story. "Now" punctuates the sequence ("Yes, we are going to suffer now"; "life is evil now"), working against the serial and undifferentiating "and." "Now," the sonnets suggest, is the only time-word those in the midst of war can recognize. Yet the word weaves through the diegetic and nondiegetic features of the poems, uniting the reader with the poet. "Tonight in China let us think of one," Auden urges in the moment, writing of Rilke, remote in time and place, and addressing readers similarly distant.

The other time-oriented adverb common to these sonnets, as to Shakespeare's sonnets, is "when." "When" indicates a relation to time but asks us to locate it with reference to the verb tense that follows. Auden marks time with particular complexity in the famous dead soldier sonnet 28 (*EA* 258). "When this campaign is tidied into books" anticipates a future order, however skeptically, but the sonnet immediately takes us to a past, "When / He turned to dust in China." (While a rare place-name arises here, it is not certain that he is Chinese, thus he is located, more than a symbol, but never identified.) Sonnet 23 (*EA* 260) also turns us back to the future, "When all the apparatus of report / Confirms the triumph of our enemies," only to make a plea, a first-person plural imperative, to recall the past: "let us remember."

The sonnet form, then, with its disjunctions, broken temporalities, and surprising connections, is crucial to Auden's creation of an experience more episodic than plotted, more dramatic than panoptic. The reader feels what it is to be "A mountain people dwelling among mountains" (*EA* 263) rather than a skyhawk reflecting impersonally on the spectacle of history. The reader is "he" and "me," "you" and "I," "them" and "us," connecting their "here's" and "now's."

Sonnet Traditions of "In Time of War"

Auden wrote Petrarchan and Shakespearean sonnets throughout his career. But these traditions tend to emphasize the I/You form of address and, while they reflect on time, are removed from the pressures of history. In writing "In Time of War," Auden chose instead to shift between third-person and first-person plural pronouns, a practice established by George Meredith in *Modern Love*. To write sonnets, rather than epics or chronicles, "in time of war" is also to invoke, however indirectly, war sonnets by Thomas Hardy, Rupert Brooke, Wilfred Owen, Ivor Gurney, and others who foregrounded the experiences of anonymous men. Auden's debt to Hardy and Owen has often been noted but seldom detailed. His irony and cultural critique also owe something to Siegfried Sassoon, a major influence on Owen. Sassoon's "Dreamers," for instance, which imagines trench soldiers remembering their childhood—"things they did with balls and bats"[28]—anticipates Auden's metonymic compression, mixed idiom, understatement, and appeal to the everyday. Sassoon's "They" works against partisan Us/Them alignments, reframing the dichotomy as one between the heroic rhetoric proposed by civilian culture and the actual losses and sufferings of the soldiers. Like all these First World War poets, Auden in his "In Time of War" sonnets focuses on suffering and its affront to the fictions of war and valor. "They are and suffer" (sonnet 17) may take inspiration from Ivor Gurney's "Pain," about the Somme in 1917. From Milton's "Late Massacre," Auden may have learned to read contemporary war in a biblical perspective, though he eschews the prophetic call to vengeance. Auden's depiction of the dead soldier in "Far from the heart of culture he was used," published on its own in 1938, may be read in counterpoint to Rupert Brooke's "The Soldier." By the time Auden was maturing as a poet, certainly the subject of "war" was deeply associated with the sonnet form.

Combatants wrote most of the well-known sonnets of World War I. Auden, in these sonnets, neither lover nor soldier, found another affiliation in Rainer Maria Rilke, to whom he alludes but whom he never names in "When all the apparatus of report" (sonnet 23). It is the only time in the sequence when Auden uses a form of the first-person *singular* (albeit in the objective case: "Let me think of one"), so the allusion gains a special status and points to Rilke's "Sonnets to Orpheus." This sonnet about Rilke, standing out from the rest of the sequence, can certainly serve as Auden's apology for poetry and his sense of the artist's role in time of war. Auden addressed these matters directly in writing a review of Spender's translation of Rilke in September 1939, just after Britain's declaration of war. He quotes Rilke's use of "we" to address the task of the artist, which is not to concern "ourselves with the distresses of others" but to present a shareable portrait of "the suffering within us" and thus offer a "clearer meaning to endurance" (*Prose* II 26). Rilke clearly also represents for Auden the strength of resistance in the poet who "refuses to understand" public hate and destruction, a theme he elaborates on in his 1940 portrait of Rilke in "Poet in Wartime" (*Prose* II 73). But while Auden aligns himself with Rilke, he is not imitating him in "In Time of War." He is, instead, conversing with him, though indirectly since, in contrast to Rilke, Auden does not employ direct address. "You" in "In Time of War" appears only implicitly, in the rare imperative. And while Rilke turns away from history, "refus[ing] to 'understand,'" Auden turns toward history to gauge the distress of the soul. He certainly reveals the perverse logic of war and thus the unreasonableness of its justifications; but through the sonnet form Auden *seeks* to understand the reality of war in all its absurdity, to get past the "lies."

Rilke's importance for Auden's project in "In Time of War" may have as much to do with the tradition of sonnets as with the particular ideological or ethical choices of the artist (Rilke's "we") in separating himself from partisan conflict. Rilke stands for a kind of writing in contrast to "the apparatus of report" (*EA* 260), a kind of writing skeptical toward official rhetoric. Instead, Rilke takes up universal themes and creates enduring forms against the dehumanizing and destructive conditions of modern history. Rilke's sonnets, with their minimal use of metonymy and their large abstractions (Exultation, Desire, Lamentation), may have provided Auden the permission to introduce a didactic rhetoric of Truth, Wrong, and Folly into this intimate form, at a time when most poets were abandoning such abstraction. More specifically, Rilke likely provided Auden with his sky/earth dichotomy, a trope that runs throughout Auden's war sequence and indeed throughout his poetry. Rilke also anticipated the theme of technological warfare and its way of isolating man from the world. Indeed, Rilke's sonnet I.18, "Behold the Machine," which takes the airplane as its example, and sonnet I.23, which continues this imagery of blind flight, may be read as direct precursors to Auden's imagery of Japanese bombers in sonnets 14 and 15, though Auden applies them differently.

Auden never names Rilke in these sonnets, and in this he most particularly follows him. The conscious avoidance of names is a prominent theme of Auden's war sonnets. It is also one of the reasons that pronouns are so important. "Erect no gravestone for him. . . . We do not need to look for other names," writes Rilke,[29] and Auden echoes it in sonnet 24: "No, not their names. It was the others who built / Each great coercive avenue and square" (*EA* 261). In keeping with this pact against names, both poets make use of pronouns that lack proper noun antecedents and suspend or break anaphoric structures. While Rilke's title suggests poetic address (sonnets *to* Orpheus), the third-person and first-person plural prevail in the first part of his sequence. Only later does Rilke employ an "I" with which we might associate Auden's "one" at his tower in sonnet 23 (*EA* 260). More often Rilke positions himself in relation to an inclusive "we," human and subjugated, longing for freedom and flight, not the unique orphic poet he names in his sequence's title.

But if Auden's sonnet 23 is a tribute to Rilke and his "completed" tower of poetry, in sonnet 13 (*EA* 256) Auden seems to be in dialogue with this master, calling him away from his orphic meditations and even his "refusal to understand." "Praising is what matters!" writes Rilke in *Sonnets to Orpheus*,[30] and Auden answers, "Certainly praise: let the song mount again and again," then turns back to history in the next quatrain: "But hear the morning's injured weeping, and know why." Rilke addresses an abstract or absent being, but characteristically he can't bear to listen and finds the voices from the historical and social world oppressive. Auden may have learned from Rilke something about using the imperative to activate the reader's attention, but he directs us toward historical suffering, where Rilke focuses on his inner distress. In sonnet 13 Auden finds his position, then, within a tradition, and adapts the form to his own time and needs. He will not simply refuse to understand, attending to Orpheus's higher music; he will on the contrary cause us to *hear* present injuries and demand answers. Auden's unique stance between the imperatives of poetry and those of history turns in sonnet 13 on the word "hear" as its imperative calls up a pun on "here." Charles Berger has noted the pun on "hear" and "here," which gives further immediacy to present suffering. Auden must also have intended an elegiac pun in "the morning's weeping," which creates a continuous keening overlay to the matter-of-fact, past perfect of "Some people have been happy; there have been great men."

Not Forster, then, but Shakespeare, Hardy, Owen, Sassoon, and Rilke helped Auden choose a poetic form and shape it to his subject. Auden's sonnet "To E. M. Forster" belongs where it was first placed, apart from "In Time of War," as a foreword to the travel-diary by two young English writers anxious about their position in a postcolonial reality. Only later, in "Sonnets from China," does it become an afterword to the sonnet sequence. The choice of sonnets has been mostly treated as incidental. But as a genre of dramatic feeling rather than documentary realism, it deeply informs Auden's orientation toward history.

Reading for Pronouns

My argument for the dramatic nature of Auden's sonnets in "In Time of War" assumes the value of close reading and attention to form, and here I invite the reader to follow the text as I comment on Auden's pronouns. In observing the jolts, disjunctions, and reversals within and across sonnets in the sequence, we begin to understand how Auden builds up to a borderless "we" that is not just imagined from a mountaintop but felt and lived within "the mountains of our choice." As is often noted, the first twelve sonnets offer a kind of Western genealogy of the modern world. Auden dramatizes enlightenment and secularization, and the shift from feudal structures to contemporary fascist uprisings. He follows the course of individuation (when "they" becomes "he"), perverted into narcissism and violence. But he presents these episodes, not as textbook chapters outlining a myth or recording a predictable narrative, but as vital moments of internal as well as social change, parables of the experience of history. "They wondered why the fruit had been forbidden; / It taught them nothing new" (*EA* 251), begins sonnet 2. Through free-indirect discourse Auden brings the reader close to the unnamed figures. "They" will shift and point to other subjectivities as the sequence continues, but the pronoun remains tied to this original pair seen close up.

The first-person plural enters the sonnet sequence in 9 (*EA* 254) with the advent of the modern world. The first "Us" and "Them" relation, then, is not between dichotomous enemies or aliens, not between Chinese and Japanese or between East and West, but between Western culture's past and present (including its involvement in the East). The sonnet form marks gaps and parallels to tell a story of the past as both fixed and persistent, absent and present, closed and yet everywhere.

> They died and entered the closed life like nuns:
> Even the poor lost something; oppression
> Was no more a fact; and the self-centered ones
> Took up an even more extreme position.

Who are "they"? Linking the pronoun to the previous sonnets, "they" becomes associated with Adam and Eve, and this creates an ironic reversal; death, the result of their forbidden knowledge and expulsion, brings them to another cloistered purity, "the closed life," which they enter "like nuns." More broadly, "they" are the past, all the "he's" and "they's" that have preceded this sonnet. The end-stopped finality of the opening line is soon belied by the halting caesura and ambiguous enjambments of the third and fourth lines. The past is "closed," it seems, the relation asymmetrical. The past is not dead, just sequestered and sanctified; it exists in an unchanging and idealized space inaccessible to the present either for blame or guidance. Yet the present feels answerable to it. Ironies abound in this first quatrain; for instance, self-centeredness becomes an "extreme" position. The sharp social hierarchies of the past become muddied for us. The past provides a moral standard not because it is better than the present, but because we idealize it. Indeed, the achievements of the past given in the previous sonnets hardly uphold this estimation of the achievements of civilization. If the first stanza of sonnet 9 sequesters the past from the present, the second and third stanzas emphasize the opposite effect, that of dispersal and absorption.

> And the kingly and the saintly also were
> Distributed among the woods and oceans,
> And touch our open sorrow everywhere,
> Airs, waters, places, round our sex and reasons;
>
> Are what we feed on as we make our choice.
> We bring them back with promises to free them,
> But as ourselves continually betray them.

Here the Us/Them dichotomy of past and present becomes bidirectional in a troubling way. The distinction dissolves into reciprocity, confusing the pronouns. Though the past is cloistered and inaccessible to us, its heroes "touch our open sorrow everywhere," a notion reinforced in the geographical trope of "woods and oceans." An unsettling chiastic syntax and other mirroring devices enter the poem to confuse identity. "They" enter the present, indicated by the temporal conjunction "as": they are "what we feed on as we make our choice." Yet the connection is broken in the next use of "as," now a term of identity instead of time, meaning "in the role of": "As ourselves continually betray them." "We" of the present invoke the ideals of the past without living them out. The final stanza frustrates connections of past and present even further when "knowledge" becomes a mutual space that action cannot realize: "They hear their deaths lamented in our voice, / But in our knowledge know we could restore them." Is the sentence merely redundant or richly ambiguous? Repetitions and parallelisms force "us" and "them" into constant relation. Since hearing is assigned to this past, is the verb "know" theirs or ours? Auden's turn to conditional and subjunctive tenses at the end of the poem ("They could return to freedom: they would rejoice") distinguishes the lies of the present with the possibilities of the future. Throughout this sonnet, then, we see what is typical of the sequence: a constant interplay among points of view and subject positions that seeks to close the gap marked by pronoun distinction. Sonnet 9 does not lecture on the present's condition in relation to the past but dramatizes it through the entanglements of syntax and form. The rhyme scheme helps to turn us from uneasy negations, rigidities, and sorrows ("oppression" / "positions" / "oceans" / "reasons") to confident freedoms and aspirations ("choice" / "voice" / "rejoice"), though the next few sonnets will dampen this aspiration with the emergence of economic oppression, the abuse of power, and the lesson of "many ways of killing."

The initial sequence of genealogical parables ends more conclusively if still ironically in sonnet 12 (*EA* 255–56): "And the age ended, and the last deliverer died / In bed." Perhaps echoing Vico, Auden leaves the age of Gods and the age of Heroes to enter the age of Men (or simply men). But power has gone underground. Who is "they" in "they were safe"? Does the pronoun point to the population or to the tyrants? In modern times "They were safe" from the gods, but the age of men brings on "power" even more brutal and obscure. The beginning of sonnet 12 marks the end of one tyranny. But the close of the sonnet marks a new turn to horror, a secular age of "free" power "without remorse . . . [which] ravished the daughters and drove the fathers mad."

In sonnet 13 (*EA* 256), "Certainly praise: let the song mount again and again," Auden suddenly shifts to the present tense, marking a major reorientation of the sonnet sequence. But which present? The lyric present of "praise" with its celebration of nature's renewal and its recursive "again and again," or the historic present, which presses against the poet's "buoyant song" and repeats the errors of the past even if it is "quick" (alive, high-speed) and "new"? The address is to "us," marked in the imperative: "certainly praise." The praise is for life, but also for art (where life in art "blossoms out in a jar") as a replacement for religion. But this "us" born in secular crisis is urged to praise in uncertainty and "hear," "know," and even "weep." The second stanza's admonishment, heard in the spondaic rhythms and daunting abstractions and negative constructions, overtakes the Rilkean song. Humanity has "again and again" failed to realize its potential. Echoing Rilke, Auden's "we" here speaks as the authority in a majestic we but also collectively of all poets, with allusions to Rilke especially in the images of the first stanza. But Auden is humbled by the limits of his power in the actual world and its immediate present tense, its "morning's injured weeping." Instead of marking a transcendence of time, the word "still" here is loaded with irony directed at old idealities betrayed: "still, all princes must / Employ the Fairly-Noble unifying Lie." This is a transitional stanza, acknowledging the shadow that history casts (from the previous twelve stanzas). The lines are jagged with caesura, and the rhymes tighten in the middle of lines; "still" reminds us of the precarious state of the present and its unfulfilled promise against "the will of the Unjust." To whom is this poem addressed? Rural China is objectified as a "passive flower-like people" and industrial Europe as "the quick new [and 'false'] West." The "We" of "our buoyant song" is all poets (and their invisible listeners) in history, at least since Rilke, who may sing like gods or about angels but make nothing happen.

How does this "we" of buoyant songsters relate to sonnet 14 (*EA* 256–57), "Yes, we are going to suffer, now; the sky," which turns fully to the historic present, to the "now" that supplies the fulcrum of the sequence? "Yes" makes the poem dialogical, but to what and to whom is this "yes" answering? Is it an internal acknowledgment of the foreboding at the end of the previous sonnet? Or is it a counterforce to our denials of history, as in answer to the implicit "no, it can't happen to us, only to other people; the war is in China, far away." Auden withdrew this sonnet from "Sonnets from China," perhaps because it focuses on Japanese aerial bombing (also depicted in the cartoon frontispiece of *Journey to a War*), on a "they" and a "we" more historically localized than Auden wanted for the later version. This is in keeping with a general pattern of Auden's late revision of his poetry, which tends to remove personal reference and concrete experience. In this case we may regret Auden's choice to abandon the poem since it is certainly one of the most dramatic in the sequence. The sonnet creates a vivid and intense sense of what it means to live "in time of war" while using pronoun ambiguity to keep that sorrow and anxiety "open" to many subjectivities. Douglas Kerr has argued that Auden is "speaking as a Chinese" in the "we" of this sonnet. Since this "passive flower-like people" have just been mentioned in the previous sonnet, the connection seems valid. However, in the context of *Journey to a War* this "we" also links to Auden and Isherwood, who had been close to bombing sites and felt the threat and civilian chaos around them even if they did not suffer. Their "refuge is a sham," especially as they could see the signs of war everywhere. The Nazi bombing of Guernica just a year before would certainly also be on Auden's mind in this sonnet. Like Picasso, he imagines it from below and with a multicentered perspective that pulls the audience into the panic. The borderless sky terror remains unfixed but vivid, becoming urgent and immediate rather than general and abstract. This unromantic and nontranscendent "sky" hangs at the end of the first line and menacingly above everyone's head, regardless of location. Rather than describe and illustrate, Auden uses the tools of the sonnet to impress this sky-searching anxiety on the reader. The poem thus has the force of Yeats's opening to the sonnet "Leda and the Swan": it creates a "A sudden blow." Time and space converge on the reader's present. The subsequent line describing the sky that "Throbs like a feverish forehead" collapses not only geographic distance but mind and world, making the event an inward one by using the conceit of the body, part of the wound of our "open sorrow." Auden reinforces the inward/outward movement in the next line's simile: "like a conscience all the guns resist." After the rhyme of "sky" and "cry" comes another coordinated pair, "exist" and "resist."

The visceral linking in sonnet 14's octave of personal feeling (somatic and psychological) and public crisis prepares for the broader moral reflection that will take up the sestet: "The private massacres are taking place; / All Women,

Jews, the Rich, the Human Race." The poem's immediacy makes these general reflections vivid. Culpability is, first, intimate and only subsequently universal. The desire to exclude and annihilate the other cuts across lines of gender, class, race, and ideology, and across the divide of public and private. Having exposed the logic of hatred in its nihilistic extreme, Auden can turn to a universal "we" as the basis for correction: "We dwell upon the earth." Auden has built up from an immediate and experiential scene of human suffering, through an inclusive list of targeted groups, to a philosophical and contemplative "we," of earthly habitation. The point is that we all dwell somewhere specific, and that we all *dwell* and are vulnerable and culpable. "Yes, we are going to suffer now" is at once local and universal. Using the sonnets, Auden creates a language that is neither journalistic nor didactic but draws on energies of both modes.

As if to test and reinforce the inclusive vision at the end of sonnet 14, Auden's next sonnet repositions the reader within the earth/sky dichotomy. While 14 began by looking up, sonnet 15 (*EA* 257) imagines the perspective of the pilots in those bombing aircraft. Auden's emphasis on "skill" reinforces a central theme of the sequence: how technology erases moral awareness. The pilots are autistic, "remote like savants," remote from the gaze of the earth dweller, and remote in their attitude toward the earth. They have become their machines. The sonnet is marked by the compounding ironies, their technological "freedom" a kind of imprisonment. "They chose a fate" that eliminates choice, and they "turn away from freedom and become / Bound." Simile extends the emphasis from politics to class and reinforces irony while maintaining the local focus on the pilots. "Bound like the heiress in her mother's womb," they enter a deterministic economy that paradoxically links them to "the [helpless] poor." Technology's promise to make us "free" of the earth leads us, the sequence argues, to Hegelian bondage.

Auden fully enters the "now" of wartime in sonnet 16 (*EA* 257), "Here war is simple like a monument," perhaps the most famous of all the sonnets, but also the one that deviates most from the formal norms established in the sequence. Its foreshortened couplet—the only closing couplet in all of the twenty-seven sonnets—reasserts the simultaneity of the global perspective of "In Time of War" even as the poem insists on the reality of place and locality.

> And maps can really point to places
> Where life is evil now:
> Nanking; Dachau.

In breaking the form with a pulled-in line near the middle of the sequence, Auden puts special pressure on the lyric moment, a present framed by "Here," its first word, and "now" at the end of the penultimate line. These adverbs suspended from their referents are common in poetry, calling up the instinctive rules of implication and the reader's interpretive drive. "Here" may at first be understood within the narrative scene. That is, read in the context of *Journey to a War*, the telephone, the map, etc. are all part of the war in China; we understand "here" as journalistic report, in keeping with the book's assignment. But "here" in lyric, no matter how specific, is never fixed in context; it hovers, assignable to other "places." In sonnet 16, the opening "here" hangs in ironic suspension since what we encounter are images of deterritorialization and substitution: phones, maps, monuments, plans. The poem hinges on the conceit of placeless and faceless modern warfare—"A telephone is speaking to a man." Without any claim to documentary authenticity, this poem contrasts the unreality of war's conduct with the reality of suffering and evil in the next stanzas. The enjambment makes the point of contrast and mocks at strategy: "There is a plan / For living men in terror of their lives." Auden arrives at the riveting final arrhythmic couplet, rhyming "now" with "Dachau," after the deferral of several "and's" and "but's." The reality of suffering arrives in the poem with such force at the end, in part because of the surprise of names after all the anonymity. Auden seems to be imitating and converging news headlines; he certainly knows these names are loaded: "Nanking; Dachau" in a line by themselves feel like large print. East and West, in the foreshortened line, become one "here" and one "now."

The next two sonnets reinforce the reality of bodies rather than places. War robs victims of their personhood and agency, making them merely figures of suffering. Here we see Auden using the anonymity of pronouns with special thematic force. "They are and suffer; that is what they do" (*EA* 258). Auden's sonnet confronts the challenge of how to imagine the pain of others. "A bandage hides the place where each is living," Auden writes in sonnet 17. While a "time of war" collapses distance in 16, in 17 the agonized bodies, though proximate, "lie apart like epochs from each other," inverting the space-time logic and equivalence that has threaded these poems. Auden has come up against the limits of his boundless, humanistic "we" and the empathic power of his shifting pronouns. The limit is marked in the *volta*: "we stand elsewhere" ends the octave. Pain isolates. "Only happiness is shared."

The body and spatial politics organize the next poem as well, Auden's famous sonnet 18 on the dead soldier (*EA* 258), "Far from the heart of culture he was used," which Isherwood mentions in the diary as something Auden composed on a prompt. Here Auden moves from the group image of suffering to a focus on a single body. The opening location reminds us of how "centre" (his later revision of "heart") and periphery keep moving for the poet as he reaches out to connect to others. The figure may be far from the cultural center where we live, but in the poem he is focused and magnified, as proximate even as "lice." But bringing us this close, the poet then presents us with something worse: absence rather than anonymity. Even the lice have "abandoned" the soldier because he is dead and perhaps decayed. We share the soldier's bed; we are invited to gaze "under [his] padded quilt" where he "closed his eyes." We sense the human connection of sleep, which all men require, however near or far the heart of culture. But the line break jolts us awake, for the soldier has "closed his eyes / And vanished" (as if instead *we* had closed *our* eyes, which we do by turning away) from this padding, even as it is evoked. Auden nods to a sentimental trope. Like Thomas Gray he memorializes the unsung, but a callous simile undermines and forestalls the romantic homage: "His name is lost for ever like his looks." This anti-chronicle compounds negations and absences: "abandoned," "closed his eyes," "vanished," "will not be introduced," and the ironic "no vital knowledge" that registers the death. The soldier's "looks" are lost not only because he has been defaced by war but also because he does not *appear*. We cannot empathize here. There is nothing behind the pronoun but a gap.

But the *volta* in 18 again seeks linkage, seeks a meaning to this death and a use for our gaze other than false sentiment. "He neither knew nor chose the Good, but taught us" anticipates a direct object: taught us what? The poem will not supply the didactic answer directly. Instead of a *what*, the matter of the lesson, we get a *how*, a *when*, a *why* and a *that*: "And added meaning like a comma, when . . ."; "that our daughters / Be fit to love the earth." A comma has no semantic content, but it has an illocutionary force, like a dynamic mark in a score. The ungrammatical comma seems a mimetic gesture here, but it disappears in later versions of the poem. With or without the actual comma, the simile tells us something important: this dead soldier *gives us pause* and registers as an untidy gap in the campaign records. He teaches by example rather than axiom, as this iconoclastic sequence does. This puts him at the center of the heart of culture and crucial to its survival, "that, where are waters, / Mountains and houses, may be also men."

While the first eight sonnets of "In Time of War" contain no first-person pronoun, the sequence has, as we have seen, sought forms of connection through its constant variation of subject position. "We" enters the sequence in sonnet 9 but roves, pointing to various groups (*EA* 254). The last six sonnets are dominated by the first-person plural, as if to register the cognitive result of the effort to connect many points of view. The sequence enters the realm of choice and community: "Nothing is given: we must find our law" (*EA* 261). On the one hand, this is the kind of rhetoric Auden would use in "September 1, 1939" and later reject. But here it is less an axiom than a project for the future.

The mountains of China become an image for the sequence itself, in which we have "wandered" "amazed" and "articled to error" rather than holding a steady clear course (sonnet 27, *EA* 262). Throughout, these sonnets have been concerned with a process of learning through error, of being taught, corrected, and reminded. Yet the didacticism of the sequence relies on more than propositions; these sonnets are not spoken from the mountaintop. Though error is the condition of life for "mountain people dwelling among mountains" and while we are not "perfect like a fountain," the same but never the same, the sonnet sequence gives form and grace to error. The "intricate maze" of our dreams eludes us, but a mazelike structure has informed this sequence as "we" labors through it. The sonnet sequence is no sage, synoptic vision; neither is it a mere diary of disorientation. The pronominal linkages across difference give shape to the episodic verse. A set of conceits also binds the poems: the idea of our earthbound and vulnerable natures, despite our impulse to soar and subdue, the need to relearn the "proper discipline" of love. The pronouns register familiar Audenesque topoi: the relation of the individual to the group, the reciprocity between private and public experience, the disdain for "names," and the importance of every living person. But the sequence is also a conversation with the reader. The rhetoric of the sonnets often registers this openly with call and response—with "yes" opening one poem, "no" or "but" opening others, so that thought is kept vital and supple.

The didactic nature of "In Time of War," then, differs fundamentally from the universalizing rhetoric of the "Commentary" that follows. "Commentary" is best considered not as a capstone to the sonnet sequence but as a work on its own (it was first published in 1938 in the journal *Commentary*). In contrast to the pronoun-dominant sonnets, "Commentary" is noun heavy, between proper nouns ("Shanghai") and abstract nouns ("The Third Great Disappointment," EA 265). "Commentary" looks down at the experience of China, and at the human record in general, from a high promontory. Auden would later write in an afterword to the 1973 edition: "The verse Commentary is, I know, far too 'preachy' in manner and, were I to preach the same sermon to-day, I should do it very differently. I have always believed, however, that, among the many functions of the poet, preaching is one."[31] But the sonnets are not preaching. They give us the sense of life that Auden finds expressed in José Ortega y Gasset's *Towards a Philosophy of History*, just two years later: "Life is gerundive, not a participle: a faciendum, not a factum. Its mode of being is formally a being difficult, a being which consists in problematic toil.... To be free means to be lacking in constructive identity, to be unable to install oneself once and for all in any given being" (*Prose* II 128). Sonnets, with their gaps, shifts, inversions, are the perfect form for "wandering lost."

6

Poet and Audience

But play, you must,
A tune beyond us, yet ourselves.

—WALLACE STEVENS, "THE MAN
WITH THE BLUE GUITAR"

LIVE PERFORMERS OFTEN remark on the double nature of the audience relationship, intimate and collective. In discussing both the experience of performing and the experience of hearing Schubert's *Winterreise*, a lyric song cycle, Ian
Bostridge writes: "It is sometimes said that the measure of a great singer is that
it feels as if he or she is singing to you alone; . . . the address to the individual as
well as to the mass—is a crucial part of the aesthetic transaction."[1] Such an intimate relationship is more commonly associated with the experience of poetry.
But poets can also create the opposite effect; more in line with the concert
hall, they make us feel, even in the privacy of reading, that we are part of a large
congregation or mass. What is the special social presence of poetic audience,
and how is it different from or a model for other kinds of human community?
Is the audience one or many? What various relations does a poet establish or
imagine with an audience when she says "we"? How is this related to the classic
tension between poetry and rhetoric? In this chapter I argue that while we tend
to think of poetry as intimate address, poets do conceptualize large assembled
audiences and often draw on metaphors of performance to create a feeling of
gathering, even as they retain the sense of intimate address.

The practical experience of literature is usually a solitary affair, for both
writer and reader. But the ideal scene of reading, often figured in literature, is
the exquisite, transparent meeting of two solitudes, together in a room outside time and space. This, the reader knows, is an illusion of presence that
overlooks all the gaps, frameworks, and contingencies which condition the

literary encounter. A great deal of John Ashbery's poetry addresses this illusion and its paradoxes, often through the voice of the first-person plural. The social relation formed in literature (if it exists) is distinct from other social relations, may even seem a turning away. But as Ashbery and many before and after him prompt us to consider, literary forms of being-together not only evoke other social relations (erotic, contentious, communal, or otherwise) but may also offer some lessons for the common sphere about open, heterogeneous, and flexible modes of relation and community. Poetry, as opposed to narrative fiction, has a special position here as it emphasizes subjectivity over exposition of a story or character. The poem presents an individual mind in action but activates the reader's own exploration. But writer and reader are in a sense ghosts to each other, the reader or readers a conjuration in the mind of the poet, the poet an effigy arising from the words on the page. What kind of community can be formed in that meeting of phantoms? Part of our reading experience is often the sense that others' eyes have passed over these words, others have engaged with this speaker, and that we are linked in some way not only to the writer but also to readers. Certainly no community with an essence can endure in the posterity of a work, though such a community may have given rise to a poem. But performance metaphors can give form and aggregation to the transient and local communicative bonds that make up literary experience.

While figures of interiority prevail in representing the scene of reading, many poems imagine poetic encounter in larger and more public spaces—a theater, a church or commemorative site, a courtroom, a classroom, a rally, or the boards of a municipal ferry. Individual poems sometimes move between these two ideas of audience, creating a sense of communicative bonds but also of a boundless gathering. In this chapter I want to touch on the complex social formation of literary encounter and literary audience, and especially consider how metaphors of performance and assembly, whether explicit or implied, aggregate poetic audience as a present collective even while maintaining the sense of personal address traditionally associated with poetry. These metaphors, along with the tendency of so many poets to venture into dramatic literature, suggest how much this intimate genre yearns for the larger community of theater, ritual, stadium, or other group transport.

These subtleties in the phenomenology of reading have little direct bearing on the social aspect of literary audience except in the way they imitate and model other social interactions. In a practical sense, literature can certainly be a prompt to actual working community as writing and reading causes like-minded individuals to gather in conversation. The poetry reading is a live performance that embodies this community-creating power of art, and spoken-word models of poetry attempt to bring back the oral tradition in which poet and audience coincide. Benedict Anderson has explored the role prose fiction played in the remote formation of a national sense of community. Literature has been instrumental in the formation of emergent communities seeking to voice themselves, to appear for or to resist a hegemonic culture. But literature can also bring about a hypothetical, untethered community, as it forms a network unknown to itself and unlinked to identity, "unavowed" (to use Maurice Blanchot's term) and without goals or objectives. Such a projective community is horizon-less, or rather forms new horizons in each encounter of text and reader, forming an "us" of what Giorgio Agamben called "inessential commonality, a solidarity that in no way concerns an essence."[2] Literary formations of community are not "accomplished once and for all, but [in an] infinite series of modal oscillations."[3] Such a vision of community draws on the endless web of particular encounters but still imagines a kind of combinative power, without consensus or exclusions, without regulating institutions, but holding to the interplay of many and one. These recent ideas of virtual and shifting community are abstract, even mystical, and riddled with paradox. But they are not alien to poets who, by definition, seek an unidentified audience and hope to reach not only one but many. The trope of theater often presents this sense of virtual community for reader and writer. Sometimes the poet does want to suggest simultaneous presence for this relational network. If the audience for a poem forms a "we" like a chorus, if the poem is designed to bring about such a congregation, it does so virtually and as a hypothetical suturing of the many "personal encounters" that make up its history and potential reach.[4]

What Auden said about opera in "Cav & Pag" guided his thinking about poetry as well: "Every encounter with a work of art is a personal encounter; what it *says* is not information but a revelation of itself which is simultaneously a revelation of ourselves" (*Prose* IV 794). Yet this "personal encounter" is implicitly multiple and widely disseminated. (*Cavalleria Rusticana* and *Pagliacci* are among the most popular operas in the repertoire, which is why there is a community of those who recognize the abbreviation.) This personal and yet inclusive aspect of art's audience is perhaps behind Northrop Frye's sense of literature as both intensely private, something "overheard" (in Mill's sense), and at the same time analogous to a "chorus." Frye writes: "There is, as usual, no word for the audience of lyric: what is wanted is something analogous to 'chorus' which does not suggest simultaneous presence or dramatic context."[5] As Heather Dubrow points out, Frye "is divided between two models for lyric. . . . On the one hand, his expressed commitment to rhetoric as the guiding principle behind genres leads him to emphasize a model for lyric in which the poet is performing the poem for an audience; . . . on the other hand, . . . he joins Mill, Sidney and many others in the drive to locate that mode, disengaged and unmediated, in a world of transcendent truth."[6] Against the choral model, Dubrow shows how the different auditors may be disaligned, or dialogic, interrupting each other. She evokes poetry's affinities with theater, complicating Frye's model by connecting lyric and soliloquy.[7] Not only the chorus, but also devices of side participants, bystanders, and disrupted speech, all connect to lyric practice.

While literary community may indeed be only virtual, scattered, and non-coinciding, existing merely as potentiality and in a hypothetical network of local, transient encounters or implications, the metaphor of performance allows the writer and reader to congregate this community in imagination, to give image to a wish. In the figure of a performance gathering (theatrical, oratorical, pedagogical, or ceremonial), I argue, poets often suggest this double nature of audience relation, solitary and yet choral, intimate and one-on-one, yet also a gathered, kinetic plurality. I am interested here in exploring the rhetorical and representational strategies—genre and mode, forms of address, metaphors of public utterance and performance—that affect the sense of the audience, or multiple audiences in relation to each other, as "we."

Poetic address helps to imagine and constitute an image of audience, whether intimate or public, and it often carries with it implications about the space and time of relation between speaker and audience. The shift in critical attention from lyric "I" to "you" has coincided with a new emphasis on understanding language and literature as communication and performance. The emphasis on address has also brought forward the social dimension of the genre against accusations of solipsism, narcissism, and aesthetic detachment. The possibilities and implications of poetic address as communicative gesture, its "publically intimate" quality, have been richly explored.[8] Even so intimate a poet as Baudelaire reminds us—in his "To the Reader," a poem that maintains the "we" form throughout in addressing his "brother and twin"—that his "*hypocrite lecteur*" takes its word origin from "actor."[9]

W. R. Johnson anticipated this connection between lyric and drama in *The Idea of Lyric*:

> Greek lyric, then, is a peculiar fusion of the forms of epideictic oratory and of something like drama: that is, the dramatic . . . moment of rhetorical encounter, in which both poet and audience participate as they contemplate together the possible shapes of inward movements of the soul that they have felt or feel or may feel but cannot see or name or, in a full sense, know. For the purpose of containing, ordering, clarifying, this situation of discourse, the pronominal form, so far from being mere rhetorical artifice, is a natural, perhaps *the* natural form; . . . The private and the public, the merely personal and the truly universal, resist one another, yes; but from that struggle comes lyric poetry, both monadic and choral, at its best.[10]

Tropes and scenes of performance in poetry often create an illusion of simultaneity and an effect of gathered plurality for their audience. At the same time, the poetic genre can turn the performance metaphor toward the personal power of art, reaching into the thoughts and feelings of each audience member individually and creating something that seems uniquely for him.

"Caliban to the Audience": Auden as Echo

Auden worried not only about *what* poetry is, but also for *whom*, and what his relation to that audience should be. In "The Poet & the City" (1962), he would assert that the characteristic style of "Modern" poetry is an "intimate tone of voice, the speech of one person addressing one person, not a large audience; whenever a modern poet raises his voice he sounds phony" (*DH* 84). Yet even Auden's poems dealing with private experience seem aware of a group audience (even if, in the postwar years, only the group who "Read *The New Yorker*," *CP* 338). This may be a simple result of early fame, but it also has a generic dimension. While Auden abandoned the writing of plays after the mid-1930s, he retained many of dramatic art's generic features for some of his poems, including the sense of assembled audience. Theater, which offers a different model of public speech than oratory, had a lasting effect on his didactic style. Poetic rhetoric is shaped by the kinds of speech communities it imagines and imitates. Auden wrote in a variety of genres and styles, addressed to a variety of listeners, not just to one abstract, hypothetical audience. And when Auden mixes genres, as he does in *The Sea and the Mirror*, he also implies a range of audiences. Most readers of the work have focused on the opposition of art and life that constitutes the thematic focus. But the relation of individual to community forms another crucial theme of both Shakespeare's *The Tempest* and Auden's poetic "Commentary" on it. Auden's choice in aligning his poetry with dramatic structure, and his formal decisions in the work more broadly, connect to this theme. It also allows him to approach his readers as a hypothetical community. Who says "we" in *The Sea and the Mirror*, and to whom, inside or outside the world made by art? In connecting drama and poetry, Auden found a way to layer the idea of audience, making it person-to-person but also choral, without the "phony" or demagogic voice. Critics have stressed the dualistic concepts organizing *The Sea and the Mirror*, but the more practical, dramatistic features are just as important, even in this nondramatic text.[11]

T. S. Eliot wrote "Three Voices of Poetry" in 1953, more than ten years after *The Sea and the Mirror*, but his distinctions are useful in analyzing Auden's relationship to audience and his changing sense of poetic address. Eliot saw the three voices of poetry—overheard, addressed, and dramatic—as frequently overlapping, and this is certainly true in Auden. We have explored the first voice, "the poet is talking to himself—or nobody" in connection with *The Orators* and the figure of Narcissus. Eliot's second voice is meant, he says, "to be overheard by other people," but he notes that even when the address is to a lover, the second voice has "a conscious social purpose—poetry intended to amuse or to instruct."[12] This second voice dominates in Auden's work, even, as we have seen, in his love poetry. It is certainly the dominant voice of political poetry's quarrel with others. But Eliot's third voice, the dramatic voice that has "divided loyalties," and where the poet "is everywhere present, and everywhere hidden," also speaks in Auden's poetry, not only in his explicitly dramatic works but also in the dramatic structures to which his poetry often alludes.[13]

Auden's interest in drama aligned not only with his dialectical thinking but also with his desire for community. He contributed most of the choruses in the plays he wrote with Isherwood, and he extracted some of these and published them separately as poems. The imprint of their origins in theater still shapes our reading of some of his extracted lyrics. As David Kurnick has shown in *Empty Houses*, studying the theatrical efforts of Henry James and James Joyce, a writer's experience of theater, even when he fails at it, often influences his work well after the direct involvement in theater ends. Some poems are choral in nature rather than simply oratorical, as if the audience itself was on the stage, united in feeling. What Auden said about his aims in drama, in a Group Theatre program in 1935, carries over into some of the poetry he would write years later: "Drama began as the act of a whole community. Ideally there would be no spectators. In practice every member of the audience should feel like an understudy" (*Prose* I 128). When Auden described the "community" of theatre he listed among its essential participants not only actors, producers, and other contributors but also, highlighted in capital letters, "AUDIENCE."[14] The world of the drama becomes our world; the players are mirrors of ourselves, and our presence animates them. While Auden relinquished this ideal in practical terms, abandoning dramatic writing except for opera and oratorio, he continued to find ways to suggest drama formally and rhetorically. He attempted to close the gap between author and audience and at times to re-create the sense of a plural community that is immanent in theater, on the stage and with the audience. In this way we can consider Caliban's speech at the end of *The Sea and the Mirror*, dominated by the first-person plural, as a late transformation of the chorus model from Auden's plays of the thirties. It would be a mistake to suggest that Auden offers the reader-writer collaborative model of poetics that has always been an aspect of experimental poetry. We never forget who is framing the illusion and directing its meaning. But in "Caliban to the Audience," the player is not only a mirror but also an echo of audience.

By associating his poetry with theater, Auden carries forward the image of live performance and creates a sense that an audience is addressed in a particular but transferable here and now. The same feeling for local audiences applies to other circumstances in which the poet performs or participates, whether entertaining friends, addressing an English journalistic public from abroad, teaching a college class, or attending church services. These life groups and circumstances shape not only the poet's ideas of community but also his voice. Auden often remarked on the loss of community in modern life, especially in individualistic America. The writer's task, then, became not so much to respond to the needs of an existing community as to create community within and through the world of his art, or at least to offer an image of possible community. The figures of performance that arise in *The Sea and the Mirror* and other midcentury works help gather up the sense of audience as an assembled yet pluralistic presence.

Writing on light verse in 1938, Auden remarked: "The problem for the modern poet, as for everyone else to-day, is how to find or form genuine community, in which each has a valued place and can feel at home" (*EA* 367). The problem arises, the essay argues, because traditional local communities have disappeared, giving freedom to the artist to explore the private life but also dangerously isolating him and limiting his reach. The focus on community stands in stark contrast to his later idea of art in "The Poet & the City": "art . . . is concerned with *singular persons*, as they are alone and as they are in their personal relations" (*DH* 88). But what Auden actually meant by finding or forming community was already ambiguous in the late thirties, since he did not write to summon a working community or offer a blueprint for one. The poet forms, rather, a virtual or possible community. In "Squares and Oblongs" (1957), Auden thinks of his art both in person-to-person terms and in light of a broader community that may be a cause or a result of art (or both):

> Like an image in a mirror, a poem is a pseudo-person, i.e. it has uniqueness and addresses the reader face to face or person to person, but, like all natural beings and unlike historical beings, it cannot lie. In writing a poem, the poet can work in two ways. Starting with an intuitive idea of the kind of community he desires to call into being, he may work backwards in search of the system which will embody it most justly, or starting with a certain system, he may work forward in search of the community which that system can most truthfully embody. In practice, he nearly always works simultaneously in both directions, modifying his conception of the ultimate nature of the community at the immediate suggestions of the system and modifying the system in response to his idea, as it becomes increasingly clear, of the future needs of the community. (*Prose* IV 64)

But like many writers of his generation, Auden in the thirties was more divided about the nature of his audience and of his poetic authority. Is he one with the common man or a superior teacher? Is shared ideology the basis for genuine community? The mixture of camaraderie and condescension often led to ambiguous pronoun use. For whom does the poet speak when he says "we"? This confusion became clear in "Brothers who when sirens roar" (1932), later titled "A Communist to Others," a poem Auden would ultimately reject as "rubbish." Valentine Cunningham, writing in a "Symposium on 'A Communist to Others,'" observes that the poem "is characterized by deep confusion. Its pronouns prove, strictly, unreadable, and so both its addresser and its addressee remain decidable."[15] Theater work led Auden to confront the problem of audience more directly. The "dream of a public poetry," as Alan Jacobs has called it,[16] led Auden to his work with the Group Theater in London. In experimenting with medieval forms, Auden hoped to revive drama as a community activity. Auden's heavy use of the chorus was not only a way of inserting second-voice poetic passages into a dramatic form but of getting the audience on the stage by proxy. A chorus represents the public local to the narrative, but it also becomes a surrogate for audience, figuring audience as community, just as "play" becomes a trope for "life." "You who have come to watch our play. . . . We, too, have watched life's circular career."[17] The chorus in *The Dog Beneath the Skin* speaks insistently in the second person, flagging and confronting the audience as well as reflecting and contextualizing the play's action. But the audience and chorus are also natural collaborators or allies: "We would show you at first an English village: You shall choose its location."[18] To capture a popular audience, Auden knew, the artist must in some sense pander to the tastes of those looking for simple entertainment. But he imagined a balance of approaches, not a reduction of the whole; high and low forms could be "interspersed," reaching multiple audiences. This mixed manner would remain a characteristic of Auden's writing in all genres throughout his career. Auden wrote to Stephen Spender on June 28, 1935: "The audience. The theatre going audience is a bourgeois one. I must not let them yawn, I must not keep their minds too long at a stretch (i.e. scenes like the financier and the poet must intersperse more serious stuff). The average level of appeal must not be much higher than the average level of response. There must even be something to keep the young man who has come with his girly by mistake, thinking it was a detective story."[19] But clearly Auden could not satisfy himself as an artist within the strictures and audience demands of the theater as he defined them. And in truth, rather than treating playwriting as a generic challenge separate from the poetic one, Auden wrote poems for the dramas. And he discovered that, perhaps in part as a consequence, the Group Theater was not attracting much of a bourgeois audience at all, only a more limited, avant-garde one that might enjoy a flirtation with the common. If the plays posited a diverse community *in potentia*, they failed to bring such a community into being. In that case, rather than bringing poetry to the theater, theater might just as well be a metaphor in his poetry, modeling the idea of community through image and form.

In a continuing search for ways to form community in writing, Auden experimented with collaborative travel books, cabaret songs, verse epistles, and other popular, social genres that might still contain cultural critique. In each of these genres he developed a style and manner of address that brings audience into the scene of writing.[20] This background of career-long reflection on the nature of and relation to audience is important to understanding Auden's aesthetic and rhetorical choices in *The Sea and the Mirror*, choices that reflect its diverse social world and complex, layered sense of the audience as a community.

——————

Whatever else Auden's *The Sea and the Mirror: A Commentary on The Tempest* is about—the limits of art, the dualities of power, the need for grace, the Second World War, and the dangers of *gesamtkunstwerk*, "l'affaire C"—it is about audience and the poet's relation to audience. The issue of art's relation to audience frames *The Sea and the Mirror*, and the "Commentary" creates a context for the addresses, soliloquies, and asides that follow and precede these framing passages. Art may be frivolous—and the emphasis on "trucs" in this work suggests the extent to which Auden has moved away from thinking of his work as serious intervention into history—but it is still a means of imagining community, potential community, not the indigenous, vernacular-specific one that Larkin yearns for.[21] Like Shakespeare's original, this is a metafictional work, though in this case we have drama hosted by lyric poetry and prose instead of lyric poetry inside of drama. The audience collaborates to embody "the real," a direct, dialogical challenge to the artist's solipsism and withdrawal from the world. Auden embodies this challenge not only in the dialectic of Ariel and Caliban but also in the generic shift from poetry to prose in chapter 3, where the first-person plural prevails.

But what or who is the audience, *The Sea and the Mirror* implicitly asks, and in what ways might the audience for art present potential community in other spheres? Is an audience an undifferentiated mass or crowd, Stevens's "a million people on one string,"[22] or a multiplicity of single, invisible listeners, drawn close to the mind of the performer? Or is it an ordered, hierarchical cross-section of society, from groundlings to royals? A "mob of men" or a congregation joined together out of common love for something outside itself? What is the special social presence of audience, and how is it different from other kinds of human collectivity? And what is the nature of the special human relationship between performer and audience? Does the performer see the audience as an antagonistic "Them" or a companionable "We"? Does the artist convene audience, or does audience compel art? Or is the relationship reciprocal? How does the relationship to audience differ from, or model, other kinds of human connection? *The Sea and the Mirror* is a "Commentary" in the form of a poetic representation of a drama; how do the two (or three) generically determined kinds of audience, one standing behind the other but in different spatial, temporal, and conceptual relations to the text, merge and collapse the inside/outside logic of their auditory frameworks? We can think about Caliban's speech as a postproduction talkback, but the tag "Commentary" frames the entire work, complicating our position in relation to the drama.

"All we are not stares back at what we are" (*SM* 6)—the eloquence and compression of the statement masks its complexity. The simplicity of its chiasm tricks us (pronouns are tools for linguistic sleight of hand) into accepting something deeply ambiguous. Who or what exactly are "we"? In one sense the line, spoken by Prospero as he packs to leave the island and return to Milan, means that the ideal world art creates in its mirror reminds us of how short we fall from the ideal. But in another sense the line, which rises out of its dramatic situation, might be construed merely as a social fact—it announces the presence of the other and the other's gaze on us—or even a practical fact of actor/audience relations. It can mean many things in terms of the relationship between the ideal and the real, moral perfection and human fallibility. It can certainly refer to the experiential mirror of performance, the audience staring back at characters in a play, and the actors staring back at the audience. Auden is both actor (empathically impersonating various characters through acts of lyric ventriloquism) and commentator (bringing insight to a prior text). Auden evokes Brechtian frame-breaking devices in *The Sea and the Mirror*, most prominently the liminal figure of stage manager, who reminds the audience they are watching a play. But Auden also involves the audience in the illusion. These effects are not really modern; they are present in the Elizabethan drama as well, and were already emerging in the medieval morality plays that Auden imitated in his Group Theater work. As Thomas Bethell has argued, in Shakespeare's time the audience was sitting on the stage: "It would have been impossible for actors so closely beset with audience to create and sustain an illusion of actual life."[23] Like Bethell, Auden saw this exploitation of conventions as a valuable counterpoint to the realist theater that had grown up from Ibsen. The analogy Bethell makes with the Marx Brothers could be extended to *The Dog Beneath the Skin* and other moral comedies produced by the Group Theater. As Bethell writes of Shakespeare, "the audience are vividly aware of acting in progress and the communication, through their cooperative goodwill, of a work of dramatic art. If the one type of production is more realistic [Ibsen], the other is essentially more real."[24] This sense of "the real" is less a product of illusion than an effect of audience involvement. Caliban's address to the audience makes this most explicit and extends the point to the encounter of text and readers. By addressing the audience directly, then, Auden's Caliban speech introduces a kind of "real" that counters the mirror ideal of mimesis. Of course the opposite could and has been argued, that the real is not so much discovered on a new plane as deferred. The point, perhaps, is that Auden creates ambiguity in the sense of the real by enfolding performance into commentary. The "Commentary" merges art and life even as it thematically examines their intersections. (No one has privileged access to the real; we only have commentary.) The overlapping realities help link the figures of community—that of the characters, that of the fictional audience of a play, and that of Auden's readers. *The Sea and the Mirror* is framed at the front by Brecht's fourth wall of alienation effects and at the back by Henry James's free-indirect discourse. They represent two modes of modernist realism. While the Brechtian thrust is collective and external—the theater back in the street, in the home of the audience, provocation to action and consequence—the Jamesian thrust is absorptive—a single narrative that at the same time contains within it, through free-indirect discourse (a form of ventriloquizing), a web of perspectives. James's prose seems an odd vehicle for exploring the group sense of audience. In "At the Grave of Henry James," Auden celebrated a writer who "ignored the / Resentful muttering Mass" (*CP* 309). But Henry James found a way to keep plurality in play. Auden attempts something like this dialogical Jamesian interiority in the voice of Caliban.

In discussing the meaning and intention of *The Sea and the Mirror*, critics have made use of Auden's notes on Shakespeare from his time at Swarthmore and later at the New School. But what has gone largely unremarked is the possible impact of the actual audience (community) that Auden was addressing at this time, not a theatergoing audience for the most part but a college- and lecture-going audience. Whatever role he might aspire to as an artist, he had an actual and assured role as a visiting professor of literature, as a commentator—at the University of Michigan, at Swarthmore, at Bennington College, and eventually as a public lecturer at the New School. When Auden says "we" in this period, he is at least partly invoking the American academic community and those who came to it from the broader public. As Auden trades the bullhorn for the blackboard, theater is both subject matter and rhetorical guide. The classroom had been Auden's stage before. But the environment of a secondary-level boarding school in the early thirties, when he is still young and relatively unknown, is different from a university or college setting in postwar America, when he is a mature and famous poet. The American college scene did not carry the same burden of hierarchical culture and tradition. Auden was older and more esteemed, a public intellectual and authority in literary culture. His New School lectures on Shakespeare are at once confident and informal, and reports suggest this was his style in undergraduate teaching as well. Auden found American college students ill-read and underprepared but open and generous, eager to express opinions. In many ways Auden approaches America as a latter-day De Tocqueville, interested in a social structure different from Europe's. In his essay on James and America, "The American Scene," Auden reflects on "the unequal distribution of intellectual gifts ... since they refuse to face it, the institutions of Higher Learning in America cannot decide whether they are to be Liberal Arts Colleges for the exceptional few or vocational schools for the average many, and so fail to do their duty to either" (*DH* 320). This ambiguity as to audience arises in chapter 3 of *The Sea and the Mirror*, which addresses now the masses, now the exceptional reader or young artist.

Early Auden remarked that "Teaching is a political activity, a playing at God the political father, an attempt to create others in one's own likeness" (*EA* 401), but he resisted this demagoguery. In his memoir of Auden's year at Michigan (1941–42), Robert L. Chapman made a survey of those who remembered Auden "as a teacher, host and man."[25] Chapman emphasizes how Auden discouraged the students from taking notes but, on the other hand, insisted on memorization. ("Six cantos of the Divine Comedy," according to his letter to Ursula Niebuhr, December 19, 1941.) His focus, then, was not on his own ideas but on the works he was teaching. A friend and admirer of Reinhold Niebuhr, Auden would nevertheless remark that the theologian "had a tremendous grasp of history and theology but sometimes 'wrote as if he thought he were God Almighty.'"[26] The comment seems a self-directed warning against the pedagogue's tendency to act like Prospero.[27] Chapman found Auden's pedagogical style free-ranging and associative; he was also a good listener and a "spontaneous blackboard" diagram designer (or at least he gave the impression of spontaneity; his notebooks suggest a great deal of preparation). Auden was also, by all accounts, a lively participant in the academic community. This was just as true at Swarthmore where he composed much of *The Sea and the Mirror* and made the now-famous chart of the play as a teaching tool. He took an active interest in student drama, inevitably bringing his interest in theatrical audiences into connection with academic audience. It is not difficult to imagine Caliban's speech as a certain kind of classroom performance, associative in its structure, alert to the point of view of the listener, aware of the diversity in the audience, ultimately turning to that special student who has the promise of an artist. Caliban speaks for both the author and for his readers; he's an intermediary of sorts, like a teacher, ironic as that might seem since in Shakespeare he is the most recalcitrant student of language. Auden's "we" in chapter 3 of *The Sea and the Mirror* might be understood, then, as a pedagogical "we."

In calling *The Sea and the Mirror* a "Commentary," Auden has already shifted the focus from artist to audience.[28] In this regard it is worth comparing Auden's earlier didactic "Commentary," the one that followed his sonnets "In Time of War." That "Commentary" spoke from a lofty position, beginning with a gaze at the planets, something Prospero might write. Though the "we" of the China "Commentary" may refer to Auden and Isherwood as well as humanity more broadly, the speaker is nonetheless removed from and looking back at the turmoil that the sonnets have described. He gazes upon "man," "little upon his little earth" despite his large "forebrain." The poem ends in italicized words from the disembodied "voice of Man," speaking back to the cosmos with a prophetic and moral vision. But Auden became wary of this undramatic, detached voice. His best work offers nuanced voices, listeners, and situations, providing an active and diverse sense of speech community. So in calling *The Sea and the Mirror* a "Commentary" Auden may be deliberately wrenching the term from its usual associations and redefining a mode he had used earlier. Here the idea of literary commentary, literary encounter—an animated and interactive relationship between artist and reader—replaces the idea of an impersonal, synoptic viewer offering detached observations on the state of mankind.

We might also think of the genre of "commentary" in a broader sense, as naming the exegetical nature of all literature and calling up the community formed by this intertextual world. In opening remarks for his New School lecture on *The Tempest* in 1947, Auden observed that the play succeeds more as "myth" than as words.[29] Thus all verbal realizations of it become commentaries on the myth. Authorship is in that sense communal; cultures re-create mythic archetypes and give them meaning in new contexts, and commentary is reiteration. Auden is certainly aware that long before he wrote *The Sea and the Mirror*, the play had been appropriated for its archetypal modeling.[30] Professional commentators have a role in this refashioning of archetypes. Auden was an avid reader of literary criticism and aligns himself with that liminal writing by addressing the theater critic in the opening. Furthermore, the New School audience was primarily adults, even peers (such as Marianne Moore); in that sense it was a place less for definitive exegesis than for interventions in a long conversation.

As a commentator Auden would seem to abjure the orphic power of the poet, becoming an audience member, putting his own writing in the service of another authorial power. Yet Auden is no Rashi. His relation to Shakespeare is interested but hardly devout. He is making corrections. He is also, thereby, modeling for the reader an interactive relation to his own text. Auden was interested in secondary forms more generally—in "New Year Letter," he decenters his own text with disproportionate annotation. In *The Sea and the Mirror*, he receives a canonical text as an individual in a different time and place, thus inevitably altering it, exemplifying his earlier adage: "The words of a dead man / Are modified in the guts of the living" (*SP* 89). In this way all of literature is "commentary"—that is what literary history and indeed literary transmission and reception are—a conversation across time and space. While lecturing on the play Auden mentions earlier treatments by Dryden, Renan, Browning, and Wilson Knight. But the "commentary" that Auden cites most extensively and uses to close his lecture is Rilke's "The Spirit Ariel."

Rilke, the modern exemplar of the orphic poet, seems an unlikely precursor to a commentary with a clear civil motive. Rilke wrote "The Spirit Ariel" in 1913, in a time of crisis. Yet as we saw in connection with the sonnets "In Time of War," Auden had already identified Rilke as a guide in thinking about the artist's relation to society. Rilke himself was no stranger to theater, having written at least two plays. Rilke's commentary (Rilke's subtitle was "On Reading Shakespeare's *The Tempest*") is addressed to an ambiguous "you" who seems to be the poet-as-Prospero facing the prospect of life without his spirit, the spirit that has been "free" in order to serve, the spirit without which the artist is "powerless, ageing, poor." Auden imitates Rilke's example with his own monologue for Prospero addressing Ariel, in which the magician still clings to a modicum of power. But in the 1947 lecture Auden quotes Rilke's second stanza, a stanza in parenthesis in Rilke's version, which shifts from the "you" to "me."

> Now he terrifies me,
> this man who's once more duke.—The way he draws
> the wire into his head, and hangs himself
> beside the other puppets, and henceforth
> asks mercy of the play! . . . What epilogue
> of achieved mastery! Putting off, standing there
> with only one's own strength: "which is most faint." (*Lectures* 307)

Auden concludes his lecture on *The Tempest* with this passage. Rilke provides the example for author-as-audience, the author not only as explainer-expositor of the text but as interrogator and student of the myth. Since Auden had been reading Rilke in the late thirties, it is likely that the German poet provided a source, in addition to Henry James, for the Caliban speech in Auden's poem. Indeed, the syntax and parenthetical digressiveness of Rilke's poem, at least in translation, share something with James's prose. We would expect Rilke to be a model for Ariel. But Rilke speaks to a "you" who may be himself in the guise of Prospero. "Once long ago somewhere you freed him / with that same jolt with which as a young man / you tore yourself toward greatness."[31] After a long meditation on the history of Prospero and Ariel ("you" and "he"), Rilke suddenly shifts to "I," distancing himself from the Prospero figure he has addressed as a version of himself. "(Have I loosed him, already? This man . . . terrifies me.)" Rilke's last stanza is entirely parenthetical and shifts focus and address very much in the way Auden does in chapter 3 of *The Sea and the Mirror*. Rilke's "epilogue," which is a commentary on Shakespeare's epilogue to *The Tempest*, captures the paradoxical effect of the wall-breaking strategy of theatrical epilogue. The rejection of illusion relinquishes magic and exposes the traps, yes, but that very rhetorical gesture of standing naked is a "mastery achieved."[32] It brings the world, and the reader, onto the stage, dissolving the very distinction between what is real and what is artificial. But Rilke has little to do with the spirit of Caliban.

———

If Auden's work is a "commentary" it is also, according to John Fuller, an attempt at "completion" of a work in which Caliban in particular "doesn't fit," according to Auden.[33] By allowing Caliban such a long soliloquy, Auden breaks not only the proscenium frame of theater but also the formal boundaries of the poetic work, generically and proportionally. Auden draws a new, wider circle of art's boundaries; this is not the perfect "arbitrary circle" of love poetry but the more problematic circle that involves the "tohu-bohu" of human plurality (*SP* 121). In order to make this point I will focus on two aspects of the work: the permutations of the first-person plural in this sequence, culminating in Caliban's insistent use of the pronoun, and the formal invention and variety in the work, which becomes a poetic underscoring of the plurality of voices that form the community of the poem. Caliban's echoic voice enfolds the diverse characters, as well as the audience, into this circle.

How should we understand the role of the Caliban-commentator in Auden's broader "Commentary" on *The Tempest*? For John Boly, in *Reading Auden: The Returns of Caliban*, Caliban represents the possibility of the reader's independence from the authority of the poet, his power to talk back: "In addition to the docile effigy, his poetry offers the reader another role, that of the auditor. . . . The main task for poetry is to maintain the possibility of an auditor's alternative reading, as a noncompliant, dissenting respondent."[34] In a sense the ambiguity of Caliban, as individual subject and as echo of audience, is an embodiment of Auden's complicated relation to his own audience, and to the "we" he would both invoke and establish in his work. But Caliban without Ariel is merely a creature of the swamp, a figure of chaotic impulses. He needs the creative ordering that can form a genuine community for him to join, however recalcitrant his participation. Thus Ariel is a crucial figure and partner in Caliban's interactions with the audience. Caliban is never autonomous. He must "fit."[35]

Caliban's speech in chapter 3 is often treated in isolation. Its generic distinction and its structural separation from the other speeches make this approach valid. Yet just as "In Time of War" takes on a greater significance when viewed in the mosaic of *Journey to a War*, so Caliban's speech benefits from comparison and coordination with the instances of address and relationship that precede it. Almost all the lyrics that make up *The Sea and the Mirror* are in some form of address, which is not surprising given the dramatic framing. Even Antonio's speech at the beginning of chapter 2, along with all his subsequent asides, which threaten rather than form human bonds, is addressed to Prospero in his absence. Antonio's negations are predicated on his brother's existence and vision; he is not autonomous, and indeed, Auden's Antonio uses the first-person plural often to indicate he is part of a group even as he sets himself apart. Gonzalo's meditation is a "farewell" to the island, and in the course of his reflections he makes imaginary address to his lonely and discouraged soul: "Here I am" and "All is well." The work's structure takes society as a given, community as a project.

The first-person plural goes through many permutations in *The Sea and Mirror* arising from these various voices and contexts of address. Yet "we" also provides a kind of thread suturing the various fragments of the community. In Caliban's speech the full ambiguity of reference in "we" is most pronounced. All these "we's," which converge in Caliban's speech, offer an antithesis to the Brontë epigraph for *The Sea and the Mirror*, in which "my own soul can grant my prayer" (*SM* 1). Brontë's pronoun is "I," and the words involve the self-worship and self-circulation of imagination. There is no audience necessary in Brontë's idea of creation, which forms a romantic circle of art as self and soul. But the force of the commentary is against this solipsistic vision. The array of addresses that follow the epigraph already calls into question Brontë's Ariel-oriented vision of artistic autonomy. Yet subsequent lyrics, even as dramatic monologues, can hardly be called communal or even dialogical, and Antonio's retorts are soliloquies, heard only by the audience and himself. He represents the continuing counterforce to genuine community, and the reason it remains unrealized. Only when we get to the Jamesian free-indirect discourse of chapter 3, with its many relative clauses, do we move beyond Antonio's fatalistic negations. Caliban's otherness is fundamentally different from Antonio's; it is the otherness not of an antagonist but of the audience. Brontë's question proposes an autonomous art; Antonio's retorts propose self without community. Caliban's address insists on audience, treating it as an unavowed community, not conforming to fixed traditions or goals, complex and divided in relation to society, yet forming a pluralized unit.

———

Caliban's speech in chapter 3 stands on its own, but it is better read as part of a sequence, and not only in terms of plot. Auden wrote to Annie Dodds: "My own feeling is that every new work one writes should, among other (and more important) things attempt to solve a new technical problem for oneself of metrics, diction, genre, etc." (January 20, 1945).[36] Auden's diverse work of the forties is ample evidence that he follows this imperative. In *The Sea and the Mirror*, he used this challenge to create a kind of dramatic form of forms, each poem's metrics and diction fitting to character and stance. If we take aesthetic form as an example of what Auden meant by a "system which will embody ... community" (*Prose* IV 64), we may see each poetic unit of the work as a part of the constellation of relations that projects an idea of community in *The Sea and the Mirror*. The drama that arises implicitly in the lyric sequence, in juxtaposed voices and worldviews, gets replayed in the prose of chapter 3 as one voice engaging many perspectives. The generic choices in *The Sea and the Mirror* draw attention not only to artifice but also to performance. These lyrics are ritualized speech *acts*. The turn to prose here parallels the turn to poetry in book 3 of *The Orators;* both invest genre with meaning in dialogue with other generic meanings.

Across all the frameworks of address, *The Sea and the Mirror* probes the various meanings of "we." The story as Auden tells it begins with Ariel's self-delighting narcissism and Prospero's surrender of autocracy. It moves to inescapable human connection and the command to love thy neighbor. Auden's dedication of *The Sea and the Mirror* to James and Tania Stern already predicates the poem upon an idea of human love and marriage as a model of acknowledging the other. The dedication offers a rebuke, then, to Prospero's master/servant paradigm.[37] The "stage manager to the critics" (*SM* 3–4) is in a sense a foreshadowing of "Caliban to the audience." While the stage manager addresses the critics, he does not offer the expected defense of art; his speech could just as easily be labeled "critics to the stage manager." The stage manager is in the business of fostering illusion; he is in on all the tricks of art and aims to reach from the stage back out to each "in his own backyard." The critic's job is to expose and interpret those mechanisms and to aid the transition from art to life; to talk back to art. The "we" in this opening poem puts both stage manager and critics in the position of audience. "We are wet with sympathy now; / Thanks for the evening." The stage manager is mimicking the audience and perhaps echoing the critic in whom he has produced this effect. Auden's constant inversions of priority between art and audience (and their proxies) remind us that the aesthetic must yield to the ethical life. The last stanza of "Stage Manager to the Critics," eleven lines long, deviates from the previous ten-line stanzas, even as it keeps a rhyme in lines 9 and 11, as the others do 8 and 10. What is missing is the couplet that sits in the middle of the previous stanzas. Instead, the fifth line of the closing stanza picks up the rhyme from the third line, and then the poem loosens, or rather reduces to a closure of word repetition. The manager, unlike the magician, knows that neither art nor life can be fully encircled.

The formal irregularities of the first lyric prepare us for the coordination between character and prosody throughout *The Sea and the Mirror*. The subsequent poems, which enter us into the dream-life of the story, are mostly, as I've said, forms of address—Prospero to Ariel, Stephano to his belly, Ferdinand to Miranda, Alonso to his son, etc., and so they invoke drama even without dramatic structure and emphasize speech as communication rather than private reverie or language game. We have already examined the modulating "we" in the stage manager's address. Prospero to Ariel similarly complicates pronoun reference. With "Prospero to Ariel" (*SM* 5–12), Auden invites the audience to forget the stage and enter the illusion. Unsurprisingly, Prospero's address to Ariel is a series of imperatives even as he is packing and Ariel is now "free."[38] He compels Ariel to listen to his drawn-out, sententious speech in which he imparts the wisdom he has gained—the rhetoric does not match the modesty of the claims. Prospero's speech is dominated by the first-person singular, culminating in the biblical "I am that I am." But the phrase quickly turns in the next line, where suddenly his relation to Ariel is invoked: "your late and lonely master." Having shifted to second person, Prospero moves on to first-person plural. "We have only to learn to sit still and give no orders / To make you offer us your echo and your mirror." Is this a royal "we" (in which case it is ironic), or does it speak for all who respond to the spirit of art? The line anticipates Caliban's role as well as Ariel's, for if Ariel offers the *artist* an echo and a mirror, Caliban does the same for the *audience*, merging artist and audience. And the turns in authority are multiple: here we have a passivity that compels, an offer that is the insubstantial stuff of mirror and echo—the play of identity and image, of self and other, is circular and elusive.

In Caliban's prose address to the audience (*SM* 27–53) we are most aware of speech as social performance. Prospero's sententious monologue on the lessons of the island barely acknowledges his listener except as a captive. Caliban's speech is an antimonological monologue, digressing and turning in the way of conversation. While challenging in terms of its length, it incorporates many points of view so that it never feels like oratory. Whereas "I" dominates Prospero's speech to Ariel, Caliban's favored pronoun is "we." Yet the meaning and tone of that "we" is faceted. On the one hand, Caliban's "we" can be paradoxically aloof and condescending. But with his talent for impersonation, Caliban addresses the audience as a plurality. In Caliban we find a new sense of "mirror" and "echo," terms that have threaded through the entire lyric sequence of *The Sea and the Mirror*. Caliban's speech inverts the structure of performance; he is not a *surrogate* for the audience but its "echo," giving the audience priority over the performing voice. It is broadly conventional to give prologues and epilogues to minor characters speaking of or for the author in first-person plural as "our author."[39] But the strategy also grants a degree of independence to the audience. As with the stage manager and the critics, Caliban remains a liminal figure, and as with the audience itself, he is neither wholly inside nor outside the world of art.

The medium of Henry James's prose brings Caliban closer to Auden than to Shakespeare. It is clear that Auden identified with James in many ways and was reading him just before writing *The Sea and the Mirror*, though his essays and poem about James would come a few years later. It's not hard to think up reasons why Caliban would speak in prose, the genre associated with the ordinary, though in Shakespeare's play his idiom is more often poetry. But late Jamesian prose is anything but primitive. Caliban's speech in Auden captures James's class refinement in the archly French "*tout le monde*" and other embellishments of speech that suggest disdain toward the common sphere. James no doubt attracted Auden as an expatriate figure and as an observer of human plurality but contemptuous of the mob.

Auden once said that he aspired to write "the thoughts of a wise man in the speech of the common people" (*Prose* I 165).[40] Caliban's speech is in many ways the opposite, embodying, at least at first, the "thoughts" of the audience (a kind of "common") in the elite speech of Henry James, an artist, as Marianne Moore put it in "An Octopus," "damned by the public for decorum, not decorum but restraint."[41] (And Moore was fully aware of the paradox here, that Jamesian "restraint" involved more, not fewer, words, than a conventional prose style.) Shakespeare's Caliban is a figure of rapacious impulse, of anti-art. But in Auden life and art are hard to distinguish. Auden would quote James just a few years later: "It is art that makes life, makes interest, makes importance." But Auden qualifies James's point, reminding us in this review that James was "no esthete" but one for whom "the interest itself of human life was always the single dreadful choice it offers" (*Prose* II 243). In his address to the Grolier Club, Auden gives further indication of James's importance, for James represents artistic integrity. And he reminds us of the distinction between magic (Prospero's conception of art) and writing. "Magic, black or white, is not art, for magic is a means of ruling children and all who cannot rule themselves, one kind of fraud and force, while art, like all kinds of truth, is one of the pleasures of free men" (*Prose* II 302). This statement in the context of an address on Henry James surely looks back to *The Tempest*, to Prospero, and to Auden's "Commentary," *The Sea and the Mirror*, a few years before. Auden admired the personal integrity of the artist, who is at once cosmopolitan and alone. James, like Caliban, "doesn't fit in" and stands solitary, unmarried and unabsorbed into the circle of society/the state. James's realism is that of a mind so fine no idea could penetrate it, whereas Ariel with Prospero imposes concepts and represses the individual (Caliban). Yet in contrast to Antonio's creed, Jamesian individuality is not atomic or antagonistic to community.

Auden adapts a number of formal and stylistic characteristics of Jamesian prose for Caliban's speech. Jamesian free-indirect discourse realizes Caliban's claim to be the "echo" of audience, and his syntax absorbs plurality. Initial nouns are succeeded by pronouns surrounded by clouds of adjectives and prepositional clauses far from their original referents and verbs. Those nouns are deferred and then preceded by a series of adverbs. The turns and shifts of angle, avoiding rigid divides, stand in contrast to Ariel's schematic imagination. Caliban's address to the audience is a kind of tour de force in marking out difference while maintaining a sense of something whole. His style embodies an idea of audience at once individuated and communal. As James Phelan writes of James, "the narrator is almost a collective or community consciousness, if indeed anything like a community is presupposed in James' fiction."[42] Caliban himself becomes as much a conduit for the audience in all its plurality as a single allegorical archetype of natural man, even as he uses italics and other devices to imitate a live voice. He resists the univocal schema of Prospero, which Ariel had implemented; he imagines the community of the audience not as an ordered totality but first as a mass or swarm. Caliban is the anti-orator and improviser. His speech meanders and turns on itself, his performance more important than the content of his statements. Dashes, parentheses, italics, and other devices mark live thought and utterance, not premeditated rhetoric or song. The speech is propelled by a series of questions, internalized to generate yet more thought. This fragmented, shifting, and overlapping performance is contrasted in the end to the "perfected Work" of divine creation, which cannot be possessed or retained, "which is not ours" (*SM* 52).

Any attempt to track the shifts in orientation of Caliban's speech will confront its turgid and twisting quality. A focus on pronouns offers a path, but hardly a straight path, through his language. Among the many remarkable features of chapter 3 of *The Sea and the Mirror*, the labile structure of address stands out. "You," "I," "We," "He" are constantly reassigned as Auden reflects on the experience of art from many angles and gives texture and meaning to the idea of audience. Points of view get tangled up in these mobile pronouns. The first remarkable sentence establishes address in terms of an "I" (Caliban) addressing a plural "You" (Audience), about its wish to address a third person, a "him" ("our late author"). But the syntax of this long sentence—its twelve prose lines like the hall of mirrors in an Ashbery poem—complicates the structure of address. A push-pull relation develops between Caliban and audience: "my reluctance is, I can assure you, co-equal with your dismay." Yet the relations formed by dramatic art will, a few pages on, be compared to marriage. Despite his reluctance, Caliban presents himself to the audience as "your echo," suggesting subservience and complicating the notion that he is speaking "to the audience." Rather, as the section develops, he presents himself as a proxy of the audience speaking to the author, the counterpart of the audience's narcissistic relation to the "mirror" of art (*SM* 6).

Caliban in a sense addresses a society that with regard to the play they share has become a tentative community. But it is not a stable or lasting one. As Caliban turns to first-person plural with the qualifier "We must own" in the second paragraph of his speech, he troubles the most minimal meaning of the pronoun (We = I + another or others). On the one hand this "we must own" sounds like an editorial "we" (later, "we submit") marking a turn in argument, more than a voice of common feeling. But what does "we" mean when "I" is not origin but echo? And what is being acknowledged (owned) or proposed (submitted)? The structure of the address is the structure of a begged question. The last line of the second paragraph responds explicitly to Shakespeare's epilogue (in which Prospero sets the audience free) and turns the "you" of the epilogue's address around: "we are, we submit, in no position to set *anyone* free."

Caliban is not a cipher, however, and does not disappear entirely as echo; he adheres to audience as a metaphor, as a point of view. Caliban *as* the audience rather than *to* the audience might be a better title in this sense. Caliban's recalcitrance becomes the recalcitrance of audience, neither wholly inside ("he doesn't fit") nor wholly outside the circle of art. Caliban represents, in this respect, the independence of the work of art from the artist. Yet this independence has no special allegiance to audience, either. As the speech proceeds, Caliban changes alliances and turns the mirror once more, becoming the indifferent messenger of the author's address to an ephebe, one who in many ways resembles Auden himself.

Caliban's first gesture gathers and generalizes rather than differentiates audience. Art has a wide scope, yet "our native Muse" paradoxically elevates her diction with French. "She invites, dear generous-hearted creature that she is, just *tout le monde* to drop in at any time." Caliban's supercilious manner here and throughout the work marks the feigned nonchalance of the impersonator, skeptical about the sincerity of the claims he mimics. The impulse of the muse toward inclusion becomes in Caliban a version of *noblesse oblige*. She is motivated as much by aesthetics as social conscience ("to make *every* shade of the social and moral palette contribute to the general richness"). Auden demonstrates the elegance of this aesthetic of inclusiveness with a bit of brinksmanship: a one-paragraph sentence of eighteen lines. The passage ends by describing what it does: "she can skate full tilt toward the forbidden incoherence and then, in the last split second, on the shuddering edge of the bohemian standardless abyss effect her breathtaking triumphant turn." Inclusive (or co-opting) as the muse may be, the audience speaking through Caliban reasserts its difference. "We most emphatically do *not* ask that she should speak to us or try to understand us." The "we" (addressing "you," the late author) soon unravels into an "us" and "them." Indeed, difference asserts itself in the social world of audience as a challenge to the abstract unities of art. "Without a despised or dreaded Them to turn the back *on*, there could be no intimate or affectionate Us to turn the eye *to*." Art may seek to bring all into a circle, but life, beginning in the theater house ("*chez nous*"), depends on exclusions and stratification. "For without these prohibitive frontiers we should never know who we were or what we wanted." Caliban paradoxically represents this message of distinction as a sweeping proposition. The text vacillates between the assertion of picket fences and their erasure under the universal urges of "commercial hope" and "erotic nostalgia." What unifies us, what we have in common, Auden suggests, is private desire, not political and social solidarity. Acknowledging that "the Whole" has interest only in relation to "the partial and contrasted," the speech turns to "our auditorium" and begins to make distinctions where it has previously spoken (through Caliban) as one voice. Caliban's "we" becomes increasingly protean.

Once the audience no longer speaks as one voice, Caliban too separates himself out and relinquishes his role as an echo of the audience. He has no opinions of his own; he is only a turning mirror or faceted echo chamber. But he asserts his presence briefly as an "I" that is not quite transparent, carrying a message from "our late author" to a "strange young man," the aspiring artist of a new age. The author's message unsurprisingly places Caliban again in dialectic relation to Ariel, the "He" competing with Caliban's "I." By the end of this long section Caliban addresses the audience again. But this time he is not an echo of the audience. The "we" at this turn is instead an alliance with Ariel. He speaks "on behalf of Ariel and myself" to address a neutral plurality—many yet one—in which he does not include himself: "you, assorted, consorted specimen of the general popular type." This body, addressed with the utmost condescension, as Auden wants us to hear, is sheepish humanity in its struggles and longings, its "Journey of Life."

This pathetic "you" ("the general popular type") is given voice in quotation rather than free-indirect discourse. "We" is kept at a distance: "'O Cupid,' Cupid, howls the whole dim chorus, 'take us home.'" "'Release us,' you will beg." Caliban speaks now from the world of art that holds this audience captive. Caliban also makes a place in his speech for the elites of civilization (echoing their own self-love, the "smaller, but doubtless finer group among you, important persons at the top of the ladder"): "'O yes,' you will sigh, 'we have had what once we would have called success.'" A catalog follows of exceptional "I's." The once holistic audience is breaking apart. "These several private regions," it concedes, "must together comprise our public whole," but "... without in short our devoted pungent expression of the partial and contrasted, the Whole would have no importance."

Behind the performance of *The Tempest* that the audience has just seen is "the first performance in which the players were their own audience" (*CP* 441)—the circle of life with its "incorrigible staginess" around the circle of art. It is worth remembering in this context that Auden also originally imagined this as a final performance. He drafted a stanza announcing a blitz, once again evoking aerial bombardment: "Ladies and gentlemen, please keep your seats / An unidentified plane is reported / Approaching the city" (*SM* 95). The darkening of the lights in the theater is likened to a wartime blackout, of which there were many even in New York, let alone in Auden's former homeland. Though Auden did not keep these lines, the sense of death as "the other side of the wall" (*SM* 4) is strong throughout. In the fear of death, at least, we find the commonality prefigured in the audience as community.

———

The "incorrigible staginess" continues into the final lyric of the sequence, called "Postscript (Ariel to Caliban. Echo by the Prompter)" (*SM* 55–56). The words resonate with Auden's epigraph to *Another Time*, dedicated to Kallman: "Every I must weep alone."[43] The postscript as a kind of love poem begins where the epigraph to Kallman left off. "Weep no more but pity me," says Ariel. Here again pronouns are featured and proper nouns are absent, making the poem at once too intimate for names and broad enough to bring the audience in. You and I weave around each other, the neutral Prompter's "I" impartially uniting them in their separateness and sorrow into a "we" of brotherly empathy." The postscript is lyric-dramatic in that it contains a dramatic address with an answer that is ambiguously an echo or a reply. We might hear it as a reply, "I can sing as you reply / . . . I," in which the prompter might stand in for the now silent Caliban. Or the "I" might be the dropped word of Ariel's speech, since Ariel is never an "I"—Ariel's sentences are mostly imperatives ("weep," "Wish," "never hope"), but the Prompter's "I" turns them into confessions. What seems most important here is the creation of a "we" that emerges from I/You exchange: "What we shall become / One evaporating sigh / . . . I," imitates the evaporation of the self as it becomes a "we" but also keeps the I in play, now well outside the reach of Antonio.

One job for the poet, Auden had argued in his comments on light verse, is to "call into being" a community that is "integrated and free."[44] *The Sea and the Mirror* seems to have that ambitious project in mind. But such a community begins in a simple act of sharing one's vision with another. As he wrote to James Stern on July 23, 1942, "Perhaps the real wish is not for an audience, but because one thinks one has had a vision in which suffering is turned into joy, one wants to share the joy with others, i.e. one would like to be able to do the same for someone else, as books which one has loved have done for oneself. The rest is bread and butter, and the desire for self-respect."[45] The convergence of voices in the echoic duet at the end of *The Sea and the Mirror* suggests a joy that comes from the close meeting of poet and reader. The figure of drama embodies both motivations for art: the gathering of a fractured society into community, and the intimate sharing of that vision with another.

7

Crowds, Publics, Congregations

Enjoying a crowd is an art.

—CHARLES BAUDELAIRE,
PARIS SPLEEN

The genuine saying of We has been manifest ever again and in the way of life of
the human race though also, of course, more and more endangered. What was
and is said thereby is directly opposite to what Kierkegaard designates as the
"crowd"—the opposite as the clear shape is to its caricature.

—MARTIN BUBER, "WHAT IS COMMON TO ALL"

CHANGING REPRESENTATIONS OF the crowd in modern poetry reflect
changing history but also changing theories about the nature of "crowd mentality." Does human plurality, when gathered in a mass, whether physical or virtual, become something more than the sum of individuals and local contacts?
Is the crowd "nothing," an "it" that acts apart from the will of its individual
members, or a "we" melding the many into one? How might this "we" retain
fluent relations among persons rather than simply forfeiting personhood to
collective identity? Does the crowd become a unified entity with a drive and
even a will, or is that merely an affect, a product of the spectator's imagination? Does a crowd have a voice? Certainly there are instances when we might
say that a crowd, or at least a large group, appears to speak *as* a group—in
political rallies, sports chanting, in church services, audience response. Some
of this coordination may be (or at least seems) spontaneous, not guided by
a single speaker. Intellectual debates about the sociology and psychology of
the crowd resonate in poetry, and central to those debates is the question of
whether the crowd is more than a numerical agglomeration, whether it has a
consciousness, and even a voice apart from the plurality of individuals who

constitute it. For the first modern philosopher of crowds, Gustave Le Bon, the crowd is a psychological phenomenon that involves the evacuation and de-individuation of reason and agency to make room for a group mentality. The crowd has a "mental unity" that is predicated on the dissolution of individual consciousness and will. Freud essentially repeated Le Bon's theory, with a focus on mass psychology, in "Group Psychology and the Analysis of the Ego" (1921). Freud identifies group psychology with self-love but also with abandonment of the ideal of self-sovereignty.[1] Theodor Adorno and others repeated Freud's idea and read his essay in retrospect as a prophecy of fascism. Diverse thinkers emerging from the thirties—Ortega, Burke, Weil, Arendt, Niebuhr—expressed concerns about the voice and spectacle of the masses, concerns that are reflected in the poetry of their time.[2]

In the context of the philosophy of consciousness, removed from ethics and politics, John Searle's "Collective Intentions and Actions" asks whether there can be such a thing as the will of a group. While his focus is on coordinated groups rather than apparently spontaneous crowds, some of his analysis has relevance for both. He begins with an intuition he will test, that group intention might precede individual choice: "Collective intentional behavior is a primitive phenomenon that cannot be analyzed as just the summation of individual intentional behavior."[3] Searle recognizes the general resistance of cognitive scientists to acknowledging this intuition: "How could there be any group mental phenomenon except what is in the brains of the members of the group? How could there be a 'we intend' that wasn't entirely constituted by a series of 'I intend's?" Searle makes a distinction, however, between consciousness and intentionality and action. He acknowledges that "There cannot be a group mind . . . all consciousness is in individuals."[4] "Collective intentionality," on the other hand, can arise with a "background sense of the other as a candidate for cooperative agency" that does not require speech or conscious reflection.[5] Searle's argument for "we-intentions" is suggestive but insufficient for crowds, where gathering is the first condition of their being. Whether "group" (more neutrally) or "crowd mentality" is fact or illusion, and whether it is the result of agglomeration or arises in circumstances where there is already a convergence of like-minded individuals, remains much debated. But the idea that there is such a thing as a unified psychology of the group or crowd survives. Most of the essays in the recent collection *Crowds*, by Jeffrey Schnapp and Matthew Tiews, build on Le Bon's principle. They explore the investment in the idea of crowd collectivity and analyze its use and development in modern culture.

Some recent work in psychology has tried to refute Le Bon's theory. In a recent article in the *New York Times*, "Crowds are not People, my friend," author Maggie Koerth-Baker cites Clark McPhail as one of the first people to actually document and study, not just theorize, how people behave when they come together in large gatherings (December 18, 2012). He doesn't even like to use the word "crowd."

> It's too weighed down by inaccurate stereotypes. For years, sociologists thought a crowd behaved like a herd of animals: at some point, it reaches a critical mass and the will of the crowd overrides individual intelligence and individual decision making.
>
> But that's not what happens. Groups of people are still made up of people. They can behave in helpful and intelligent ways, or they can behave in dumb and dangerous ways. But in either case, a crowd's behavior depends on what individuals are thinking and how they interact with one another—not some overpowering collective consciousness. "Crowds don't have central nervous systems," McPhail said. And that is true whether the crowds you're talking about are physical or virtual.[6]

McPhail's view is shared by Robert Brandom, who writes in *Making It Explicit:* "We may be thee and me. We may be all that talks and all that moves, all that minds or all that matters. . . . But we are not some organically united system or structure ruled by overriding determinant forces."[7] Brandom identifies the valid meaning of "we" in relation to two principles that preclude crowds: "sapience," the recognition of each other as beings who reason and understand; and discursiveness in "we-saying"—both qualities we associate with community but not with crowds.[8] "Collective mentality" continues to be an active area of research in philosophy and cognitive psychology. The notions of "distributed cognition" and "collective emotions" focus on cooperative and collaborative systems rather than crowd agglomeration, but some of the reciprocal cognitive processes these studies propose, in which individuals propel a collective mentality yet are also propelled by it, may also be relevant for apparently disorganized and spontaneous crowds.[9]

Whether or not the crowd in fact develops a will and agency independent of its participants may be in doubt, but the spectacle of its agglomeration gives the impression of a unified entity, as Ortega y Gasset argued in *The Revolt of the Masses.* This spectacle has tremendous persuasive power, indeed is often enhanced by those wishing to recruit a populace to a collective force. The visual phenomenon of the crowd creates an epiphenomenon of crowd identity. The epistemological "wisdom of crowds"[10] may be a statistical phenomenon rather than a cognitive or psychological one, but the *appearance* of the crowd and the effects of crowd activity, whether physically manifest or virtually constituted in the media and the imagination, often lead us to perceive it as an entity with its own drives.[11] Whatever the psychological and social truth about crowd consciousness, crowds have tremendous affective power over the imagination, for participants and spectators alike. Hubert Dreyfus and Sean Dorrance Kelly, in their book *All Things Shining*, explore the allure and also the dangers of crowds in the recovery of a sense of the sacred in modern culture. For sport, as for religion, one sees the "importance of community" in the sense of value that crowds awaken in spectator-participants. "The sense that one is joined with one's fellow human beings in the celebration of something great reinforces the sense that what one is celebrating really is great. . . . Whether it is in the church or in the baseball stadium, the awesomeness of the moment is reinforced when it is felt as shared with others. When it is also shared *that it is shared*—when you recognize together that you are sharing in the celebration of a great thing—then the awesomeness of the moment bursts itself forth and shines."[12] Dreyfus and Kelly identify this feeling as a "whooshing up" that involves a surrender of the sense of control and choice, which in this way is antithetical to the Enlightenment drive to mature, independent choosing and control. "When I find myself rising as one with the crowd . . . there is an important sense in which I am not the source of my own activity," writes Dreyfus and Kelly.[13] As such, "the power of the whooshing up phenomenon is revealed to be Janus-faced."[14] How to distinguish the awesome feeling at a Martin Luther King rally, for instance, from the awesome feeling at a Hitler rally? Dreyfus and Kelly recommend the principle of *poesis*, which they associate with skill and judgment in our interactions with the world, coming from a mature, focused awareness of the physical reality and a rich knowledge of circumstance and environment, such as an artisan develops for his masterwork. Such *poesis* can allow us to be discerning in our actions and evaluations even as they become instinctual and as we yield to the intensity of the moment. Dreyfus and Kelly are of course referring to *poesis* in the Aristotelian sense of making and doing, and in Heidegger's sense of being's self-unfolding—building and thinking coordinated with dwelling. But the connection of *poesis* to *poetics* is suggestive of the role poetry might play in helping us to navigate the power of crowds and to restore the sense of meaningful communities of value.

———

Poets have been both repulsed and fascinated by crowds, particularly in the industrialized city where crowds present a challenge to the ideal of the solitary, autonomous poetic subject. And this debate about the identity, cognition, and force of the crowd has been central to literary representation. For many the crowd has seemed a unified being, a quantitative phenomenon taking on a qualitative feature as a single entity. The crowd, we might say, is the poet's opposite, the presence that most threatens or invites his being, insofar as his inward and distinct subjectivity is the essence of his creative identity. Poets express not only revulsion but also attraction as the crowd offers an opportunity for expansion. For William Carlos Williams the combination of beauty and fear inspired by the crowd is related directly to the paradox that the crowd is many and yet one; he registers this paradox in his subtle shifts from plural to singular verbs, articles, and pronouns. And like Dreyfus and Kelly, Williams sees the crowd as Janus-faced. In a poem from *Spring and All*, "The crowd at the ball game," his view shifts abruptly from delight to horror.[15] The crowd of spectators "delights" "uniformly" in the beauty of the game. Williams's gaze is not on the game but on the crowd that it activates. The crowd "are beautiful" "in detail," that is, a glorious plurality rather than a mass. But Williams switches pronouns and the verbs become singular. The crowd that was a plural "them" of idle potentiality becomes an "it," and with this switch the poet recalls the crowd's capacity for collective violence as individuals become a mob. "It smiles grimly, its words cut." "It is beauty itself," but "it is / deadly, terrifying." At the end of the poem Williams converts his dread of the crowd into a frozen moment in the poem so that this seasonal "it" "without thought" becomes a thing of permanent beauty for the mind of the artist, and the "detail" of the many becomes a new unity, not of mass but of art.

Crowds, when perceived as uncountable hordes, inassimilable within a public sphere of face-to-face encounter and I/You dialogue, produce an effect of the numerical sublime, appearing as a force of nature or of the supernatural. Beyond counting, they become one mass. Blake's "multitudes" of orphan children in "Holy Thursday" gather force for the speaker first as "Thames waters" and then as a "mighty wind," associated with divine power.[16] The numerical sublime may have a negative effect as well as an exalting one as vast numbers threaten the subject's sense of his own reality. Wordsworth may have celebrated "a crowd, a host of daffodils" as an antidote to loneliness and joined them in memory, but he was oppressed by "the endless stream of men and moving things" in the city. Wordsworth's urban crowd becomes ghostly and unreal, a "second-sight procession" that is "nothing" but also something that undermines the foundational being of the self and drives the poet to reestablish his identity on a spiritual basis.[17] By contrast, Baudelaire's flâneur is animated by the crowd and animates it in turn. The crowd is not the poet's threatening Other but a series of others he may briefly become, without losing his autonomy. At the same time, the crowd for Baudelaire is a medium through which he moves, partaking of its pleasures without wholly dissolving into it. He can "take a bath of multitude" and still preserve his "solitude." Baudelaire writes: "Multitude, solitude: identical terms, and interchangeable by the active and fertile poet. The man who is unable to people his solitude is equally unable to be alone in a bustling crowd."[18] For him "enjoying a crowd is an art" that involves a release of pride and narrow ego into the crowds around him, to merge his flesh with the crowd. Baudelaire's pleasure involves maintaining a sense of plurality in the crowd. He can reanimate the crowd by meandering through it, entering into each figure briefly, serially, transiently, chameleon-like, so that he is joined to it, apart yet a part of the whole. But for Baudelaire there is no identification with the crowd as a solid entity. He does not become a man of the mob, like Carl Sandburg, nor does he withdraw in alienation, like T. S. Eliot. Rather, he finds in the crowd the freedom from his own narrow selfhood. Whitman similarly expands the self by absorbing the crowd and giving himself to it. The image of the crowd may dissolve distinction, but in just this way it also overcomes separation and individual death. In "Out of the Rolling Ocean, the Crowd, came a drop gently to me," Whitman imagines a brief encounter with a lover, "the drop"; they form an integral "we" of love before returning to the mass that absorbs them without dissolving their connection: "Now we have met, we have look'd, we are safe, / Return in peace to the ocean my love, / I too am part of that ocean, my love, we are not so much separated."[19] Once he establishes the distinctness of the lovers, their unique "we" is "safe" and he can exalt in the oceanic embrace of the crowd.

As Elias Canetti has pointed out in his compendium, *Crowds and Power*, dynamic metaphors abound in the description of crowds as unified entities, giving them a quality of nature rather than history.[20] These natural metaphors characterize the crowd as having unorganized vigor, independent of human conscience and choice; they arouse affects of excitement and fear. As Canetti observed from his compilation of crowd metaphors, the crowd is above all a spectacle of insentient dynamism; it has movement, growth, force, something appealing to the mind open to change and terrifying to the mind seeking permanence and stability. In these figures the crowd is not a "mentality" but simply a "force." But an antithetical feature of the insentient crowd sometimes accompanies this organic imagery—a sense of its unreality, its ghostliness, and its zombielike aspect—eviscerating vital human consciousness. Pound's "apparition of these faces in a crowd" may be neutral, but it is a provocation to the poet to convert apparition to artistic substance, to capture it and make it permanent and vivid in art.[21] For Eliot the crowd was something more troubling, a phantom-like horde. "The crowd that flowed over London Bridge" has again become a natural force (like Thames waters in Blake), but without vitality.[22] Eliot's crowd is a phenomenon of numbers rather than faces, "so many," seen as one inhuman motion until an unsettling corpse eventually spins out from this ghostly flow and stops the poet-observer. The crowd is not chaotic but disordered, a swarm, a phenomenon of movement without a consciousness or soul, something visible and yet strangely insubstantial, even hallucinatory, from which the poet-spectator cannot turn away. Eliot impersonates this crowd in his anti-apocalyptic "The Hollow Men," where the crowd is given a terrifying collective pronoun: "We are the hollow men / We are the stuffed men." Their hollowness itself is the figure of a negative crowd mentality, "leaning together," "Shape without form."[23] They can only say "we"—there is no I and Thou relation possible among them.

With populist poetry and the labor movements in the thirties, a Whitmanesque reverence for crowds and for "the people" returned, an emphasis on plenitude and solidarity rather than vacuity or debilitating force. In *The People, Yes,* Carl Sandburg would celebrate "the roar and whirl of street crowds, work gangs, sidewalk clamor."[24] "Who will speak for the people?" he asks in his refrain. In contrast to Eliot's horror, "I am the people—the mob—the crowd—the mass" is a proud assertion in Sandburg.[25] Answering the fear of an insentient and inarticulate (though vocal) crowd, he becomes the articulate voice for the crowd. Archibald MacLeish found in the crowd the hope for change. Like Sandburg, he stands apart in his "Speech to a Crowd." He is the orator who awakens the crowd to itself: "Tell yourselves the earth is yours to take!"[26] Wallace Stevens in "Farewell to Florida" writes in ambivalent regret that he must abandon the private romance with the muse and return to the "slime of men in crowds," but the responsibility to acknowledge and answer to the image of men in masses was irrefutable even to him.[27] This was an age of crowds, not just of masses but also of the amassed, and the voice of the crowd collective must be answered in some way.

The evocation of "the people" takes on darker shades by the late thirties, with authoritarian leaders and crowd seducers of fascism. The crowd loses all plurality, and the spontaneous swell is replaced by the imposition of the state, preempting all other voices. For the wary, the crowd is now a passive and vacuous body with no distinct will of its own but catalyzed or manipulated by a demagogue. It becomes a "we" by virtue of a negative daemon, an epiphenomenal force associated with violent and destructive impulses, which fill the void left as ethical individuals surrender themselves to a mass identity and to an idealized leader who offers them vicarious action or release and the satisfaction of collective egoism. Jeffrey Schnapp has pointed out that Fascist propaganda manipulated crowd images, tightening and rearranging them to erase distinction and chaos and support an idea of rallied oneness that extended beyond the public square into the public imagination.[28] As this glamorous crowd aesthetic, deployed for political ends, coincided with horrific acts of crowd violence, anti-Fascist writers turned the aesthetic and moral imagination away from crowds. Nathaniel West's dark narrative *The Day of the Locusts* (1939) became the more representative vision of the crowd for the American imagination. Inverting Whitman, West sees the crowd as a soulless and violent mass drive with the destructive power of a swarming plague. In a quieter, though no less anxious sense, Wallace Stevens in "United Dames of

America" would write of "the mass," hinting at Whitman: "There are not leaves enough to cover the face it wears."[29] The poem struggles to distinguish the orator's "singular man of the mass" and "the face of the man of this dead mass and that" from an abstract "central face," which would be the ideal figure of human nobility, "our faces circling round a central face." The poem is constantly pulled back from this transparent, abstract hero by the fear of its hollow guise, the orator's figure of mass man. And so the poem vacillates, finds meaning in vacillation itself, over the abstract face of humanity. "There are not leaves enough to crown, / to cover, to crown, to cover—let it go."

Auden's Crowds and Chimaeras

In 1948, speaking on "Poetry and Freedom" at the University of Virginia, Auden offered one of many versions of his definition of the three "human pluralities": "there are crowds, there are societies, and there are communities" (*Prose* II 496).[30] Auden defined a crowd as "a collection of people whose common bond is that they are together. There is a *we*, but there are no separate *I's*" (*Prose* II 492). He had made a similar remark in his lecture on *Julius Caesar* in 1946, and as with so many of his lectures on Shakespeare, we sense the weight in it of the contemporary European crisis. Auden's postwar liberalism is clear: "In a community . . . 'I' precedes 'we.' . . . The individual is a contradiction in a crowd. The 'we' precedes the 'I'" (*Lectures* 127). At this point it is obvious that Auden dislikes crowds and desires community ("something I can join," *Lectures* 126). During and after the war he will seek aesthetic forms that foster and represent sacred community—especially liturgical and congregational forms. In his lecture on *Coriolanus,* he sees community "threatened . . . by a crowd, because its members are incapable of saying 'I,' and have no fixed desires, only fluctuating ones" (*Lectures* 245). Communities are formed in I-Thou relations and small clusters of association and meaningful bonds. Auden identifies the crowd not just as numerous, then, but as false, a collective ego without interpersonal connection that extinguishes the individual, replacing his "I" with a "we" that has no real integrity but is easily manipulated. This "we" may arise from the point of view of the spectator or the participant. For Auden in the forties, as for many of the philosophers and theologians he knew or read, the private, freethinking individual was the prerequisite to the health of the public sphere; fascism, in identifying the vulnerability of individual conscience and will, had replaced community with collectivity, the self with state power embodied in an idealized leader who takes up the narcissistic drive of the group.

Auden in the forties abhorred the crowd mentality even as he also abhorred the solipsism of the romantic self. Crowds for him are never benign, though there are passive crowds and violent crowds, spectators and rioters. The crowd phenomenon itself bothered him. In the 1948 speech in Virginia he includes, as examples of crowds, "ten people watching something in the road, six people in a railway carriage, sixteen people at a lynching, whatever you like" (*Prose* II 492). Regardless of the cause that activates their assembly, Auden is troubled by a crowd because it weakens the drive to ethical action.

Auden closes his speech to the UVA gathering by describing a "very nice cartoon by Charles Addams . . . in the *New Yorker*" (496). "The picture is of a street in a rather good neighborhood in New York . . . a little demure man struggling with an octopus which has come out of an open manhole." What makes this an "extremely significant cartoon" for Auden is the moral it offers about crowds and individuals. "There is only one individual. In order to become individual ourselves we should have to conjure the octopus out so that we could fight with it." "The lookers-on in the picture are a crowd because none of them dare step forward unless others do. They can only be a *we*. None of them is an *I*." The octopus might be any monstrous, unpredictable, and unequal force—of nature or of human power. For postwar readers it must inevitably have been associated with Nazi victimization of the Jews. The octopus is not just a sublime power that the crowd watches in paralyzed fascination as it devours a neighbor; it is a crowd image in itself with its many arms, emerging as if out of nowhere, but all part of one body. Our ethical responsibility must be to do all we can to rescue the one overwhelmed by that force. But the crowd is passive and absorbed in its spectatorship. Is this collective lack of will the result of crowd agglomeration, which somehow saps the will of individuals, or is it only a reflection of the weak-willed individuals who gather in the first place? His idea of a "chimaera" says both.

By the time he wrote "The Virgin & the Dynamo," Auden's feelings about crowds were certainly negative. "A crowd loves neither itself [as society does] nor anything other than itself [as a community does]; its existence is chimerical. Of a crowd it may be said either that it is not real but only apparent [a multitude that we mistakenly perceive as a swarm, something encouraged by fascist propaganda], or that it should not be" (*DH* 63). Auden equivocates here. Is the crowd a neutral thing, an illusion in the sense that it is really only a multitude of individuals, or is it something more frightening and potent, a chimaera that arises through agglomeration of the multitude and then acts on everyone in it? "A crowd is composed of n > 1 members whose only relation is arithmetical. They can only be counted" (*DH* 63). And yet this numerical phenomenon can say "we" even without a "who" saying it. Crowds trouble Auden in part because they do not form meaningful and lasting bonds internally through I/Thou relations that he saw as fundamental to the health of

"It doesn't take much to collect a crowd in New York," copyright © 1941 by Charles Addams,
renewed 1968, reproduced by permission of the Tee and Charles Addams Foundation.

the *polis*. The crowd not only lacks human bonds, it undermines them. The
crowd doesn't just stand by as the octopus swallows the individual; the crowd
is the octopus.

Auden's thinking about crowds, and even his imagery, is influenced profoundly by Kierkegaard and by contemporary followers of Kierkegaard including Charles Williams, Rudolf Kassner, Reinhold Niebuhr, and later, Hannah
Arendt. All these thinkers echo Kierkegaard in that they seek to understand
the nature of evil in the modern world in connection with what they see as its
relation to an impersonal social order and herd mentality. In "New Year Letter"
(1941), Auden would echo Kierkegaard's warnings about the loud impersonal
impact of the mass and its "immanent imperative."

> By which the lost and injured live
> in mechanised societies
> Where natural intuition dies (*CP* 223)

But what is Auden's investment in "the metaphysics of the Crowd" (reinforced by the capital letters)? The "Voice" isn't just Hitler's or Stalin's but "our[s]." Auden makes clear that the "evil *Daimon*" is not something external but something within our mechanized society, a potentiality activated where human feeling atrophies. The crowd is a false god, but that does not leave it without power. Kierkegaard's idea of the crowd centers on paradox—that crowds are formed out of weakness and human passivity but take on a dark potential as they amass; they are chimerical and yet dangerously consequential. The "unreal" becomes a force.

But Auden's thinking about crowds and publics was not always so negative. His early poetry made a place for both the aesthetics and politics of the crowd. He may not have liked joining mass rallies—"Now we're due to parade on the square . . . / Shout ourselves hoarse" (*SP* 23)—but they commanded his attention. He was moved by the spectacle of multitudes and drawn to the rhetorical power of large numbers. Like others in the thirties, Auden sometimes saw crowds as figures for un-ignorable human need and potential for action in political or social solidarity. If he marked imploring weakness in the masses (as in *The Orators*), he also imagined their brotherhood and saw crowds embodying the beauty of common man. Auden's provocative remark in "The Poet & the City" (1962) that "the poet is bored to death by the idea of the Common Man" carries a particular note of self-revision (*DH* 84). In the early thirties Auden was sometimes enthusiastic about crowd experience, identifying it with his art. He had compared poetic rhythm favorably to the charging pulse of a large gathering. In "Writing" (1932), he argues, enthusiastically: "The urge to write . . . came from . . . the need for group communication," and further, "just as in a crowd we are much more easily carried away by feeling than when alone, so metre excites us" (*Prose* I 16, 19). The remark suggests a zest for this self-transcending state of group excitement, a state Elias Canetti would later locate as a topos, "the rhythmic or throbbing crowd" that arises from exuberance at immediate increase.[31] And even later Auden makes the analogy between crowd formations and poetic formations. In "Squares and Oblongs," he writes: "As members of crowds, every feeling competes with every other, demanding inclusion and a dominant position to which it is not necessarily entitled, and every word demands that the system shall modify itself for its sake, that a special exception shall be made in its case" (*Prose* IV 63). This jostling must gradually convert to "community," he argues, as the system of the poem emerges, but it is an important part of the process.

The films in which Auden collaborated in the mid-1930s often involved crowd scenes, deemphasizing personal lives as the camera speeds past individual faces, blurring them into a whole. One of Auden's voice-overs for *By the Sea* similarly focuses on convergence and a shift from individual motives to collective desire: "On the terminus now every kind of person is converging each with his own idea of freedom. People who work, people who read adventure stories or understand algebra, people who would like to be rich or brilliant at tennis, people like you and me, liable to catch cold and fond of their food, are brought all together here by a common wish: a desire for the Sea!"[32] The individual voice in the narration creates counterpoint but not antithesis to the crowd. The sublimity of the crowd comes from relinquishing reason's atomizing sense of singleness and embracing an indeterminate human expanse. In his enumerations of groups and types, Auden can sound surprisingly like Whitman, even like Sandburg, though he maintains a satirical edge that undermines sublimity, especially in *The Orators*. Later, in "The Fall of Rome," Auden's crowd fascination is still apparent: the "flu-infected city" suggests a troubling contagion and debilitation, but we feel a certain anxious thrill at the beautiful final image of "herds of reindeer" moving across the landscape, perhaps suggesting nomadic hordes (*CP* 331).

Auden's attention to crowd spectacle is intermittent and never emerges as an aesthetic focus. Auden was no Whitman ("crowds of men and women attired in the usual costumes, how curious you are to me!")[33] Auden read Baudelaire enthusiastically, but he could not "bathe" in the crowd.[34] His 1937 poem "As I Walked Out One Evening" employs the strategy of the flâneur, but Auden is washing his hands alone at the end of the poem. Yet Auden was not indifferent to the aesthetic power and moral compulsion in the spectacle of multitudes. In his poetry immediately after *The Orators*, crowds are less about weak people submitting their will and conscience to an idealized leader and more about the demands and needs of masses. They are less a threat to individuality than a provocation to work for a greater good. At least some readers understood Auden in this way. Auden's poetry was the primary inspiration behind Archibald MacLeish's images of the masses in "Poetry and the Public World" (1939):

> We live, that is to say, in a revolutionary time in which the public life has washed over the dikes of private existence as sea water breaks over into the fresh pools in the spring tides till everything is salt. The world of private experience has become the world of crowds and streets and towns and armies and mobs. The world of many men equaling man, of every man equaling men, has taken the place of the world of the lonely walker, the self-searcher, the single figure staring by night into mirrors, into stars. . . .
>
> What happens in his morning paper happens in his blood all day, and Madrid, Nanking, Prague, are names as close to him as the names by which he counts his dearest losses.[35]

Much later, in "The Poet & the City," Auden would insist that art "is concerned with *singular persons*" not "anonymous numbers," but his poetry occasionally bears witness to the latter (*DH* 88). The multitude must be acknowledged. In wartime and after, he had seen the damage crowds do when they become a "mob": "the mob is active, it smashes kills and sacrifices itself" (*DH* 82). Crowds are dangerous not only because they are passive before a mob but also because, in dissolving individual thought and conscience, they always contain the potential to become mobs. Auden sees crowd power as turned in on itself—as in Europe's self-destructive embrace of fascism. And the detached spectatorship of "the public" creates the space for this agonistic, self-destructive mob action. But rather than simply turn to the solace of the private life, Auden continued to imagine humanity in large groups, often sympathetically. In his introduction to Cavafy's poetry, when he is discussing the Hellenistic ruler Demetrius Soter, Auden echoes Reinhold Niebuhr on the dangers of collective identity: "In most poetic expressions of patriotism, it is impossible to distinguish what is one of the greatest human virtues from the worst human vice, collective egoism" (*F&A* 341). But Auden's sense that the focus on the individual led to an atomized society was as strong as his anxiety about the dangers of collectivism and crowd mentality. His most lasting commitment to human plurality seems to have been forged in the religious liberalism that emerged in the forties where the *I* retained its voice within the choral *We*.

Gathering Multitudes

The visible and audible needs of the masses hold a powerful sway over Auden's imagination in the thirties. In this, if little else, Auden echoes the writing of Ortega y Gasset, who remarked on the visibility of the modern mass.

> Perhaps the best line of approach to this historical phenomenon may be found by turning our attention to a visual experience, stressing one aspect of our epoch which is plain to our eyes. I shall call it the fact of agglomeration, of "plenitude." Towns are full of people, houses full of tenants, hotels full of guests, trains full of travellers, cafes full of customers, parks full of promenades, consulting rooms of famous doctors full of patients, theatres full of spectators, and beaches full of bathers.[36]

Ortega's view of society and culture was essentially aristocratic, and he would associate this spectacle of plenitude with a "thinning" of folk culture and the emergence of "mass man" (and what Marcuse would later call "one-dimensional man"). Auden would later come to some of the same conclusions about mass culture, though without the nostalgia for aristocratic distinction. But in the thirties, for Auden, the spectacle of multitudes was more a prompt to action than a cause for withdrawal from the public realm (*DH* 80). Auden's sestina "Hearing of Harvests" (*SP* 29–30) is a call to "rebuild our cities, not dream of islands," and its image of humanity is one of big demographic numbers, not individual lives. His repetition of "so many" offers an imaginary spectacle of "gathering multitudes" even if an actual crowd is not portrayed. He does not make his appeal on the basis that each one of the sufferers is a unique person. And the relentless reshuffling of priorities in the poem's sestina form drives forward this connective vision against the island mentality.

Before the war, Auden's sense of crowds is not darkened by the idea of a collective will overtaking the mass. In "The Good Life," he writes: "There is no such thing as a community of will, nor has the will of the majority any effectiveness apart from the material power it is able to wield" (*Prose* I 112). When Auden evokes crowds in the mid-thirties they are not usually threatening monsters or chimaeras but overwhelming forces of nature. Later Auden would make sharp distinctions between nature and history, identifying history with choice rather than necessity. But in the thirties organic metaphors prevail. This is particularly clear in "Out on the Lawn" (*SP* 30–33) where the protected environment of the small community, "equal with colleagues in a ring" though it enables a vision of *agape*, must be deferred in order to permit the natural course of history, the destruction of old orders, and the regeneration of man. The shelter of the *hortus conclusus* and its remote morality gives way to the invasive force of numbers, in competition with the ivy's growth.

> The creepered wall stands up to hide
> The gathering multitudes outside
>   Whose glances hunger worsens;
> Concealing from their wretchedness
> Our metaphysical distress,
>   Our kindness to ten persons.

The first-person plural in this poem is a self-deprecating and self-sacrificing group of intimates, based on the inhabitants of the Downs school, though they may stand for other elite, protected communities. In "Out on the Lawn," the multitude comes to preempt the face-to-sky and face-to-face relations so important to the formation of this intimate community. "Gathering multitudes" might be construed as a crowd, is even one definition of a crowd, but here it is organic, not, as it will later be seen, "chimerical" or monstrous. As a natural force the gathering multitudes become one moving body, a river or ocean, pressing in on the complacencies of the privileged community and the private life.

Soon through the dykes of our content
The crumpling flood will force a rent,
    And, taller than a tree,
Hold sudden death before our eyes
Whose river-dreams long hid the size
    And vigours of the sea.

While Auden doesn't explicitly tie the "gathering multitudes" to these floods, he does so implicitly by repeating the image of breaking down barriers and of regeneration. Elias Canetti identifies sea and river as salient "crowd symbols." "The sea is multiple, it moves, and it is dense and cohesive."[37] In Auden's poem the flood is an annihilating force "hold[ing] sudden death before our eyes" but also a regenerative one. Auden emphasizes the rejuvenating value of this new opening to the multitudes, even as old orders are destroyed. He shifts then to a different crowd symbol, that of wheat, a forerunner of the rebirth of cities. "When the waters make retreat / And through the black mud first the wheat / In shy green stalks appears," the group of friends will not hoard their safety but yield "our privacy" to this wider belonging. Corn and wheat are also crowd symbols, according to Canetti.[38] The multitude is an active and strong mass, quite distinct from the passive figure of the speaker ("on my back") at the beginning of the poem.

Auden's association of multitudes with nature is more ambivalent a few years later in "As I Walked Out One Evening" (*SP* 66–68). The multitudes have become "crowds upon the pavement," standing not as Baudelaire's figures of modern life but as "fields of harvest wheat." The harvest metaphor emphasizes mortality over plenitude and keys the reader to the *carpe diem* theme of the poem. The hyperbolic seducer, overheard by the speaker, makes a cynical reference to teeming multitudes when he evokes the "brimming river" of life. Auden draws the Eliotic speaker away from this cynical vision and toward humility and the commandment for brotherly love. The "crowds" have been humanized to "neighbor[s]," however "crooked" this brotherhood might be. Auden would make that river a mysteriously "deep" symbol at the end of the poem, after the crowds and lovers have left.

With the rise of fascism, which shocked Auden long before any large public outcry arose, the poet's crowd imagery becomes more disturbing. In "Easily, my dear" (*SP* 34–37), the "desperate" are converted to an army, becoming superhuman as a mass: "ten thousand of the desperate marching by / Five feet, six feet, seven feet high." (When he republished the poem as "A Bride in the 30's," Auden changed the number to "ten desperate million" [*CP* 129].) Auden may be recognizing a link between Germany's economic suffering and the rise of militant fascism; the crescendo march suggests fascist displays of crowd power in films and posters. The language anticipates "The Shield of Achilles," especially with its seven-line stanzas; the rhymes provide the elegance of love poetry, but the pulled-in lines that close each stanza create a sudden alertness against the pleasing lull. It is not only "the desperate" and "grouped invalids" that Auden observes against the landscape but also important rivals: "Hitler and Mussolini in their wooing poses." These dangers draw the speaker out of his private pleasures into the public realm. It is clear from the above images that "the crowd" does not have much intentionality or agency of its own for Auden, but is rather constituted by the public faces that manipulate the faceless masses and incite their destructive energies. As he would later write in his lecture on Julius Caesar: "The negative impulse is easier for an orator to instill in a crowd. A crowd is passive, and therefore notoriously fickle" (*Lectures* 128).

But not long before this, in "Spain," for instance (*SP* 54–57), Auden himself had taken on a wooing pose, captivating the reader with adjectives and three-syllable words that mirror the temporal triad of the poem. Here he represents the crowd as a redemptive force, greater than individual will or desire. The disembodied voice "I am Spain" has something of the chimerical quality he would warn against in later work. But in "Spain" organic crowd images prevail, where "the many" who answer the conscience-call ("Yes, I am Spain") "have heard and migrated like gulls or the seeds of a flower," and this activated crowd—the International Brigade—has the power to redeem "the corrupt heart of the city" and make way for a civil society marked by healthy public activities, by "the beautiful roar of the chorus under the dome." It was a poem like "Spain" that provoked Archibald MacLeish to applaud Auden's example of "public speech" and to rebuke his contemporaries for their self-indulgent lyric narrowness. But crowds do not articulate themselves, and in giving them voice, the politician and even the poet can do great harm, as Auden knew well. He makes the analogy in *The Prolific and the Devourer*: "The Dictator who says 'My People': the Writer who says 'My Public'" (*EA* 394).

What particularly troubles later Auden about crowds is the lack of verbal exchange that is so essential to the health of the public sphere. As Martin Buber would write in 1951, "For the word always arises only between an I and a Thou, and the element from which the We receives its life is speech, the communal speaking that begins in the midst of speaking to one another."[39] Crowds, by dissolving the I-and-Thou into the mass, preclude speech. Crowds do not deliberate, they "roar." The problem of the crowd and its modern manifestation as "the public" was for Auden, among other things, a problem of voice and of language. Crowds "mutter" in "At the Grave of Henry James" ("The resentful muttering mass," *CP* 309), they "mumble" in *For the Time Being* (*CP* 349). Crowds are a threat to civil discourse; in "In Sickness and in Health" they speak "a foreign language of revolt" (*SP* 121). And Auden revolted against his own capacity to provoke that noise with his speech. The public is not a group of free individuals speaking to one another but a mechanized and impersonal voice. Crowds and publics create opportunities for tyrants and false prophets to speak in their place, as if speaking for them and through them. We can see the kernel of this discontent with the inarticulate crowd in some of the first poems Auden wrote in America. In "In Memory of W. B. Yeats," we hear the barking "dogs of Europe" and the "brokers" "roaring like beasts" (*SP* 89–90). Against this din Yeats's poetry "survives" within the underground river of the private life, for which poetry is the "mouth." In later work Auden would prefer a "sotto-voce" (*CP* 620). He would continue through the fifties writing poems in an oratorical style, but his image of the collective audience is a congregation rather than a crowd.

————

In moving to America, Auden wrestled with his ambivalent feelings about crowds. On the one hand, America represented the freedom of individuals to pursue their personal happiness; on the other hand, the spectacle of crowds was everywhere, and popular art forms, especially in song, were thriving. America was a place of great numbers and great injustices, he would observe, especially to "negroes" and to immigrants, whose numbers were swelling as displaced persons sailed to New York or sought visas in vain (*DH* 320). "Refugee Blues" (*SP* 91–92) uses a simple form to explore a complex subject: it sets the fact of being numerous against the fact of exclusions, and the promise of American openness against the reality of American attitude and policy toward suffering minorities within and abroad.[40] No poem of Auden's deals more fully with the spectacle of multitudes and large numbers. But the crowd identity shifts within the poem from sympathetic to frightening as the poet's focus on neutral multitudes shifts to bureaucracies and, ultimately, terrifying armies.

"Refugee Blues" differs from early work not only in its transition from positive to neutral and negative crowd images within the same poem, but also in its insistence on the single over the collective in relation to the crowd. (Auden's cabaret songs for Hedli Anderson written a couple of years before did not directly address social issues.) The choice of the blues is significant as an American folk form that features the individual whose suffering resonates with the audience; in this it differs from gospel and work songs, other American choral forms Auden might have chosen, that emphasize the chanting group. The blues singer is not the voice of the crowd, though his suffering is representative and the repetitions of the form are based on call and response. Nor does he incite a crowd. Auden departs from blues convention in using the first-person plural, but the "you and me" keeps the poem focused on the personal experience of this very public matter of refugees. In this poem there is an "I" and a "You" that "precedes" the "we" and longs to be acknowledged. Auden would write later, in "The Poet & the City," that mass culture had "destroyed naive popular art" (*DH* 83). But Auden showed considerable interest in American folk genres when he immigrated, and his adoption of the blues suggests his attraction to a form emerging out of the suffering of a living community. By writing the blues, Auden protests anonymous modernity and its impersonal voice. The blues is a performing art, thus associating writing with the bodily presence of the singer, in contrast to the impersonal and absent language of print media and other mass culture forms. "Refugee Blues" also yokes a traditionally black form to a European immigrant story. Auden is not simply replacing one form of suffering with another. He is implicitly widening the focus of protest to include America's Jim Crow exclusions.

Auden's later review of immigrant writer Anzia Yezierska's *Red Ribbon on a White Horse* gives some insight into the form and themes of "Refugee Blues." The experiences of impoverished immigrants on the Lower East Side not only revealed the indifference of Americans to the spectacle of suffering but also exposed the fallacy that "the fellowship of suffering" could provide a coherent and lasting group identity. The latter sort of community easily dissolves. As he would write a few years later in connection with Yezierska: "Open a door through which many but probably not all can escape one at a time and the neighborly community may disintegrate, all too easily, into a stampeding crowd" (*Prose* III 179). In "Refugee Blues," Auden eschews the image of immigrant experience as crowd solidarity or demographic function (the immigrant as "algebraic cipher"). Instead, he presents refugees as isolated and exposed individuals. By not specifying "you and me," Auden draws the reader into the position of the immigrant. The treatment of human beings as numbers rather than faces creates the condition for indifference and exclusion that the poem laments. Yet the spectacle of multitudes is an important aspect of the pathos of "Refugee Blues."[41] The poem compels us by its crowds even as it presents the plight of the refugee within the single blues voice. Just as the constitution of the mass images changes in the poem, so too the nature of the address, the identity of "you and me" alters and indeed widens.

Auden's life is always relevant in reading his poetry, to understand his motive if not his meaning. Chester Kallman's Jewish heritage, Auden's émigré status, and enduring homophobic laws may well have contributed to the feeling of exclusion the poem conveys. But Auden and Kallman were hardly refugees, and they suffered very little if at all under these conditions. On the contrary, America was most welcoming to Auden—" the U.S.A., so large, / So friendly / and so rich," as he would write in "On the Circuit" (1963) (*SP* 260).

But more broadly, at least in 1939, America was not so friendly to outsiders. American policies and public opinion on a broader scale may be more relevant to "Refugee Blues" than Auden's personal autobiography.

America had been parsimonious in welcoming immigrants in the war years. Although thousands of Jews had been admitted into the United States under the combined German-Austrian quota from 1938–41, the U.S. did not pursue an organized and specific rescue policy for Jewish victims of Nazi Germany until early 1944.[42] One can read this 1939 poem as a direct appeal on behalf of refugees. Some 38,000 Jews had left after the Nazi takeover, and by 1938, after the Kristallnacht pogrom, another 36,000 left, and 77,000 in 1939.[43] Roosevelt had convened a conference in Evian, France, in July 1938; 1939 marked the first time the U.S. filled its combined German-Austrian quota (which now included Czech refugees). However, this limit did not come close to meeting the demand; by the end of June 1939, 309,000 German, Austrian, and Czech Jews had applied for the 27,000 places available under the quota. These are the circumstances surrounding "Refugee Blues," and they explain why the poem responds not only to refugees in the U.S. (and the demographic "threat" communicated in the media) but also to crowds of the vulnerable and displaced flooding Western Europe. The multitudes ignored or turned away in the rich U.S. were the same that were vulnerable to the vicious mobilized crowds and armies of Europe "Looking for you and me, my dear, looking for you and me." In the poem refugees are not just numbers but faces of the Other to whom we have responsibility, as if they were ourselves.

Auden's internal structure in "Refugee Blues" highlights his central concerns: first, the interplay between numbers and faces, between mass phenomena and individual experiences, and second, the public's inclination to turn its back on vulnerable minorities. The first two lines of a blues song rhyme, and Auden uses them to depict multitudes or public representatives. The last line, the refrain, is the emotive core in blues form, the feeling corresponding to the situation presented in the first two lines. Here, individuals enter Auden's poem, figures of an excluded minority. Yet, paradoxically, this very minority "is coming more and more to stand for Everyman," as Auden would say of Yezierska's characters (*Prose* III 183). Auden's poem builds toward this transfer from the particular minority to a universal We, while resisting an impersonal, demographic image of humanity.

Auden's dislike of the demographic view of humanity can be heard even in the first lines. Is he echoing Gogol's *Dead Souls* when he writes of "ten million souls" in the opening stanza—"Some are living in mansions, some are living in holes"? To those for whom humanity is a matter of numbers, these are statistical concerns, not matters of justice or morality. But the word "souls" reinstates what the large number refuses, and it introduces a background of social stratification to the condition of race, ethnicity, and immigrant outsiderhood. "Say this city has ten million souls" opens the poem, inviting the reader to examine not a hypothetical situation but a guesstimate. "This city" may be New York, America's most populous at around seven million in the war years. But "ten million" creates a feeling of infinity, of endless zeroes swallowing the world. This mind-boggling number (which the reader is commanded to "say") is the challenge of the poem, against which the exclusion of the refugee is a particular crime. All are accounted for in the census, whether "living" in "mansions" or "holes" (rhyming with "souls"); zeroes take on force. Only the immigrant laments, "Yet there's no place for us." Rather than dwell on these statistics of injustice within the social order, Auden draws our attention to the disorder of refugee presence and its threat to the demographic view of society. This threat becomes more salient as the poem continues; neither geographic orders (the atlases of line 5) nor organic orders (the old yew trees of line 7) can absorb the fact of displacement. As each stanza's couplet presents another public refusal of the immigrant's appeal, the unrhymed, odd-numbered third line offers the refrain, the lament of those the order will not or cannot absorb.

The poem turns midway from the refugee's plight in America to the European condition that has motivated their flight. This turn heightens our sensitivity to their predicament and hence enhances the drama of the poem. More importantly, the change of scene alters the image of the crowd, from a passive and neutral body to a destructive one, specifically, the crowds in various cities in Germany and Austria on Kristallnacht. Though crowd power focuses his imagination, Auden sees crowd violence as a force activated by a particular demagogue, "Hitler over Europe." Auden exploits the black dialect (its idiomatic use of "over") as if in mock echo of Hitler's slogan, *Deutschland über alles*. The cabaret grotesque, "Saw a poodle in a jacket fastened with a pin" (92), also suggests the Weimar atmosphere and the inversions of racial hatred in which Jews were depicted and treated as vermin. The refrain here is not "you and me" but something more historically particular, a racial category: "German Jews." But Auden would not leave the reader with this image of suffering as something that happens only to others.

Auden further broadens his scope in stanza 10, away from historical particulars and toward "the human race," here contrasted unfavorably to the animal world. The realms of fish and birds represent the condition of nature: freedom in necessity ("as if they were free"). There are no individuals in this form of freedom, in schools and flocks. Auden calls on another kind of freedom, belonging to moral choice and its consequences in history, a state, that is, as he would later write, "an immediate datum of consciousness unavailable in the animal world, a kind of freedom that must reconcile itself to justice and 'the love of my neighbor as a unique and irreplaceable being'" (*Prose* III 548).

The politicians and their representatives in the poem lack this consciousness and refuse to recognize the unique being of the refugees.

The expansion of the poem and its mounting sense of demographic disaster continues in the final stanzas, where Auden takes the spectacle of numbers and its contrast to individual being to the level of the sublime. Large numbers work their own contrast in the conclusion of the poem. The penultimate stanza is a "dream" of an infinite and open place, "a building with a thousand floors, / A thousand windows and a thousand doors." It might well echo the rhetoric of "the American dream" (a new phrase in currency in the thirties). This makes the closing refrain, with its return to exclusion, "not one of them was ours," a specific indictment. Auden in New York would certainly have been aware of the words of Emma Lazarus welcoming the "huddled masses yearning to be free" to the open arms of America. Against this plenitude, marked in thousands, is a parallel number to describe the reality of the refugees' position—the refugee is not only excluded from this abundance but persecuted and hunted by thousands:

> Stood on a great plain in the falling snow;
> Ten thousand soldiers marched to and fro:
> Looking for you and me, my dear, looking for you and me.

It is unclear whether the image in the closing stanza is part of the "dream" of the previous stanza—a dream turned nightmare. The austere imagery anticipates the punning "plain without a feature" and "million boots in line" of "The Shield of Achilles." In any case, it is a dream of historical reality, inviting the reader to take the position of the speaker's vulnerability. The fact of being numerous in stanza 1 has been replaced by the fact of being pursued by a mobilized army on a vast, shelterless terrain.

———

Other reckonings with the paradoxes and betrayals of American democratic promise would follow. In fact, Auden increasingly saw America with a Jamesian ambivalence, anxious about egalitarian leveling and vulgarity. "At the Grave of Henry James" (1941 long version, SP 128–32) can be read as a meditation on the artist's place in a bovine society dominated by "the / Resentful muttering Mass, // Whose ruminant hatred of all which cannot / Be simplified or stolen is still at large; / . . . / Preserve me master from its vague incitement." Implicitly, Auden is turning to Henry James as a defense against his own earlier attraction to the "roar of the crowd" and the applause of the many. James is also a defense against the "milling mob of fears" within, which war "excite[s]." Auden's "I" addresses James's "you," and at the end of the poem "our calling" forms a "we" of "me . . . and all writers living and dead." But in the course of the poem Auden uses the first-person plural to speak for many of his generation—"our dreams." Thus, like the novelist, he recovers a sense of common humanity even as he turns from the inarticulate horde. James was deeply disturbed, if also grimly fascinated, by crowds, especially in New York. *The American Scene* describes "the whole quality and *allure*, the consummate monotonous commonness, of the pushing male crowd, moving in its dense mass—with the confusion carried to chaos for any intelligence, any perception; a welter of objects and sounds in which relief, detachment, dignity, meaning, perished utterly and lost all rights."[44] James's abhorrence of the crowd can be heard in these lines of Auden's poem about him: "Our theatre, scaffold, and erotic city / Where all the infirm species are partners in the act / Of encroachment bodies crave." The artist provides a voice of clarity in contrast to the "knotted mass / Of the improperly conjunct." Here, Auden is describing the "plural numbers" of the dead, since he stands imaginatively in Cambridge Cemetery. But to be part of a crowd is for Auden already to be dead, to be without being, given over to a soulless "we."

The Public

Like many twentieth-century thinkers, Auden saw the crowd developing a terrifying new form in modernity. Mechanization, the spread of mass media, and its promotion of a bodiless public opinion destroyed local community and personhood. The crowd was now a virtual, not just a physical, phenomenon; it wasn't a throng but a "mass." In "The Poet & the City," Auden is nostalgic for a time when art concerned itself with the "Public Realm" (what Jürgen Habermas and others call "the public sphere") where "a man could disclose himself to others" (*DH* 80), and much of Auden's poetry looks to restore that civil function to art. But Auden was also a participant in the world of radio broadcasting, writing radio sketches with Isherwood and later involving himself in war propaganda for radio while in Spain;[45] he was certainly attentive to the "waves of anger and fear" building up to World War II. Mass media was a fact of modernity, and Auden did not turn away from it. But like many thinkers of his time, he began to connect the unspeakable evil of Europe's recent history with the phenomenon of mass society and the manipulation of mass media.

By the late 1940s Auden had made a distinction between "crowds," which have bodily presence and thus local and visible manifestation, and a media-constituted "Public," demanding deference to an impersonal generality easily manipulated. Crowds may become mobs. But crowds have a positive side; they offer a bodily medium of self-transcendence and group immersion. They are perceivable and direct, and thus can be gauged. A crowd has edges. "The public" is something more frightening because measureless, placeless, and impalpable. If crowds turn men to monsters, "the public" turns them into automatons, into "neuter atom[s]" (*DH* 321) that allow the monsters their opportunity. Auden's growing sense of the importance of the sensuous body in the ethical connection of men to each other and to Christian truth rebelled against the disembodied collective brought about by media and mass culture.

The Double Man marks a point at which Auden sees the end of the possibility of community as a local realization. "The Machine" and its loud voice have removed men from the public sphere and instead created a virtual connectedness "among the crowd" in which, paradoxically, each man is alone.

> The secret that was always true
> But known once only to the few,
> Compelling all to the admission,
> Aloneness is man's real condition. (*CP* 237)[46]

But the "machine," if it exposes the aloneness of everyone, also offers "the crowd" a dangerous alternative to facing the freedom of this aloneness, offers a new collective dominion, "the Public." Auden's ideal in embracing "aloneness" may be "to achieve a real unity [of man] through a common recognition of diversity," but the emergence of "the Public" threatens this ideal (*Prose* II 52). The media and other institutions fostering "the public" obviate physical presence and replace local social connections and even crowds with a faceless and pliable abstraction immune to ethical qualm and difficult to attack because phantasmal. "A crowd has a generalized stink," Auden wrote in "The Poet & the City," "The public is odorless" (*DH* 82), a sterilized and abstract form of the crowd. Because odorless, the influence of the public is harder to detect, even within the private realm, and more toxic. Public opinion and bureaucratization could erase the individual and his moral center: "Our researchers into Public Opinion are content / That he held the proper opinions for the time of year," Auden writes in "The Unknown Citizen," imitating the fickle voice of bureaucracy (*SP* 93). The chimaeras of "the public" seem at once to be the cause and the result of this evisceration of individual conscience. There was no longer a space apart from the herd. No "I" stands behind the public, yet its consequence is formidable in creating a conduit for violent and repressive orders. Auden may be the "abstract intuitive" type, but here he sees the danger of removal from the world given us through the senses.

Auden's thinking on the subject of "the public" comes from a variety of sources. The first may have been Baudelaire, whose *Intimate Journals* Christopher Isherwood was translating in the thirties and for which Auden would write an introduction in 1947.[47] But it is only after reading Kierkegaard that Auden begins to emphasize the daemonic nature of "the Public." By the 1940s many social philosophers expressed the view that mass media and mass culture

had helped form a new, malevolent form of crowd mentality. Niebuhr, Kassner, Williams, Arendt, and others were reacting to the manipulation of mass
culture and media as a central instrument of evil in modern times. Auden,
following Kassner in particular, called this evil "chimerical," not to dismiss it
but to demonstrate the real power and consequence of a phantom entity. The
problem is that this attracted him as a concept yet seems to have little force as
a poetic image since he is not prone to a mystical but rather to a practical and
ethical view of evil. "The public" is not a fruitful dramatic subject for Auden
until he contains it in a Christian frame where it is once more linked to the
ancient image of the crowd.

Auden's "The Chimaeras" (*CP* 612–13) is symptomatic of the problem he
had converting this idea of the daemonic "public" into a poetic image. It is not
a successful Auden poem, but it shows his effort to give dramatic and affective
literary form to the phantom phenomenon of "the public."[48] The poem derives
its diagnosis and even much of its wording from Rudolf Kassner, as Mendelson has pointed out.[49] Kassner himself took the concept of the crowd chimera
from Kierkegaard but put greater emphasis on its metaphysical aspect. These
thinkers associate the crowd with the formation of ideology, that is, of unconscious and pervasive concepts mistaken for given conditions. The hidden work
of ideology usurps the ethical and reasoning power of the individual, who in
joining the crowd surrenders his moral reasoning to the unreality of a "public"
identity. "The public" takes on a mystical character, an evil in the Augustinian
sense in that it works by negation and absence. The metaphysics of the crowd
is an epiphenomenon. In calling this daemonic force "chimerical," Auden
marks the daemon an illusion, a false god, but an illusion that becomes a real
force on historical bodies and minds, like an ideology.

"The Chimaeras" is much more than a transcript of these ideas, however.
The poem is more dramatic than expository as it mixes Christian mysticism
with Kafkaesque paradoxes. Strategic pauses, repetition, and paradox promote
the dramatic effect. Auden addresses the reader prophetically, casting the evil
in a sublime light even as he employs colloquialisms ("ugly customers") to
acknowledge the ordinariness of the evil. Auden chose an unusual form for
"The Chimaeras." He has often used three-line stanzas, but in this context they
suggest a certain demonic presence. Dante has been suggested as a model
for the poem's end,[50] but in contrast to Dante, Auden refuses rhyme, as if to
register the incoherence and disharmony of this paradoxical phenomenon
of public being. Several stylistic features of "The Chimaeras" help articulate
the uncanny, devouring quality of this phantom force. Auden is especially
focused on articulating the peculiar absence/presence of the modern, media-
formed herd mentality. For instance, the first half of the poem uses dashes
abundantly—a device Auden rarely employs elsewhere. Dashes can function

in many ways in poetry, but here they mark an absence, a gap or incompleteness, and a silence. Dashes mark the intrusion of the inarticulate into individual voice. They also mark the lack of logical transition; they register a sense of speed and surprise as ordinary life is taken over by these mysterious forces. Grammatical devices also embody the chimera. Double negatives turn contradiction into paradox and introduce the mystery of an entity arising out of the insubstantial Void. Negative prefixes mark absence devouring substance: "indescribable, uncountable, unreal." Each adjective builds to a greater negation of "being"—the word they modify in each case. Being for Auden is tied to faces and thus to individuals, whereas the chimeras arise from a faceless mass and are an epiphenomenon of demographic reality. But once engendered, their unreality, however insubstantial, becomes a force. These negative attributions lead to the idea of negation itself as phantom agency, always plural since it is connected to herd mentality. "Not liking what they are not is what now they are." Auden's attempt here to create an idiom of nonbeing is awkward and unconvincing in the end, especially as compared with the great poetry of double negation, from Shakespeare's *King Lear* to Wallace Stevens's "The Snow Man." In fact, Auden shifts after the first three stanzas from a stance of mystical fascination to one of ethical instruction and abandons the metaphysical *via negativa* for a didactic voice of warnings. Yet the poem nevertheless represents Auden's attempt not just to convey the ideas of Kassner and others but also to embody and reproduce in language a phenomenon that philosophy identifies and analyzes. The insertion of personal pronouns, especially "we" ("We prod or kick or measure and are lost"), changes the perspective of "The Chimaeras." The first part of the poem registers the shock of recognition; the poem then shifts to warning and moral assessment. The "we" that arises at the end of the poem stands outside the reach of negation, restored to "heart," "Mind," "worth." It is not the anonymous, without origin, and usurped "we" of "public speeches" but a call to conscience in direct address, the restoration of human choice and responsibility, the individual returned to the public sphere. The chimeras can only speak as "we." The broader "we" at the end of the poem is not the voice of the collective but of the common. But the poem seems finally confused about the source and nature of this chimerical power.

Auden's metaphysics of evil in "The Chimaeras" depends on an externalized daemon; and here is a paradox since it is precisely this externalization of responsibility that allows the work of the chimera. Thus the second half of the poem doubles back on the reasoning self: "do not let your goodness self-deceive you." This rhythm and rhetoric of cancellation continues to the final line in "it is good that they are but not that they are thus." Auden's instruction here complicates ethical responsibility for others. His imperative, "walk on," might seem to mirror the very problem of public indifference to atrocity and suffering (just as "Musée des Beaux Arts" implicates those who turn away). But "walk on" in this case denotes a power of refusal. Not to join the crowd, not to stand and gaze with the spectators as the octopus devours its victim, not to follow those possessed by the daemon of the public, becomes an act of will. "Walk on" instructs the reader to avoid a chimera that steals the moral agency of the mobile individual. "They" indicates the chimeras themselves here, an absence constituted by ideas that have been transformed into hollow ideologies; through the channels of public media they silence individual voices. They perpetuate blind assumptions and undermine moral reckoning. "The Chimaeras" offers a warning concerning the surrender of mind and heart, thought and choice, to the phantom of public opinion. But Auden is not a poet of metaphysics, and as the "multitudes" of the thirties receded and he lived in small American communities or island retreats, he ceased to be a poet of crowds.

Liturgical Forms

Auden's schematic imagination is not well matched to this inchoate, modern, and secular daemon of the mass. He needed to contain this random and negative process within a greater pattern that could give meaning and coherence to history. In order to do so he connects present history and his own artistic vision to biblical narrative and thus links the modern "public" to the more palpable, primitive figure of the crowd. Furthermore, the forms of Christian ritual, combining local assembly and universal community, embodiment and transcendence, individual reflection and choral expression, suggested to Auden a strong counterpoint to this impersonal, secular, and disembodied unit of "the public." In Christian ritual Auden found a form for community that could resist romantic individualism and modern collectivism. Here, crowds might become congregations, formed in bonds of faith. The virtual connections among Christians are referred to sacred time, rather than being merely secular and chimerical. One hears this effort in "Anthem," written for the dedication of St. Matthew's Church in 1944. "Let us praise our Maker," he begins, calling for "the whole creation . . . / Phenomena and numbers" to announce "in one / Multitudinous oecumenical song" their "gratitude and joy" (CP 330). It's an anthem not for a crowd but for a boundless and unified community, "peaceable and plural." The poem is an unrhymed sonnet, but the language is bound through a medieval alliterative verse form that makes the lines break in the middle, creating balance in the long single sentence, "as one feeling fabric, all flushed and intact." Auden's liturgical poems do more than imitate Anglican ceremonies, then. Readers who complain of the abstraction and sermonic tone in Auden's later poems overlook the very concrete force of their sound and rhythm. Auden's late poetry is not image-rich, but his poetic arguments are embodied in their forms as much as in their words.

In his book *Ritual and Experiment*, Jacob Korg discusses the way T. S. Eliot and other modern poets reflect the conflict Mircea Eliade describes between the historicist view of history as a linear sequence of unprecedented events, which must be individually interpreted, and the archaic or traditionalist belief that history conforms to a cyclical, repetitive plan determined in the original moment of creation.[51] Auden's sense of ritual as a form of virtual gathering precedes his return to Christianity, of course. We can see in Auden's 1939 "In Memory of Sigmund Freud" an early, secular attempt to counteract the "Generalized Life" with a pagan funerary rite that calls up a sense of community. The elegy is in first-person plural throughout, and its allusions to collective mourning in time of war make this "we" particular to time and place: "When there are so many we shall have to mourn / . . . For every day they die / Among us" (*SP* 100). At the same time this sense of congregation allows the defense of "differing lives" that was Freud's legacy. Here, the private unconscious abides in a layered, if not timeless dimension and becomes an eternal, collective space. Auden's later use of liturgical forms, which draw on Christian narrative and ritual but integrate them with contemporary history and innovative technique, also reflect this conflict of the historic and the eternal. Auden believed in his early days that "poetry is a rite." He was drawn to verse drama because it combined the individual and the collective, and "poetry is a medium which expresses the collective and universal feeling."[52] The performance of the liturgy also suggests immediacy and localized voices. While "we" or "our" may be general in such moments, a sense of congregation and presence arises in the ceremonial rhetoric and in italics suggesting response.[53] Worship is communal, Auden believed, and he attempts to bring this quality to his poetry, where the door remains open and the ritual unbounded by time and space (*Prose* III 574). But Auden also saw what Korg calls "experiment" as an important aspect of his responsibility as an individual artist, the "I" of the present, to renew the intellectual life of the culture rather than simply perpetuate the collective "we" traditions of the past. In turning to the forms of Christian worship, he draws on the power of ritual to create community, the idea of collective devotion that engages rather than evacuates individual feeling and thought. And he turned those forms toward his own time.

The roar of the crowd is nothing to this vociferous "Public" that drowns out the poet's *sotto voce*. Auden found an alternative musical model in the oratorio, which offered a voice at once public and meditative, with room for both the individual and the group. The chorus in the oratorio *For the Time Being* begins by expressing a state of discouraged drift, but it rises in celebration and triumph against the defeatist voice from the "purple rostra" and of "the general loquacious Public" (*CP* 361). The chorus develops an affirming "we" that stands against the coercive "we" of public sentiment. In congregational and liturgical forms like this, Auden sought an alternative collectivity to mass media and the disembodied "we" or the divisive "we" of class stratifications. The first-person plural in this oratorio is impressively scaled and diverse, and we are meant to hear that variation in the range of full and semi-choruses, soloists and chorus together, responsive reading, the "Tutti," and representatives from different stations (shepherds, wise men). We hear a frightened crowd where there is no "personality" but only a "mumble" (*CP* 349). We hear a semichorus speaking of their desolation, the multitude like wheat "sifted / And cast into the void" (*CP* 350). We hear the prosaic and detached, analytical "narrator" speaking of the "familiar tribulations" that "we have been through . . . before" (*CP* 351). His didactic "we" describes the state of affairs ("We can only say that now It is there and that nothing / We learnt before It was there is now of the slightest use," *CP* 352). There's the "we" of the fugal chorus, the voice of mechanized man, and the "we" of the conversing shepherds, "What is real / About us all is that each of us is waiting" (*CP* 376).

Auden's Christianity shaped his feelings and ideas about human plurality, counterbalancing his political liberalism with a strong sense of congregation. The importance, to ethical awareness, of the capacity to say "I," and to recognize the other as equally an "I," recurs in Auden's writing. In the words of the wise men in Auden's *For the Time Being*: "Love's possibilities of realisation / Require an Otherness that can say I" (*CP* 384). In liturgical form and Christian ritual he found a way of connecting his aloneness with a voice of sacred community, "in solitude, for company." Auden said that Anglicanism "implanted in me what I believe to be the correct notion of worship, namely that it is first and foremost a community in action, a thing done together, and only secondarily a matter of individual feeling or thinking."[54] But to write poetry *is* first and foremost a matter of individual feeling and thinking. By adapting Christian forms to his own poetic invention and sense of contemporary reality, he sought a way of coordinating his ideas of individual conscience and freedom (man's "aloneness") with his desire for connection to the multitude, where individual ego adheres to a greater good. The community of the faithful was open to anyone and practiced locally, but the symbolic dimension of ritual released this community from the confines of time and space, without the chimerical effect of "the public."

Ecclesiastical forms offered a layered relation to audience and among members of the community. On the one hand, Auden presents himself as a worshipper, joined with other active worshippers. But there are also echoes of the pulpit. Here, the "roar of the chorus under the dome" was not cheers in a sports arena but hosannas in a cathedral formed in a "co-inherence," as Charles

Williams called it, of the one and the many, of I and We. Auden remained a civil and often a didactic poet, but he sought forms in which he could avoid the role of the demagogue and the crowd crystallizer. Liturgical compositions interwove the individual and the collective voice, integrating sermon and chorus. As participatory forms they give structure to the intuitive life rather than usurping it. Here seemed to be a kind of group assembly that did not require the surrender of the ethical self; instead, it provided a spiritual framework for ethics. Here too was a form that would satisfy Auden's aesthetic attraction to multitudes while overcoming the seductions of the collective ego. The oratorio may have been collaborative in origin (Auden worked with Britten for a time) but is not collaborative in form. The audience is not sharing in the creation of the work or in the formation of meaning. But rhetorically at least, the oratorio offers a figure of group participation rather than of group subjugation.

In his essay "Greatness Finding Itself" (the greatness involving the embrace of something larger than the self), Auden repeated his ideas on the poles of theology that come together in his Anglican faith and hence in liturgy. It is perhaps unsurprising that this English belief system is revived in him when he comes to America, where democracy forms around this dialectic of "I" and "We." Again, he is searching for the proper structure of plurality, one that can maintain the sense of both "I" and "We."

> One might say that, in conjugating the present tense of the verb *to be*, catholicism concentrates on the plural, protestantism on the singular. But authentic human existence demands that equal meaning and value be given to both singular and plural, all three persons, and all three genders. Thus, protestantism is correct in affirming that the *We are* of society expresses a false identity unless each of its members can say *I am*; catholicism correct in affirming that the individual who will not or cannot join with others in saying *We* does not know the meaning of *I*. (*Prose* IV 289)

To represent this I/We interaction in his work, Auden needed a more expansive and dramatic form than the poems in his single voice had allowed, one that would emphasize the ritual and communal dimension of his art.

"Horae Canonicae" and the Metaphysics of the Crowd

In *For the Time Being*, Auden had adapted the quasi-dramatic form of solo and chorus. The work was designed for performance as an "oratorio," though it quickly became clear to both Auden and Benjamin Britten that the complex speeches were ill-suited to a musical setting. In contrast, Auden based "Horae Canonicae" on daily prayers and meant his poem to be read rather than sung, though the Anglican hours are part of ritual practice and often made in immediate communion with others. They are *offices*, to be *done*. The roots of the word *liturgy* contain the meanings "work" and "public." But these prayers are also meant to connect worshippers everywhere, to bring them into a community formed in ritual time. The performed and collective aspect of the prayers becomes part of the poem's meaning. The form of this poem is a defense against the momentum of the crowd, which is at the heart of its story; the crowd event that surrounds the Crucifixion motivates the communal longing for redemption. Thematically, "Horae Canonicae" does not simply present a spiritual counterforce to the evil of the crowd. That would be a form of Manichaeism. Instead, Auden tries to incorporate the crowd into a coherent and meaningful history, to give it a purpose, rather than oppose it as a random threat. Following the gospel of Mark, the biblical prompt for the canonical hours, he identifies the role of the crowd and its self-destructive drive in bringing about the necessary awareness of human error and atonement, and the subsequent invigoration of ethical and spiritual life. The crowd with its clamoring "Crucify him!" is fundamental to the process of grace.[55] It resonates for Auden with contemporary attitudes and events of the war years, both in Europe and America. The crowd is sacrificing itself in killing Christ whose being centers on incarnation. Historically, as Auden knew, Christ's crucifixion took place at a point when the Romans had suppressed Jewish uprising; the remaining community was debilitated and cowed. Yet it is not the Jews who kill Christ in Mark's narrative but *the people* more broadly, the weakened multitude stirred up by jealous priests. Their call for Christ's death is a form of humanity's suicide since Christ had united god and man. Auden saw this self-destructive crowd pattern repeating itself in history, though unique in each event. The momentum of the crowd and the revulsion from the violence it enables are the focus of "Sext" and "Nones," which form the heart of Auden's sequence. They are very much reflections on a post-Nuremburg era.

Pronouns enact the struggle of the narrative in "Horae Canonicae." The canonical hours become for Auden a study in the modulations between *I* and *We*, where the individual awareness emerges, finds the other, loses itself in the crowd, recovers itself in dissociation from the crowd and in personal conscience, and returns to the group formed of individuals in community. Auden registers these permutations of pronoun through carefully selected and implemented prosodic forms that again work to embody in lyric the emotional narrative of sin, sacrifice, and redemption. Though "Prime" and "Nones" first appeared in the volume *Nones*, the canonical sequence, as we know from Auden's letters to Ursula Niebuhr, was planned as a whole. Not only the connection of the hours to each other, but the context of the sequence in *The Shield of Achilles*, helps us see its meaning. Section 1 of *The Shield of Achilles* depicts a pastoral landscape of middle earth. Section 2, which includes the title poem, deals with history, art, and politics. Section 3, "Horae Canonicae," introduces sacred time, which is manifest in each historical moment. *The Shield of Achilles* appears to turn its back on "the public" that Auden once hoped to address. It is addressed to "Earth, sky, a few dear names," and each of the bucolics is dedicated to one or two of those dear names—it is thus focused on nature and on the private life's more intimate "we." But by the time we reach the magisterial poem "The Shield of Achilles," we are in a world that is anything but bucolic, a faceless and placeless world of mass armies and dehumanized victims where the private life does not exist. Here, Auden's horror of mass media and the public can be heard. Many parallels to "Horae Canonicae" arise as "The Shield of Achilles" presents a desacralized crucifixion. "A crowd of ordinary decent folk" (*CP* 595) anticipates the crowd that forms in "Sext." "The Shield of Achilles" laments the loss of vital community and its dance of unity, calling into question the cultural axioms that perpetuate war. This "iron-hearted" culture (*CP* 596) requires a spiritual awakening. In this sense the title poem, "The Shield of Achilles," makes way in the volume for "Horae Canonicae." Its "hours" are "ours."

Auden's central concern in his treatment of the canonical hours is the struggle of individual awareness and conscience in the web of history. The individual's relation to God is only addressed insofar as it is lived in historical time, in his relation to other men united in common guilt and complicity with evil, and in a shared future. Each of the "hours" is a meditation on this fact of interrelation in various formations—as societies, crowds, and communities. Pronoun choice and placement is a crucial tool for Auden as he unfolds this narrative. By modulating pronoun positions but returning continually to the first-person plural, Auden works toward a group image in which the plurality of individual will and agency is kept alert within the congregation. What mars Auden's rhetoric throughout "Horae Canonicae," however, is a conflict between worship and instruction, between the participation in ritual through exemplary struggle and the effort to explain, in which case Auden becomes a didactic interpreter rather than a member of the congregation in free communion.

"Prime" (*CP* 625–26), a syllabic poem, imagines Adam's buoyant awakening to consciousness and links it to the modern self's own coming into awareness of history—and into ethical responsibility—with each new morning. Auden had already imagined this moment of self-discovery and self-creation in his essay "Purely Subjective": "I wake into my existence to find myself and the world that is not myself already there, and simultaneously feel responsible for my discovery" (*Prose* II 184). "Prime" seems to claim our attention in sound that overrides syntax. But Auden loses confidence in such mimetic effects of threshold awareness, and his rhetoric quickly becomes more propositional than dramatic: "my name / Stands for my historical share of care / For a lying self-made city." The self is not an autonomous entity but, in the very taking of breath, becomes part of a larger human city. The opening scene of "Prime" may be Ischia but it is also New York, London, or any place where "self-made" men accrue wealth and destroy what they create with it. Auden deliberately postpones the pronoun to build into his poem a phenomenology of being prior to selfhood. "I" is the last thought of the first stanza: "I wake," which takes on the full weight of modern awareness of history. The pronoun "I" moves to the middle position in the second stanza, "I know that I am here," and the first position in the third stanza, "I draw breath." The sequence creates the impression, then, of a self-conscious relation to environment. But at the end of the third stanza the pronoun becomes plural, "Afraid of our task, the dying," and the reader is reminded of the congregation even as the focus remains on a single speaker. The three-stanza structure of the poem organizes the awakening into a preview of the narrative of fall and redemption. While "Prime" anticipates in its last stanza the burden of guilt and social responsibility that "Horae Canonicae" will explore, it nevertheless creates an orphic arousal of the single voice. The sense of primary vision can be felt in the gusty lines with their *s* and *l* sounds. The considerable internal rhyme in place of end-stopped lines causes words to merge and counteracts the divisions of syntax. Auden poetically manipulates grammar, sound, and syntax, then, in order to convey Adam's primal awareness, prior to the differentiations of the rational and social mind.

"Terce" (*CP* 626–27), composed more than three years later, also uses a three-stanza form. The thirteen-line stanzas inscribe the foreknowledge of the crucifixion into the nonverbal, spatial dimension of the poem. "Terce" describes a world approaching the terrible event, a world of judge and hang-man, a world of action and choice, desire and depravity, of private yearnings and fallibility. Auden contrasts this historical world, which "does not know" the meaning or consequence of its choices and actions, to the eternal truth that "knows already" human guilt and the intervention of grace. The section begins in the third person (perhaps appropriate to the title) and builds toward the first-person plural. An "I" emerges in quotation only after the poem acknowl-edges: "we might all be anyone." "Terce" deals with man in a social dimension, not just in a spiritual or natural dimension as in "Prime." And instead of a lyric mode, the first stanza of "Terce" is narrative exposition. Auden focuses here on the catalog of social types, each with its "historical share." Auden uses paren-theses to mark the isolation of the self in relation to the social order, sectioning off the hangman's dog and wife. But the momentum of the poem is away from this segmentation toward empathy. By using quotations, the poet causes us to speak the words of others in the first person, to position ourselves differently in relation to the hierarchy of work, the tensions of erotic connection, and economic grasping. The quotation marks drop out and the "I" falls away, but as an impersonal "we" resumes, voiced by an interpreter-sermonizer, the pronoun indicates the plurality of unique voices. Auden thus avoids a generalized notion of collective guilt with which no one identifies. "Terce," with its trinity of hangman, judge, and poet, ends, "We shall have a good Friday." On Good Friday the only principle of brotherhood is mutual guilt, the bond of Christian community for Auden along with tradition, but each of us participates in that guilt uniquely.

In "Sext" (*CP* 627–31), again the poem has three sections; the dominant pronoun is "you." Where "Terce" put the reader in the position of "anyone" participating in history, now the reader is urged to "know" and "watch" humans intent on their vocations, "forgetting themselves in a function." For this one section, Auden drops the formality of the capitalized lines, perhaps to register the domain of the ordinary and the purely human. He loves this image of work. The reader is not part of a spectator-crowd but witness to an act of intense concentration in which, perhaps following Buber, an "I" loses itself into an "It." "How beautiful it is, / that eye-on-the-object look." We are in the world of Aristotle's *poesis* and his megalopsych. But Auden is not willing to see work alone as redemptive, nor does it protect us from the lure of the crowd; there are dangers in substituting an "It" for a "You" or "Thou." As Auden's attention shifts in section 2, with parallel language, from the prolific to the devouring, from makers to administrators, the poem grows more sinister and asks us to embrace a paradox. Human division and repression, through strength, justice, and intelligence, play a part in the formation of civilization, but these qualities also ultimately lead to the destruction of civilization, which must be remade in shock and forgiveness. What is most immediate here for Auden in "this death" is the spectacle of war and genocide—the suicide of the city rather than the sacrifice of God. The increased punctuation in the free verse couplets of section 2 of "Sext"—here commas and elsewhere parentheses—mark the struggle to acknowledge this negative principle in history. The parentheses bring us closer in, activating our awareness, impressing upon us the difficulty of what we are asked to acknowledge.

The third section of "Sext" is in many ways the heart of the poem, just as the crucifixion is the central point of the Christian story in the Gospel of Mark. Here, Auden struggles to understand the metaphysics of the crowd, how a holistic entity, the crowd, can arise from individuals with their unique experiences. Terrible as it is, this crowd-being is superior to the "exoskeletons" of social stratification and distinction formed by the administrators in section 2; it brings men closer to each other in their culpability and weakness.[56] Auden brings together what has been fragmented—"someone," "anyone" into "the crowd," which also has its own distinct "share" in the crucifixion, converting its evil into a necessary catalyst of conversion to community. The crowd and its guilt are the thematic crux of the story for Auden, who does not focus at all on Christ's death or resurrection. He introduces the crowd at the exact middle of his text. The conceptual difficulty of crowd identity prompts Auden's complex syntax and heavy use of parentheses, giving what was earlier a breezy, invitational free verse a heightened, momentous tone.

What is the nature of crowd-being in "Horae Canonicae"? Being would seem to involve personhood, and crowds dissipate that state in their accretion of numbers. Auden slows down to reflect on this question—no listing at this point, and no epiphany, but a gradual pondering. Auden's poem pauses to take in this paradox of many dissolved into one, an entity without a conscience that undermines the ability of those gathered to act or feel independently. This is not the spectacle of "gathering multitudes" in "Out on the Lawn" (*SP* 32) or the "unintelligible multitude[s]" of "The Shield of Achilles" (*CP* 594). These multitudes are now spectators themselves, and they form a crowd not as a visual or demographic phenomenon but as a center of recognition in the meditations of the hours. The crowd imagined here, since it is connected with the crowd gathering to urge on the crucifixion, has an immediate and physical character quite different from the "unreal" public. But the crowd in "Sext" is not a community; community is reserved for later in the poem and is formed in the recognition of original sin.

Auden's language in section 3 of "Sext" becomes almost mystical as he dwells on the metaphysics of the crowd, more compelling to his imagination than the divinity of Christ, which he does not mention. The first couplet introduces the contradiction of "life-giving Earth" and death-dealing man, removing the crowd to a placeless "anywhere"—simultaneous and metaphysical. Auden gives the crowd a face (eyes and mouths, thus combining the prolific and the devourer of 1 and 2) but makes it "expressionless, perfectly blank" as this personless crowd-face obscures the face of the other as ethical being. This crowd phenomenology is underscored in the chimera-like chiasm: "the crowd sees only one thing / (which only the crowd can see)." Auden frames the boundaryless crowd in parentheses and in his ritual structure. The paradox and abstraction of the crowd presses on through the two-line stanzas, punctuated with pauses but few full stops. The crowd has a metaphysical "epiphany of that / which does whatever is done." Its inclusiveness ("the crowd rejects no one") is built on a negation, on complicity, not love: "only because of that can we say / all men are our brothers." Auden stresses the unity of the crowd as well as its negativity by repeating and pairing "one" and "only."

Having located the crowd uncomfortably "anywhere" in the opening line (not a mere abstraction but a recurrent and ever-present reality), Auden invokes the ritual of the canonical hours to make the crowd immediate to the imagination. And he shifts suddenly to first-person plural here. The "we" of the loud and angry crowd shouting "Crucify him" connects to the "we" of the brotherhood of man in mutual guilt—thus a crowd is converted to a sacred community and brings forth a special knowledge. Auden also uses "we" to indicate a universal in the Christian community, to press the point that the crowd is "us," come "to worship / the Prince of this world," "at this noon, on this hill, / in the occasion of this dying." For once, this "we" seems less that of the pontificating priest than of the "surprised" congregation. The "here" and "this" and "now" invoke an epiphany albeit in unceremonious lower case in counterpoint to the crowd's phantom being.

"Nones" (CP 632–35), though it was the first poem Auden composed for the sequence, seems propelled narratively by "Sext." It opens with the first-person plural that has been established and embedded in narrative: the collective witness to "this dying." The "we" of crowd collectivity is transforming into the "we" of Christian guilt, as in the gospel of Mark 15. As the crowd disperses it does not simply shake off this epiphany in a numb forgetfulness. The "we" speaking here is not the crowds of "infinitely many" mouths. It is a "we" known to solitude, a "we" of individual rather than collective reflection, "left alone with our feat," not only without god but without community, man confronting his guilty agency within the space of individual thought after the daemon that devoured it has departed. This "we" is predicated on individual guilt, in precise contrast to the crowd, which was predicated on the surrender of individual conscience. Importantly, though, the move away from the crowd of "Sext" is not a retreat back into the "I" of Adam's discrete being, which never arises in this poem. Auden mocks the drive to externalize guilt: "'It was a monster with one red eye / A crowd that saw him die, not I'." While this is true in one sense—the crowd overtakes the individual will—it does not exonerate anyone. The poem refuses this exculpation of "I" and insists on "we" throughout the poem, a "we" reanimated with individual choice and shared guilt.

Auden uses internal rhyme in "Nones" to reinforce the shock of recognition: "we are surprised by the ease and speed of our deed," he writes, creating ease and speed in the line. But the stanza as a whole is about the suspension of agency, the culture's reflection on what it has wrought. Ownership of the deed is stressed in the personal pronouns: "Outliving our act we stand where we are." Stupor, denial, retreat, aimless wandering are registered in a string of labyrinthine prepositions—"on," "over," "down," "through," "to," leading back to "a room . . . where our Double sits / Writing and does not look up." We are back to an image of human agency, of *poesis,* man "forgetting [himself] in a function." "All men are brothers" returns to the immediate encounter of writer and reader—of writer as reader. There is no hiding in the universal brotherhood, as there is in a crowd.

Agency, which flourished in "Sext," is now a burden haunted by responsibility for "this death": "We shall always now be aware / Of the deed into which they lead." But "Nones" also awakens the participants to the details of the sensuous world, a kind of rejuvenation after the previous withdrawal from all such noticing into the crowd's phantom being. Auden's plural nouns decenter effects—"brooks run," "telephones ring"—while ordinary lives slowly resume. Punctuation, internal within the line or occasionally marking an end, an edge, reins in the expansive feeling. Rhyme is dangerous; it leads us into conclusions as often as it discovers new direction. Auden makes us wary of rhyme in the first stanza, as "some chance rhyme / Like *will* and *kill*, comes to pass / Before we realize it." The moment is self-reflective, inclusive of the guilty poet. Indeed, the poet becomes exemplary of the guilt. In the second stanza the rhymes distance the speaker from his subject and take on a random character, "red eye" rhyming with "not I," "Collect" rhyming with "wrecked" to link the beginning of a line to its end. These rhymes mark dead and death-dealing orders, the work of the devourer. More negative rhymes arise in stanza 3, marking the recursive and negating character of repetition: "our projects under construction / Look only in one direction," but rhyme looks back: "rusted kettles . . . / buried nettles." Rhyme increasingly disappears from the poem as the ruin of an old order, the focus of meditation in "Nones," yields to the healing body. Our creaturely nature and sensuous being reawaken from the stupor of grief. The last stanza contains no rhyme, internal or end; recursive structures have been dropped and replaced by a continuous present. Again, sound and verse form more than rhetoric and imagery, do the work of making this experientially immediate.

Having dropped all rhyme in the last stanza of "Nones," Auden turns to something close to prose in "Vespers" (*CP* 635–37), though it has a spatial pattern if not an auditory one. "Prime" led with the pure orphic exuberance of Adam's awakening; here we arrive at Adam's grave and a familiarity with death and history. Auden's orientation is civil rather than orphic. "Vespers" is a disputation, presenting the struggle to reconcile politics and art. The dialogue between the utopian and Arcadian impulses suggests not only rival ideologies of the postwar era but the range of Auden's own thinking over the years. The pronouns of "Vespers" vary—you, I, he, our—but the momentum is again toward reconciliation and community, a "rendezvous between accomplices" in common guilt. This is a "cement of blood" that has nothing to do with race or lineage.

But "Horae Canonicae" is a cycle, and in "Compline" (*CP* 638–39) Auden begins the turn back to lyric's single voice, restoring internal rhyme. "Compline" is a poem of personal reflection more than convocation. The poem stresses free individuals in open, loving relation—"libera / me, libera C (dear C)." The "we" this time is "all poor s-o-b's who never / Do anything properly" (including poets). But the connection is not only negative; common recognition is the prelude to the forming of bonds (and we may remember that singing and dancing were important in the oratorio as well): "That we, too, may . . . join the dance / As it moves in perichoresis." *Perichoresis* is a crucial term for this sequence, not only as it turns back to its Greek meaning—to dance around—but as it evokes the Christian appropriation—the movement between one and many in the Trinity.

With "Lauds" (*CP* 639–40), "Horae Canonicae" closes in a tight lyric form, turning back from the prose of "Vespers." As if to mark a restored harmonious order or the circle of a dance after the story of a broken world, we have two rhymes and a refrain in three stanzas. In sharp contrast to the phantoms of the crowd of "Sext," here "men of their neighbors become sensible" in body and in mind, and plural and singular conscience converge to create congregation: "in solitude, for company." The line is original with Auden though it takes on a liturgical resonance in italicized repetition. It expresses the dialectical terms by which a community is distinguishable from a crowd. In "Horae Canonicae," then, we see Auden trying to solve the problem of the modern poet—to find or form genuine community—by way of a liturgical model.

8

Invitations to the Common

> Though nearly all the poems written in the last nineteen hundred years are the joint product of the Poet and the Historian, the collaboration is one of uneasy tension.
>
> —AUDEN, "READING"

General, Universal, Impersonal

When Wallace Stevens concludes, "we live in an old chaos of the sun,"[1] or when T. S. Eliot reflects, "we have lingered by the chambers of the sea,"[2] these poets cue us to closure and to the widening import of the experiences and feelings their poems have shared, even through their fragmented voices. Summative, epigrammatic, aphoristic statements contribute to poetry's eloquence as well as its reach and *gravitas*. These may be "momentary stays against confusion" arising out of historical circumstance, but they speak beyond their historical moment, bringing poet and reader into common ground at least for the term of exchange, even when the statements are paradoxical or enigmatic. ("We love the things we love for what they are.")[3] "We" propositions often introduce the philosophic mind, requiring our transhistorical assent to the incontrovertible voice of reason and quieting the emotional drama of a poem. By saying "we," the poet bridges the meditative and the communicative frameworks—self-dialogue, group alliance, oppositional stance, address to audience, these forms of convening open out to an unbounded and impersonal context. Matthew Arnold may address a lover, "let us be true / To one another," but in closing "Dover Beach" he presents not only a historical but a universal condition: "we are here on a darkling plain / Swept with confused alarms of struggle and flight."[4] "We" here makes the scenic details symbolic. But in modern literature especially this transfer to the common is often edgy and self-conscious. With what authority can the writer speak for all of us?

Virginia Woolf, in her famous essay announcing that "all human relations shifted" in 1910, writes in the first-person singular because "I do not want to attribute to the world at large the opinions of one solitary, ill-informed, and misguided individual."[5] The summative "we" can sound coercive or clubby. The movement toward an unbounded "we" in modern poetry often proceeds in struggle and doubt. As Rosanna Warren has written of Geoffrey Hill: "No I, no you, no we, can be trusted to remain the same even in the course of a short passage in these poems, and in the struggle to track them, the reader is jarred into an uncomfortable, radicalized vision of selfhood and its relations."[6] These shifts test each extension from the particular to the general; they locate more restrictive, interlocking "we's" and acknowledge the aspirational and prospective character of the universal more than its logical necessity.

Yet poetry has never really surrendered its aim to speak for the most universal human experiences, and the plural first person remains a way to indicate its reach. Helen Vendler is skeptical that "we" is an acceptable way of achieving this "desired all-purpose abstraction."[7] She observes that Wallace Stevens's "'we' is perhaps tarnished for us by its long use in 'high sentence.' It belongs to the rhetoric of sermons, of political oratory, of moral verse." Stevens, she suggests, preferred the impersonal forms of "one" and "he."[8] But in fact, Stevens did often speak "of ourselves and of our origins"[9]; his verse is full of successful "we" propositions that strive for the universal even as they resist the didactic. This "we" is a potential community, based on a "search" that is both individual and common; it is not a creed for the collective:

> If ever the search for a tranquil belief should end,
> The future might stop emerging out of the past,
> Out of what is full of us; yet the search
> And the future emerging out of us seem to be one.[10]

By the mid-twentieth century, broad, abstract, and general statements concerning all of us, if discouraged during modernism, became commonplace in poets of a philosophical turn such as Robert Penn Warren, Richard Wilbur, Howard Nemerov, and Allen Tate. Even so scrupulous a poet as Elizabeth Bishop made frequent use of the summative pronoun: "our knowledge is historical, flowing, and flown."[11]

Vendler and Johnson have emphasized a connection in lyric between the individual and the universal, largely bypassing the "we" of the historical group. The "stripping away" of the social and biographical particulars of "a socially specific self"—the sloughing off of the contingencies of the historical person—makes room for a revelation of "soul," for Vendler.[12] W. R. Johnson is less abstract in his account of poetry's reciprocal "universality" in relation to its particulars: "The poet dramatizes the universal, makes it vivid and plausible; and, at the same time, he universalizes an experience that was peculiarly his own, thus rendering it clear and intelligible. It is the delicate and yet powerful fusion of the individual and the universal that characterizes lyric poetry."[13] For both Vendler and Johnson, poetry's ability to communicate these universals depends not only on abstract words and symbols but on what Johnson calls its "pronominal dynamic." Neither critic finds lyric's universality in the erasure of the "I" or in such antirhetorical modes as hermeticism, on one hand, or "snapshot" objectivism on the other. For Johnson, the modern forms of impersonality in poetry (certain imagist practices, for instance) fail to activate their universals or invite community. Such poetry may be expression, he argues, but it is not discourse. "The disintegration of pronominal form entails the disintegration of emotional content . . . a totally unrhetorical poetry will be, as we have come to know all too well, a poetry void of passion, void of choosing, void of rational freedom. . . . What is essential . . . to lyric is rhetoric, and essential to this lyrical rhetoric . . . is the pronominal form of lyric identity, the dynamic configuration of lyrical pronouns that defines and vitalizes the situation of lyrical discourse."[14]

What I have been showing throughout this book, and will continue to discuss here, is the way poetry sometimes makes its reach for universals a dramatic process that involves not only singular "you's" and "I's" but a scale of "we's" and group affiliations. It wants to resonate for unknown readers whose situations are unique but for whom something fundamental in the poem remains true, if differently true, for them. Poetry can keep its inclusive "we" open and flexible, a space of the common, a space Buber says is "on fire" with the dynamism of human speech.[15] It achieves this by checking narrower configurations and often pressing against the voice of the hegemon; it moves cautiously and in degrees from the particular to the general, testing the impersonal for unconscious personal bias, recognizing many "we's" and frames of communication along the way, and widening or qualifying its scope but also infusing it with broad human emotional concern.

There is no single rhetoric of universality, of course, and the general, the impersonal, the abstract, and the universal do not all belong to one class of concepts. Impersonality does not necessarily produce universality, and the latter may arise without any of the other rhetorical strategies. Poetry can convey its aim of inclusiveness not only through *abstraction* (its stripping away or symbolic refiguring of social and historical particulars) but also often from *generality*, especially in its employment of epigrams, aphorisms, and other summary propositions and questions (Yeats's "How can we know the dancer from the dance?") that move out from a dramatized utterance and give it explicit thematic meaning.[16] General propositions have certainly been one of the ways lyric has always enhanced its authority, despite Ezra Pound's warning to "go in fear of abstractions."[17] And the pronoun "we" is often part of such generalizing rhetoric, giving wide epideictic force to state-ments. When Auden writes, "we are lived by powers we pretend to under-stand" in his 1939 "In Memory of Ernst Toller" (*CP* 247–48), he performs a choral function while producing the elevated atmosphere of disinterested wisdom. The urge to find meaning in human experience implies a move to generality. He might have said "Man is lived," but the impersonal form seems relatively inert. In saying "we," he opens out a drama of inclusion. In the course of the poem, Auden has already addressed the German expres-sionist playwright personally as "Ernst" several times, in declarative and interrogative sentences that dramatize the communication and probe the meaning of Toller's suicide. This makes the mourning immediate and partic-ular. The "we" takes up the speaker and Toller, certainly. And Auden's "we" throughout the war years and immediately after encompasses a traumatized Europe. Elegy often confronts the fragmentation caused by death and aims to heal and reestablish community. In this poem of 1939, "we" is not only Auden and "Ernst" but also a contemporary world in distress, fearing "the enemy bullet" and anxious for "our friends." By saying "we," Auden projects communal hope against the fractious present. All these "we's" enter into the generalization "We are lived by powers we pretend to understand" and give it heightened, situational impact, not just impersonal authority. The proposition extends beyond the circumstances that give rise to it but never loses touch with those circumstances. The closing qualifier to this general proposition, "but existence is believing / We know for whom we mourn and who is grieving," converts the negations and uncertainties of the poem into an affirmation that, while local to the deceased, speaks to the human condi-tion, experienced personally by every reader but common to all. Indeed, the modern elegy offers a compelling example of how poetry evokes universals while retaining particularity and group affiliation. "In Memory of Sigmund Freud" (*SP* 100–103) mourns "this doctor" (who is also a Victorian type), and whose life's work was the study of what he saw as universal tendencies in the private psyche. He was both a great generalizer and an enemy of "the Generalized Life." In remembering him, Auden uses the first-person plural throughout, evoking a suffering wartime community ("there are so many we shall have to mourn"), a general rhetorical "we" that stands in for the orator ("of whom shall we speak?"), and a modern point of view that lends perspec-tive while retaining diversity. "'To us . . . he is no more a person / Now but a whole climate of opinion / Under whom we conduct our differing lives." As the poem develops, the first-person plural moves out from the occasion and context of Freud's death to his legacy, involving a set of universalizing prop-ositions about the private life: "he would have us remember . . . / Because it needs our love."

For those critics who wish to retain the claim of "universality" for poetry, one answer has been to distinguish "universality" from "generality." Robert von Hallberg admits, "General propositions themselves have few advocates among poets."[18] (Though poets delight in making commonplace books, made up of such propositions, and drawing on them for epigraphs.) "Generality can be defined statistically; some texts . . . refer more widely than others," he remarks.[19] "Generality is a practical matter; universality is an intellectual one."[20] We might add that generality is a rhetorical matter, universality a hermeneutic one. Yet von Hallberg goes on to recover not only universality but also generality, by showing the ways poetic language achieves a broad thrust through figurative language. And here we may wrestle with definition, for "to generalize" is a verb that may be transitive or intransitive, leading to some confusion about the status of general propositions in poetry. As a transitive verb "to generalize" suggests a natural function of inductive reasoning. The derived generality has validity insofar as it is tested and conforms to relevant particulars on its horizon. It is an activity of the reader, triggered by the very nature of literature. Without an object the verb "to generalize" suggests thinking in abstractions and broad principles; it can be linked to deductive reasoning when the abstraction colors the interpretation of a particular. Poetic thinking requires a constant interplay, a momentum from the individual to the reader that produces generality always inflected with or cognizant of difference and distinctness so that generality does not become inert, etiolated proposition, a view from nowhere held by nobody.[21]

To generalize from a narrow group of "I's" to a universal "we" risks obscuring the diversity of "you's," of course, and covering up distinction. One solution has been to avoid generalization, to cling to particulars as impersonal points of connection. "Unrestrained individuation"[22] may seem to lead to fragmentation, but for many modern poets particularity was the back door to universality. "The local is the only universal," William Carlos Williams frequently repeated, extrapolating from Dewey.[23] In "Against the Weather," he wrote:

> Being an artist I can produce, if I am able, universals of general applicability. If I succeed in keeping myself objective enough, sensual enough, I can produce the factors, the concretions of materials by which others shall understand and so be led to use—that they may the better see, touch, taste, enjoy—their own world differing as it may from mine. By mine, they, different, can be discovered to be the same as I, and, thrown into contrast, will see the implications of a general enjoyment through me. . . . [Art] closes up the ranks of understanding. It shows the world at one with itself.[24]

Williams, in striking contrast to later Auden, seeks a universality that does not rely on generalizing or homogenizing rhetoric. He avoids language that erases the here and now of human experience. The generalizing function is left to the reader; the emphasis is on the world's diversity and the infinite networks of connection across time and place. For Williams these networks are achieved by an intensification of the sensuous particulars. But for W. R. Johnson, persons discursively present must animate the sensuous reality, at least in pronominal form. "To generalize," in Johnson's ideal, is a directive mode of thought, epideictic and dramatic, requiring agency in pronouns, not just inert propositions.

If "the general" has aroused suspicion, so has "the impersonal." In her early poetry, Bishop used "we" not only as a generalizing pronoun but also as a form of the impersonal when narrating a dream or experience: "We'd rather have the iceberg than the ship / although it meant the end of travel."[25] (Later Bishop's "we" may more clearly indicate the presence of a companion in the narrative.) Michael Hofmann argued that in Bishop's early work she uses "we" negatively as a suppression of the motivating "I,"[26] and similar points have been made about the modernist poets who influenced her, such as Moore, Stevens, and Eliot. In Eliot's "Interlude in London," "we" creates authority by depersonalizing experience and allowing the reader's inclusion in the story.[27] Maud Ellmann has argued that such gestures of impersonality cover up personal drives and desires, and Hofmann implies the same for Bishop.[28] But we discover different effects if we focus on the poems themselves rather than their biographical background. Ellmann and Hofmann reflect an attitude developing in the late 1960s in which the generalizing "we" became associated with Cold War conformity and the repression of personal life and political struggle in favor of an impersonal Everyman.

But "impersonality" as a means toward the discovery of universals has many thoughtful contemporary defenders. The pronoun "we" may indeed play a role in making the impersonal an active condition of mind. Sharon Cameron's reconsideration of impersonality reanimates the concept, replacing absence and passivity with decreation and ecstasy. Impersonality is less a state than an ideal, an active self-abandonment in the movement toward universality. Impersonality for Cameron is thus aporetic; it obtains in the struggle to depersonalize, which is not a single achievement but a constant effort, a performance in which the ego is sloughed off. There is no room for subjective personhood in the ideal of the impersonal.

The principle of impersonality in modern poetry is most fully associated with T. S. Eliot. Any "we" that he offers may be taken as impersonal and not attached to any historic collective. In "Little Gidding," Cameron reveals, pronouns may mark phenomena as experience, "without being experienced as someone's." "If 'we' pluralizes experience, the 'See' undoes the plurality. The recognitional moment is not properly experienced as collective, though it is also not properly experienced as personal."[29] The impersonal, so bound up with dissociation from personal experience, would seem to be outside, even antagonistic to, the social, which relies on intersubjectivity. And yet the intellectual and emotional state of the impersonal opens out from the personal to acknowledge the limits of one's own power to articulate a truth.[30] And as it moves toward articulation it inevitably reintroduces the personal, acknowledges it along with its "condition," its necessary saying-together. Though function words such as "we" may indicate the impersonal, as an ideal it stands outside language. (Eliot saw the impersonal as an ideal, while Auden saw it as a human failure to connect to history.) Insofar as the impersonal can be spoken, then, it must enter a realm of persons, of You and I meeting in the common. However, this meeting must not become univocal in its quest for the universal. As Simone Weil asserts, "There is no way from the collective to the impersonal."[31] The impersonal, that is, cannot be a collective ego or group identity. But this does not mean the process of discovering the impersonal is void of personal pronouns. Weil's pronouns are "nomadic" or "migratory," according to Cameron.[32]

Peter MacDonald wrote *Serious Poetry* before Cameron's essays appeared, but he anticipates her understanding of impersonality. MacDonald wants to vigorously separate impersonality from the persuasive collectivity of the first-person plural, which courts the reader with the promise of familiarity rather than universality. Like Cameron, MacDonald considers the nature of the impersonal in Eliot's *Four Quartets* and its relationship to personal pronouns. Many poets, he argues, use the force of personality to create an audience's sense of community. For MacDonald, Larkin's poetry "is held to speak to 'us' and for 'us' and is written by a 'personality' with whom 'we' can identify."[33] But the poet is not so much everyman as one-of-us, with the sense of inviting an in-group familiarity. Of Larkin's first-person plural that swells in "Church Going," MacDonald writes that it is literally a vehicle: "The 'personality' that hitches a ride there becomes ours in giving itself to us, and offers the most exquisite 'frisson' of contemporary literature: the feeling that the 'personality' and the reader are on intimate terms, and are even, for the moment, united. If words are not the obedient vehicles of this thrill, they are simply getting in the way."[34] But he continues, suspiciously combining these quotes to give one note: "Poems, and the 'personalities' that make themselves 'ours,' present a much more appealing, and less forbidding, subject than a series of works that rely on form for authority." "But there is a problem with 'our,' and this problem hinges on the very authority which much critical writing renders invisible. Who are 'we'? and, more problematically still, when are 'we'?"[35] The essential job of serious poetry is "to work against the grain of opinion, or in complex and guarded relation to it, so as to create an original order in which language overpowers the 'weight of judgment or opinion' through the individual (and essentially unrepeatable) form."[36] Form, for MacDonald, is individual and yet impersonal and thus becomes an alternative inclusiveness to Larkin's narrow in-group "we." Eliot's *Four Quartets*, he argues, invoking I. A. Richards, propels the reader to "general truth," but "the poetry is more important than the 'us' whom it may (or may not) be capable of 'saving.'"[37] MacDonald distinguishes poetry's mode of general but unrepeatable formal truth from the philosopher's, which relies on the content of truth propositions.

> "The language of poetry" as a medium for communication is not quite the same medium as that in which "logical propositions" are framed and understood; but Eliot's clear implication here . . . is that the communication of wisdom is a matter of finding common ground between poet and reader in poetic language, almost a collaborative process.
>
> In light of this, Eliot's "we," like his "you" or "I," are important indicators and are implicated in the "humility" that conditions "wisdom."[38]

MacDonald seems to be arguing, then, that the pronouns in Eliot's poems do not create illusions of personality that might (as in Larkin) recruit the reader to an assumed community of the knowing. Rather, they operate as markers of the more direct interaction between poetic language and reader, mediated in the impersonal dimension of "form," which does not rely on the poet's personality as an intervening voice to transmit experience.

Auden in the 1950s is trying to affirm a universal that allows for historical distinctness. His postwar work continues a struggle between history and form that is central to modernism. While Auden's Christianity and the Christian-inflected philosophy he was reading provided him with a conceptual framework for exploring this tension, he still needed to find a rhetoric and stance that could embody poetically, and convey as feeling, this difficult rendering of historical experience into meaningful and universalizing form.

Bondage to Clio and the Discourse of Man

"If not a poem had been written," Auden would often repeat from the late thirties on, history would be more or less unchanged. "For poetry makes nothing happen" (*SP* 89). But this does not mean that Auden severed all relations with history or that his "we" was not embedded in history. Auden's poetry is often addressed to historical trauma, and the "we" arises from this collective shock. If poetry seeks to understand and move the human heart, it must reckon with human embodiment in time and with the social forces and ethical choices that shape a life. And while poetry may seek to address "all of us" in our common humanity, past, present, and future, it must acknowledge and account for the fact that "each of us" lives uniquely in time. The first-person plural can be a flexible and mobile register that engages and motivates a reader in the search for general truths. But it can also seem coercive or presumptive, removed from circumstance, setting down principles and imperatives more reasoned than felt.

A consensus was emerging in the fifties, at least among poet-critics: Auden's poetry after the war lacked the vigor of his earlier work. Philip Larkin's complaint that Auden's American writing was characterized by "loss of vividness" and "abstract windiness" echoed Randall Jarrell's complaint that the poetry had taken on "that flatness and vagueness and deadness of a bad essay."[39] Auden's poetry since his move to America, many argued, relied on theory and generalization, removed from local concerns, and had little dramatic energy. Auden's tendency to pile up sententious "we" propositions certainly contributed to the sense that didactic rhetoric had overtaken his verse. One cause of his bad habits, as these critics saw it, was the heavy helping of philosophical prose, often quasitheological, that Auden was taking in, especially in his activity as a reviewer. Auden had become, as Philip Larkin put it, "a reader rather than a writer."[40] The work of John Fuller, Edward Mendelson, and others has documented the extent to which some of Auden's poems may indeed be seen as versifications of ideas derived from Charles Williams, Martin Buber, Reinhold Niebuhr, Paul Tillich, Charles Norris Cochrane, Rudolf Krassner, Eugen Rosenstock-Huessy, Simone Weil, and other wartime and postwar cosmopolitan thinkers with a theological orientation toward history. Christian liturgical *rituals*, as we have seen, offered Auden a form for imagining spiritual community against the fragmentation and crisis of contemporary history. Judeo-Christian social *philosophers* offered a lens for interpreting that history and a moral direction for the future. Not only the ideas but the rhetoric of this intellectual prose enters Auden's work in many poems—its synoptic and schematic divisions of history into "ages," its presiding forces of Nature and History, its talk of "Destiny" and "Necessity," of "humanity." Larkin and Jarrell may exaggerate the extent to which Auden's later poetry suffers from this "abstract windiness"—there are numerous moments of vibrant diction and imagery, narrative and dramatic movement, portraiture, verbal wit, and modern eloquence in the later work. The sonnet "Our Bias," for instance, manages to use an inclusive first-person plural, epigrammatic phrasing, and even abstract allegorical figures such as "Time" within a lively linguistic frame of fresh conceits and arch understatement. But there is little question that the proportion of Auden's poetry devoted to setting down general propositions about history and moral choice, removed from experience and derived from his reading, had increased. Auden's later poetry has had many defenders, notably Edward Mendelson and Alan Jacobs, who argue that the excellence of Auden's postwar work should not be measured in terms of the same poetic principles that shaped his earlier poetry. He is working in different rhetorical modes and with different ends in mind, especially the aim to identify broad principles for interpreting recent history. Certainly the modern social and religious philosophy Auden was reading and reviewing influenced his *style* as much as his *thought* in the forties and fifties. But this influence reverberates variously in his work and is manifest quite differently and with variable success, as Auden shifts from liturgical to Horatian models for addressing community, with their differing registers of civic voice.

I do not intend here to tackle the broad range of Auden's strategies of generalization. Rather, I want to look at a specific problem for Auden: how to reconcile the fact of historical particularity with the imperative of poetic universality. We can see the tensions present in Auden's later work between two kinds of impersonality: general proposition and documentary fact. In his strongest later poems, Auden eschews the documentary ideal as too detached from meaning and purpose, but he also tests his abstract universalizing impulse against the historical contingencies of human knowledge and experience. I explore his increasing resistance to the documentary mode and its form of impersonality as he seeks a more subjective yet comprehensive interpretation of history. In "Memorial for the City" and "Homage to Clio," Auden works out two different ways to say "we." One way evokes an indeterminate community, congregated in the wake of historical trauma and searching for general truth; the other presents the individual poet as representative figure in a reckoning with historical meaning. As Auden turns between these poems from liturgical to Horatian rhetoric, his pronouns change, from a sermonic to a more dialogical first-person plural. Auden's "we" in "Memorial for the City" is a collective subject with a social being (as well as an abstract pronoun with an inclusive referent), but in later poetry "we" increasingly encompasses everyone's singular encounter with history and posits a potential community through a more individual but representative poetic address. Both forms of "we," orator and everyman, present pitfalls for Auden.

It is helpful to put Auden's propositional language in its wartime and postwar intellectual milieu. Mark Greif, in *The Age of the Crisis of Man*, has investigated the swelling of the kind of intellectual prose that Auden was reviewing during the war and afterward. Greif acknowledges how hollow and boring this "discourse of Man" can be for our reading, accustomed as we are to a relativistic, perspectival orientation that emphasizes locality and particularity. Phrases such as "the dignity of man" seem to have little vital significance, too vague and inclusive to be debatable; they are universals easily recruited to partisan interests or at least encouraging inertia and passivity, a feel-good ethics with little at stake and often with nefarious consequences. But Greif distinguishes "cant" (where words really don't mean anything and are a matter of "default thought" rather than thought-provoking ideas) from what he calls "empty" discourse, which creates the potential for conversation and community. "An empty discourse is one that behaves as if it wishes to be filled with a single inductive or deductive answer—a definitive argument meant to persuade all hearers and end inquiry through complete satisfaction—but in fact generates the continuation of attempts or tacitly admits to unanswerability."[41] While we may no longer feel engaged by such "empty discourse" and while its suitability for poetry can be questioned, "the discourse of Man" can be distinguished from cant, among other ways, through its inner contradictions. For example, this discourse often acknowledges perspectival limits to historical knowledge even as it uses an impersonal, universalizing language. Greif argues that the work of Reinhold Niebuhr, Hannah Arendt, Lewis Mumford, and others (many of whom Auden reviewed and revered) should be understood within J. L. Austin's speech-act framework, as performance rather than description. Such a discourse impacts the world through utterance of its desire and search for explanations, rather than registering and naming *a priori* reality. "The underlying utterance," Greif writes, "remains both collective and imperative. 'We must give a new or renewed statement of what man is.' One does not, in fact, expect to stop others from giving answers; one anticipates ever more answers. The proliferation of answers, not their conclusion, seems to be the underlying point."[42] The "discourse of Man," then, though it deals in general propositions, offers itself as conversation more than definitive description. Many of the books Auden was reading and reviewing in the postwar period can be taken as early examples of this style of motivated thought and argument. Auden's commitment to Christianity may have been final, but Christian ideas in the arena of contemporary philosophy and theology were not revelation but propositions to be tried on for their value in understanding and responding to modern history. If Auden viewed these models in the way Greif suggests they were intended, we can see why he might appropriate them for poetry, where the illocutionary features of language abound, and affect is as important as final truth. Poetic statements have a different status as truth claims from the impersonal statements of philosophy—they may seem to want to be filled by definitive meaning, but their rhetorical context works against such closure, and their style is part of their meaning. Poetry makes propositional statements in a provisional and experimental spirit since it is the form, the voicing, and the dramatization of thought, more than the substance of propositions, that determines its power.

    A common theme in the genre of works Auden was reading is that "man's" knowledge is always embedded and limited, that his truth cannot be perspective-less and above history. Modern culture needs an engaged and problem-solving, not an impersonal and dissociated, response to history.

One studies the past for the sake of the present and future. This does not preclude an abstract and comprehensive framing, but it warns against totalizing schemata that only appear disinterested. The shift from an impersonal subject, "Man," to the personal "We" is often a way of registering this ambiguity since "we," though it may be inclusive, retains a sense of a speaker embedded in a specific communicative framework. This ambiguity arises in many of the passages Auden quotes from writers of the forties and fifties.

In 1941, for instance, Auden quotes a caveat from Niebuhr's *Christianity and Power Politics:* "The Renaissance thought that it had found methods of extricating the universal man from the particular man, imbedded in the flux of nature. . . . As a consequence the tragic character of human history, in which man is perennially betrayed to use his freedom for destruction as well as construction, is not understood" (*Prose* II 109). Niebuhr often favored the third-person impersonal "man": "Man is not divided against himself so that the essential man can be extricated from the nonessential . . . man is a finite spirit lacking identity with the whole, but yet a spirit capable in some sense of envisioning the whole so that he easily commits the error of imagining himself the whole which he envisages" (*Prose* II 133). But the detached philosopher readily yields to the concerned theologian. Niebuhr argues that liberalism needs Christianity and the idea of original sin in particular to return the "I" of free choosing to the "We" of tradition and universal brotherhood, without the error of mistaking one for another. Auden summarizes Niebuhr's argument: "The Catholic emphasizes the initial assent, the Protestant the continuous process of voluntary assent. The former is therefore always in danger of identifying the eternal with some particular historical social form; the latter is always in danger of ignoring the concrete realities of a historical situation altogether" (*Prose* II 134). The principle of original sin, of human fallibility in the dimension of history, becomes the principle on which a universal "we" is built, a principle opposite to the romantic focus on the transcendent soul that identifies the self with the universe. But Niebuhr tended to shift to "we" when presenting himself as an engaged intellectual, bringing Christian theology to contemporary Western politics. For instance, in *Christianity and Power Politics* (1940), concerning why the Christian church is not pacifist, he moves around in his pronouns as he guides the reader through his arguments. This persuasive oratorical maneuver, so common in wartime and midcentury writers (Marianne Moore's "In Distrust of Merits," for instance, a work likely influenced by Niebuhr), forms a bond with auditors and readers. "Do we not know that the sinful will-to-power may be compounded with the most ideal motives and may use the latter as its instruments and vehicles?"[43] As if to discount his own "will-to-power" in the presumptive "we," he shifts to the first-person singular, "Even as I write," and to the impersonal, "one is reminded . . ." But soon he returns to "We cannot fully trust the motives of any ruling class or power."[44] Niebuhr's "we" may be indeterminate, but it is still local and urgent in comparison to the impersonal "man." It speaks in absolutes yet against the collective and the generalized life, and against the hubris of superior knowledge. It calls for civic spirit and concern for others but resists exclusive group affiliations or really any social embodiment of the collective vision. It tends to be a "we" rallied in resistance to such a vision, if also in resistance to the narrow preoccupations of "I." "We must declare that no historic community deserves the final devotion of man." As Auden writes, "Cognition is always a distinct historical act accompanied by hope and fear" (*Prose* II 214).

Such evocations of a boundless "we," in the name of arguments that question the ability to extricate the universal from the particular, arise often in the work Auden reviews and cites. "One must not be I, but still less must one be We," writes Simone Weil.[45] Yet while she uses the impersonal "one" here, she often, and in all the many passages Auden includes in his *Aphorisms*, uses "we" in a general sense, meaning all of us, but also each of us on our own, a plurality seen in a shared condition or imperative, not a collective mass. This "we" is aspirational, qualified, dynamic—not a fixed and agreed upon Logos. For instance in the aphorisms Auden cites, Weil uses "we" to acknowledge subjectivity in a deontic mode: "We have to endure the discordance between imagination and fact. It is better to say, 'I am suffering,' than to say, 'This landscape is ugly'"; "A hurtful act is the transference to others of the degradation which we bear in ourselves."[46] In Auden's poetry as well, a "we" invoking a local, modern experience often moves into an impersonal, generalizing "we" standing for all of humanity. History is both the impediment to universal knowledge and the inescapable condition of man, the context in which discourse arises as speech act, and the constraining perspective through which humans encounter general truths. Auden admonishes, "The louder the voices grow that demand strong beliefs, universal values, and nothing more, the more necessary it becomes to warn, 'It is not enough that a belief should be strong—it must also be true. It is not enough that a value should be universal—it must also be really unconditional'" (*Prose* II 153). For Auden, as for many of the thinkers he cited, these issues were bound up with, and even symbolized by, pronouns, which position us in relation to one another and to our environment. Auden was especially influenced in this sense of pronominal paradigms by the work of Eugen Rosenstock-Huessy.

Eugen Rosenstock-Huessy, a religious philosopher Niebuhr had recommended to Auden, became one of the poet's most extensive and direct influences over a thirty-year period, perhaps because language is at the core of his philosophy. In the introduction to a translation of his work, *I Am an Impure Thinker*, Auden wrote:

> Rosenstock-Huessy has uncovered many truths hidden from his predecessors. . . . Whatever he may have to say about God, Man, the World, Time, etc., Rosenstock-Huessy always starts out from his own experience as a human being, who must pass through successive stages between birth and death, learning something essential from each one of them.[47]

While Rosenstock-Huessy's writing deals in abstract paradigms, he also presents himself as a representative thinker rather than an impersonal authority; he writes as someone living in history. Both the abstraction and the subjectivity appeal to Auden as a way to reconcile poet and historian. Over several decades Rosenstock-Huessy worked out a schematic theory of human awareness and choice in relation to language, a grammar of history, which he mapped specifically onto pronouns. He built on Martin Buber's *I and Thou* (1921) and developed a more complex axial thesis in which all personal pronouns are included and in which every person is involved in all pronoun positions.[48] Rosenstock-Huessy argues that pronouns delineate a fundamental grammar of human understanding that involves human interactions with others and with the universe, spatially and in time.

For Rosenstock-Huessy, linguistic structures form and gain meaning in social reality and conversely serve as a guide to that reality. Grammar, he says, is the "Baedeker of social relations." "We" is perhaps the most important axis for this philosopher. "We" requires communication. "All 'we's are historically created by a successful fusion of some speaker and some listeners."[49] By definition, then, "we" cannot sponsor absolutes, though it may express ideas as if they were universals; and, if these ideas continue a forward-looking "thou" momentum, "we" may remain open to new voices. While Rosenstock-Huessy emphasizes the "we" that forms and changes traditions, the most important mood is the imperative. It is the mood that sets human consciousness and society in motion. Not the I but the You comes first, and its imperative propels us to the future of community, to We. In his section on pronouns, Rosenstock-Huessy leavens his sociolinguistics by breaking into verse:

> Man is beyond the It and I.
> The "I" is boundless; "It" asks "why?"
> By "you" I'm changed into your "thee,"
> And all together sing their we.[50]

These lines amount to little more than a mnemonic jingle, outlining his axes of relation, but they share features with many of Auden's pronoun poems, from "Another Time" (1939) to "Aubade" (1972). It is often Auden's weaker poems that show Rosenstock-Huessy's rhetorical influence most obviously, as in these cases where the philosopher-historian's ideas are transcribed into verse. But Rosenstock-Huessy's fundamental ideas about the need for subjective and purposive historical vision, and the sense that historical flourishing or crisis might be understood in terms of relations marked pronominally, become infused in Auden's social imagination. The best poems don't just set down but struggle with the pronominal scheme and relation of universal to particular.

The Poet, the Historian, and the Camera Eye: "Memorial for the City" and "Homage to Clio"

The uneasy tension between the poet and the historian is a theme in Auden's wartime and postwar poetry, and it also informs his rhetorical choices. The poet's disposition, Auden suggests, inclines him most toward his inner life— his sense of beauty in the natural world and in his own creations—and toward ideas of transcendence and permanence. But the pressure of the *polis*, of men pressed together in conflict or cooperation, in sheer proximity, requires his "collaboration" with the historian. History is the dimension of the *polis*, of men in crowds, communities, and societies, to use Auden's terms. But what does the poet bring to this collaboration? Why is he not merely displaced by the historian in times of public crisis when everyone's attention is on urgent public events rather than nature or private satisfactions?

Auden wrote several poems at midcentury that grapple with these questions, which he understands at least in part as a problem of rhetoric. How shall the poet speak of history, and how shall he address the *polis* without becoming merely topical? What role can subjective feeling and thought, what role can imagination, have in the approach to history? Rosenstock-Huessy clearly helped Auden formulate a historical understanding that would justify the poet's subjective feeling and thought, and his preference for the symbolic over the literal and factual. The impersonal facts and patterns of historical reality have meaning in the network of relations formed through time by experiencing subjects. This emphasis offered Auden a new way of "collaborating" with the historian. History was not just a series of fragmented events, one thing after another, nor an inevitable chain of relations to be seen only in terms of impersonal logic. It was a consequence of choices and aspirations made by individuals living in time and forging a future. Rosenstock-Huessy's "man" is always in this sense "we" rather than "he," and the past, if it is "they" externally, is also "we," a community formed in the network of imperatives. Literature then becomes relevant both as a symbolic and subjective mode of expression, and as an institution with traditions and conventions that connect a human community over time.

Rosenstock-Huessy had a particular antagonism toward the documentary mode and especially the camera, which recorded facts as fragmented, impersonal surfaces rather than internalized and felt realities. Auden latched on to this idea, forswearing documentary modes that had once fascinated him. Photography externalizes history, offers itself as transparent record, an eye without an "I," indeed without any internal pronouns, "you" or "we." It belongs to the impersonal, external realm of He and They. But what is the artist's responsibility to history? In presenting a subjective view of history, he may wish to transfigure fact to symbol, but the external truths of his individual encounter with the social and natural world (the I/It relation) also have a claim on the intellect and challenge the poet's readiness to say "we." Camera objectivity may flatten reality and present it only as visible surface, but it also records particularity and thus the distinctness of events and conditions, whereas the symbolic imagination wants to generalize. In "Memorial for the City," Auden would explicitly reject the camera's way of seeing. But Auden's dismissal of the camera has a defensive quality about it, and he would face the "unique Historical fact" and even its visual embodiment more directly, if without consummation, in "Homage to Clio."

While Auden frequently acknowledged his incapacity for representing the sensory dimension of life, he had long recognized the importance of the sensorium through collaborative and mixed-media projects. Photography in particular played an important role for Auden as part of a documentary thrust in the thirties. His own photographs in *Letters from Iceland* and *Journey to a War* are far more than supporting illustrations, however. In many ways, as Marsha Bryant has shown, these books were antidocumentary in their orientation, but the camera was still a legitimate medium for Auden. Through angle, cropping, juxtaposition, and other means he was using photography as an expressive, even a subjective medium, often revealing features of the scene or person that diary notations or official rhetoric passed over or characterized differently. Auden the cameraman made bold choices of subject matter and angle that challenged norms of reportorial photography and exposed the camera's intervention, connecting an "It" with an "I." Still, photography, while it localized subject matter, also seemed to present history impersonally, without intervention, and without pronouns. In "A Bride in the 30's," the photograph album captures what the narrow focus of the self-absorbed lovers cannot see in the moment. Even "Musée des Beaux Arts" has its visual evidence. Yet by the time Auden is writing "Memorial for the City," he has rejected documentary style and indeed the whole visible realm as superficial and incapable of penetrating the meaning of history. It might capture facts, freezing them into "eternal facts," but it could not capture "historical fact[s]," in which events are linked to human relations and ethical choices. The visual realm for Auden was

"Greek," belonged to "Homer's World, not ours," and was purely spatial in its understanding, in contrast to the Christian, internalized experience of time, which he associates with music. The Greeks understood the world externally and formally in terms of Fate and Destiny; the Christians saw it verbally, internally and morally, in terms of Choice, Error, and Grace. Auden had decided that the truths which concern him are invisible ones, truths of a moral and spiritual nature discovered in discourse, truths that the camera cannot access and, in fact (he felt), distorts.[51]

Auden's repudiation of the impersonal writer-as-camera-eye is most explicit in his often-cited late poem "I Am Not a Camera" (1962), where he evokes Rosenstock-Huessy to answer Isherwood's 1945 declaration on the first page of Berlin Stories, "I am a camera."[52] Auden used Rosenstock-Huessy's aperçu, "Photographic life is always either trivial or already sterilized," as the epigraph for his poem (CP 841). The camera's truths were either too narrowly particular or too impersonal. It cannot convert the phenomenal "It" to "Thou"; it deals with vision but not Vision.

> To call our sight Vision
> implies that, to us,
> all objects are subjects.

These ideas about the subjective view of history and the shallowness of the impersonal documentary mode become particularly focused in two poems, "Memorial for the City" and "Homage to Clio," in which Auden reflects on the imperatives of history and eschews the impersonal perspective, trying to identify a place for the symbolic and literary imagination in the interpretation of history. Both of these poems make significant use of the first-person plural as they consider the meaning and perspective of history, and the place of the individual in the historical community, but they differ substantially in their approach to rhetoric. In the first Auden writes as an orator in a time of public crisis, in the second as a lone poet addressing the muse of history. "Memorial for the City" opens up history for the subjective, literary imagination by linking the historical city with the eternal city central to a Christian understanding of time. Auden eschews the impersonal "eye of the camera" and evokes a "we" of modern Western tradition and Christian community, in the congregational style similar to what he had employed in "Horae Canonicae," though without the narrative arc. "Homage to Clio" is in many ways a return to the concerns of "Memorial," but it deals more directly with the poet's own situation as a representative subject. Here, Auden's "we" is at once wider, evoking the common condition of man without allusions to specific historical episodes, and narrower, speaking for poets and their special relation to the muse of history. In the struggle to find a place for the poet in the account of historical time, Auden acknowledges what he had repressed, the superior capacity of the camera eye to represent the "the unique / Historical fact" (*CP* 610). In this sense at least, "Homage to Clio" might be taken as a palinode to "Memorial for the City."

While "Memorial for the City" was dedicated to Charles Williams at his death, it draws from Rosenstock-Huessy's history of the Christian world and his arguments about the immanence of the universal and eternal in the historical and particular. A quotation from Juliana of Norwich, previously cited by Charles Williams, provides the epigraph: "*In the self-same point that our soul is made sensual, in the self-same point is the City of God ordained to him from without beginning*" (*CP* 589). The epigraph speaks of "our soul," not "the soul" or "a soul" or even "our souls." It establishes the double perspective of the incarnational understanding of history, connecting man's historical cities to an eternal brotherhood in the city of God. But while the epigraph cites the saint of Norwich, *England*, it is the Christian convert of Norwich, *Vermont*, whose ideas are presented, especially his particular version of the idea that the "now" has an eternal meaning, not just a historical reality. In *Out of Revolution: An Autobiography of Western Man*, which forms the basis of section 2, Rosenstock-Huessy emphasized the need to invest subjectively in history, to recognize it as *our* history. But this perspectival, engaged relation to history does not isolate us since history is motivated dialogically, directed toward the forging of a future, and connected to an eternal dimension of human value. The Christian City of God is not an alternative to the City of Man but a dimension that gives the historical world meaning and value.

While Auden, with Rosenstock-Huessy, eschews the impersonal at a thematic and narrative level, however, he has learned from Eliot how form may be a means of connecting the reader to the poem's vision without the intervention of "personality." Indeed, the strategic use of pronouns is itself a formal matter as much as a rhetorical one. Auden also creates an impersonal connection of his meaning to the reader through his verse form, which varies importantly through the work and introduces a level of experience for the reader that does not rely on images.

Section 1 of "Memorial for the City" (*CP* 589–90) begins in a civic voice and introduces a contemporary "we" appropriate to a war memorial service. In this section Auden offers two perspectives that are captured in two pronoun positions—the first is impersonal, carried by "she," "he," "they," "it." The second is "ours." The first perspective is the nonhuman, impersonal, and detached perspective of crow and camera and what it "open[s] onto." That is "Homer's world," an archaic worldview spatially and visually oriented, and "not ours" in a double sense: pagan instead of Christian and thus deterministic and without spiritual meaning. In Homer's world there is no difference between nature and history; both are given, not chosen. "The assumption of the *Iliad*, as of all early epics, which is so strange to us, is that war is the normal condition of mankind and peace an accidental breathing space . . . around them all indifferent and unchanging, the natural world of sky and sea and earth. That is how things are; that is how they always have been and always will be" (*F&A* 17). It is striking how many lines in "Memorial for the City" Auden dedicates to this view in the process of rejecting it.[53] Indeed, the first line, "The eyes of the crow and the eye of the camera open," suggests something filmic with "open" emphasized as the line ending. The "camera roving" in the next stanza similarly creates this film documentary orientation. Auden's essay "Hic et Ille" points out that "From the height of 10,000 feet, the earth appears to the human eye as it appears to the eye of the camera; that is to say, all history is reduced to nature" (*DH* 101). Humans are indistinguishable from sheep, and there are no historical values. In the poem, too, he is sampling the poetics of the impersonal and its way of collapsing together nature and history, though he will go on to suggest that this "open" eyed perspective is in fact blind, and worse, it "lie[s]." This perspective is not without its poetry—indeed, a poetry that recollects the imagist style with its hard, dry, un-emotive rendering of things and its criterion of impersonality: "Plum-blossom falls on the dead." "The hard bright light composes / A meaningless moment into an eternal fact" suggests again the visual thrust of the still moment. Auden underscores the spatial bias of this perspective and indeed its camera ideal: "On the right a vil- lage is burning, in a market-town to the left / The soldiers fire, the mayor bursts into tears." The reportorial voice is "dedolent" (archaic: meaning "unfeeling") like the sea in which the "tankers" sink. After its catalog of images, the imper- sonal pulls in with curt, indifferent reductions and equalizations mimicked in syntax: "One enjoys glory, one endures shame; / He may, she must. There is no one to blame." The first-person plural is conspicuously absent from this section of the poem, which relies, where there are pronouns at all, on "one," "it," and "he." Auden could be writing a voice-over for a documentary film, as he did in the thirties. But he heightens the poetic eloquence of this impersonal voice in order to render what it denies, the bitterness and terrible inhumanity of a world understood only in terms of nature and fate, not man, god, and history. The poetry reverberates so that this impersonal world is internalized, felt, and thought, not just seen. Auden optimizes sound and syntax to create an aural-verbal intensity over the visual bias. He wants us to hear, in the internal rhymes, "The cries of the whipped and the sighs of the lovers" under the "roar of the waterfall," and to claim them as "ours."

Appropriately, in the third and fourth stanzas of section 1 the pronoun shifts back, the external facts again connected to feelings of "grief" and suffering, owned and given meaning, given historical as well as spatial dimension. Aud- en's "we" is a boundless polity but not a transcendental identity—it speaks from "our time" with the sense that perception will change over time. "We" evokes those living in contemporary history and speaks from that perspective. If the first-person plural is strong in this section, the second person is implicit throughout, the imperative that brings human identity and purpose into being and propels the relations that constitute history. Unlike the impersonal world of the poem's beginning, this is a world of discourse and thus of the formation of meaning in community. The project of the poem is clear: to convert the hopeless vision, "our past is a chaos of graves and the barbed wire stretches ahead into our future" (the line stretches out and breaks over the margin), into a meaningful order based not on utopian ideas of history but on the principle of grace. Hope comes from an imperative (thou) that "ordains" the connection of the human city to the City of God. As in many classic elegies, the poem ends in a rebirth.

The "city" of the title is not specified but stands in for Europe's decimated *polis* and civil society, and more broadly for all earthly cities that by definition have or will come to ruin. In this sense the "we" for whom the poet speaks is not exclusively his local community but all humans living in the modern, "Post-Vergilian" world, which stands in ruin. "Memorial for the City" does not dwell on loss or indeed on a Christian promise of an afterlife. Auden's focus is on history as a center-less process of fallible man linked to an eternal center of divine purpose that makes a future imaginable. This memorial service resonates with the language of resolve and exhortation that was heard on the airwaves throughout the war. The focus is not on death and ending but on hope: "Whoever the searchlights catch, whatever the loudspeakers blare, / We are not to despair." If this were Churchill's speech (and it seems to allude to his May 8, 1945, speech celebrating the end of World War II), it would refer to national resolve; Auden's hope rests instead on the eternal City, not as an escape from the earthly one, but as a guarantor that our actions and choices are not isolated, meaningless gestures.

Auden shifts the reader to his Christian double vision in part through changes in the formal structure of the poem. Those focused on the abstract rhetoric of Auden's postwar work overlook how often Auden finds his originality and symbolic subtlety in prosodic techniques, sometimes derived from other works but always fitted for the particular purpose of his poem. If the rhetoric of some poems suggests the quality of a "bad essay," the music of the poems is often resonant. Auden's schematic mind satisfies itself as much in prosodic pattern as in ideational constructs. The stanzas of section 1 close off in couplets, giving the language a rigidity and inevitability in contrast to section 2 (*CP* 590–92), which moves out of the present spatial reality into episodes of Christian history, where revelation (and "revolution," to use Rosenstock-Huessy's term) occurs in time as well as being informed by a timeless truth.

Here, the rhymes become internalized so that the correspondence is more than an external symmetry; it is still audible but not closural; the "facts, the acts of the City" are registered in sound, not visible as end-words. Section 2 also settles into a syllabic pattern of oddly numbered, unaccented lines, predictable and sturdy but not insistent. Section 2 shifts from the present-tense "we" of section 1 to a "they" of historical narration. Perhaps more significantly, proper nouns and names become prominent here, identifying human will and choice with a built reality, the reality of the city as opposed to nature's soulless givens. "The facts" are now "the acts of the City" since events are infused with human purpose and choice for good or ill, and given meaning in a fluent reality (not frozen camera images) with the eternal city of spiritual order. Sound integrates events, and a charged pattern of adjectives marks out the changes in human culture in the post-Vergilian world from its origins to secular modernity: "New City," "Sane City," "Sinful City," "Rational City," "Glittering City," "Conscious City" map out a narrative. This swift, potted history, derived from Rosenstock-Huessy, hardly succeeds as interpretation of the past or as poetry, perhaps because Auden's real interest and investment is in the present and in the personal, subjective view, not the external record. He will reinstate the first-person plural at the end of section 3.

Section 3 (CP 592–93) returns to the present and follows the barbed wire introduced in section 1. Here, after the previous stanza's succession of adjectives, is the postwar "abolished city," the city in ruins, but also the end of the public sphere. The flurry of prepositions—*across, between, past, around, near, behind*—returns us to a preoccupation with place and space. Auden is again asking us to see, to open our eyes, but the tone is not impersonal. Barbed wire is a figure not just of oppression but of all forms of negation, repression, and division of the common; it becomes the threat to the life of the city that depends on the commingling of the common. All that defines the integrated life of the city—humor, cuisine, rites, taste, pattern—is "erased" and "abolished" by the principle of barbed wire. The barbed wire seems an agent of the impersonal mode itself as it "neither argues nor explains" but simply imposes its negative directive. It is the antithesis of the realm of human dialogue where a "we" is formed and a future engendered. As the barbed wire moves from the outer landscape to an inner and unconscious one, moves "across our sleep," Auden replaces the impersonal mode with the first-person plural: "It trips us so we fall / And white ships sail without us." The possibility of a future emerges with this foregrounding of "we" in the last three stanzas. The return of a "pattern of the City" has been implicit throughout this section with its six-line *ababcc* rhyme scheme. Through the poem's sonic dimension Auden registers a double consciousness, linking the human struggle through history to an unknowable eternal meaning. The rhymes and recursive sounds reverberating inside the lines provide a counterpoint to the linear movement. This heightened organization of sound creates constancy within the flux of time and a sense of unity among the disparate "facts" enumerated.

The "we" emerging in the fourth stanza of section 3 is built on "our Image," the imperfect human state of error and vulnerability that the barbed wire controls and destroys, turns to a statistic, and deprives of value. The incarnation makes "our Image" not only an image of Adam but also of Christ, who takes on "*Our Weakness*" and suffers for Adam's sins. But Auden is not ultimately interested in images or even the Image. In order for the future to be possible, we need speech and discourse rather than images. "*Let Our Weakness Speak,*" closes the section, notably a revision from the manuscript's "*Let His Weakness Speak,*" an external form that would present Adam as a figure standing in the past, apart from the modern world. In moving to a ritual first-person plural, Auden makes worship more than a matter of tradition; it is ancient, immediate, and universal. He links the eternal city of Adam and Christ with the earthly city of modern imperatives. If the ruin of the city is the result of men acting as if they had the power of God, the hope of the city must be preceded by the acknowledgment of man's weakness and the power of grace. The "eternal fact" of section 1, unchangeable, spatial, impersonal, and fragmentary, has become the body that connects us to one another through time and to the resurrection—the basis of "we." By the end of section 3 Auden's poem has become a sermon with a collect, the voice of all of us.

As if to demonstrate the importance of the singular, Protestant as well as the plural, Catholic dimension of this double view of history, Auden shifts, in section 4, to the first-person singular (*CP* 593–94). But this is an iconic version of the "I" that takes plurality into itself, creating continuity out of the various exemplars of "*Our Weakness.*" These are long cataloging lines linked by anaphora, each starting with "I," curling over the printer's margins, creating rhythm. Auden gives generality to this "I" by invoking literary archetypes rather than historical figures, but their romantic stature is diminished. Through demotic phrasing and diction he emphasizes the ordinary nature of these extraordinary figures aspiring to transcendence. The momentum of section 4 is toward Rosenstock-Huessy's vision of history endowed with a spiritual and eternal concept of man. The priestly voice that dominates the work closes with a warning against the delusions of the metropolis and its earthly orientation. "I shall rise again to hear her judged." This "I," while it alludes to the resurrection of Christ and the promise of judgment and salvation, emphasizes Adam more than Christ. The *acknowledgment* of "*Our Weakness,*" rather than our delivery to the eternal City, is the main principle behind our hope. Section 4 puts the "we" back in the movement of history as an exchange between "You" and "I." The privately acknowledged "we" concludes the poem. This "we" cannot be "gathered" as a crowd collective because it retains the connection to a conscious, choosing "I." As Alan Jacobs has pointed out, the relations between the City of God and the City of Man, if simultaneous, are nevertheless "endlessly fraught and historically variable. . . . Ultimately, for Auden, it is not on public triumphs that the City of God can be built, but instead on every citizen's recognition that his or her knowledge is always partial and his or her desires often irreconcilable with the desires of others."[54] Any speaking for "us all" is predicated on this knowledge. In this way we might reconcile Auden's Christian universalism with his wariness about any claim to knowledge of absolute Truth or "the Law."

Auden's use of post-Vergilian archetypes in section 4 provides an alternative to the impersonal "camera eye" and "Homer's world" in section 1 with its visual and spatial sense of reality. Auden implicitly draws on Gotthold Ephraim Lessing's dichotomies here between the spatial and temporal arts. Again he repudiates the camera. Evoking the crowds from the "earthly City" present at the crucifixion, the voice of "*Our Weakness*" declares: "At the place of my Passion her photographers are gathered together." The Passion abides in each experience of historic oppression and suffering. But the co-presence of the eternal City in the historical moment is invisible to the photographers and cannot be represented visually. Instead, Auden sees history as a form of address, of speaking and communication rather than objectification of events isolated in space. There is no "we" in that spatial world, in the "public side of mirrors." If a universal truth undergirds the experience of history, it can be seen through a discursive and literary lens, not a documentary or visual one. But while this subjective "we" is the conceptual basis of the poem, it remains more an ideational than a dramatized, felt perspective. The poem has the majesty of its public occasion, but its "we" lacks a strong sense of emotional connection to the community it calls together.

———

Auden would eventually turn away from the quasidramatic ritual divisions of the oratorio, and the declamatory and choral forms of the memorial service, in favor of a more personable, individual voice, which critics have associated with Horace.[55] This late civic voice speaks not for "all of us" together but for "each of us." It carries something of Auden's *sotto voce* but brings it out of the domestic sphere. In his discussion of Auden's poetic style, Justin Replogle notes: "If much of his poetry is oratorical, Auden certainly knew how to write the syntax of face-to-face talk, informal and personal."[56] Auden's Everyman voice has also seemed to some a falling off from his earlier strained poetic stances, a reliance on the nonchalance of a famous poet, who goes to Schrafft's or busies himself about the house. But the individual voice works in "Homage to Clio" in part because he situates it not in personal life but in an archetypal vocational setting. The "we" of "Homage" is primarily other poets, but the meditation doesn't draw a circle around this group. Auden's "Homage to Clio" has a Horatian conversational manner that enlivens didacticism with the drama of individual emotion and thought. Horace's "*Diffugere Nives*," where wisdom is framed by a humble poet talking to himself about a condition he shares with other men, is one model for the poem. Horace was known for a style in which an individual speaker sets himself within a local community and at the same time offers didactic reflection. As Michèle Lowrie has pointed out, "When Horace gradually adopts more of a communal *nos* ('we') at points . . . there is a generic transformation from slighter to grander lyric modes and a realignment of the conception of citizenship." She continues, "Horace in his person mediates two roles, the ordinary citizen, who is one of the crowd at a parade or civic celebration, and the vatic bard, who has the special task of representing the polity to itself in all its guises. . . . The first person plural itself mediates between the individual and the group. Horace can refer only to himself with it, but it can also refer to him as representative of society or genuinely as a member of a group."[57] David Rosen has observed Auden's turn to "plain English" modeled on Horatian plain style as a way of maintaining the power of his unique voice to speak for "us all" without yielding to an impersonal and generic didacticism.[58] Auden maintains the power of plain English in part by constant oscillation in diction and style and in the interplay of generality and particularity.[59] With such gestures Auden inserts the "I" of a lively speaker (not the iconic, ceremonial "I" of Adam in "Memorial for the City") into the "we" of civil poetry. This results in a dialectic between the view from somewhere and the aspiration to a perspectiveless, universal truth, and it creates a greater didactic force than in his oratorical modes. This personal voice also makes a detour around a crucial question for Auden in America: What is the community for which he can speak? American culture emphasized the individual over the group, he found, and Americans were freer but also lonelier than other nationalities. The voice of the late poetry does not so much address or describe a given community as speak to a *potential* community, even if it is only, at first, a community of one or the virtual community of poets and readers.

In "Homage to Clio" (*CP* 608–11), Auden dramatizes the "uneasy tension" he feels in his cohabitation with the historian. He abjures the formal voice that makes the poem a public event. He is alone in the landscape; even the muse he addresses is an absence. He acknowledges that in practice there has been little "collaboration," at least with the "Muse of the unique / Historical fact," whom he repudiated in "Memorial for the City" in favor of symbols and archetypes. Instead of confronting the impersonal facts of history, the "It" of the external world, Auden here relies on personification, addressing the historian's muse. But there is nothing but "silence" on the other side of the conversation. Auden makes heavy use of "we" as he addresses this muse, but this "we" whom he speaks for does not include this unresponsive addressee, who is not human though she sponsors a human construction of knowledge; the poet does not presume any consummation or even cooperative relation to the iconic muse of history. Nor does the "we" here speak for a sacred community or the modern *polis* as it does in "Memorial." Clio may be the "Madonna of Silences," but she remains secular in her claims on our attention and singular in her relation to events. This modulating Horatian "we" remains at once narrow ("we" poets, we who live in this landscape) and applicable to all ("we [humans] . . . brought face to face / By ones"). While the poet sits alone in the landscape, his casual voice, addressed to the unanswering Clio, creates a feeling of familiarity and gives the reader a hearing before the muse, so that the reader comes to join in the poet's predicament before the silent muse.

The tone of "Homage to Clio" is one of reluctant tribute, a factor of defeat and duty (*hom-* derived from "homme," a kind of manservant). "Submission" is the first synonym the poem offers for its title. Auden is not orator but suppli-cant, not the wise minister (as in "Memorial") but the awkward penitent. He is the individual artist who feels inadequate to the imperatives of the suffering world, not the sermonizer who helps us live with that suffering, use it, and gird ourselves against self-pity. Paul Muldoon may be right that Auden is confused and confusing in his stance toward Clio;[60] he is certainly dramatically present, however, even if his struggle is unresolved. But this very struggle to address Clio makes this poem more successful than the assured "Memorial for the City," which is "abstract, public and prosaic" (to use Jarrell's words) by com-parison.[61] Auden may draw themes and stylistic features from Horace, but the encounter is his own. In answer to Larkin's criticism, we might say that Auden is here explicitly a writer, not a reader, even if the poem begins in a scene of reading. But the question becomes, what claim of inclusiveness and generality can be made with this intervening figure of the poet? How much does the poem involve *us* in this struggle with the meaning of history?

Yet if "Homage to Clio" is starkly different from "Memorial for the City" in its tone and stance, the two poems begin on a similar note: the world under-stood in terms of nature and its cycles has little meaning for us. Before he comes "face to face" with Clio he must consider the place of writing in nature, and it is clear that, in the context of nature, his book, like all human artifacts, has no value at all. Insofar as we are among nature's creatures, "we" is "singular" (all of us in the same way, not each of us uniquely, are subject to its laws), and discourse is noise. Auden cannot converse with Aphrodite and Artemis, the divinities who preside in this realm. Again Auden is distancing himself from

Homer's world, in contrast to "ours," the post-Vergilian world not of nature and fate but of human choice, purpose, and morality, where "we" is plural, not singular.

"Homage" situates the poet in a local landscape he shares with an unspecified community that includes others: "Our hill has made its submission and the green / Swept on into the north." Nature here is an environment, and the "us" is a regional community experiencing a change in season. The hill's "submission" shows that nature is subject to time and change. He robes nature's struggle in the metaphors of battle. But Auden is not a romantic poet in this vein, forgetting history in his solitary encounter with nature's losses and renewals. The analogy, the pastoral displacement of war into the aesthetic "combat" of color "which they all win," is meant to highlight a *difference* from history. In history, by contrast, there are winners and losers. Quickly enough "our hill" becomes generic, and the "tribal outcry" is the new generation of birds or of "chirping" nature poets. Auden's sense of exclusion from this tribe—"to observation / My book [the one he is reading, but perhaps also the one he is writing] is dead"—has a tone of superiority about it. He will not be a nature poet because man's moral and spiritual life does not belong to nature. But if not to nature, does his book belong to history?

Auden's book doesn't seem to be of much use to Clio either, if her silences are anything to go by. Auden uses the first-person plural throughout "Homage," but he is not speaking for a region or a generation. Clio is the muse of plurality, the muse we all face but only "by ones"; she presides over the story of lives that "only can be once." This is of course a dramatic shift from historical thinking in the thirties, when history is understood as a struggle of groups. But in the allegorical figure of Clio, Auden assembles a "we" that is not simply atomized. If history can't be generalized, the *muse* of history can be, is by definition an abstraction. Auden thus, through allegory, gives the reader a vicarious struggle in imagination without pretending to represent everyone's encounter with history.

While Auden admits the failure of poets to answer the imperatives of history, the encounter with Clio animates the theme and gives a feeling of immediacy to the struggle it describes. The encounter with the muse becomes a symbolic action with dramatic interest and movement. The variable syllabics, 10–12 alternating with 8–10 syllables, without end rhymes, and filled with caesura and enjambment, subdue song and heighten the conversational mode. The poem is dialogical even without an explicit countervoice—full of questions, shifts of argument, assertions of doubt, and qualifications. "Are we sorry?" he asks, but the "we" here, because voiced by a spokesman of this one-by-one encounter, shifts to "I," making the poem itself a face-to-face drama: "If I don't know how I shall manage, at least I know"; "How shall I describe you?" / "I dare not ask you." The address to a deity is a figurative move—the real audience is not this silent muse but the poet himself, the community of one, and the reader who overhears and recognizes the poet's predicament, putting himself in the poet's place. As Rainer Emig has argued, the poem "reiterates the connection between 'I' and 'You' [that] throughout history is one of tension, potential betrayal and struggle, but also one of fulfillment. This fulfillment need not be a merely personal one, but it can—via acknowledgement of history as tensional—encompass both a politics of skeptical humanism and a faith that is not so much doctrinaire as understanding."[62] There is no communion with the addressee, a remote figure who is marked above all by her silence throughout, her refusal either to answer or to offer speech. Where "Memorial" followed Rosenstock-Huessy in understanding history as generated by discourse, "Homage" confronts the refusal of the muse of Time to lend him words or respond to his questioning.

The silence of the muse rejects not only the state's "generalized life" but also the poet's myth-making and pattern-making drive. But if she does not provide for the poet, that leaves two other art forms as the proper attendants of this spirit: photography and music, forms covering the spatial and the temporal dimensions of experience, respectively. In "Memorial," Auden cast aspersions on the view of history as a set of discrete and immutable (spatial) facts. In "Homage to Clio," he tends toward the reverse: the subjective and generalizing vision of the poet is inadequate to representing historical experience. Charles Altieri's observation is relevant here: "At the end of the sixth stanza there emerges a problematic 'we,' not sufficiently anchored to what is present."[63] In this poem Clio is a symbol for what resists symbolism, or at least resists the generalizing impulses of poetic thought.

If Horace provides a rhetorical model and some of the initial imagery for "Homage to Clio," the poet's Lessing-like struggle with her silence suggests another, and more surprising, link to Keats. Auden may not be conscious of the parallel, but a comparison of "Homage to Clio" with "Ode on a Grecian Urn" reveals much about Auden's concern with speech and silence and with the relation of spatial and temporal orientations toward life. "Homage to Clio" is a kind of ekphrastic poem, one that wishes to *speak out* before the silent object. It is also a romantic crisis poem, set in a landscape and tracking the turns of a struggle between the individual and the universal. Rainer Emig has observed that Auden's Clio "is the absence that invites completion," a phrase that certainly resonates with Keats's great odes, and with "Ode on a Grecian Urn" especially, which pays homage to a "sylvan historian" and a "bride of quietness." Except that in this *paragone*, Auden spurns the Greek model of "phallic pillar and navel stone," the forms of Greek ideal beauty Keats admired. Keats's urn may be "a friend to man," but here "pictures are no help." But is

Auden telling the truth here? Or has he seen Vermeer's *Allegory of Painting*, in which the artist is depicted, back turned to us, portraying a woman dressed as Clio who seems to take no notice of him (or the viewer, for that matter). She is demure, her eyes half-closed. She carries a musical instrument and a book. Vermeer describes Clio and himself in archaic costume with laurel crown, backed by a map. These are not Auden's tokens of history; he must find his own way. "How shall I describe you?" he begins (like Keats, hurling epithets and questions at the silent urn). The spatial reality and iconic tradition in which nature and her arbiters, Artemis and Aphrodite, prevail is rejected in favor of a verbal, bookish orientation. Yet the visual nevertheless comes back to challenge him. What, after all, can it mean to be "brought face to face" with Clio if the visual is not relevant? History is aurally present in the "superfluous screams" of the marginal, but it is also visually present. "What icon / Have the arts for you . . . ?" Auden asks rhetorically, and we presume the answer is "none." But surprisingly, given his repudiation in "Memorial" of the camera eye and indeed of photographers gathered at the scene of the Passion, he arrives at a different answer. "I have seen / Your photo, I think, in the papers, nursing / A baby or mourning a corpse." These are specific people, but they have representative, even iconic force; they present demotic versions of the nativity and the *pietà*. Is this the allegorical imagination finding its symbols in the documentary mode? Or is this the return of Auden's repressed documentary mode and an acknowledgment of the power of the impersonal? Auden gives photography its due as a proper servant of Clio, certainly superior to the poets, whom she does not "bless" or "ever read." Poetry might regain some authority and access to Clio through its kinship with music, if only it could cure its retentive and abstracting habits of mind. In the understated rhythms and reduced oratory, in the dramatic movement of the poem, Auden "find[s] the time" to sound Clio's silence, perhaps not in words but in silent (syllabic) measures.

Auden asks forgiveness of Clio on behalf of a "we" that includes noisy discursive beings, but he "dare not" ask for approval or even attention. The poem returns to reading and writing but without any consummation or consecration with this muse. He cannot as a poet "face" history, pay her homage in terms that she would recognize. If Clio is not pagan (not Artemis or Aphrodite), neither—despite Auden's efforts to align her with the Virgin—is she Christian. As the muse of the "unique Historical fact," she resists all dogma. The poem ends without speaking as "we," only as an "I" to a "You."

9

The Future of Us

And the child
We took on a trip
Said

"We're having the life of our times."
—GEORGE OPPEN, "QUOTATIONS"

MY AIM IN THIS BOOK has been to open up a topic largely ignored in the study of poetry, and even in language more broadly. As the scope and richness of the speaker's "we" across poetry in all its variety became clear to me, I chose to focus on Auden's example, though I have had in mind others, especially Wallace Stevens and Elizabeth Bishop. I might also have taken George Oppen as my case study. A close contemporary of Auden (Oppen was born in April 1908), he was similarly concerned with human pluralities in political, ethical, and philosophical terms. Perhaps no other poet of Auden's generation has so deliberately employed the first-person plural. But this practice only emerged when Oppen returned to poetry in the 1960s after a twenty-five-year hiatus, when he moved away from the impersonal, documentary style of his early work. And while Oppen had his devoted followers from that period on, it is only in this century that his work has commanded wide critical attention, influencing a new generation of poets. We might loosely argue that while Auden's "we" can be heard through the twentieth century, Oppen's "we," embedded in a more experimental style, has taken hold in the twenty-first. There are of course many similarities in their usage. Both poets are wary of the abstraction "the people." Both poets modulate their social gestures, with one group relation displacing or superimposed on another. Both employ poetry in order to awaken in their readers emotional and spiritual, not just material, forms of human interest and connection. But Auden, for all his evocations of groups in the thirties, became increasingly a poet of liberalism, in which, as he put it, "I precedes we," though in ethical terms "you" may precede "I." Auden's career-long critique of romantic individualism increasingly included a parallel warning against the loud, aggregative "we" that silenced the *sotto voce* of individual conscience. "We" in late Auden is grounded in a Christian reading of history and a Christian obligation of brotherly love more than practical togetherness or solidarity. Oppen's work, though similarly concerned with individual agency, goes beyond a critique of individualism; the "bright light of shipwreck," the failure of "the singular," is his starting point, leaving a "we," "bewildered," unformulated, and elusive.[1] "We" is not, as in later Auden, a collection of "isomorph[s]" (*CP* 239) that congregates in worship or reflection. When Oppen says "I" it is sometimes as an "androgynous chorus"[2] or a sense of the self as part of a group ("I am one of those").[3] Whatever the scale of relations, being is always already being "with"—"We are pressed, pressed on each other"[4]—and one effort of the poetry is to discover meaningful unity within this condition of proximity, for "we have chosen the meaning / of being numerous."[5] This "we" in Oppen is less a clear outcome of this choice than a conceptual and ethical horizon. It is easy to see why Oppen's poetry, more than Auden's, appeals to a generation of poets with both communitarian and globalist (rather than liberal and cosmopolitan) viewpoints. While Auden often writes in the first-person plural, an "I" joining others, Oppen tends to write in the plural first person, as one who is already part of the greater, though various, presence of others, although "Humanity" remains a horizon concept rather than an a priori principle.

Recent poetry is catching up with both Auden and Oppen, after a long silencing of the civil tongue. Especially since 9/11, American poets are reclaiming a civic voice for their twenty-first-century art and experimenting with old and new ways of saying "we" inclusively. (Auden's "September 1, 1939" became a kind of hymn in the immediate aftermath of the attack.) "We" universals, common in Auden-influenced postwar formalist writing, are creeping back in, though with renewed self-consciousness.[6] In the December 2010 issue of *Poetry*, Jane Hirshfield wrote: "I suppose some would say it's terribly old-fashioned, or terribly arrogant, for a person to use 'we' in a poem to speak of 'us all,' but it's a concept I still believe in—that certain experiences are universally and profoundly human, and that one of the possible tasks of poetry is to name or evoke them."[7] Oren Izenberg offers a recent effort to refresh poetry's claim to universality within a ground of social being, and Oppen is one of his salient examples. He argues for what he calls a "new humanism" that can be the "ground of social life" without resorting to the untested general propositions of a neoclassical style (e.g., Johnson's "Vanity of Human Wishes") or to the figure of the exemplary self, the poetry of experience as it was established in romanticism and carried forward in confessional poetry. (We might think of Lowell's "Skunk Hour" with its troubled regional and dynastic "we" and skewed, alienated personal vision.) Izenberg sees universality as a resistance, a project still involved in the negative: not just against *sententiae* but also against the inward-looking subjectivity of the confessional mode.

> [The poets of this new universality] will also demand that our concepts of personhood identify something real: not political fictions we could come to inhabit together, or pragmatic ways of speaking we might come to share, but a ground on which the idea of a "we" might stand. This poetry, I argue, is an important site for the articulation of a new humanism: it seeks a reconstructive response to the great crises of social agreement and recognition in the twentieth century.[8]

Izenberg's new humanism lives more as a project than as an achievement in the work he analyzes (from Yeats to Bob Perlman), which may be the point (notice his word "might"), since poetry understood within the "ground of social life" must be a restless, open poetry, embedded in an interactive model of communication. Agreement, in order not to be coercive, must constantly recognize the other.

Experimental forms and stances have emerged with the contemplation of this new humanism, in which the "we" does not so much succeed as displace the lyric "I." Many contemporary poets—C. D. Wright, Forrest Gander, Juliana Spahr, Jorie Graham, Timothy Donnelly, Rachel Du Plessis, Mark Nowak, Peter Meers, and others—want to acknowledge and arouse a feeling not only for the universal or "the common" but for "everybody" in a compressed world, and not just as subject matter but as a physical, economic, social, historical, and political presence. They want urgently to address human disparities, injustices, displacements, indifferences, etc. that have arisen in a hierarchical, corporate, remotely connected but socially divided, and global reality. They seek to reorient us to this urgent social condition at the very level of language, often wrenching us out of the habitual "I" position into more collective orientations. Suspicious of the rhetorical authority of the poet and of the power of plain English, they often prefer a style in which the reader feels called directly, even collaboratively, into the meditation. Auden has not been the adequate model for such a revolution of consciousness. A more radical poetics has been called for, and Oppen has provided one model.

I will return to the nature of Oppen's "we" and the recent poetics that has followed from it, but the presence of Auden's "we" in poetry of the late *last* century has many distinct manifestations.[9] Auden's heirs, without his Christian belief system, have found that loving their neighbors is difficult. From Larkin's lyrics on "lying together"[10] to Tony Harrison's verses on "versus," the "we" has come up against limits, of will and of words. Auden's most direct American successor is James Merrill. His late "Self-Portrait in Tyvek™ Windbreaker"[11] presents a contemporary mass-culture "we" of synthetic, trademarked group identity and global pseudosolidarity, a "we" that erases personhood. Merrill cringes at the cheery "wave" of the "smiling as if I should know her" teen-ager who, "wearing 'our' windbreaker, assumes" a kinship of taste and value based on the printed map of "Mother Earth." What really underlies this "dumb jacket" of simulated first-person plural? (The "wave" that is the jacket's countersymbol is both the crowd motion and the flux of life.) Despite the commercial fictions of the global village, the singular, mass "we" is linked (as it is in Auden) to dehumanizing nature and to death, which both isolates us and lumps us together. "We?" he asks sardonically, "A few hundred decades of relative / Lucidity glinted- through by minnow schools / Between us and the red genetic muck—." It's hard to find much comfort or community in a "we" so primordial. ("Yet I return her wave, like an accomplice," Merrill relents.) Like Auden (and he seems to have taken some notes from "Caliban to the Audience" here), Merrill registers the encounter with the other through shifts in linguistic register, high and low. Merrill's imagination retreats from the post-modern clutter and the prehistoric muck into the memory of the smaller, more intimate community of pre-fascist Naples, preserved in the songs of Robert Murolo. Merrill turns at the end of his poem to the transhistorical, one-to-one community of art, to an intimate "we" address where the self is not lost in the laws of the state or the "wave" of the masses but dissolved into a sky beyond words, beyond nature and society, blazed by imagination.

Auden flirted with modernist style in the late twenties and thirties, but in later work he aimed for "the thoughts of a wise man in the speech of the common people" (*Prose* I 165). He used the language he found around him and in the tradition, sometimes prosaically, sometimes with remarkable eloquence, even as he brought out its troubling assumptions and evasions. But Auden was also an important model for poets seeking to break with the language of the tribe. Some of Auden's heirs have followed Auden's earlier, more radical style, and their speaking self becomes fractured, pluralized, made permeable, distanced, or otherwise complicated. John Ashbery's floating pronouns, both "you" and "we," have received the most critical comment in this regard. Adrienne Rich, another poet Auden chose for the Yale Younger Poets, pursued the "dream of a common language" through more politically oriented innovations. Her attempt to unite lyric's private and public gestures led her to create new, flexible uses of the first-person plural. But her journey away from old masters, which, as Aidan Wasley argues, parallels Auden's own journey, is still a dive alone.[12] Rich is "not like Jacques Cousteau with his / assiduous team," though the ladder is familiar to many: "We know what it is for / we who have used it."[13] Difficult, often painful internal and interpersonal communication precedes unity and is what we share. ("We are our words, and black and bruised and blue," she writes in "The Demon

Lover.")[14] In "In Those Years," Rich reflects, "people will say, we / lost track / of the meaning of *we*."[15] But she immediately shifts her pronouns: "of *we*, of *you*." The "great dark birds of history" wrench the speaker out of solitude, but the I/ You relation remains primary and local as a stance against that darkness; the "we" of civic imperatives does not, should not, evacuate the personal. Rich remains a lyric poet with a voice centered in the experience of the individual in relationships, intimate or remote. And her debt to Auden is clear even in her later poetry. In "Inscriptions: History," she quotes (unattributed) Auden's "Canzone," a love poem, with its classic, epigrammatic "we": "*When will we learn, what should be clear as day, / We cannot choose what we are free to love*."[16]

Like Auden, Rich as a love poet feels the forces of division that are "within us and against us, against us and within us," a troubling chiasmus turned on love's absorbing, reciprocal gaze. As in Auden's epithalamia (and Rich admired "In Sickness and in Health"),[17] the experience of love—transient, inevitably disappointed, burdened by the pressures of a fractured world, weighted with the truth of human error and the limits of commitment—can nevertheless provide a figure of connection and lead out into the embrace of a broader social hope. In her "Twenty-One Love Poems," Rich creates her own premises, alert to gender and socially engaged, in which an ecstatic intimacy can be experienced within a fragmented and oppressive public world. The poem ends by drawing a circle, one that embraces rather than excludes, like Auden's "arbitrary circle of a vow" (*CP* 317). But the opening lines of the sequence are richly ambiguous in their meaning and their address: "No one has imagined us. / We want to live like trees."[18] The poet invites the reader to "imagine us" as "no one" else has, and as a transpersonal, optative "no one." But conversely, the phrase "no one has imagined us" highlights the verb *imagine*—no one has imagined us because we are not just a figment of the imagination; we are palpable, particular, and real. This duality of the possible and the real *us* recalibrates and broadens the place of the ideal in love poetry. The "us" of these poems moves between private and public, personal and general, in order to bring touch and intimacy to humanistic vision, for "without tenderness / We are all in hell." Like Auden, Rich is bold in her use of the propositional "we," in which she posits human universals, anchored in personal experience and tested and strengthened by the knowledge of our time.

———

George Oppen, too, is fond of philosophical "we" statements. Human togetherness is not only a given the self must avoid or engage but a preconceptual phenomenon that restructures the self. And the process of conceptualizing is, at the level of the poem, less narrative or argumentative than serial and digressive.

Oppen's most elemental "we" is usually his shared life with his wife, Mary, from whom he was inseparable from the age of eighteen. Of his daughter, too, he says "We seem caught / In reality together."[19] But these little collectives stand as the emblems of other forms of human togetherness, real and aspirational. Other specific "we's" enter, generational ("how we loved them once, these mechanisms, we all did"),[20] regional ("the sense of where we are who are most northerly"),[21] cooperative (his army unit), and so on. Like Auden, Oppen often employs generality, a philosophical "we" that can make him sound similarly sermonic. But Oppen's phenomenological language gives his propositions a more searching quality, in contrast to Auden's epigrammatic thrust (however tentative). Oppen's generalizations become part of an unfinished, enjambed meditation on a subject that thwarts language—"We want to say // 'Common sense' / And cannot. We stand on / That denial / Of death that paved the cities."[22] As we saw, Auden contextualizes and modifies his "we" in many poems, but in Oppen this becomes a consistent strategy. By moving into quotation and anecdote Oppen localizes the "we" as soon as he evokes it, insisting on perspective even as he reaches out for absolutes. His "we," he reminds us, is made up of many overlapping, horizontal communities. He declares, in a spliced, collaborative sentence: "There are things / We live among 'and to see them / Is to know ourselves.'" Six lines later he has localized the address: "You remember that old town we went to, and we sat in the ruined window, and we tried to imagine that we belonged to those times—."[23] Peter Nicholls reveals how "the poem's drama occurs at the level of the pronoun and that it is ultimately to these 'little words,' these aptly named linguistic 'shifters,' that so much importance here attaches."

> Section 1 begins with what must be an all-inclusive "we," but by section 3 there are "others" whom "we" encounter, a difference clarified in terms of generations in section 4. With section 6, "we" may be "pressed on each other," but far from being all-inclusive this is now a populist "we" implicitly oppressed by some vaguely defined other ("We will be told at once / Of anything that happens").[24]

Oppen's shipwreck of the autonomous self formulates a problem that recent poets have confronted: the multitude has no core, yet it provides the image of human connection toward which the imagination is propelled. Not only the meaning but also the form that follows from this meaning is not obvious, or perceived in the same way by all or all the time. But the oneness of the many, while manifest, is hard to interpret or explain without invoking an essence. How can plurality be maintained within it? There is a danger to explaining, which requires detachment. The poet's sharp vision creates a distance in which "the people" become "them."[25] One need only leaf through Carl Sandburg or Archibald MacLeish to see this tendency. Oppen emphasizes "proximity rather than identification" in his sense of the self's relation to the many, but there are ontological and ethical implications to this compaction.[26]

The temptation remains not only to enable connection and community through art but also to imagine humanity as a corporate whole, and this often involves poets in a turn from the "ground of social life" to impersonal dimensions of earth and sky against which "the human" becomes a single "we." Louise Glück's "Wild Iris" speaks for the inward journey of the self, but the pressure to yield the self to a wider unity is voiced in a different plant persona, "Scilla" (perhaps a version of Whitman's grass), where a host of blue flowers suggests the earth and sky's defiance of the singular: "Not I, you idiot, not self, but we, we."[27] Inhuman measures and phenomena can create a background that erases individuality. An alien "It" of the impersonal cosmos rather than an antagonistic "they" of the social realm incorporates an inclusive human "we," of "Humanity." This strategy informs Tracy Smith's *Life on Mars,* which was featured on the PBS *NewsHour,* where essayists often use "we." In Smith's "It & Co.," "It" seems to designate what she describes in another poem as "the largeness we cannot see," a largeness that modern telescopes make palpable but that drifts off into metaphysics. That invisible "largeness" beyond the boundaries of the human seems to be what helps us form ourselves as a group, helps us become "Us & Co.," the title of the concluding poem of Smith's volume. Smith seems to use the organizational title in a spirit less of irony than of revision, reclaiming it for an uncommoditized ideal of human connection. The title presents more trouble than help, however, in conceiving of "us all" collectively. But Smith's main basis for incorporating "us" seems to be the fleetingness of individual life and its small scale in the universe. This is a "we" of Nature, not of History, Auden might say. The abstractions and metaphors of the poem leave "one" with little sense of what "Us & Co." really amounts to other than words and vague sentiments. Oppen's phenomenological struggle with the concept of "us" is lacking here. Jorie Graham's 2015 prose poem "We" (the title is part of the first sentence) is more compelling in situating "us" in a matrix of time: a desperate awareness and shared burden in human history and its near-apocalyptic damage; an acceptance in nature's flow, void of memory and expectation; and a hope in literature where writer and reader meet and "the universals keep."

Tim Donnelly's *Cloud Corporation* is explicitly echoing Oppen, though unlike Oppen he brings the conundrums of our social being into a voice baffled and assaulted by the modern condition, not just straining to understand it. Donnelly finds forms that both evoke the environment of mass existence and offer counterpressures to the corporate versions of connectivity (Internet, global capitalism, etc.). He is a lot more suspicious than Tracy Smith of the cosmically incorporated "we" and our ability to escape the atmosphere of commerce. "We" amounts to "a congregation of bodies / united into one immaterial body, a fictive person / around whom the air is blurred with money."[28] The ambiguities of the subject "we" are multiplied in its range of cases: the objective (us), the reflexive (ourselves), the possessive (our), and the majestic plural (ourself). Donnelly's title offers an unredeemed and a redeemable image of our collective reality. Living in New York, Oppen's "city of corporations" that manufactures desire, and living on the Internet's "cloud" that "connects" us by absorbing us into a soulless, all-knowing computation, Donnelly suggests that "we" has taken on a demoralizing, dehumanizing, and faceless unreality, a pseudopersonhood. And yet poetry too is a cloud formation, its world is imagination, and its ability to imagine potential community, to give a body to what seems insubstantial, is part of its power. So one cloud might provide an antidote to another, if not simple redemption. Like poetry, a cloud seems like fog when you are in it, but seen from a distance, a cloud has form and substance. This duality between the debased and the poetic, between an "us" reduced to manufactured desires and an "us" of conscience and aspiration, finds expression throughout Donnelly's book, perhaps most explicitly in "Claire de Lune." This villanelle with its repetitive formal unity (its incorporation of words into pattern) enacts an idea of collective self-assessment. The alternating lines establish division within this body that allows the plurality of the first-person plural to assert itself, however agonistically. "We revolt ourselves; we disgust and annoy us."[29] The grammatical strains of the villanelle's permutations create collective confusion and irony; "we" are in mutiny against our own coercions. "We become like those who seek to destroy us." The summation of the villanelle is really a second turn of the screw, however. The self-disgust itself seems to generate the self-destruction when we are not just like the enemy but are becoming the enemy: "We disgust and annoy us / into those we become we who seek to destroy us." Is there any hope for community in this portrait of a hollow, incorporated, evasive, opiated, and eviscerated "we," in this "cat-and-mouse world" of capital? The poet is unique yet part of the group, and this introduces a dialectical element into an otherwise static I/We dichotomy. "Notice the group photo in which I stand / apart from but attached to. I feel I should die if I let myself / be drawn into the center no less than if I just let go."[30] The strangely hanging preposition "to," where "group" might be the object, reminds us that the group is only abstractly an entity and has no living "center."

This labile and unsettling "we" has many habitations in poetry, where our aspirations, our idealizing tendencies, are both expressed and checked, where potential communities are imagined, falsifying and exclusive ones deconstructed and revised. This contemporary "we" does not simply promulgate particular communities of race, class, or gender, nor does it simply speak in general terms about the human condition. Rather, it begins as a critique of poetry's long association with individualism and starts from the sense of common humanity as "one big self," as C. D. Wright puts it in her lyrical documentary work. But it resists any metaphysical essence that might invite a feel-good universality while evading the ground sense of our common existence. This poetics of togetherness explores what it means to be "one with others" (the title of another Wright volume), to take social inclusiveness, rather than privacy, as a starting point for poetry. For these poets the fact of social oneness is foundational to their new subjectivity. It starts from a ground sense of connection and combination rather than from a univocal, top-down perspective.

In what sense is a multitude a "we" without recourse to metaphysics? George Oppen addressed this question directly, but with hesitance: "The shuffling of a crowd is nothing—well, nothing but the many that we are, but nothing."[31] Oppen resists the romantic notion of a transcendental unity of man, an abstract human oneness that coexists with social atomism. But, perhaps wary of totalitarian control, he also resists the temptation to find identity in the manifest crowd, precisely because that identification is prevalent and appealing—in solidarity parades, in collectivist rallies, in mob actions, and in political and media manipulation of public opinion. Some recent poets show less wariness about the bridge between the personal and the collective. Indeed, they have learned to love crowds. Juliana Spahr's critical work *Everybody's Autonomy: Connective Reading and Collective Identity* (2001) and post-9/11 prose poems in *This Connection of Everyone with Lungs* (2005), among other volumes, articulate a ground-level communal poetics that we might call a form of crowd-sourcing in the way it calls to the reader to share in the collective subjectivity of the poem. "We come into the world. / We come into the world and there it is" begins one prose poem from *This Connection of Everyone with Lungs*.[32] This seems a familiar, propositional "we" with abstract, universalizing force. But the simple sentences are characteristically followed by long convoluted ones in which the pronoun "we" gathers up many referents and experiences. The first-person singular and regional community adheres to the universalizing plural "we" as the poem takes a local, autobiographical turn while opening into postlapsarian allegory: "We immersed ourselves in the shallow stream. / We lied down on the rocks on our narrow pillow" (7). Spahr's poetry moves along the gradations of "we" from intimate writer/reader relations to localized memories to public demonstrations and transcultural, even transhuman linkage. Collective identity is underwritten by constant attention to local or virtual connection, to horizontal links and communitarian values, but the focus remains on the holistic, combinative reality undermined by a destructive and divisive capitalism. Spahr's mixed prose-poetry work "We," for example, uses a Stein-ian repetitive style of verbal permutations in order to puzzle through this being singular/plural. For Spahr, the sense of "we" is not abstract but bodily, and "we" is an irreducible state of being, a sensuous and even an erotic knot. The long poem, which first appeared in prose in *The Chicago Review*, closes her book *Fuck You—Aloha—I Love You*, a volume dominated by a variable first-person plural voice. Spahr writes:

> We examine the light we have
> written and are confused because
> we can't see the singular in it and
> then we realize there is no personal
> story without we.[33]

Where Oppen's writing is phenomenological and wary of ideology, Spahr's is increasingly political and often topical, collaborating with invisible listeners but also with explicit allies, in poems full of antagonisms and calls for partisan solidarity. Spahr's poetic movement is a tool for a political movement, con-cerned especially with environmentalist, feminist, and economic themes. Her Commune Editions series, which publishes poets of like-minded collectivist and collaborative sentiments, calls for a poetry dedicated to arousing read-ers in an "era of global struggle."[34] In keeping with contemporary dialectic, the poems shift between global and local ideas of "we," between decrying a vast impersonal but hostile capitalist "system" and celebrating a ground-level engagement of bodies with each other, pressed together privately or publically, but always with a mind toward contemporary political reality. In her most recent book, *That Winter the Wolf Came*, "I" appears almost always amidst other bodies. The second poem of the book recalls, in prose diary form, how she spends her Saturday nights participating in a rally (part of the Occupy movement), accompanied by her son. This poem imagines a nar-rative within a mass movement, but other quieter and more lyrical poems seek to conceive the "we" more horizontally, in a chain of connections. Her "Calling You Here" at first murmurs to the reader, but her big public themes quickly begin to shout out, so that lyric becomes oratory. Spahr's poetic address calls the reader to a calling, to join her in turning outward to identify with others, human and nonhuman. The "we" she voices is emergent and fluid, a social ecology, not a static collective entity. The poem moves lyrically toward a hypothetical "we" developed in the combining of "you's"; it brings others into unison and turns them toward others, serially projecting new externalized "you's" that might similarly become absorbed into the momen-tum of "we." Other authors in the Commune Editions series, Joshua Clover and Jasper Bernes, similarly press the poem into political work, especially concerning income inequality and capitalist despoliation. A socialist vision underlying this "we" rings unapologetically through these books, testing and updating ideas of fraternity. Jasper Bernes's *We Are Nothing and So Can You* is a found title whose graffiti source, he claims, "rings a change upon a . . . line of Eugene Pottier's original French lyrics for 'The Internationale,' 'Nous ne sommes rien, soyons tout!'"[35] Many other politically oriented poets have moved to "we" as the dominant subject position. Philip Metres and Mark Nowak, for instance, invoke "we" on behalf of an embattled working class. This agenda-driven, topical poetics may be artistically limiting, but *The New American Poetry of Engagement: A Twenty-First Century Anthology* offers a range of impressive civic voices and styles of collectivist thought often featuring the first-person plural.

One of the most innovative and nuanced recent imaginings of togetherness comes from Nathaniel Mackey, whose "we"-dominated *Splay Anthem* won the National Book Award in 2006. His poetry is clearly prompted by the same distressing global history of exclusion and violence that motivates the poets of the Commune Editions. He acknowledges, as many poets of the previous generation do, that everything is in a sense political. But he has found a different, more archetypal way of probing the meaning of being numerous and the difficulty and rewards of togetherness. He pushes against any codified notion of collective identity and reflects on "we"-being in a lyrical voice and allegorical rather than journalistic or didactic mode.[36] There is no clear key to such allegory, which seems part jazz improvisation and part Buddhist koan, discovering its direction as it goes, without definitive origin or end, tracing the boundary of the ineffable "we." Here is a new (or renewed, in that it draws on many traditions), flexible, and dramatic approach to togetherness, balancing real and ideal, a palimpsestic "we" with many localities and scales of relation, from the most intimate to the most global. Mackey's unit of "we" is neither clearly exclusive nor inclusive but open, adjustable, and indeterminate; strengthened and changed as it is broken and repaired. His use of African mythology and African American music inflect this "we" with racial history, but he deliberately avoids narrowing his serial meditation to any particular narrative of divisions and oppressions, while alluding to many along the way.

Splay Anthem is part of a long, Whitmanesque work in serial form, carried over several volumes. It "braids" together two poetic stances, that of the recursive and traditional "Andoumboulou" (ancient tribe) and progressive "Mu" (of opening gates). The poems form an episodic journey of "crab auspices," more sideways than forward, following the human social rhythms of merging and separation. Boundaries of self and other, individual and group, are blurred; interior and exterior, dream and reality, local and global, sound and sense fade in and out. The poems put stress on "we" often through enjambment (in a way that recalls Gwendolyn Brooks's "We Real Cool") or through first words that thrust a line forward. (If the rhythms are jazz inspired, the alliterative and stress-based character of the lines also gives the feeling of *Beowulf*). This "we" is sometimes nostalgic, sometimes proleptic. The archetypal protagonists (male and female, sometime partners, but as much to suggest alterity as to focus the we on *eros*) search out this condition of union. "We" becomes ecstatic, then codifies, breaks down into discrete identities and dissolves into dust. It is sometimes a "limbo" (and Mackey's rich wordplay here suggests not just a betweenness but a barrier one must go under), sometimes a "verge." It is known more in *via negativa* and subjunctive moods of unrealized states than in assertion and denotation, a potential that is not utopic. Mackey makes each arrival a departure, as a mentorlike "Annuncia" becomes "Nunca" in the give and take, the joining and breaking apart of love. Above all, "we" in Mackey flourishes when it is not fixed in identity, when it is not a tight "web" we weave and are caught in, and not a "nub" that ties off life's flow, but a braid that also sometimes "frays" or "splays." Thus "we" is not one sustainable state but a fluid process of being singular/plural.

For Mackey, the poet's "we" is "an invitation";[37] the sense of togetherness is variable, a union of lovers, of brothers, of humans, in continuous modes of connection:

> "We," for example, can sometimes be an idealization or be subject to idealization, whether that of the romantic couple, some larger collectivity such as family, tribe, or nation, or the Gnostic apprehension of unity . . . but my recourse to "we" has not done away with the other pronouns. "I," "he," "she," and "they" still abound. "We" is often merely a matter of number, simply indicating more than one, but it also signifies a sought-after quality, state, or condition, romantic oneness, utopic sociality or millenarian arrival, if not all of these at once. It's an aim, an aspiration, an object of pursuit and a source of fulfillment, or if not, disappointment, "They the would-be we" in "Song of the Andoumboulou: 60," for, as I said in "Destination Out," "we" was never a swifter fiction.[38]

This song of we moves deliberately at an abstract level that can take in textures and moods of different locations while it drives on with its own internal promptings and rhythms.

Mackey initiates first-person plural early, in the second poem of *Splay Anthem*, after the speaker is aroused into song and love initiates the journey with its dreamlike beauty and resonance. As if to emphasize that this is not a journey of one or even of two alone, not a beginning, but part of a continuum with other voices and other journeys, Mackey's title quotes another writer, making tradition into jazz collaboration:

Beginning with Lines by Anwar Naguib

    —*"mu" sixteenth part*—

    A boat that sails to
    heaven on a river that
        has no end,   high above
    all but the elect among whom
        we of late no longer
        numbered. Ythmic ship
                        we
        stepped aboard, stood
            aboard, or so we
                    thought . . .[39]

The perspective from a plane, where one might see the "Lit city" as a unity, "thought we saw the heavenly city," descends into a more uncertain knowledge, the subjunctive mood and separation of the real from the imagined: "No sooner thought than / what we saw stood only / in / thought." "Fit venue we sought, / saw, / thought we / saw."[40] The passage quickly shows us the instability of this boat they have stepped into and the ambiguity of its load and direction. In another interview he explains:

> "We" runs the gamut from the he/she couple to larger groupings—you mentioned "nation"—that the title *Splay Anthem* evokes. One of the things that makes the anthem "splay"—an awkward anthem, a disturbed anthem—is the fact that one is of more than one mind in this desire to be a part of a "we," whether it's a couple, a nation, or some other collectivity. This ambivalence splays the anthem, the unifying song of whatever the collective is. The collectivity that these poems seem to be about or to chronicle in some way, the lost tribe that sometimes goes by the name of the Andoumboulou, seems to be some renegade group whose relationship to established collectivities is a fugitive one. This lost tribe is in flight from such established groups and seemingly in search of some alternative way of bonding. The alternative that they seek is marked by the word "splay." This is an anthem that wants to open out, that is ungainly—I think "ungainly" is one of the synonyms for "splay"—that is wary of the harmonies and the symmetries of conventional, bonded ways of public belonging.[41]

Stylistically, it's hard to imagine a poetry more in contrast to Auden of mid- to late career, though thematically and even structurally this poetry has something in common with Auden's archetypal, though personally and historically prompted, poems such as "The Quest" or "Atlantis," which emphasize the journey over the destination. The poem shares something too with "phe-nomenal Oppen," but it eschews both the documentary and the propositional modes as such, absorbing them into a lyric motion where feeling itself is the story. Like Oppen, Mackey shares a sense of the shipwreck of the singular, indeed he employs the same metaphor of boat and water, but he sets out on a new kind of boat, the ship of "we," on its diasporic journey.

The episodes of *Splay Anthem* offer ecstatic transport and lakes of dread, braids and frays, until the final section finds the archetypes run into a "nub." This "nub" is only very loosely a figure for our contemporary post-9/11 Amer-ican reality—a collective that is constricting, defensive, stifling. The elegiac mood, resonant with 9/11's apocalyptic feeling, closes the poem, though it suggests a new birth as much as a finality:

> Nub no longer stood but lay and we
> lay with it, earth-sway cradling our
> backs [. . .]
>
> [. . .] Nub, no longer standing,
> filled the air, an exact powder, fell
> as
> we ran thru it, earth-sway swaddling
> our
> feet.[42]

It is a place where we might begin to reflect, to quicken, to reimagine.

———

How do we profit from this scrutiny of first-person plurals? Maybe just from an awareness of the pitfalls of the pronoun—in an imperative to listen to ourselves, or at least to "ourself," and go back to the face-to-face encoun-ters, even the face-offs, that are the foundation of any community. The idea of "We" these poems show derives from horizontal clusters of relation. An inclusive "we" in poetry can express a desire to connect, the sense of moti-vated speech that is ready to yield up the personal familiar to a cognitive and emotional process. "We" can of course be seductive and even subjugating, aimed at coercing or at least disarming the other. But when the poem dra-matizes its struggle with the personal, when it becomes interactive or self-questioning, the first-person plural revitalizes civic poetry and animates the space of the common.

Such a "we" is not a totality; it returns us constantly to the particular, attend-ing to the growth of a single blade of grass, perhaps, but investing dialectically, as Whitman did, in the gathering of these leaves, building toward more sat-isfying modes of togetherness. Poetry's first-person plural suggests how the genre might propose or project open, reflective, splayed community, create a sense of potential in "us" that is not predicated on consensus, domination, or the mentality of the crowd. Poetry can keep the first person in the first-person plural, even when it isn't always first, and keep the plural from becoming too incorporated, too singular, too constricting—from becoming a nub.

NOTES

Chapter 1: Speaking of Us

1. Auden, *Forewords and Afterwords*, 51 (hereafter cited in text as *F&A*).

2. Whitman, *Complete Poems*, 194.

3. Ibid., 196.

4. Johnson, *Idea of Lyric*, 189.

5. Ibid., 194.

6. Patrick Henry, quoted in Marshall, *American Experimental Poetry*, 153.

7. This is a famous punch line from a well-known joke based on *The Lone Ranger*. Ivins posted the column "'We' is not me or a lot more of us" on July 21, 2002. The old joke about Tonto and the Lone Ranger highlights the trouble with pronouns and has been cited by several linguists. The joke turns on both the inverted power structure and the ambiguity of the pronoun "we." The two characters are riding together in a canyon when the Lone Ranger notices an Apache party flanked across the top of the cliff. "We're in a heap of trouble," observes the Lone Ranger, "we'd better head for the hills," to which Tonto replies, "What do you mean by 'we', *kemosabe?*"

8. Rand, *Anthem*, chapter 11 (n.p.).

9. Obama, "Remarks by the President."

10. For a discussion of how English indicates these distinctions without morphological markers, see Scheibman, "Inclusive and Exclusive Patterning."

11. Stein, *Lectures in America*, 213–14.

12. Auden, *Selected Poems*, 89 (hereafter cited in text as *SP*).

13. See Culler, *Pursuit of Signs*; Waters, *Poetry's Touch*; Keniston, *Overheard Voices*; Vendler, *Invisible Listeners*; Hedley, *I Made You to Find Me*; and Pollard, *Speaking to You*.

14. Stevens, *Collected Poetry and Plays*, 444.

15. Arnold, *Works*, 59.

16. Celan, *Selected Poems and Prose*, 396.

17. Emmanuel Levinas, for instance, argues that "we" is constituted in an interruption of history in that history is generated in struggle and opposition, in conflict with or oppression of the other. See *Entre Nous*, 37.

18. Celan, *Selected Poems and Prose*, 72.

19. Bishop, *Poems, Prose, and Letters*, 162.

20. Johnson, *Idea of Lyric*, 178.

21. Ibid., 177.

22. Rich, *Poems*, 196. But it is worth noting that some readers, including other poets, have found Rich's "we" coercive. Alice Notley, for instance, remarks in response to a question about

Rich's writing on women's poetry: "I don't like the way she uses the pronoun 'We.' I think she emotionally blackmails you with it. And I never feel like I'm part of her 'We'" ("Walking That Stretch for a Second").

23. Archibald MacLeish's volume *Public Speech* includes the poem "Invocation to the Social Muse."

24. Cary Nelson prefaces *Repression and Recovery* with this comment: "Those of us who study and analyze modern poetry are gathered together in the collective 'we' that recurs throughout the book" (xi).

25. Bogan to Rolfe Humphries, July 8, 1938, in *Selected Letters*, 157.

26. Cowley, *Dream of the Golden Mountains*, x.

27. Stevens, *Collected Poetry and Prose*, 135.

28. Lowell, *Collected Poems*, 387. A number of recent critics have commented on Cold War culture as promoting a set of norms rather than forming a social entity. See, for instance, Edward Brunner's *Cold War Poetry*, Deborah Nelson's *Pursuing Privacy in Cold War America*, and Justin Quinn's *Between the Fires*. See also Quinn's "Auden's Cold War Fame."

29. Buber, *Knowledge of Man*, 105.

30. Ibid., 106–7.

31. Nancy, *Being Singular/Plural*, 3.

32. Ibid., 2.

33. Ibid., 65.

34. See Émile Benveniste's "Subjectivity in Language," the second lecture in *Problems in General Linguistics* (325–31).

35. Nancy, *Being Singular/Plural*, 34.

36. Ibid., 70. Jean-Luc Nancy, Giorgio Agamben, Maurice Blanchot, and others have in fact reflected quite a bit on the role of literature in creating a concept of community that avoids absolute unity. See, for instance, Nancy, "Literary Communism," in *Inoperative Community*, 71–81. Agamben in *The Coming Community* and Blanchot in *The Unavowable Community* have both weighed in on the question of how language codifies and instantiates community, and they have tried to bend language against itself to create more supple ideas of community. Blanchot proposes an open, discursively flexible ethical relationship with others. Agamben's "whatever singularity" is one of the latest attempts to think about individualism open to community, or a community that does not stifle particularity.

37. In *Poetry's Touch*, William Waters claims that this lack of context in poetic discourse makes the insights of linguistic pragmatics irrelevant. However, the ability to imagine context surely answers this objection.

38. This argument is in line not only with Blanchot and Agamben but with the earlier work on prose of Benedict Anderson, *Imagined Communities*.

39. Cavell, *Must We Mean What We Say?*, xxvi.

40. Cavell, quoted in Greif, "Cavell as Educator," 102.

41. Cavell, *Must We Mean What We Say?*, 96.

42. Ibid., xxvi.

43. Edward Mendelson emphasizes Auden's ambivalence about groups in *Early Auden*: "He longs for the release and self-forgetfulness a group can provide, but he must reject all existing opportunities for that release while hoping for something better in the future" (25).

44. There are important related areas for considering poetry and the first-person plural that I am *not* taking up here. Collaboration, for instance, is central to Auden's art and clearly related to the issue of plural subjectivity, but its creative and cognitive operations are beyond the scope of this study. I do not spend much time on the issue of coterie, so important in the rhetoric of Auden's early poetry, since a number of critics have taken up this topic, most recently Lytle Shaw. I do not much discuss "we" in the context of a collective fictive persona, as in Eliot's "The Hollow Men." Nor do I much discuss the "we" in which a poet writes exclusively in first-person plural when describing an experience he has shared with an unnamed and unaddressed intimate. See, for example, Edward Hirsch's "Uncertainty."

Chapter 2: The Demagogue and the *Sotto Voce*

1. Such essays as "Hic et Ille" and "The Virgin & the Dynamo" in *The Dyer's Hand* (hereafter cited in text as *DH*), and "The Protestant Mystics" in *F&A*, are significant examples. Critics have of course noted Auden's pronoun use in local instances. Two particularly subtle analyses of his pronoun use can be found in Stan Smith's *W.H. Auden* (10–11) and Susannah Gottlieb's *Regions of Sorrow* (177).

2. Recent studies in pragmatics have documented the nuanced ways that the first-person plural is employed in political speech. See, for instance, Proctor and Su, "The 1st person plural in political discourse."

3. Kierkegaard, *Living Thoughts*, 26.

4. Mendelson, *Later Auden*, 79.

5. Auden, *The English Auden*, 165–66 (hereafter cited in text as *EA*).

6. Larkin, "What's Become of Wystan," 418.

7. Auden, *Collected Poems*, 885 (hereafter cited in text as *CP*).

8. Auden to Mrs. E.R. Dodds, July 11, 1939, Bodleian Library archive. Partially cited in *Map of All My Youth*, 100.

9. Auden, *Complete Works of W.H. Auden: Prose*, vol. 1, 425 (hereafter cited in text as *Prose* followed by the volume number).

10. Mendelson, *Later Auden*, 78.

11. Mendelson, *Early Auden*, 322.

12. Auden, *Lectures on Shakespeare*, 245 (hereafter cited in text as *Lectures*).

13. Auden's "Aubade" (1972), which reflects back on so much of his art, may remember these lines when it ends with a modified motto, spoken not by the poet but by the "City" of "Human Time": "*Listen, Mortals, Lest Ye Die*" (*CP* 885). The imperative is to tell the truth about the past and listen to the tale.

14. Quoted from the Berg Collection manuscript in Mendelson, *Early Auden*.

15. Auden would later write of "utter patience" in the "The Hidden Law" (*CP* 262). In drafting "September 1, 1939" Auden evoked a "law" but found no "verbal definitions" for it and abandoned the stanza. But we might consider that he has returned to it in "The Hidden Law." The "lie"/"die" rhyme and the scene "in a bar" also connect back to "September 1, 1939."

16. Mendelson publishes the English spellings but notes "odour" in the Berg Collection typescript, along with other changes from English spelling.

17. April 1, 1967, Berg Collection. Mendelson writes that the letter was unsent (*Early Auden*, 330).

18. Constance Rourke's *American Humor: A Study of the National Character* had been published in 1931.

19. Mendelson, *Later Auden*, 79.

20. Eleven years before he had said the task of the poet is to create "private spheres out of public chaos" (*Prose* I 4); and much later, in "The Poet & the City," he would say that poetry is "concerned with *singular persons*, as they are alone and as they are in their personal relations" (*DH* 88). Of course those private spheres might form an intimate community, but in 1938 he had something broader in mind.

21. Auden to Mrs. E.R. Dodds, August 7, 1939, Bodleian Library archive.

22. In "Aubade" (1972), Auden would return to this "*sotto-voce*" with similar ambivalence. He does not dictate laws to a "public" but rather, in his conversations with himself, "sing[s] verses *sotto-voce*, / made on behalf of Us all" (*CP* 885).

23. Berlin notebook, Berg Collection.

24. Mendelson, *Later Auden*, 360.

25. Simone Weil, quoted in Auden, *A Certain World*, 283.

Chapter 3: Song of My Selves

1. Boas, *Handbook of American Indian Languages*, 39.

2. Whitman, *Complete Poems*, 123.

3. See especially neuroscientist David Eagleman's *Incognito: The Secret Lives of the Brain*. Eagleman begins his study with a number of literary examples and moves on to a chapter called "Democracy of the Brain" in which he uses the political model as his central trope. The brain is "*e pluribus unum*" and "the brain runs on conflict" like representative democracy (a two-party system of reason and emotion) or a cabinet of rivals (106). He is especially interested in those parts of brain function that are "secret"—following Carl Jung, "In each of us there is another whom we do not know" (7). For a more traditionally Jungian antecedent, see Samuels, *Plural Psyche*. See also Paul Bloom's *How Pleasure Works*, his article "Song of My Selves" (which cites Whitman) in *The Atlantic*, and his follow-up column "First Person Plural." These writings argue against a strictly dualistic view of human cognition, emphasizing healthy plurality and interrelation of partial selves over duality and opposition in the mind.

4. See Kacewicz, Davis, and Pennebaker, "Pronoun Use Reflects Standings in Social Hierarchies." The identification of high status with the use of "we" might suggest group orientation, but it also suggests a figure who feels confident to speak for and to direct the group according to his own position. This is just one example where modern uses of the first-person plural are really modifications of old modes of imperiousness.

5. Shakespeare, *King Lear*, 161.

6. Dickinson, *Poems*, 342 and 351. Paul Crumbley has developed this argument about Dickinson. "Where the 'We' supersedes the orthodox 'I' in the speech of royalty, Dickinson's speakers assume that the self is plural to begin with; a unified 'I' represents for her an unfortunate decline in stature.... For Dickinson, 'We' is the norm, not the exception" ("Emily Dickinson," 247–49).

7. Arnold, preface to *Poems*, x.

8. Whitman, *Complete Poems*, 123.

9. Cavell, *The Senses of Walden*, 108.

10. Bloom, "First Person Plural."

11. See the many self-portraits "as" or "with" by Jorie Graham, Yusef Komunyakaa, and Charles Wright, among others; Cees Nooteboom's "Self Portrait of an Other" provides a recent prose example.

12. Cohen, *Thinking of Others*, 67.

13. Ibid., 76.

14. Tze-wan, "Towards a Phenomenology of Pronouns," 6 and 18. See also *Stanford Encyclopedia of Philosophy*, s.v. "Heidegger," http://plato.stanford.edu/entries/heidegger/#Bei; and s.v. "Existentialism," http://plato.stanford.edu/entries/existentialism. Alan Marshall draws some related connections, in his discussion about Robert Creeley, between Heidegger's idea of "anxiety" and its social implications. See Marshall, *American Experimental Poetry*, 215.

15. Bertacco and Gibson, "Skepticism and the Idea of the Other," 119.

16. Yeats, *Poems*, 236.

17. Auden, *Double Man*, 3.

18. Pleshette DeArmitt has explored this defense of narcissism in Rousseau, Kristeva, and Derrida. See *Right to Narcissism*.

19. Yeats, *Poems*, 8.

20. Greenberg, *Quest for the Necessary*, 1–2.

21. Mendelson, *Early Auden*, 94 and 95.

22. Ibid., 111.

23. Auden, *Juvenilia*, 185.

24. In *Later Auden*, Edward Mendelson distinguishes between narcissism and self-regard. Auden began to think that he "had been foolish to believe he could love only the world of the Alter Ego, that he really wanted someone like himself. Self-love was paradoxically an escape from narcissism and its insistence on the irreconcilable differences between the self and others" (57).

25. Jacques Derrida, quoted in DeArmitt, *Right to Narcissism*, 2. She goes on to discuss Derrida's defense of narcissism in terms of the self-love that makes ethical action possible. For Derrida, there can be no ethical action toward the Other, toward Thou, if self-love, the recognition of the "I," does not precede it.

26. Stephen Spender, quoted in Firchow, *Contexts for the Poetry*, 131.

27. Yeats, *Essays*, 492.

28. Recent literary theory and literary history have looked again at this old contest between rhetoric and poetry, seeing it as central to modernism and its aftermath. Robert von Hallberg, for instance, devotes separate chapters in *Lyric Powers* to the "orphic" and "civil" power of lyric. Peter Nicholls and Robert Scholes see the quarrel between rhetoric and poetry as productive of modernist poetics. See Nicholls, "Poetry and Rhetoric"; and Scholes, *Paradoxy of Modernism*, 95–119. Charles Altieri discusses the return to rhetoric as a move away from modernist efforts to produce a new poetic realism and pursue an ideal of impersonality (see *Art of Twentieth-Century Poetry*).

29. Altieri, *Art of Twentieth-Century Poetry*, 146.

30. Smith, introduction to *Cambridge Companion to W.H. Auden*, 2.

31. Replogle, *Auden's Poetry*, 101.

32. Smith, *W.H. Auden*, 63.

33. Replogle, *Auden's Poetry*, 105.

34. Davenport-Hines, *W.H. Auden*, 103–14.

35. Auden, foreword to *The Orators*, vii.

36. Ibid., viii.

37. In "Some Modernists in Early Auden," Gareth Reeves makes clear that *The Orators* does not consistently subject the old school ways of oratory to sinister parody. Old styles in fact find a place in Auden's new language. And, conversely, the modernists come in for critique as detached voices. However, in the author's "compulsion to interrogate other voices" (Reeves 304), it is difficult to establish the line between absorbed strategy and mocked strategy, between ideas taken up and ideas presented in parodic extreme.

38. Boly, "*The Orators*: The Artist in the Thirties," 130.

39. Lehman, "In the Cool Element of Prose," 50.

40. Jarrell, *Jarrell on Auden*, 34–35. The entire chapter discusses Auden's "we/they" system.

41. Edward Mendelson, in "The Coherence of Auden's *The Orators*," sees the odes as more or less recapitulating the shuttle between exhortation and defeat introduced in book 1. I am arguing that while *The Orators* has no clear narrative, the generic progression from prose (book 1) to mixed genres (book 2) to poetry (book 3) may suggest stages of transformation within the purgatory of language and point toward alternative modes of thought and interaction.

42. Replogle, *Auden's Poetry*, 106.

43. Psalm 23:2.

44. Cited in Fuller, *Commentary*, 121.

45. Baudelaire, *Intimate Journals*, 31.

Chapter 4: Private Stuff and Public Spirit

1. Plato, *Essential*, 746.

2. Shakespeare, *Midsummer Night's Dream*, 103.

3. In her essay "Steerforth's Arm: Love and the Moral Point of View," Martha Nussbaum traces this antipathy of moral philosophy to romantic love through Kant, Spinoza, and Adam Smith. But she suggests that certain writers of fiction—Dickens and James in particular—navigate the tensions between moral and erotic perspectives in their characters' stories and in the reader's relation to those stories. Nussbaum discusses this figure of the "wise spectator" who for Adam Smith represents the moral point of view (341).

4. As the theory of lyric has turned its attentions increasingly to the social aspect of poetry, pushing back against its reputation for inwardness and privacy, critics have begun to emphasize the ways that love poetry models social intercourse. Many of those who want to argue for the social and ethical import of poetry point out that its utterances, abstracted from historical contingencies and local particularities, become "analogical" or paradigmatic interpersonal or social events, demonstrating human choices and gestures. Helen Vendler writes in *Invisible Listeners*: "The lyric . . . conveys ethical import less by narration of character in action than by believable tonalities (which may be of any sort—appealing or truculent or repellent), tonalities that are

invented and expended as the poet structures and elaborates the emotions of his fantasy" (7). As William Waters points out in *Poetry's Touch*, the apparent addressee is not always the primary intended audience, and in "the vast body of European poetry in the courtly love and Petrarchan traditions" (28), address is really better understood as performance. In many love poems the speaker withdraws from the act of address into an act of observation or reflection, "interrupts the continuum of relationship in order to present the relationship" to an overhearing audience, which may foremost be the beloved (33). "In an account of reading lyric, there will be places where the participant roles of speaker, intended hearer, and bystander meet together or away, and these are moments of wonder" (51). In these convergences, I want to add, the ambiguity of the pronoun "we" often comes into play. For Waters these are moments of "intimacy" for the reader as well as for the subjects. Heather Dubrow has challenged this assumption that lyric address always creates an effect of intimacy for the reader; see *Echoes of Desire* and "Towards a Reevaluation of Immediacy." Dubrow questions both the assumption of lyric presence and the binary of deixis (here vs. there) and demonstrates the layered, modulated use of "here" in Petrarchan poems and in modern examples. A similar argument can be made for the deictic pronouns "you" and "we."

5. Whitman imagines a pair of particular lovers, briefly united, who fall back into an immersion in the flood, the "one" that dissolves all human distinction. In "We Two, How Long We Were Fool'd," Whitman starts all nineteen lines of the poem with "We," and its meaning goes out into the flux and comes back as lovers' joy, indistinguishable for the merge. Two is repeated, so that the merging can be enacted again through a series of tropes of natural fusion. Lovers entwining become a figure for the unity of the universe, of love and death, "we are Nature," and the unity of two individuals dissolves back into undifferentiated being.

6. Shakespeare, *Sonnets*, 383.

7. Ibid., 499.

8. Vendler, *Art of Shakespeare's Sonnets*, 282.

9. Shakespeare, *Sonnets*, 453.

10. Vendler, *Art of Shakespeare's Sonnets*, 191.

11. Shakespeare, *Sonnets*, 459.

12. Frost, *Poetry*, 118–19.

13. Love's "we" may also be conceived as ternary or triangular, internally so, as in Freud, or socially as René Girard and Eve Sedgwick have argued, involved in spectacle or in homosocial dynamics.

14. Frost, *Poetry*, 260.

15. This study will not take up the complex issue of Auden's ideas about homosexuality and the particular structure of homoerotic desire in the poems. It will focus instead on the connection in his writing between *eros* and civic virtue. (The connection was perhaps formed in response to the prohibition of homoerotic love in the public sphere, but Auden's personal motivation is not my subject.) Auden reflected at various times on the psychosocial dynamics of his sexual preference, seeing it sometimes as a form of solipsism or a foreshortening of adult social engagement, at other times simply as a variety of the I/Thou relation that structures human interaction. Richard R. Bozorth in *Auden's Games of Knowledge* discusses the love poetry with reference to Auden's homosexuality, his revisions of Petrarchanism, and his use of parable as an anti-universalizing mode. He addresses the issue of pronouns in terms of their ability to mask gender and sexual preference.

16. Spenser, *Shorter Poems*, 662.

17. Donne, *Poems*, 177.

18. Mendelson, *Early Auden*, 139–40.

19. For a discussion of Hannah Arendt's ideas about promising and forgiving, and their importance for Auden, see Gottlieb, *Regions of Sorrow*, 147–60. See also Arendt, *Human Condition*, 230–47.

20. Auden, "Epithalamium for C. Day-Lewis," appendix 1.

21. Levinas is revising Martin Buber and Émile Benveniste, who emphasized reciprocity in the I/Thou relationship. See Neve, "Ethics and the Place of the Other."

22. Auden, *Another Time*, 107–10. For a discerning analysis of this poem and also "In Sickness and in Health," I refer the reader to Susannah Gottlieb's article "With Conscious Artifice."

23. Searle, *Speech Acts*, 57. Also, "The Logical Status of Fictional Discourse," 326.

24. For a full discussion of Auden's developing ideas about love and the shift from *eros* to *agape*, see Cole, "Love and Other Gods."

25. Mendelson, *Later Auden*, 179.

26. "Jumbled in the common box" of January 1941 is darker; the "we" of the lover's address offers no shelter from the "ragged rascals": "Once we could have made the docks, / Now it is too late to fly" (*SP* 125). All protective circles have been squared by the universal fact of the coffin.

27. Marriage is also the subject of several of the operas Auden would write in collaboration with Kallman. For a discussion of this thematic focus and its implication for ideas of collaboration, see Sastri, "A Marriage of True Minds."

28. Auden, *The Sea and the Mirror*, 14–15 (hereafter cited in text as *SM*).

Chapter 5: Tribes and Ambiguities

1. Eliot, in "Little Gidding": "our concern was speech, and speech impelled us / To purify the dialect of the tribe."

2. Kipling, *Collected Poems*, 340.

3. Ibid., 791.

4. Fussell, *Great War and Modern Memory*, 79–80.

5. See Joshua Greene's *Moral Tribes: Emotion, Reason, and the Gap between Us and Them*. Using insights from psychology, economics, and neuroscience, Greene describes what he calls "the tragedy of common sense morality," an extension of the classic "tragedy of the commons." The tragedy of common sense morality is that difference, and oppositional perspectives, trump common interests and values. He proposes a "metamorality" in which in a sense we all become moral philosophers, able to see beyond our limited perspectives. But the trouble with Greene's argument is that he bases cooperation among groups on a higher-order reasoning that seems to put emotion aside. Although Greene ignores it, perhaps literature, which often invites us to take on emotionally the perspectives of others, has a role to play in achieving this "metamorality."

6. Connolly, *Identity/Difference*, 64.

7. Tolson, *Harlem Gallery*, 146.

8. Brooks, *Selected Poems*, 73.

9. Brooks, *In The Mecca*, 44.

10. Jarrell, *Jarrell on Auden*, 34 and 35.

11. Fussell, *Great War and Modern Memory*, 79.

12. As Auden would say in his 1960 lecture, "Brothers & Others": "The members of a society with a primitive self-sufficient economy can think of those outside it as others, not brothers. . . . But, first, money and, then, machinery have created a world in which, irrespective of our cultural traditions and our religious or political convictions, we are all mutually dependent. This demands that we accept all other human beings on earth as brothers, not only in law, but also in our hearts. Our temptation, of course, is to do just the opposite, not to return to tribal loyalties—that is impossible—but, each of us, to regard everybody else on earth not even as an enemy, but as a faceless algebraical cipher" (*DH* 235).

13. The numbering refers to "In Time of War," reprinted in *EA, SP,* and *Prose* I. Because of omissions and reordering, the numbering in "Sonnets from China" differs even in poems that were otherwise unchanged.

14. Marsha Bryant notes that the intersection of a war on fascism and a continuing imperialist relation between West and East makes this opposition especially unstable, with shifting alliances. "In the United Front against fascism," China is an ally and Japan an enemy. She quotes Auden and Isherwood's dispatch for *New Masses*: "For us, in Canton, in Hankow, along the Yellow River, the Japanese were 'the enemy'; the Chinese anti-aircraft were 'our' guns, the Chinese planes 'our' planes, the Chinese army was 'we.'" But Bryant asserts that in another account, for *Harper's Bazaar,* Auden and Isherwood follow the orientalist logic that opposes "European observer and Asian observed." She quotes Said's characterization of the orientalist vision as an "us" (West) and "them" (East) mentality; but she goes on to see that the authors "wrench themselves from their culture's interpretive framework" so that "us" and "them" sometimes intersect. (See Bryant, *Auden and Documentary*, 157 and 161.) I argue that this is a deliberate strategy and frequent device in the sonnet sequence.

15. My text for the photographs in *Journey to a War* is Auden's *Prose* I. In his notes, Mendelson writes: "The arrangement of the headings in this section attempts to reconstruct the arrangement that the authors asked for but did not entirely receive" (*Prose* I 828).

16. Bryant, *Auden and Documentary*, 131.

17. Bryant notes, "European embassies, businesses, and missions make it difficult [throughout the diary] to mark with certainty what is 'Chinese'" (Ibid., 129).

18. Charles Berger treats all the short poems in *Journey to a War*, the opening ones along with "In Time of War," as if they were one group, and he approves the removal of "To E.M. Foster" to the end of "Sonnets from China" as a mark of the poet's real intention, to emphasize the moral failings of imperialism. Like Berger, Stuart Christie sees the dedicatory poem to E.M. Forster as the key to the whole work. I disagree.

19. Douglas Kerr quotes "Night falls on China; and the great arc of travelling shadow . . ." and remarks: "thrilling as this is, it is a view of the orient available only from space." While this is true, it must be noted that the lines are from the didactic "Commentary," not from the sonnets. Kerr is speaking of the "Commentary" when he calls the perspective "olympian vantage . . . generic 'human cry'" ("Journey to a War," 290).

20. The characterization of the work as an "occult imagining" also ignores the textual and contextual differences between "In Time of War" and the later "Sonnets from China,"

which Christie mistakenly dates as 1938 while citing the 1966 versions. They are not at all the same work.

21. Auden's comment to the BBC is perhaps the best introduction to the sonnets "In Time of War" because of the way it emphasizes gerunds and avoids subjects: "War is bombing an already disused arsenal, missing it and killing a few old women. War is lying in a stable with a gangrenous leg. War is drinking hot water in a barn and worrying about one's wife. War is a handful of lost and terrified men in the mountains, shooting at something moving in the undergrowth. War is waiting for days with nothing to do, shouting down a dead telephone, going without sleep and sex and a wash. War is untidy, inefficient, obscene, and largely a matter of chance" (*Prose* I 490).

22. Hynes, *Auden Generation*, 344–45.

23. Hynes quotes Geoffrey Grigson's appreciation of the sonnets at a time of Chamberlain's appeasements. Chamberlain did not although he "might have *felt* human history . . . [whereas] reading these sonnets, I did feel life instead of death" (Grigson, quoted in Hynes, *Auden Generation*, 348).

24. Auden's parataxis is frequently noted, but I am particularly indebted to Nausheen Eusuf for some of these extrapolations on "and" in Auden's war sonnets.

25. Lanham, *Analyzing Prose*, 29.

26. Bishop, *Poems, Prose, and Letters*, 166–67.

27. Jarrell, *Jarrell on Auden*, 35.

28. Sassoon, *War Poems*, 8.

29. Rilke, *Sonnets to Orpheus*, 91.

30. Ibid., 95.

31. Auden, *Prose* I, 830.

Chapter 6: Poet and Audience

1. Bostridge, *Winter Journey*, 153.

2. Agamben, *Coming Community*, 18.9.

3. Shaw, *Frank O'Hara and the Poetics of Coterie*, 8.

4. Reader-response criticism and reception aesthetics have relevance here as well, though "interpretive communities" are more hermeneutic than social. R.M. Berry has put Stanley Cavell's skepticism in conversation with these and related ideas about the principles determining what constitutes something as art. See "Is 'Us' Me?"

5. Frye, *Anatomy of Criticism*, 249.

6. Dubrow, *Challenges of Orpheus*, 69.

7. Ibid., 85.

8. William Waters (*Poetry's Touch*), Jane Hedley (*I Made You to Find Me*), Anne Keniston (*Overheard Voices*), Helen Vendler (*Invisible Listeners*), Heather Dubrow (*Challenges of Orpheus*), John Emil Vincent (*John Ashbery and You*), Natalie Pollard (*Speaking to You*), and many others, including myself. Pollard, in *Speaking to You*, sums up the discussion: poetry is "busy with you's," that is with "meanings made with and against others" (69).

9. Baudelaire, *Flowers of Evil*, 4–7. I am here concerned less with the practical matter of audience than with the poet's way of imagining and hailing audience, the rhetoric of audience. Thus although Pound, echoing other modernists, could express his indifference to the public

and write in *Poetry* in 1913: "I beg you, my friendly critics, / Do not set about to procure me an audience," and declare that "the artist is not dependent on the multitude of his listeners," his rhetoric often reverberates with a sense of large public import and audience or communal gathering (Pound, *Selected Poems*, 25). Thus W.R. Johnson calls Pound "the great *choregos*" who can "talk to all of us, *for* all of us" (*Idea of Lyric*, 194).

10. Johnson, *Idea of Lyric*, 73.

11. See Arthur Kirsch's introduction to *SM*, xi–xxxiv, for discussions of the dualistic principles at work.

12. Eliot, *On Poetry and Poets*, 97.

13. Ibid., 103 and 112.

14. Cited in Mendelson, *Early Auden*, 266.

15. Cunningham, in *Map of All My Youth*, 185.

16. See Jacobs, "Auden and the Dream of Public Poetry."

17. Auden and Isherwood, "The Enemies of a Bishop," in *Complete Works of W.H. Auden: Plays*, 78.

18. Auden and Isherwood, *The Dog Beneath the Skin*, in *Complete Works of W.H. Auden: Plays*, 191.

19. Auden to Spender, June 28, 1935, in *Map of All My Youth*, 64.

20. For a discussion of Auden's use of Augustan rhetorical tradition and its relation to the engagement with audience, see Jeffrey Donaldson's "The Company Poets Keep." Donaldson discusses the issue of Auden's anxiety about a fragmented society and the lapse of poetic authority. See also Patrick Deane's "Within a Field That Never Closes."

21. Larkin, "What's Become of Wystan," 418.

22. Stevens, *Collected Poetry and Prose*, 136.

23. Bethell, *Shakespeare and the Popular Dramatic Tradition*, 29.

24. Ibid.

25. Chapman, "Auden in Ann Arbor," 507.

26. Ibid., quoting Auden, 511.

27. Auden complained to Ursula Niebuhr about the lack of preparation and resistance to criticism among American students. On the other hand, his syllabus for a two-credit course, "Fate and the Individual in European Literature" (1941), suggests he expected a lot from them. The readings covered everything from Greek drama to Eliot's *Family Reunion* and included an international cast of writers and philosophers (*Poetry Foundation*).

28. Christopher Nealon in *The Matter of Capital* argues that "a camp mixture of pleasure and dismay derives from the mismatch of speaker and occasion, in a personified scene of live address.... Commentary, study, commonplace book: the secondary status of forms ... seems strange for a poet, almost a disavowal of the traditional primacy accorded to 'poetry' as a high, or intensified, or immediate literary form. For Auden, though, this secondary is exactly poetry's saving grace" (61–62).

29. In making this point Auden cites C.S. Lewis, who is discussing George MacDonald, thus putting the idea of "commentary" into play. Lewis writes: "Myth does not essentially exist in *words* at all ... what really excites and nourishes me is a pattern of events, which would equally delight and nourish if it had reached me by some medium which involved no words at all—say by a mime, or a film" (*Lectures* 296).

30. Ibid., 297.

31. Rilke, *Uncollected Poems*, 41.

32. Ibid., 42.

33. Kirsch quotes Auden's letter to Theodore Spencer: "Caliban does disturb me profoundly because he doesn't fit in; it is exactly as if one of the audience had walked onto the stage and insisted on taking part in the action. I've tried to work for this effect in a non-theatrical medium, by allowing the reader for the first two chapters not to think of the theater (by inversion, therefore, to be witnessing a performance) and then suddenly wake him up in one (again by inversion, introducing 'real life' into the imagined)" (introduction to *SM*, xxx).

34. Boly, "*The Orators*: The Artist in the Thirties," 2. See also Boly, *Reading Auden*: "Caliban stands for the rights of the otherwise silenced text. Ludic voice against violence of the 'author'" (193).

35. It is possible that Auden had read Archibald MacLeish's famous call for the poet's voice in the work of social transformation, especially since Auden features prominently in that work. MacLeish writes: "To establish the negative revolutions . . . it is necessary first to destroy the authority of the unseen sayings of the mind. . . . Caliban in the miserable and besotted swamp is the symbol of this revolution. As long as the unseen beauty in the air retains its voices and its seductive music and its stinging whips, the revolutions of the gangs are clumsy, blundering, grotesque and foolish. They can bellow and threaten and boast and gesture with their arms, but in the end the invisible voices in the air, the invisible power of the ideal will matter to them. They have one hope of success and only one—the destruction of the whole system of ideas, the whole respect for truth, the whole authority of excellence which places law above force, beauty above cruelty, singleness above numbers" (MacLeish, *Irresponsibles*, 111). But Auden in his "Commentary" on *The Tempest* presents a Caliban who is fully alert to the voices in the air, even if he remains skeptical of their authority.

36. Auden to Mrs. E.R. Dodds, January 20, 1945. Bodleian Library archive.

37. Arthur Kirsch and others emphasize the Christian idea of the inadequacy of human imagination and need for higher order as referent of truth. But the poem has a secular meaning as well, rejecting romanticism (from Rousseau to Hitler) in favor of an idea of art in and for plural community.

38. The epilogue of *The Tempest* puts Prospero in relation to the audience, which is structurally parallel to Ariel's relation to Prospero. Both beg for freedom from a "spell." Auden considered a different option from the address he finally chose, and his notebooks show him persisting with it over several drafts. Prospero's address, "kiss me Caliban," would have retained Prospero as the center. It does not seem that the long prose monologue by Caliban came until rather late in the compositional process (Auden, MS and Notes for *The Sea and the Mirror*, Poetry Collection manuscripts, University of Buffalo).

39. The convention of a poet speaking in the first-person plural with reference to his creative work is well established in neoclassical poetry. See, for instance, Dryden's prologues to his long poems.

40. These words are in quotation marks but not ascribed, and no one has located their source.

41. Moore, *Complete Poems*, 76.

42. Phelan, *Companion to Narrative Theory*, 124.

43. Arthur Kirsch has identified it with an early draft of *For the Time Being*, where the same words were given to Simeon (*SM* 105).

44. Auden, introduction to *Book of Light Verse*, xxiii.

45. Auden to James Stern, *In Solitude, for Company*, 79.

Chapter 7: Crowds, Publics, Congregations

1. DeArmitt, *Right to Narcissism*, 8–9.

2. For a fuller discussion of crowd collectivity and the psychology of mass gathering, see Poggi, *Art and Politics of Artificial Optimism*; Plotz, *The Crowd*; Schnapp and Tiews, *Crowds*; Nickels, *Poetry of the Possible*.

3. Searle, "Collective Intentions and Actions," 401.

4. Ibid., 406.

5. Ibid., 415. Especially in the past couple of years, philosophical studies in social cognition have developed into a rich interdisciplinary field, and the "interactive turn" in cognitive research has led to increased interest in "we-intentionality," but literary criticism has not yet drawn from these insights. "We-mode cognition" and the communicative dynamics of the first-person plural goes well beyond the notion of herd mentality. Sometimes (and literature represents this) we make sense *with* others, forming a combinative or collective viewpoint that suggests a first-person plural subjectivity. Such an approach does not compete with individualism, but in taking into consideration (representing to ourselves) the viewpoints of another or others, we enter into a "we-mode" intentionality that some cognitive theorists find irreducible. See especially Gallotti and Frith, "Social Cognition in the We-Mode."

6. Koerth-Baker, "Crowds Are Not People, My Friend."

7. Brandom, *Making It Explicit*, 3.

8. Ibid., 644.

9. For an online bibliography on collective mentality, see http://philpapers.org/browse /collective-mentality.

10. The notion of the wisdom of crowds is derived in part from the work of economist Friedrich Hayek. James Surowiecki develops the idea in *Wisdom of Crowds*.

11. William Egginton analyzes the ambivalence and deception of phenomenal crowd power, its lure and danger, in his essay "Intimacy and Anonymity, or How the Audience Became a Crowd," in *Crowds*. The crowd "haunts the general good of universal reason with the terror of unified unreason; it haunts the freedom of individual desire as the desire for something more, for shared affect, for community, for greater good" (110).

12. Dreyfus and Kelly, *All Things Shining*, 13

13. Ibid., 202.

14. Ibid., 203.

15. Williams, *Selected Poems*, 57–58.

16. Blake, *Complete Poetry*, 13.

17. Wordsworth, *Major Works*, 303 and 472.

18. Baudelaire, *Paris Spleen*, 20.

19. Whitman, *Complete Poems*, 141.

20. See Canetti, *Crowds and Power*.

21. Pound, *Selected Poems*, 35.

22. Eliot, *Complete Poems and Plays*, 39.

23. Ibid., 56.

24. Sandburg, *The People, Yes*, ii.

25. Sandburg, *Selected Poems*, 173.

26. MacLeish, *Public Speech*, n.p.

27. Stevens, *Collected Poetry and Prose*, 98.

28. See Schnapp, "Mob Porn," in *Crowds*.

29. Stevens, *Collected Poetry and Prose*, 188.

30. For other versions of Auden's statement on these "human pluralities," see *Prose* III 162–63 and 226.

31. Canetti, *Crowds and Power*, 31.

32. For an analysis of Auden's early voice-over texts for film, see Jonathan Foltz, "Vehicles of the Ordinary."

33. Whitman, *Complete Poems*, 189.

34. "It is not given to every man to take a bath of multitude" (Baudelaire, *Paris Spleen*, 20).

35. MacLeish, *Time to Speak*, 88.

36. Gasset, *Revolt of the Masses*, 11–12.

37. Canetti, *Crowds and Power*, 80 and 83.

38. Ibid., 85.

39. Buber, "What Is Common to All," 106.

40. Auden's attraction to the blues form with its tragicomic effects and its folk associations can be seen in a letter to Annie Dodds written in 1939, during his trip through the American Southwest with Kallman: "Heard fragment of a spiritual the other day:

> You can't get to Heaven in a limousine
> 'Cause the Lawd ain got no gasoline
> Ain gonna grieve ma Lawd no mo
>
> You can't chew terbacca on the Golden Floor
> 'Cause the Lawd ain got no cuspidor.
>
> You can't go to Heaven on a pair of Skis
> 'cause you'll skid right past St. Peter's knees." (Auden to Mrs. E.R. Dodds, June 8, 1939, Bodleian Library)

41. Auden's preoccupation with the moral import of faces is everywhere in his poetry: "huge hurt face accuses / And pardons nothing" in "The Sphinx" (*CP* 175); "Faces along the bar" in "September 1, 1939" (*SP* 96); "Easily, my dear"; "The Summer Holds"; "Sonnets from China" (late numbering) VIII, IX, XI, XII, XX; "The Shield of Achilles"; "The faceless machine / Lacks a surround" in "The Age of Anxiety" (*CP* 450) are just a few.

42. "The United States and the Holocaust," United States Holocaust Memorial Museum, www.ushmm.org/wlc/en/article.php?ModuleId=10005182.

43. This is echoed in "New Year Letter": "A little crowd smash up a shop, / Suspended hatreds crystallise / In visible hostilities" (*CP* 198).

44. James, *American Scene*, 65.

45. Carpenter, *Biography*, 211.

46. Kathleen Bell's essay in *Map of All My Youth* discusses this more broadly (101 ff.).

47. "In a society which has become a public, a gifted man like Baudelaire is placed in a peculiar position: his gifts enforce a clarity of consciousness which makes it impossible for him to join the crowd; they compel him to raise those questions which the public by tacit consent represses" (*Prose* II 313). Auden uses this introduction to extend Baudelaire's view of the public to his own time and place. His aversion to urban mass culture here, as opposed to primitive rural association, is extreme: "The members of a traditional society—say a Chinese peasant village—are not fully developed individually, but they have not lost their potential capacity to become so, and one can therefore say that, as far as they have gone and as far as one knows, they are individuals. The members of a public—say, the evening crowds on Times Square—have been offered the possibility of full development but have rejected it, and by this rejection have lost the right to be called individuals" (312–13). Baudelaire would be unlikely to follow Auden in this condemnation of the urban crowd.

48. Jarrell responded: "It's quite a nice Graves poem. . . . But how extraordinary that Auden should have written [it]" (*Jarrell on Auden*, 80).

49. Auden, *Later Auden*, 367.

50. Fuller, *Commentary*, 423.

51. Korg, *Ritual and Experiment*, 7.

52. Mendelson, *Early Auden*, 259.

53. See Korg, *Ritual and Experiment*. Surprisingly, Korg does not discuss Auden though he makes reference to him.

54. Auden, quoted in Sharpe, "The Church of England: Auden's Anglicanism," 82.

55. Gospel of Mark 15:13–14.

56. As Adrian Caesar has argued in "Auden and the Class System": "A richly ambivalent gloss on 'brotherhood' is given when we are told that 'joining the crowd' 'is the only thing all men can do.' But we, as an audience, know that the crowd watching the death of Christ were not so worshipping; 'brotherhood' for Auden remains an abstract possibility, but it depends on the individuals within the crowd to join in belief" (76). And yet, as Alan Jacobs has argued, Auden insists on embodiment ("Auden and Theology," 178).

Chapter 8: Invitations to the Common

1. Stevens, *Collected Poetry and Prose*, 56.

2. Eliot, *Complete Poems and Plays*, 7.

3. Frost, *Poetry*, 119.

4. Arnold, *Works*, 401.

5. Woolf, "Mr. Bennett and Mrs. Brown," 194.

6. Warren, *Fables of the Self*, 272.

7. Vendler, *Soul Says*, 2–3.

8. Vendler, *On Extended Wings*, 68.

9. Stevens, *Collected Poetry and Prose*, 106.

10. Ibid., 121.

11. Bishop, *Poems, Prose, and Letters*, 52.

12. Vendler, *Soul Says*, 3.

13. Johnson, *Idea of Lyric*, 33.

14. Ibid., 23.

15. Buber, *Knowledge of Man*, 106.

16. Yeats, *Poems*, 221.

17. Pound, *Literary Essays*, 5.

18. von Hallberg, *Lyric Powers*, 195.

19. Ibid., 189.

20. Ibid., 191.

21. Thomas Nagel's recent book *The View from Nowhere* (1989) articulates a method of cognition and argument that constantly proposes an impersonal view even as it accounts for layered subjectivities. Human beings have the unique ability to view the world in a detached way. We can think about the world in terms that transcend our own experience or interest and consider the world from a vantage point that is, in Nagel's words, "nowhere in particular." At the same time, each of us is a particular person in a particular place, each with his own "personal" view of the world, a view that we can recognize as just one aspect of the whole. How do we reconcile these two standpoints—intellectually, morally, and practically? To what extent are they irreconcilable and to what extent can they be integrated? Nagel's ambitious and lively book tackles this fundamental issue, arguing that our divided nature is the root of a whole range of philosophical problems, touching, as it does, every aspect of human life. He deals with its manifestations in such fields of philosophy as the mind-body problem, personal identity, knowledge and skepticism, thought and reality, free will, ethics, the relation between moral and other values, the meaning of life, and death. Excessive objectification has been a malady of recent analytic philosophy, claims Nagel; it has led to implausible forms of reductionism in the philosophy of mind and elsewhere. The solution is not to inhibit the objectifying impulse but to insist that it learn to live alongside the internal perspectives that cannot be either discarded or objectified. Reconciliation between the two standpoints, in the end, is not always possible.

22. Theodor Adorno, quoted in von Hallberg, *Lyric Powers*, 199.

23. Williams, *Autobiography*, 391.

24. Williams, *Selected Essays*, 197–98.

25. Bishop, *Poems, Prose, and Letters*, 4.

26. Hofmann, "Mostly Middle," 15.

27. See Rosen, *Power, Plain English*, 128.

28. See Ellmann's *Poetics of Impersonality* and Hofmann's "Mostly Middle."

29. Cameron, *Impersonality*, 149.

30. See Paul Grimstad's "On Ecstasy," in *American Impersonal*. A surprising number of the essays in this collection direct Cameron's insights about impersonality, which focus on individual cognition, toward social imagining. Johannes Voelz, for instance, in "The Recognition of Emerson's Impersonal," asks how impersonality "enables the social world it appears to eradicate" (Arsić, preface to *American Impersonal*, x).

31. Simone Weil, quoted in Cameron, *Impersonality*, 130.

32. Cameron, *Impersonality*, 128.

33. MacDonald, *Serious Poetry*, 4.

34. Ibid., 7. Natalie Pollard makes a similar critique of Larkin: "Larkin himself rarely uses the second-person pronoun, preferring instead the inclusive 'we' or 'one' which holds a body of yous together, as if they stood as one, sharing the same perspective and position: 'And we are nudged from comfort, never knowing,' 'What will survive of us is love'. . . . Such addresses tend to enact an evasion of you that as Virginia Walker Jackson complains, 'converts the isolated "I" into the universal "we" by bypassing the mediation of any particular "you"'" (*Speaking to You*, 29).

35. MacDonald, *Serious Poetry*, 9–10.

36. Ibid., 5.

37. Ibid., 107.

38. Ibid., 127.

39. Jarrell, *Jarrell on Auden*, 50.

40. Larkin, "What's Become of Wystan," 417.

41. Greif, *Age of the Crisis of Man*, 12.

42. Ibid., 13.

43. Niebuhr, *Essential*, 109.

44. Ibid.

45. Weil, *Reader*, 319.

46. Auden and Kronenberger, *Faber Book of Aphorisms*, 18 and 45.

47. Auden, foreword to Rosenstock-Huessy, *I Am an Impure Thinker*, i–ii.

48. In *Speech and Reality*, a 1970 compilation of his essays, his "cross of reality" forms in four pronominal positions that delineate his history of Christianity.

49. Rosenstock-Huessy, *Speech and Reality*, 109.

50. Ibid., 82.

51. See Thekla Clark, *Wystan and Chester*, 12, for a personal account of Auden's changing attitude toward the camera.

52. Isherwood, *Berlin Stories*, 1.

53. Curiously, in *The Dyer's Hand* this is also the world as seen by "The Poet," who is known for his visual imagination and his attention to nature, in contrast to "the Historian." In "Memorial for the City," Auden seems to be configuring the alignments somewhat differently, though perhaps the length of the opening scene has something to do with "The Poet's" predilections.

54. Jacobs, "Auden's Theology," 176.

55. Jacobs sees Auden as a precursor to contemporary communitarian values, and he traces these values to Horace (see "Auden's Local Culture"). But this reading overlooks the cosmopolitan self that Auden creates in his late work, in which, as Justin Quinn has argued in "Auden International," Auden constructed "an internationalized self," a "universal self" that is "a human subject basic to all cultures (through the poems, but also through his intellectual engagement with, above all, Hannah Arendt)" (159–60).

56. Replogle, *Auden's Poetry*, 206.

57. Lowrie, "Horace Odes 4," 220–21.

58. See Rosen, *Power, Plain English*, 123–80.

59. See von Hallberg's *Lyric Powers* and Spiegelman's *Didactic Muse*.

60. See Muldoon, *End of the Poem*, 343–67.

61. Jarrell, *Jarrell on Auden*, 59.

62. Emig, *Toward a Postmodern Poetics*, 114

63. Altieri, *Art of Twentieth-Century Poetry*, 149.

Chapter 9: The Future of Us

1. Oppen, *New Collected Poems*, 167.

2. Ibid., 172.

3. Ibid., 161.

4. Ibid., 165.

5. Ibid., 166.

6. See "A Highly Charged Pronoun: 'We' in Three September 1 Poems," by Pavla Veselá.

7. Hirshfield, Q&A.

8. Oren Izenberg, *Being Numerous*, 4.

9. See my essay "Lyric and the First Person Plural" for a discussion of Bishop's "we"; also my "A Whole Climate of Opinion."

10. Larkin, *Complete Poems*, 61.

11. Merrill, *Collected Poems*, 669–73.

12. Wasley, *Age of Auden*, 164.

13. Rich, *Later Poems*, 14.

14. Rich, *Early Poems*, 294.

15. Rich, *Later Poems*, 248.

16. Ibid., 279.

17. Wasley, *Age of Auden*, 172.

18. Rich, *Later Poems*, 45.

19. Oppen, *New Collected Poems*, 181.

20. Ibid., 143.

21. Ibid., 153.

22. Ibid., 178.

23. Ibid., 163.

24. Nicholls, *George Oppen and the Fate of Modernism*, 98.

25. Oppen, *New Collected Poems*, 167, 171.

26. Nicholls, *George Oppen and the Fate of Modernism*, 98.

27. Glück, *Wild Iris*, 14.

28. Donnelly, *Cloud Corporation*, 32.

29. Ibid., 14.

30. Ibid., 32.

31. Oppen, *New Collected Poems*, 168.

32. Spahr, "Her Gentle Now Don't Add to Heartache," in *This Connection of Everything with Lungs*, 6.

33. Spahr, "We," in *Fuck You—Aloha—I Love You*, 85.

34. Spahr, *That Winter the Wolf Came*, back cover.

35. The more likely source for the graffiti artist is Stephen Colbert's mock self-help book *I Am America (And So Can You!)*, of which Bernes is unaware.

36. Louise Glück (who has written of Oppen's importance as a model) offers another example of the "we"-oriented archetypal journey poem in her *Faithful and Virtuous Night*.

37. Mackey, interview by Jeanne Heuving, 215–16.

38. Ibid.

39. Mackey, *Splay Anthem*, 8.

40. Ibid.

41. Mackey, "The Atmosphere Is Alive."

42. Mackey, *Splay Anthem*, 126.

Agamben, Giorgio. *The Coming Community*. Minneapolis: University of Minnesota Press, 1993.

Altieri, Charles. *The Art of Twentieth-Century Poetry*. Oxford: Blackwell, 2006.

Anderson, Benedict. *Imagined Communities*. London: Verso, 1983.

Anderson, Quentin. *The Imperial Self: An Essay in American Literary and Cultural History*. New York: Knopf, 1971.

Arendt, Hannah. *The Human Condition*. 1958. Reprint, Chicago: University of Chicago Press, 1998.

Arnold, Matthew. *Poems*. London: Longman, Brown, Green, and Longmans, 1854.

———. *The Works of Matthew Arnold*. Ware: Wordsworth, 1995.

Arsić, Branka, ed. *American Impersonal: Essays with Sharon Cameron*. New York: Bloomsbury, 2014.

Auden, W. H. *The Age of Anxiety: A Baroque Eclogue*. Edited by Alan Jacobs. Princeton: Princeton University Press, 2011.

———. *Another Time*. New York: Random House, 1940.

———. *A Certain World: A Commonplace Book*. London: Faber & Faber, 1971.

———. *Collected Poems*. Edited by Edward Mendelson. New York: Random House, 2007.

———. *Collected Shorter Poems*. London: Faber & Faber, 1966.

———. *The Complete Works of W. H. Auden: Libretti and Other Dramatic Writings, 1939–1973*. Edited by Edward Mendelson. Princeton: Princeton University Press, 1993.

———. *The Complete Works of W. H. Auden: Plays and Other Dramatic Writings, 1928–1938*. Edited by Edward Mendelson. Princeton: Princeton University Press, 1988.

———. *The Complete Works of W. H. Auden: Prose*. Edited by Edward Mendelson. 4 vols. Princeton: Princeton University Press, 1997–2010.

———. *Correspondence with Mrs. E. R. Dodds*. Bodleian Library Archive. Oxford University.

———. *The Double Man*. New York: Random House, 1941.

———. *The Dyer's Hand and Other Essays*. New York: Vintage, 1989.

———. *The Enchafèd Flood: or, The Romantic Iconography of the Sea*. Charlottesville: University Press of Virginia, 1950.

———. *The English Auden: Poems, Essays and Dramatic Writings, 1927–1939*. Edited by Edward Mendelson. London: Faber & Faber, 1977.

———. "Epithalamium for C. Day-Lewis." In *Cecil Day-Lewis: An English Literary Life*, by Sean Day-Lewis. Appendix 1. London: Weidenfeld & Nicolson, 1980.

———. *For the Time Being*. London: Faber & Faber, 1945.

————. *Forewords and Afterwords.* Edited by Edward Mendelson. New York: Random House, 1973.

————. *"In Solitude, for Company": W. H. Auden After 1940.* Vol. 3 of *Auden Studies.* Edited by Katherine Bucknell and Nicholas Jenkins. Oxford: Oxford University Press, 1995.

————. *Juvenilia.* Edited by Katherine Bucknell. Princeton: Princeton University Press, 1994.

————. *Lectures on Shakespeare.* Edited by Arthur Kirsch. Princeton: Princeton University Press, 1994.

————. *Look, Stranger!* London: Faber & Faber, 1936.

————. *"The Map of All My Youth": Early Works, Friends, and Influences.* Edited by Katherine Bucknell and Nicholas Jenkins. Oxford: Clarendon Press, 2001.

————. *New Year Letter.* London: Faber & Faber, 1941.

————. *Nones.* New York: Random House, 1951.

————. *The Orators.* 1932. Reprint, New York: Random House, 1966.

————. Papers. Henry W. and Albert A. Berg Collection of English and American Literature. New York City Public Library.

————. Papers. Poetry Collection. University of Buffalo.

————. *The Sea and the Mirror.* Edited by Arthur Kirsch. Princeton: Princeton University Press, 2003.

————. *Selected Poems.* Edited by Edward Mendelson. New York: Vintage, 2007.

————. Syllabus for "Fate and the Individual in European Literature" (1941) at the University of Michigan. *Poetry Foundation.* Posted February 3, 2015. www.poetryfoundation.org/harriet /2015/02/found-w-h-auden-syllabus-for-fate-and-the-individual-in-european-literature.

Auden, W. H., and Christopher Isherwood. *Journey to a War.* 1939. Reprint, London: Faber & Faber, 1973.

Auden, W. H., and Louis Kronenberger, eds. *The Faber Book of Aphorisms.* London: Faber & Faber, 1970.

Auden, W. H., and Louis MacNeice. *Letters from Iceland.* New York: Paragon, 1937.

Austin, J. L. *How to Do Things with Words.* Oxford: Oxford University Press, 1962.

Bahlke, George W. *Critical Essays on W. H. Auden.* New York: G. K. Hall, 1991.

Baldwin, James. "Fifth Avenue Uptown: A Letter from Harlem." *Esquire,* July 1960.

Bandom, Robert B. *Making It Explicit: Reasoning, Representing, and Discursive Commitment.* Cambridge, MA: Harvard University Press, 1994.

Baudelaire, Charles. *The Flowers of Evil.* Translated by James McGowan. Oxford: Oxford University Press, 1993.

————. *Intimate Journals.* Translated by Louis Varèse. London: Blackamoor, 1930.

————. *Paris Spleen.* Translated by James McGowan. New York: New Directions, 1970.

Benveniste, Émile. *Problems in General Linguistics.* Translated by Mary Elizabeth Meek. Coral Gables: Miami University Press, 1971.

Berger, Charles. "Auden in Time of War." *Raritan* 17, no. 2 (1997): 79–89.

Berry, Francis. *Poets' Grammar: Person, Time and Mood in Poetry.* New York: Routledge & Kegan Paul, 1958.

Berry, R. M. "Is 'Us' Me? Cultural Studies and the Universality of Aesthetic Judgments." In *Stanley Cavell and Literary Studies: The Consequences of Skepticism,* edited by Richard Eldridge and Bernard Rhie, 30–46. New York: Continuum, 2011.

Bertacco, Simona, and John Gibson. "Skepticism and the Idea of an Other." In *Stanley Cavell and Literary Studies*, edited by Richard Eldridge and Bernard Rhie, 106–19. New York: Bloomsbury, 2011.

Bethell, Samuel. *Shakespeare and the Popular Dramatic Tradition*. Durham, NC: Duke University Press, 1944.

Bishop, Elizabeth. *Poems, Prose, and Letters*. Edited by Robert Giroux and Lloyd Schwartz. New York: Library of America, 2008.

Blake, William. *The Complete Poetry and Prose of William Blake*. Edited by David V. Erdman. Revised edition. Berkeley: University of California Press, 2008.

Blanchot, Maurice. *The Unavowable Community*. Barrytown, NY: Station Hill Press, 2006.

Bloom, Harold, ed. *W. H. Auden: Modern Critical Views*. New York: Chelsea House, 1986.

Bloom, Paul. "First Person Plural." *The Atlantic*, November 2008.

———. *How Pleasure Works*. New York: Norton, 2010.

———. "Song of My Selves." *The Atlantic*, November 2008.

Boas, Franz. *Introduction to Handbook of American Indian Languages*. Washington, DC: Bureau of American Ethnology, 1911.

Bogan, Louise. *Selected Letters of Louise Bogan*. Edited by Ruth Limmer. New York: Harcourt, 1973.

Boly, John. "*The Orators*: The Artist in the Thirties." In *Modern Critical Views: W. H. Auden*, edited by Harold Bloom, 121–33. New York: Chelsea House, 1986.

———. *Reading Auden: The Returns of Caliban*. Ithaca: Cornell University Press, 1991.

Bostridge, Ian. *Winter Journey: Anatomy of an Obsession*. New York: Knopf, 2015.

Bozorth, Richard R. *Auden's Games of Knowledge: Poetry and the Meanings of Homosexuality*. New York: Columbia University Press, 2001.

Brandom, Robert B. *Making It Explicit: Reasoning, Representing and Discursive Commitment*. Cambridge, MA: Harvard University Press, 1994.

Britten, Benjamin. *Journeying Boy: The Diaries of the Young Benjamin Britten, 1928–1938*. Edited by John Evans. London: Faber & Faber, 2009.

Brooks, Gwendolyn. *In the Mecca*. New York: Harper & Row, 1968.

———. *Selected Poems*. New York: Harper Perennial, 2006.

Brunner, Edward. *Cold War Poetry*. Urbana: University of Illinois Press, 2004.

Bryant, Marsha. *Auden and Documentary in the 1930s*. Charlottesville: University Press of Virginia, 1997.

Buber, Martin. *I and Thou*. Translated by Ronald Gregor Smith. New York: Scribner, 1958.

———. *Knowledge of Man*. London: Allen & Unwin, 1965.

———. *Martin Buber on Psychology and Psychotherapy: Essays, Letters, and Dialogue*. Edited by Judith Buber Agassi. Syracuse, NY: Syracuse University Press, 1999.

Caesar, Adrian. "Auden and the Class System." In *Auden in Context*, edited by Tony Sharpe, 69–88. Cambridge: Cambridge University Press, 2013.

Cameron, Sharon. *Impersonality: Seven Essays*. Chicago: University of Chicago Press, 2007.

Canetti, Elias. *Crowds and Power*. New York: Farrar, Straus & Giroux, 1984.

Carpenter, Humphrey. *W. H. Auden: A Biography*. Boston: Houghton Mifflin, 1981.

Cavell, Stanley. *The Cavell Reader*. Edited by Stephen Mulhall. Cambridge, MA: Wiley-Blackwell, 1996.

———. *Must We Mean What We Say?* 1969. Reprint, Cambridge: Cambridge University Press, 1976.

———. *The Senses of Walden.* Expanded edition. Chicago: University of Chicago Press, 1992.

Celan, Paul. *Selected Poems and Prose.* Translated by John Felstiner. New York: Norton 2001.

Chapman, Robert L. "Auden in Ann Arbor." *Michigan Quarterly Review* 17, no. 4 (1978): 507–20.

Christie, Stuart. "Disorientations: Canon without Context in Auden's China Sonnets." *PMLA* 120, no. 5 (October 2005): 1576–87.

Clark, Thekla. *Wystan and Chester: A Personal Memoir of W. H. Auden and Chester Kallman.* London: Faber & Faber, 1995.

Cohen, Ted. *Thinking of Others: On the Talent for Metaphor.* Princeton: Princeton University Press, 2008.

Cole, Stewart. "Love and Other Gods: Personification and Volition in Auden." *Twentieth Century Literature* 60, no. 3 (Fall 2014): 367–96.

Connolly, William. *Identity/Difference: Democratic Notions of Political Paradox.* Minneapolis: University of Minnesota Press, 1991.

Costello, Bonnie. "'A Whole Climate of Opinion': Auden's Influence on Bishop." *Literary Imagination* 5, no. 1 (Winter 2003): 19–41.

———. "Lyric and the First Person Plural." In *Something Understood,* edited by Steven Burt, 193–206. Charlottesville: University Press of Virginia, 2009.

Cowley, Malcolm. *The Dream of the Golden Mountains: Remembering the 1930s.* New York: Viking, 1980.

Crumbley, Paul. "Emily Dickinson." In *The Oxford Companion to Women's Writing in the United States,* edited by Cathy N. Davidson and Linda Wagner-Martin, 247–49. New York: Oxford University Press, 1995.

Cunningham, Valentine. *British Writers of the Thirties.* Oxford: Oxford University Press, 1987.

Davenport-Hines, Richard. *W. H. Auden.* London: Vintage, 1995.

Deane, Patrick. "'Within a Field That Never Closes': The Reader in W. H. Auden's 'New Year Letter.'" *Contemporary Literature* 32, no. 2 (Summer 1991): 171–93.

DeArmitt, Pleshette. *The Right to Narcissism: A Case for an Im-possible Self-Love.* New York: Fordham University Press, 2014.

Deutsch, Babette. "Poetry for the People." *The English Journal* 26, no. 4 (1937): 265–74.

Dickinson, Emily. *The Poems of Emily Dickinson.* Edited by R. W. Franklin. Cambridge, MA: Harvard University Press, 1999.

Donaldson, Jeffrey. "The Company Poets Keep: Allusion, Echo, and the Question of Who Is Listening in W. H. Auden and James Merrill." *Contemporary Literature* 36, no. 1 (1995): 35–57.

Donne, John. *The Poems of John Donne.* Edited by Robin Robbins. Vol. 1. New York: Routledge, 2008.

Donnelly, Tim. *Cloud Corporation.* Seattle: Wave Books, 2010.

Dreyfus, Hubert, and Sean Dorrance Kelly. *All Things Shining.* New York: Free Press, 2011.

Dubrow, Heather. *The Challenges of Orpheus.* Baltimore: Johns Hopkins University Press, 2007.

———. *Echoes of Desire: English Petrarchism and Its Counterdiscourses.* Ithaca: Cornell University Press, 1995.

———. "'Nor is here one single here': Towards a Reevaluation of Immediacy in the Sonnet Tradition." *Literary Imagination* 12, no. 3 (2010): 296–306.

Dunbar, Paul Laurence. *Selected Poems.* New York: Dover, 1997.

Eagleman, David. *Incognito: The Secret Lives of the Brain.* New York: Random House, 2011.

Egginton, William. "Intimacy and Anonymity, or How the Audience Became a Crowd." In *Crowds,* edited by Jeffrey T. Schnapp and Matthew Tiews, 97–110. Palo Alto: Stanford University Press, 2006.

Eliot, T. S. *The Complete Poems and Plays, 1909–1950.* New York: Harcourt, Brace, 1971.

———. *On Poetry and Poets.* New York: Farrar, Straus & Giroux, 1957.

Ellmann, Maud. *The Poetics of Impersonality: T. S. Eliot and Ezra Pound.* Edinburgh: Edinburgh University Press, 2013.

Emig, Rainer. *W. H. Auden: Towards a Postmodern Poetics.* London: Palgrave, 2000.

Empson, William. *Seven Types of Ambiguity.* 1930. Reprint, New York: New Directions, 1966.

Esposito, Roberto. *Communitas.* Translated by Timothy Campbell. Palo Alto: Stanford University Press, 2009.

Farr, Judith. *The Passion of Emily Dickinson.* Cambridge, MA: Harvard University Press, 1998.

Firchow, Peter. *Auden: Contexts for the Poetry.* Newark: University of Delaware Press, 2002.

Foltz, Jonathan. "Vehicles of the Ordinary: W. H. Auden and Cinematic Address." In *Auden at Work,* edited by Bonnie Costello and Rachel Galvin, 49–68. Houndsmills: Palgrave, 2015.

Freud, Sigmund. *The Future of an Illusion.* Garden City, NY: Anchor, 1961.

Frost, Robert. *The Poetry of Robert Frost.* Edited by Edward Connery Lathem. New York: Henry Holt, 2002.

Frye, Northrop. *Anatomy of Criticism.* Princeton: Princeton University Press, 1957.

Fuller, John. *W. H. Auden: A Commentary.* London: Faber & Faber, 1998.

Fussell, Paul. *The Great War and Modern Memory.* New York: Oxford University Press, 1975.

Gallotti, Mattia, and Chris D. Frith. "Social Cognition in the We-Mode." *Trends in Cognitive Sciences* 17, no. 14 (April 2013): 160–65.

Glück, Louise. *The Wild Iris.* New York: Ecco Press, 1993.

Gordon, Neve. "Ethics and the Place of the Other in Levinas and Buber." In *Dialogue and Difference,* edited by Peter Atterton, Matthew Calarco, and Maurice Friedman, 98–115. Pittsburgh: Duquesne University Press, 2004.

Gottlieb, Susannah Young-Ah. *Regions of Sorrow: Anxiety and Messianism in Hannah Arendt and W. H. Auden.* Palo Alto: Stanford University Press, 2003.

———. "'With Conscious Artifice': Auden's Defense of Marriage." *Diacritics* 35, no. 4 (2005): 23–41.

Graham, Jorie. "We." *London Review of Books* 37 no. 1 (January 8, 2015): 8–9.

Greenberg, Herbert. *Quest for the Necessary: W. H. Auden and the Dilemma of Divided Consciousness.* Cambridge, MA: Harvard University Press, 1968.

Greene, Joshua. *Moral Tribes: Emotion, Reason, and the Gap between Us and Them.* New York: Penguin, 2013.

Greif, Mark. *The Age of the Crisis of Man: Thought and Fiction in America, 1933–1973.* Princeton: Princeton University Press, 2015.

———. "Cavell as Educator." *n+1,* Fall 2011.

Grice, Paul. *Studies in the Way of Words.* Cambridge, MA: Harvard University Press, 1989.

Grimstad, Paul. "On Ecstasy: Sharon Cameron's Reading of Emerson." In *American Impersonal: Essays with Sharon Cameron,* edited by Branka Arsić, 57–72. New York: Bloomsbury, 2014.

Hedley, Jane. *"I Made You to Find Me": The Coming Age of the Woman Poet and the Politics of Poetic Address.* Columbus: Ohio State University Press, 2009.

Hirshfield, Jane. Q&A for "Sentencings," *Poetry Magazine,* December 2010.

Hofmann, Michael. "Mostly Middle." *London Review of Books,* September 8, 2011.

Hynes, Samuel. *The Auden Generation: Literature and Politics in England in the 1930s.* New York: Viking, 1976.

Isherwood, Christopher. *The Berlin Stories.* New York: New Directions, 1945.

Izenberg, Oren. *Being Numerous: Poetry and the Ground of Social Life.* Princeton: Princeton University Press, 2011.

Izzo, David Garrett, ed. *W. H. Auden: A Legacy.* West Cornwall, CT: Locust Hill Press, 2002.

Jacobs, Alan. "Auden and the Dream of Public Poetry." In *Literature and the Renewal of the Public Sphere,* edited by Susan VanZanten Gallagher and M. D. Walhout, 83–104. New York: St. Martin's Press, 2000.

———. "Auden's Local Culture." *The Hudson Review* 47, no. 4 (Winter 1995): 543–68.

———. "Auden's Theology." In *Auden in Context,* edited by Tony Sharpe, 170–80. Cambridge: Cambridge University Press, 2013.

———. *What Became of Wystan.* Fayetteville: University of Arkansas Press, 1998.

James, Henry. *The American Scene.* Edited by John F. Sears. London: Penguin, 1994.

Jarrell, Randall. *Randall Jarrell on W. H. Auden.* Edited by Stephen Burt and Hannah Brooks-Mohl. New York: Columbia University Press, 2005.

Johnson, W. R. *The Idea of Lyric: Lyric Modes in Ancient and Modern Poetry.* Berkeley: University of California Press, 1982.

Kacewicz, Ewa, Matthew Davis, and James W. Pennebaker. "Pronoun Use Reflects Standings in Social Hierarchies." *Journal of Language and Social Psychology* 33, no. 2 (March 2014): 125–43.

Keniston, Anne. *Overheard Voices: Address and Subjectivity in Postmodern American Poetry.* New York: Routledge, 2006.

Kerr, Douglas. "Journey to a War: 'A test for men from Europe.'" In *W. H. Auden: A Legacy,* edited by David Garrett Izzo, 275–96. West Cornwall, CT: Locust Hill Press, 2002.

Kierkegaard, Søren. *The Living Thoughts of Søren Kierkegaard.* Edited with an introduction by W. H. Auden. New York: New York Review Books, 1999.

Kipling, Rudyard. *The Collected Poems of Rudyard Kipling.* Ware: Wordsworth Editions, 1991.

Koerth-Baker, Maggie. "Crowds Are not People, My Friend," *New York Times,* December 8, 2012.

Korg, Jacob. *Ritual and Experiment.* New York: St. Martin's Press, 1995.

Kurnick, David. *Empty Houses: Theatrical Failure and the Novel.* Princeton: Princeton University Press, 2011.

Lanham, Richard. *Analyzing Prose.* 2nd ed. New York: Continuum, 2003.

Larkin, Philip. *The Complete Poems.* Edited by Archie Burnett. New York: Farrar, Straus & Giroux, 2013.

———. "What's Become of Wystan?" In *W. H. Auden: The Critical Heritage,* edited by John Haffenden, 414–19. London: Routledge, 1997.

Lehman, David. "In the Cool Element of Prose." In *Critical Essays on W. H. Auden,* edited by George W. Bahlke, 45–53. Boston: GK Hall, 1991.

Levinas, Emmanuel. *Entre Nous.* Translated by Michael B. Smith and Barbara Harshav. New York: Columbia University Press, 2000.

———. *Levinas Reader.* Edited by Sean Hand. New York: Blackwell, 1989.

Lewis, C. S. *The Allegory of Love: A Study in Medieval Tradition.* Oxford: Oxford University Press, 1936.

Lowell, Robert. *Collected Poems.* Edited by Frank Bidart and David Gewanter. New York: Farrar, Straus & Giroux, 2007.

Lowrie, Michèle. "Horace Odes 4." In *A Companion to Horace,* edited by Gregson Davis, 210–30. New York: Blackwell, 2010.

MacDonald, Peter. *Serious Poetry: Form and Authority from Yeats to Hill.* 2002. Reprint, Oxford: Oxford University Press, 2010.

Mackey, Nathaniel. "The Atmosphere Is Alive: Nathaniel Mackey in Conversation." Interview by Sarah Rosenthal. *Poets.org.* Posted February 20, 2014. www.poets.org/poetsorg/text /atmosphere-alive-nathaniel-mackey-conversation.

———. Interview by Jeanne Heuving. *Contemporary Literature* 53, no. 2 (Summer 2012): 207–36.

———. *Splay Anthem.* New York: New Directions, 2006.

MacLeish, Archibald. *The Irresponsibles: A Declaration.* New York: Duell, Sloan and Pearce, 1940.

———. *Public Speech: Poems.* London: Boriswood, 1936.

———. *Time to Speak: Selected Prose of Archibald MacLeish.* Boston: Houghton Mifflin, 1941.

Marshall, Alan. *American Experimental Poetry and Democratic Thought.* Oxford: Oxford University Press, 2009.

Mendelson, Edward. "The Coherence of Auden's *The Orators.*" *ELH* 35, no. 1 (March 1968): 114–33.

———. *Early Auden.* Cambridge, MA: Harvard University Press, 1981.

———. *Later Auden.* New York: Farrar, Straus & Giroux, 1999.

Merrill, James. *Collected Poems.* New York: Knopf, 2001.

Moore, Marianne. *Complete Poems.* London: Penguin, 1981.

Muldoon, Paul. *The End of the Poem: Oxford Lectures.* New York: Farrar, Straus & Giroux, 2007.

Nagel, Thomas. *The View from Nowhere.* Oxford: Oxford University Press, 1989.

Nancy, Jean-Luc. *Being Singular/Plural.* Palo Alto: Stanford University Press, 2000.

———. *The Inoperative Community.* Minneapolis: University of Minnesota Press, 1991.

Nealon, Christopher. *The Matter of Capital.* Cambridge, MA: Harvard University Press, 2011.

Nelson, Cary. *Repression and Recovery: Modern American Poetry and the Politics of Cultural Memory, 1910–1945.* Madison: University of Wisconsin Press, 1989.

Nelson, Deborah. *Pursuing Privacy in Cold War America.* New York: Columbia University Press, 2002.

Neve, Gordon. "Ethics and the Place of the Other in Levinas and Buber." In *Levinas and Buber: Dialogue and Difference,* edited by Peter Atterton, Matthew Calarco, and Maurice Friedman, 98–115. Pittsburgh: Duquesne University Press, 2004.

Nicholls, Peter. *George Oppen and the Fate of Modernism.* Oxford: Oxford University Press, 2007.

———. "Poetry and Rhetoric: Modernism and Beyond." In *The Oxford Handbook of Modern and Contemporary Poetry,* edited by Cary Nelson, 173–94. Oxford: Oxford University Press, 2012.

Nickels, Joel. *The Poetry of the Possible: Spontaneity, Modernism, and the Multitude.* Minneapolis: University of Minnesota Press, 2012.

Notley, Alice. "Walking That Stretch for a Second." Interview by Yasmine Shamma. *Jacket2,* March 18, 2009, http://jacketmagazine.com/40/iv-notley-ivb-shamma-2009.shtml.

Nussbaum, Martha. *Love's Knowledge*. New York: Oxford University Press, 1990.

Nygren, Anders. *Eros and Agape*. New York: Harper & Row, 1953.

Obama, Barack. "Remarks by the President at the 50th Anniversary of the Selma to Montgom-
ery Marches." March 7, 2015. www.whitehouse.gov/the-press-office/2015/03/07/remarks
-president-50th-anniversary-selma-montgomery-marches.

Oppen, George. *New Collected Poems*. New York: New Directions, 2008.

Ortega y Gasset, José. *The Revolt of the Masses*. 1930. Reprint, New York: Norton, 1994.

Phelan, James. *A Companion to Narrative Theory*. Cambridge, MA: Wiley Blackwell, 2005.

Plato. *The Essential Plato*. Translated by Benjamin Jowett. New York: Quality Paperback Book
Club, 1999.

Plotz, John. *The Crowd: British Literature and Public Politics*. Berkeley: University of California
Press, 2000.

Poggi, Christine. *The Art and Politics of Artificial Optimism*. Princeton: Princeton University
Press, 2009.

Pollard, Natalie. *Speaking to You: Contemporary Poetry and Public Address*. Oxford: Oxford University Press, 2012.

Pound, Ezra. *Literary Essays of Ezra Pound*. Edited by T. S. Eliot. New York: New Directions, 1968.

———. *Selected Poems*. New York: New Directions, 1957.

Proctor, Katarzyna, and Lily-I-Wen Su, "The 1st person plural in political discourse—American
politicians in interviews and in a debate." *Journal of Pragmatics* 43, no. 13 (October 2011):
3251–66.

Rougemont, Denis de. *Love in the Western World*. New York: Harcourt, Brace, 1940.

Quinn, Justin. "Auden International." In *Rainbow of American Poetry*, edited by Matthew Sweney,
157–184. Olomouc: Vydavatelství Univerzity Palackého, 2014.

———. "Auden's Cold War Fame." In *Auden in Context*, edited by Tony Sharpe, 56–68. London:
Palgrave, 2015.

Rand, Ayn. *Anthem*. Reprint of the 1946 New York edition, Project Gutenberg, 1998, www
.gutenberg.org/files/1250/1250-h/1250-h.htm.

Reeves, Gareth. "Some Modernists in Early Auden." In *Auden in Context*, edited by Tony Sharpe,
297–305. Cambridge: Cambridge University Press, 2013.

Replogle, Justin. *Auden's Poetry*. Seattle: University of Washington Press, 1969.

Rich, Adrienne. *Collected Earlier Poems, 1950–1970*. New York: Norton, 1993

———. *Later Poems: Selected and New, 1971–2012*. New York: Norton, 2013.

Rilke, Rainer Maria. *Duino Elegies & The Sonnets to Orpheus*. Translated by Stephen Mitchell.
New York: Vintage International, 2009.

———. *Uncollected Poems*. Translated by Edward Snow. New York: North Point Press, 1996.

Rosen, David. *Power, Plain English, and the Rise of Modern Poetry*. New Haven: Yale University
Press, 2006.

Rosenstock-Huessy, Eugen. *I Am an Impure Thinker*. 1970. Reprint, Essex, VT: Argo, 2001.

———. *Speech and Reality*. Essex, VT: Argo, 1970.

Rourke, Constance. *American Humor: A Study of the National Character*. New York: Harcourt,
Brace, 1931.

Samuels, Andrew. *The Plural Psyche*. London: Routledge, 1989.

Sandburg, Carl. *The People, Yes*. New York: Harcourt, Brace, 1936.

———. *Selected Poems*. Edited by George and Willene Hendrick. New York: Mariner, 1996.

Sassoon, Siegfried. *War Poems of Siegfried Sassoon*. Mineola, NY: Dover, 2004.

Sastri, Reena. "A Marriage of True Minds: Collaborative Creativity in the Auden-Kallman Libretti." In *Auden at Work*, edited by Bonnie Costello and Rachel Galvin, 111–32. Houndsmills: Palgrave, 2015.

Scheibman, Joanne. "Inclusive and Exclusive Patterning of the English First Person Plural: Evidence from Conversation." In *Language, Culture and Mind*, edited by Michel Achard and Suzanne Kemmer, 377–96. Stanford: CSLI Publications, 2004.

Schnapp, Jeffrey T. "Mob Porn." In *Crowds*, edited by Jeffrey T. Schnapp and Matthew Tiews, 1–47. Palo Alto: Stanford University Press, 2006.

Scholes, Robert. *Paradoxy of Modernism*. New Haven: Yale University Press, 2006.

Searle, J. R. "Collective Intentions and Actions." In *Intentions in Communication*, edited by Philip R. Cohen, Jerry Morgan, and Martha E. Pollack, 401–16. Cambridge, MA: MIT Press, 1990.

———. "The Logical Status of Fictional Discourse." *New Literary History* 6, no. 2 (January 1975): 319–32.

———. *Speech Acts: An Essay in the Philosophy of Language*. Cambridge: Cambridge University Press, 1969.

Shakespeare, William. *The Complete Sonnets and Poems*. Edited by Colin Burrow. Oxford: Oxford University Press, 2002.

———. *King Lear*. Edited by R. A. Foakes. London: Arden Shakespeare, 2005.

———. *A Midsummer Night's Dream*. Edited by Harold F. Brooks. London: Arden Shakespeare, 2007.

Sharpe, Tony. "The Church of England: Auden's Anglicanism." In *Auden in Context*, edited by Tony Sharpe, 79–88. Cambridge: Cambridge University Press, 2013.

———, ed. *Auden in Context*. Cambridge: Cambridge University Press, 2013.

Shaw, Lytle. *Frank O'Hara and the Poetics of Coterie*. Iowa City: University of Iowa Press, 2006.

Smith, Stan, ed. *The Cambridge Companion to W. H. Auden*. Cambridge: Cambridge University Press, 2005.

———. *W. H. Auden*. Oxford: Blackwell, 1985.

Spahr, Juliana. *Everybody's Autonomy: Connective Reading and Collective Identity*. Tuscaloosa: University of Alabama Press, 2001.

———. *Fuck You—Aloha—I Love You*. Middletown. Wesleyan University Press, 2001.

———. *That Winter the Wolf Came*. Oakland: AK Press, 2015.

———. *This Connection of Everyone with Lungs*. Berkeley: University of California Press, 2005.

———. "We." *Chicago Review* 44, no. 1 (1998): 89–91.

Spears, Monroe, ed. *Auden: A Collection of Critical Essays*. Englewood Cliffs, NJ: Prentice-Hall, 1964.

Spender, Stephen, ed. *W. H. Auden: A Tribute*. New York: Macmillan, 1974.

Spenser, Edmund. *The Yale Edition of the Shorter Poems of Edmund Spenser*. Edited by William A. Oram et al. New Haven: Yale University Press, 1989.

Stein, Gertrude. *Lectures in America*. 1957. Reprint, Boston: Beacon Press, 1985.

Stevens, Wallace. *Collected Poetry and Prose*. Edited by Frank Kermode and Joan Richardson. New York: Library of America, 1997.

Surowiecki, James. *The Wisdom of Crowds*. New York: Anchor, 2005.

Tolson, Melvin B. *The Harlem Gallery*. New York: Twayne, 1965.

Tze-wan, Kwan. "Towards a Phenomenology of Pronouns." *International Journal of Philosophical Studies* 15, no. 2 (2007): 247–68.

Vendler, Helen. *The Art of Shakespeare's Sonnets*. Cambridge, MA: Harvard University Press, 1997.

———. *Invisible Listeners: Lyric Intimacy in Herbert, Whitman, and Ashbery*. Princeton: Princeton University Press, 2005.

———. *On Extended Wings: Wallace Stevens' Longer Poems*. Cambridge, MA: Harvard University Press, 1969.

———. *Soul Says: On Recent Poetry*. Cambridge, MA: Harvard University Press, 1995.

Veselá, Pavla. "A Highly Charged Pronoun: 'We' in Three September 11 Poems." *Poetics Today* 33, no. 2 (summer 2012): 217–40.

Vincent, John Emil. *John Ashbery and You: His Later Books*. Athens: University of Georgia Press, 2007.

Von Hallberg, Robert. *Lyric Powers*. Chicago: University of Chicago Press, 2008.

Warren, Rosanna. *Fables of the Self*. New York: Norton, 2008.

Wasley, Aidan. *The Age of Auden: Postwar Poetry and the American Scene*. Princeton: Princeton University Press, 2011.

Waters, William. *Poetry's Touch: On Lyric Address*. Ithaca: Cornell University Press, 2003.

Weil, Simone. *The Simone Weil Reader*. Edited by George A. Panchias. New York: David McKay, 1977.

Whitman, Walt. *The Complete Poems*. Edited by Francis Murphy. London: Penguin, 2005.

Williams, William Carlos. *The Autobiography of William Carlos Williams*. New York: New Directions, 1967.

———. *Selected Essays*. New York: New Directions, 1969.

———. *Selected Poems*. New York: New Directions, 1985.

Wilson, Edmund. "W. H. Auden in America." In *The Bit between My Teeth: A Literary Chronicle of 1950–1965*, 355–63. New York: Farrar, Straus & Giroux, 1965.

Woolf, Virginia. "Mr. Bennett and Mrs. Brown." In *The Virginia Woolf Reader*, edited by Mitchell A. Leaska, 192–212. Orlando: Harcourt, 1984.

Wordsworth, William. *The Major Works*. Edited by Stephen Gill. Oxford: Oxford University Press, 2008.

Wright, C. D. *One Big Self: An Investigation*. Port Townsend, WA: Copper Canyon Press, 2007.

Yeats, W. B. *Essays*. New York: Macmillan, 1924.

———. *The Poems*. Edited by Richard J. Finneran. Houndsmills, Basingstoke: Palgrave Macmillan, 2003.

INDEX